# Books in English on the Soviet Union, 1917-73:

## *A Bibliography*

**Garland Reference Library of Social Science (Vol. 3)**

# Books in English on the Soviet Union, 1917-73:
## *A Bibliography*

Compiled by
# David Lewis Jones

*Garland Publishing, Inc., New York & London*

*1975*

016.947
J 76

Copyright © 1975

by David Lewis Jones

All Rights Reserved

**Library of Congress Cataloging in Publication Data**

Jones, David Lewis.
  Books in English on the Soviet Union, 1917-73.

  (Garland reference library of social sciences ; no. 3)
  1. Russia--Bibliography.  I.  Title.
Z2491.J65 [DK266]  016.947084          75-6887
ISBN 0-8240-1061-2

*Printed in the United States of America*

*I'm Rheini A'm Chwiorydd*
*To my parents and my sisters.*

# Foreword

The aim of the present volume is to list books written in the English language and which are wholly concerned with the Soviet Union. The period convered is from the October Revolution of 1917 to the end of 1973. Pamphlets, which are frequently tendentious, have been excluded in order to keep the total of items to a manageable number. Books which consider both the Tsarist and Soviet periods have also been omitted for the same reason.

The latest known edition of a book is listed but in the case of unaltered reprints the original edition only is included. The edition published in the United States is always cited first and it is followed by the British edition, and then, where necessary, editions from other countries. Translators have been omitted except in the case of works of literature where they are included when known and where different translations of the same work have been listed. There has been no attempt to establish consistency in names transliterated from Russian; the usage found in the work cited has been followed in the text of the bibliography, while in the index all the entries have been gathered under one spelling.

Aberaeron,
Pasg/Easter 1975

# *Abbreviations*

| | |
|---|---|
| **Bk.** | Book |
| **Co.** | Company |
| **Dept.** | Department |
| **FLPH** | Foreign Languages Publishing House |
| **HRAF** | Human Relations Area File |
| **L.** | London |
| **Mass.** | Massachusetts |
| **MIT** | Massachusetts Institute of Technology |
| **N.C.** | North Carolina |
| **N.J.** | New Jersey |
| **N.Y.** | New York |
| **P.** | Press |
| **Pub.** | Publishing |
| **RIIA** | Royal Institute of International Affairs |
| **U.** | University |
| **USGPO** | United States Goverment Printing Office |

# *Contents*

# CONTENTS

# CONTENTS

## CONTENTS

# CONTENTS

# CONTENTS

I    BIBLIOGRAPHIES AND REFERENCE WORKS


A    General bibliographies

1    Aav, Y.   Russian bibliographies:  bibliographies and books on librarian-
     ship printed in Russian characters in the Helsinki University Library.Zug,
     International Documentation Co., 1970.   171p.

2    Maichel, K.   Guide to Russian reference books;  ed. by J.S.G.  Simmons.
     Stanford,      Hoover Institution P., 1962-      Vol.1-
         Vol.1.   General bibliographies and reference books.   1962.   92p.
         Vol.2.   History, historical auxiliary sciences, ethnography, geogr-
                  aphy.   1964.   297p.

3    Neiswender, R.   Guide to Russian reference and language aids.  N.Y., Spe-
     cial Libraries Ass., 1962.   92p.

4    Simmons, J.S.G.   Russian bibliography, libraries and archives: a selec-
     tive list of bibliographical references for students of Russian history,
     literature, political, social and philosophical thought, theology and
     linguistics. Twickenham, Hall, 1973.   76p.

5    U.S.A. Library of Congress.  A guide to Soviet bibliographies: a selected
     list of references;  ed. by J.T. Dorosh.  Washington, USGPO, 1950.   158p.

6    Grierson, P.   Books on Soviet Russia, 1917-1942: a bibliography and a gu-
     ide to reading.  L., Methuen, 1943.   354p.

7    Horecky, P.L.  Basic Russian publications: an annotated bibliography  on
     Russia and the Soviet Union.  Chicago, U. of Chicago P., 1962.      313p.

8    Horecky, P.L.  Russia and the Soviet Union: a bibliographic guide to Wes-
     tern-language publications.  Chicago, U. of Chicago P.,  1965.      473p.

9    Hunt, R.N.C.  Books on communism: a bibliography.  L., Ampersand,  1959.
     333p.

10   Kolarz, W.  Books on communism: a bibliography.  L, Ampersand, 1964. 568p.

11   New York Public Library.  Dictionary catalogue of the Slavonic collection.
     Boston, Mass., G.K. Hall, 1959.   26 vols.

12   Schultheiss, T., ed.  Russian studies, 1941-1958: a cumulation of the an-
     nual bibliographies from the Russian Review;  pref. by D. Mohrenschildt.
     Ann Arbor, Pierian P. 1972.   395p.

13   U.S.A. Library of Congress.  Soviet Russia: a selected list of referen-
     ces:  comp. by H.S. Conover.  Washington, USGPO, 1944.   `89p.

14   Vigor, P.H.  Books on communism and the communist countries:  a selective
     list.  L., Ampersand, 1971.   444p.

15   Nerhood, H.W.  To Russia and return:  an annotated bibliography of travel-

ers' English-language accounts of Russia from the ninth century to the present. Columbus, Ohio State U.P., 1968. 367p.

16  U.S.A. <u>Dept. of State</u>. American correspondents and journalists in Moscow, 1917–1952: a bibliography of their books on the U.S.S.R. Washington, USGPO, 1953. 52p.

17  U.S.A. <u>Library of Congress</u>. Soviet geography, bibliography; ed. by N.R. Rodionoff. Washington, USGPO, 1951. 2 vols.

18  Horak, S. Junior Slavica: a selected annotated bibliography of books in English on Russia and Eastern Europe. N.Y., Libraries Unlimited, 1968. 244p.

19  Dossick, J.J. Doctoral research on Russia and the Soviet Union. N.Y., N.Y.U.P., 1960. 248p.


B   Bibliographies of periodicals and newspapers

20  Birkos, A.S, Tambs, L.A. Academic writer's guide to periodicals; Vol. 2: East European and Slavic studies. Kent, Kent State U.P., 1973. 572p.

21  Maichel, K., Schatoff, M. A list of Russian newspapers in the Columbia University Library. N.Y., Columbia U. Library, 1959. 130p.

22  Maichel, K. Soviet and Russian newspapers at the Hoover Institution: a catalog. Stanford, Hoover Institution P., 1966. 235p.

23  U.S.A. <u>Library of Congress</u>. Half a century of Soviet serials, 1917–1968: a bibliography and union list of serials published in the Soviet Union; ed. by R. Smits. Washington, USGPO, 1968. 2 vols.

24  U.S.A. <u>Library of Congress</u>. Newspapers of the Soviet Union in the Library of Congress; ed. by P.L. Horecky and others. Washington, USGPO, 1962. 73p

25  U.S.A. <u>Library of Congress</u>. Russian, Ukrainian and Belorussian newspapers 1917–1953, union list; ed. by P.L. Horecky. Washington, USGPO, 1953. 218p

26  U.S.A. <u>Library of Congress</u>. Russian periodicals in the Helsinki University Library: a checklist. Washington, USGPO, 1959. 120p.

27  U.S.A. <u>Library of Congress</u>. The U.S.S.R. and Eastern Europe: periodicals in western languages; ed. by P.L. Horecky, R.G. Carlton. 3rd ed. Washington, USGPO, 1967. 89p.


C   Subject bibliographies

28  Woronitzn, S. Bibliography of social research in the Soviet Union (1960–1970). Pullach bei Munchen, Verlag Dokumentation, 1973. 215p.

29  Schwartz, H. Soviet economy: a selected bibliography of materials in English. Syracuse, Syracuse U.P., 1949. 93p.

30  Stolz, G.  Forced labor in the Soviet orbit:  a selective bibliography.
    Y., Mid-European Studies Center, 1954.    13p.

31  Treml, V.G.  Input-output analysis in the U.S.S.R.:  an annotated biblio-
    graphy.  Durham, N.C., Duke U.  Center for International Studies,    1973.
    129p.

32  U.S.A.  Dept. of State.  Enforced labor in the U.S.S.R.:  selected refere-
    nces covering the period 1935-1951.  Washington, USGPO, 1952.    14p.

33  Critical bibliography of Communist purges and trials in the Soviet Union
    and in the "People's Democracies" since 1922.  N.Y., National Committee f-
    or a Free Europe, 1953.    38p.

34  McNeal, R.H.  Guide to the decisions of the Communist Party of the Soviet
    Union 1917-1967.  Toronto, U. of Toronto P., 1973.    330p.

35  U.S.A.  Dept. of State.  An essay on sources for the study of the Communi-
    st Party of the Soviet Union, 1934-60; by J.A. Armstrong.  Washington, U-
    SGPO, 1961.    41p.

36  U.S.A.  Senate.  Committee on the Judiciary.  World Communism:  a selected
    annotated bibliography;  ed. by J.G. Whelan.  Washington, USGPO,    1964.
    394p.

37  Akademiya nauk S.S.S.R.  Institut gosudarstva i prava.  Literature on Sov-
    iet law:  index of bibliography.  Moscow, 1960.    279p.

38  Hazard, J.N., Stern, W.B.  Bibliography of the principal materials on Sov-
    iet law.  N.Y., Foreign and International Bk. Co., 1945.    46p.

39  Solomon, P.H.  Soviet criminology:  a selective bibliography.  Cambridge,
    U. of Cambridge Institute of Criminology, 1969.    55p.

40  Movsovic, M.I.  Technical and vocational education in the U.S.S.R.:  a bi-
    bliographical survey.  Paris, Unesco, 1959.    53p.

41  U.S.A.  Dept. of Health, Education and Welfare.  Bibliography of published
    materials on Russian and Soviet education:  a research and reference tool;
    ed. by N. Rokitiansky, W.K. Medlin.  Washington, USGPO, 1960.    70p.

42  Unbegaun, B.O., Simmons, J.S.G.  A bibliographical guide to the Russian l-
    anguage.  Oxford, Clarendon P., 1953.    174p.

43  Lewanski, R.C.  A bibliography of Slavic dictionaries;  vol. 3:  Russian.
    N.Y.,  N.Y. Public Libraries, 1963.    400p.

44  Zenkovsky, S.A., Ambruster, D.L.  A guide to the bibliographies of Russian
    literature.  Nashville, Vanderbilt U.P., 1970.    62p.

45  Harvard University Library.  Twentieth century Russian literature:  class-
    ified listing by call numbers, alphabetical listing by author or  title,
    chronological listing.  Cambridge, Mass., Harvard U.P., 1965.    (Various
    paginations).

46  U.S.A. Library of Congress. Russian literature;  ed. by L.B. Voegelein.
    Washington, USGPO, 1965.    256p.

47  Lewanski, R.C. and others.  The literatures of the world in English trans-
    lation: a bibliography;  vol 2: The Slavic literatures. N.Y., N.Y. Pub-
    lic Library & F. Ungar, 1967.    630p.

48  Ettlinger, A., Gladstone, J.M.  Russian literature, theatre and art:    a
    bibliography of works in English published 1900-1945. L., Hutchinson,1947
    96p.

49  Gibian, G.  Soviet Russian literature in English: a checklist bibliogra-
    phy.  Ithaca, Cornell U.  Center for International Studies, 1967.  118p.

50  Dana, H.W.L.  Handbook on Soviet drama: lists of theatres, plays, operas,
    ballets, films and books about them.  N.Y., American-Russian Institute,
    1938.    158p.

51  Brown, G.W., Brown, D.B.  A guide to Soviet Russian translations of Ameri-
    can literature.  N.Y., King's Crown P., 1954.    243p.

52  Libman, V.A.  Russian studies of American literature: a bibliography; ed.
    by C. Gohdes.  Chapel Hill, U. of North Carolina P., 1969.    218p.

53  Magner, T.F.  Soviet dissertations for advanced degrees in Russian litera-
    ture and Slavic linguistics, 1934-1962.  University Park, Pennsylvania U.P.
    1966.    100p.

54  Senkevitch, A.  Soviet architecture, 1917-1962: a bibliographic guide to
    source material.  Charlottesville, U.P. of Virginia, 1973.    304p.

55  White, S.  Guide to science and technology in the U.S.S.R.: a reference
    guide to science and technology in the Soviet Union.  Guernsey, Hodgson,
    1971.    300p.

56  U.S.A. Library of Congress.  Soviet science and technology: a bibliograp-
    hy on the state of the art, 1955-1961. Washington, USGPO, 1962.    209p.

57  U.S.A. Dept. of Health, Education and Welfare.  Soviet medicine: bibliogr-
    aphy of bibliographies.  Washington, USGPO, 1973.    46p.

58  U.S.A. Dept. of Health, Education and Welfare.  Guide to Russian medical
    literature; ed. by S. Adams, F.B. Rogers.  Washington, USGPO, 1958. 89p.

59  U.S.A.  Public Health Services.  U.S.S.R. literature on air pollution and
    related occupational diseases.  Washington, USGPO, 1961.  5 vols.

60  Bertone, C.M.  Soviet psychology, 1950-1966: a continuing bibliography.
    No. Hollywood, Western Periodicals, 1968.    546p.

61  Forsythe, G.E.  Bibliography of Russian mathematics books.  N.Y., Chelsea,
    1956.    106p.

62  Turkevich, J.  Chemistry in the Soviet Union.  Princeton, N.J.; L.,  Van

Nostrand, 1965.    566p.

63  U.S.A.  <u>Atomic Energy Commission</u>.  Russian radioecology:  bibliography of
Soviet publications with citations of English translations and abstracts;
ed. by A.W. Klement and others.  Washington, USGPO, 1968.  131p.    Supplement 1-      1972-

64  U.S.A.  <u>Library of Congress</u>.  Manufacturing and mechanical engineering in
the Soviet Union:  a bibliography.  Washington, USGPO, 1953.    234p.

65  U.S.A.  <u>Library of Congress</u>.  Electric power industry of U.S.S.R.:  an annotated bibliography.  Washington, USGPO, 1952.    154p.

66  Prilutskii, D.N.  Bibliographic handbook on Soviet refrigeration technology. N.Y.; L., Pergamon, 1961.    135p.

67  U.S.A.  <u>Library of Congress</u>.  Soviet transportation and communication:  a
bibliography;  ed. by R.S. Janse.  Washington, USGPO, 1952.    330p.

68  U.S.A.  <u>Library of Congress</u>.  Aeronautical sciences and aviation in the S-
oviet Union:  a bibliography.  Washington, USGPO, 1955.    274p.

69  Beard, R.  Soviet cosmonautics 1957-1969:  a bibliography of articles published in British periodicals and of British and foreign books.  Swindon,
R. Beard, 1970.    43p.

70  U.S.A.  <u>Dept. of the Army</u>.  U.S.S.R., strategic survey:  bibliography.1969
ed. Washington, USGPO, 1969.    238p.

71  Parrish, M.  The Soviet armed forces:  books in English, 1950-1967.  Stanford, Hoover Institution P., 1970.    128p.

72  Dallin, A.  Red Star on military affairs, 1945-1952:  a selected, annotated list of articles in the Soviet military newspaper.  Santa Monica, Rand
Corp., 1956.    49p.

73  U.S.A.  <u>Dept. of the Army</u>.  Initial bibliography of Soviet military medicine, 1917-1950.  Washington, USGPO, 1957.    58p.

74  Fletcher, W.C.  Christianity in the Soviet Union:  an annotated bibliography and list of articles:  works in English.  Los Angeles, U. of Southern
California, Research Institute on Communist Strategy and Propaganda, 1963.
95p.

75  Braham, R.L.  Jews in the communist world:  a bibliography, 1945-60. N.Y.,
Twayne, 1961.    64p.

76  Braham, R.L., Hauer, M.M.  Jews in the communist world:  a bibliography,
1945-1962.  N.Y., Pro-Arte Pub. Co., 1963.    125p.

77  Rosenberg, L.R.  Jews in the Soviet Union:  an annotated bibliography,1967
-1971.  N.Y., American Jewish Committee, Institute of Human Relations,1971.
59p.

78  Harvard University Library.  Slavic history and literature.  Cambridge,

Mass., Harvard U.P., 1971.     4 vols.

79  Lencek, R.L.  A bibliographic guide to the literature of Slavic civiliza-
    tions.  N.Y., Columbia U., Dept. of Slavic Languages, 1966.     66p.

80  Morley, C.  Guide to research in Russian history.  Syracuse, Syracuse U.P.
    1951.    227p.

81  Harvard University Library.  Russian history since 1917.  Cambridge, Mass.
    Harvard U.P., 1966.     698p.

82  U.S.A.  Dept. of State.  The German occupation of the U.S.S.R. in World W-
    ar II:  a bibliography;   ed. by A. Dallin, C.F. Latour, Washington, USGPO,
    1955.    76p.

83  Heitman, S., Nikolai I. Bukharin:  a bibliography.  Stanford, Hoover Ins-
    titution P., 1969.     181p.

84  Sinclair, L.  Leon Trotsky:  a bibliography.  Stanford, Hoover Institution
    P., 1972.    1089p.

85  Hammond, T.T.  Soviet foreign relations and world communism:  a selected,
    annotated bibliography of 7000 books in 30 languages.  Princeton, Prince-
    ton U.P., 1965.    1240p.

86  Clemens, W.C.  Soviet disarmament policy, 1917–1963:  an annotated biblio-
    graphy of Soviet and Western sources.  Stanford, Hoover Institution P.,19-
    65.    151p.

87  Saran, V.  Sino–Soviet schism:  a bibliography, 1956–1964.  Bombay, Asia
    Pub. House, 1971.    162p.

88  Sworakowski, W.S.  The Communist International and its front organizations
    a research guide and checklist of holdings in American and European libra-
    ries.  Stanford, Hoover Institution P., 1965.     493p.

89  U.S.A.  Dept. of State.  Soviet bloc foreign economic relations:  an Engl-
    ish language bibliography.  Washington, USGPO, 1958.     31p.

90  Holdsworth, M.  Soviet African studies, 1918–59:  an annotated bibliograp-
    hy.  L., Oxford U.P., 1961.  2 pts. in 1 vol.

91  Russia looks to Africa:  a brief survey of Russian writing on Africa from
    the nineteenth century to the present day.  L., Central Asian Research Ce-
    ntre in association with the Soviet Affairs Study Group of St. Antony's
    College, Oxford, 1960.    21p.

92  Carlton, R.G.  Latin America in Soviet writings:  a bibliography.  Baltim-
    ore, Johns Hopkins P., 1966.    2 vols.

93  Yuan, T'ung-li.  Russian works on China, 1918–1960, in American libraries
    New Haven, Yale U.P., 1961.    162p.

94  Lowenthal, R.  Bibliography of Russian literature on China and adjacent

countries, 1931-1936. Cambridge, Mass., Harvard University, Russian Research Center, 1949. 93p.

95  Berton, P.A. Soviet works on China: a bibliography of non-periodical literature, 1946-1955. Los Angeles, U. of California at Los Angeles,1959 158p.

96  Bolton, A.R.C. Soviet Middle East studies: an analysis and bibliography. L., Oxford U.P., 1959. 8 pts. in 1 vol.

97  Harvard University Library. Finnish and Baltic history and literatures. Cambridge, Mass, Harvard U.P., 1972. 250p.

98  Klesment, J. and others. Legal sources and bibliography of the Baltic states. N.Y., Praeger, 1964. 197p.

99  U.S.A. Library of Congress. Estonia: a selected bibliography; ed. by S. Kuri. Washington, USGPO, 1958. 74p.

100  Ozols, S.A. Latvia: a selected bibliography. Washington, Karusa, 1964. 144p.

101  Balys, J. Lithuania and the Lithuanians: a selected bibliography. N.Y., Praeger, 1961. 190p.

102  Stanka, E. Lithuania: a selected bibliography, with a brief historical survey. Washington, Catholic U. of America, 1958. 124p.

103  Vakar, N.P. A bibliographical guide to Belorussia. Cambridge, Mass., Harvard U.P., 1956. 63p.

104  Pelenskyi, I.I. Ucrainica: selected bibliography on Ukraine in western-European languages. Munich, Bystrycia, 1948. 111p.

105  Weres, R. The Ukraine: selected references in the English language, with brief introduction about the Ukraine and the Ukrainians. Kalamazoo, Western Michigan U., School of Graduate Studies, 1961. 233p.

106  Lawrynenko, J.A. Ukrainian communism and Soviet Russian policy towards the Ukraine: an annotated bibliography, 1917-1953; ed. by D.I. Goldstein. N.Y., Research Program on the U.S.S.R., 1953. 454p.

107  Allworth, E. Nationalities of the Soviet East: publications and writing systems: a bibliographical directory and transliteration table of Iranian and Turkic-language publications, 1818-1945, located in the U.S. libraries. N.Y., Columbia U.P., 1971. 440p.

108  Foster, L.A. Bibliography of Russian emigre literature 1918-1968. Boston, Mass., G.K. Hall, 1970. 2 vols.

109  Schatoff, M. Bibliographical index of Russian publications outside of the U.S.S.R., 1961-    . N.Y., All-Slavic Publishing House, 1964-

110  Schatoff, M. Half a century of Russian serials, 1917-1968: cumulative

index of serials published outside the U.S.S.R.; ed. by N.A. Hale. N.Y. Russian Book Chamber Abroad, 1970–    Vol.1–

111   Zernov, N.M. Russian emigre authors: a biographical index and bibliography of their works on theology, religious philosophy, orthodox culture, and church history. Boston, Mass., G.K. Hall, 1973.    373p.


D   Biographical materials

112   Institute for the Study of the U.S.S.R. Who was who in the U.S.S.R.: a biographic dictionary of prominent Soviet historical personalities; ed. by H.E. Schulz and others. Metuchen, Scarecrow P., 1972.    677p.

113   Institute for the Study of the U.S.S.R. Biographic dictionary of the U.S.S.R. N.Y., Scarecrow P., 1958.    782p.

114   Institute for the Study of the U.S.S.R. Who's who in the U.S.S.R., 1961–62. Montreal, International Bk. and Pub. Co., 1962.    963p.

115   Institute for the Study of the U.S.S.R. Who's who in the U.S.S.R.,1965–66. 2nd ed. N.Y., Scarecrow P., 1966.    1189p.

116   Institute for the Study of the U.S.S.R. Prominent personalities in the U.S.S.R. Metuchen, Scarecrow P., 1968–

117   Institute for the Study of the U.S.S.R. Portraits of prominent U.S.S.R. personalities. Metuchen, Scarecrow P., 1968–    Vol.1–

118   U.S.A. Dept. of State. Directory of Soviet officials. Washington,USGPO 1960–61. 2 vols.

119   Institute for the Study of the U.S.S.R. Party and government officials of the Soviet Union, 1917–1967; ed. by E.L. Crowley and others. Metuchen, Scarecrow P., 1969.    214p.

120   Hodnett, G., Ogareff, V. Leaders of the Soviet Republics 1955–1972: a guide to posts and occupants. Canberra, The Australian National University, Research School of Social Sciences, Dept. of Political Science,    1973 454p.

121   Institute for the Study of the U.S.S.R. The Soviet diplomatic corps,1917–1967; ed. by E.L. Crowley. Metuchen, Scarecrow P., 1970.    240p.

122   Lensen, G.A. Russian diplomatic and consular officials in East Asia: a handbook of the representatives of Tsarist Russia and the Provisional Government in China, Japan and Korea from 1858–1924 and of Soviet representatives in Japan from 1925–1968. Tallahasse, Diplomatic P., 1968. 294p.

123   Lazitch, B., Drachkovitch, M.M. Biographical dictionary of the Comintern. Stanford, Hoover Institution P., 1973.    458p.

124   Turkevich, J. Soviet men of science: academicians and corresponding members of the Academy of Sciences of the U.S.S.R. Princeton; L., Van Nos-

trand, 1963.    441p.

125  Institute for the Study of the U.S.S.R.  Prominent personnel of the Acad-
     emies of Sciences of the U.S.S.R. and Union Republics.  Munich, 1963. 71p

126  Telberg, I.  Who's who in Soviet science and technology.  2nd ed.  N.Y.,
     Telberg Bk. Co., 1964.    301p.

127  Telberg, I.  Who's who in Soviet social sciences and humanities, art and
     government.  N.Y., Telberg Bk. Co., 1961.    147p.

128  Vodarsky-Shiraeff, A.  Russian composers and musicians: a biographical
     dictionary.  N.Y., Wilson, 1940.    158p.

129  Popov, V.M. and others.  Scientists of Ukrainian S.S.R. higher education-
     al institutions.  Washingtom, USGPO, 1970.    913p.


E    Miscellaneous reference works

130  U.S.A. Library of Congress.  Russian abbreviations:  a selective list.
     Washington, USGPO, 1952.    128p.

131  U.S.A. Library of Congress.  Glossary of Russian abbreviations and acro-
     nyms; ed. by Aerospace Technology Division, Reference Dept. Washington,
     USGPO, 1967.    806p.

132  U.S.A. Dept of the Army.  Glossary of Soviet military and related abbre-
     viations.  Washingtom, USGPO, 1957.    178p.

133  U.S.A. Geographic Names Board.  U.S.S.R., official standard names appro-
     ved by the United States Board on Geographic Names.  2nd. ed. Washington,
     USGPO, 1970.  7 vols.

134  Crowe, B.  Concise dictionary of Soviet terminology, institutions, and
     abbreviations.  N.Y., Oxford, Pergamon, 1969.    182p.

135  Battelle Memorial Institute.  Directory of selected scientific institut-
     ions in the U.S.S.R. with an introduction to the administration of scien-
     ce and technology in the U.S.S.R., January 1, 1963.  Columbus, Merrill,
     1963.  (various paginations).

136  Flegon, A.  Directory of Soviet sanatoria.  L., Flegon P., 1968.  119p.

137  Flegon, A.  Soviet trade directory.  L., Flegon P., 1964.    836p.

138  East European Fund.  Directory of American organizations of exiles from
     the U.S.S.R.  N.Y., 1952.    192p.

139  Simutis, A.  Lithuanian world directory.  N.Y., Lithuanian Chamber  of
     Commerce of New York, 1958.    464p.

- 9 -

F    Soviet studies in the West

140  Laqueur, W., Labedz, L.   The state of Soviet studies.   Cambridge, Mass.,
     M.I.T.P., 1965.    177p.

141  Fisher, H.H.   American research on Russia.   Bloomington, Indiana U.P.,
     1959.    240p.

142  Black, C.E., Thompson, J.M.   American teaching about Russia.   Blooming-
     ton, Indiana U.P., 1959.    189p.

143  Columbia University.   Russian Institute.   Russian and Soviet studies:   a
     handbook for graduate studies;   vol.1:   A research manual, preliminary
     version.   N.Y., 1970.    106p.

144  Fischer, G.   American research on Soviet society:   guide to specialized
     studies since World War II by sociologists, psychologists and anthropolo-
     gists in the United States.   N.Y., Columbia U., Bureau of Applied Social
     Research, 1966.    82p.

145  Coleman, A.P.   Report on the status of Russian and other Slavic and East
     European languages in the educational institutions of the United States.
     N.Y., Columbia U., American Association of teachers of Slavic and East
     European languages, 1948.    109p.

146  Columbia University.   Russian Institute.   The Russian Institute, 1946-
     1959.   N.Y., 1959.    84p.

147  Harvard University.   Russian Research Center.   Ten year report and curr-
     ent projects, 1948-1958.   Cambridge, Mass., 1958.    107p.

148  Ruggles, M.J., Mostecky, V.   Russian and East European publications in
     the libraries of the United States.   N.Y., Columbia U.P., 1960.   396p.

149  Institute for the Study of the U.S.S.R.   Institute publications,   1951-
     1968;   ed. by M. Klieber.   Munich, 1969.    160p.

150  Walker, G.P.M. and others.   Directory of libraries and special collect-
     ions on Eastern Europe.   L., Crosby Lockwood, 1971.    159p.

151  Laqueur, W.   The fate of the revolution:   interpretations of Soviet hist-
     ory.   L., Weidenfeld & Nicholson, 1967.    216p.

152  Horowitz, D.   Isaac Deutscher:   the man and his work.   L., Macdonald, 19-
     71.    254p.

G    Archives, libraries and publishing

153  Grimsted, P.K.   Archives and manuscript repositories in the U.S.S.R.: Mo-
     scow and Leningrad.   Princeton, Princeton U.P., 1972.    436p.

154  Horecky, P.L.   Libraries and bibliographic centers in the Soviet Union.
     Bloomington, Indiana U. Publications, 1959.    287p.

155  Chandler, G.   Libraries, documentation and bibliography in the U.S.S.R.,

1917-1971: Survey and critical analysis of Soviet studies, 1967-1971. N. Y.; L., Seminar P., 1972.    183p.

156  Francis, S.  Libraries in the U.S.S.R.  Hamden, Linnet Bks.,      1971.
     182p.

157  Ruggles, M.J., Swank, R.C.  Soviet libraries and librarianship:  report
     of the visit of the delegation of U.S. librarians to the Soviet Union,May
     -June 1961, under the U.S.-Soviet cultural exchange agreement.    Chicago,
     American Library Association, 1962.    121p.

158  Morachevskii, N.I.  Guide to the Saltykov-Shchedrin State Public Library,
     Leningrad.  Los Angeles U. of California Library, 1963.    48p.

159  Melik-Shakhnazarov, A.S.  Technical information in the U.S.S.R.    Cambr-
     idge, Mass., M.I.T. Libraries, 1961.    122p.

160  Simsova, S.  Lenin, Krupskaia and libraries.  Hamden, Shoe String P.; L.,
     Bingley, 1968.    73p.

161  Simsova, S.  Nicholas Rubakin and bibliopsychology.  Hamden, Shoe String
     P.; L., Bingley, 1968.    76p.

162  Gorokhoff, B.I.  Publishing in the U.S.S.R.  Bloomington, Indiana  U.P.,
     1959.    306p.

163  Book publishing in the U.S.S.R.:  reports of the delegations of U.S. book
     publishers visiting the U.S.S.R., October 21-November 4, 1970 and August
     20-September 19, 1962.  2nd ed.  Cambridge, Mass., Harvard U.P.,    1971.
     182p.

164  Bohmer, A.  Copyright in the U.S.S.R. and other European countries or te-
     rritories under communist government.  South Hackensack, Rothman,    1960.
     62p.


H    Encyclopaedias and handbooks

165  Fitzsimmons, T. and others.  U.S.S.R.:  its people, its society, its cul-
     ture.  New Haven, HRAF, 1960.    590p.

166  Florinsky, M.T.  McGraw-Hill encyclopedia of Russia and the Soviet Union.
     N.Y.; L., McGraw-Hill, 1961.    624p.

167  Freund, H.A.  Russian from A to Z.  Revolution, state and party, foreign
     relations, economic system, social principles, general knowledge.    L.;
     Sydney, Angus & Robertson, 1945.    713p.

168  Great Soviet encyclopedia:  a translation of the third edition.    N.Y.,
     Macmillan; L., Collier-Macmillan, 1973-    Vol.1-

169  Malevsky-Malevich, P.  Russia-USSR:  a complete handbook.  L., Williams &
     Norgate, 1934.    712p.

170   Malevsky—Malevich, P.   The Soviet Union today.   L., Williams & Norgate,
      1936.      102p.   (Supplement and index to 169.)

171   Maxwell, R.   Information U.S.S.R.:   an authoritative encyclopaedia about
      the Union of Soviet Socialist Republics.   N.Y.; L., Pergamon, 1962.982p.

172   Roucek, J.S.   Slavonic encyclopaedia.   N.Y., Philosophical Library, 1949.
      1445p.

173   Schopflin, G.   The Soviet Union and Eastern Europe:   a handbook.      L.,
      Blond, 1970.      614p.

174   Simmons, E.J.   U.S.S.R.:   a concise handbook.   Ithaca, Cornell U.P. 1947.
      494p.

175   Soviet News.   The U.S.S.R.:   a hundred questions answered. 5th ed. L.,
      1958.      198p.

176   Strakhovsky, L.I.   Handbook of Slavic Studies.   Cambridge, Mass., Harvard
      U.P., 1949.      753p.

177   Telberg, I.   Russian—English geographical—encyclopedia.   N.Y., Telberg Bk
      Co., 1960.      142p.

178   U.S.S.R.   handbook. L., Gollancz, 1936.      643p.

179   U.S.A.   Dept. of the Army.   Area handbook for Soviet Union by E.K. Keefe
      and others.   Washington, USGPO, 1971.      827p.

180   Utechin, S.   Everyman's concise encyclopaedia of Russia.   N.Y.,   Dutton;
      L., Dent, 1961.      623p.

181   Walsh, W.B.   Russia and the Soviet Union.   Ann Arbor, U. of Michigan P.,
      1958.      640p.

182   Walsh, W.B., Price, R.A.   Russia:   a handbook.   Syracuse, Syracuse U.P.,
      1947.      140p.

183   Whiting, K.R.   The Soviet Union today:   a concise handbook.   N.Y., Praeg-
      er; L., Thames & Hudson, 1962.      405p.

184   Fitzsimmons, T.   R.S.F.S.R.:   Russian Soviet Federated Socialist Republic
      New Haven, HRAF, 1957.   2 vols.

185   Kubijovyc, V.   Ukraine:   a concise encyclopaedia;   prepared by the Shev-
      chenko Society.   Toronto, U. of Toronto P., 1963—71.   2 vols.

I     Statistical material.

186   Bron, S.G.   Soviet economic development and American business:   results
      of the first year under the five—year plan and further perspectives. N.Y.
      Liveright, 1930.      147p.

187  U.S.S.R. <u>Central Administration of Economic and Social Statistics of the</u>
     <u>State Planning Commission</u>. The U.S.S.R. in figures: 1934. Moscow, 1934.
     276p.
     (Issues have also been produced for subsequent years;  the work was later
     published by the Central Statistical Administration.)

188  U.S.S.R. <u>Central Administration of Economic and Social Statistics of the</u>
     <u>State Planning Commission</u>. Socialist construction in the U.S.S.R.: a st-
     atistical abstract. Moscow, Soyuzorguchet, 1936.    538p.

189  U.S.S.R. <u>Central Statistical Administration</u>. The national economy of
     the U.S.S.R.: a statistical compilation. Moscow, State Statistical Pub-
     lishing House, 1956.    270p.

190  U.S.S.R. <u>Central Statistical Administration</u>. Statistical handbook of
     the U.S.S.R. (1956); ed. by H. Schwartz. N.Y., National Industrial Confe-
     rence Board, 1957.    122p.

191  Jasny, N.  The Soviet statistical handbook, 1956: a commentary.    East
     Lansing, Michigan State U.P.; L.; Sydney, Angus & Robertson, 1957. 212p.

192  U.S.S.R. <u>Central Statistical Administration</u>. National economy of the
     U.S.S.R.: statistical returns. Moscow, FLPH, 1957.    230p.

193  U.S.S.R. <u>Central Statistical Administration</u>.  Forty years of Soviet po-
     wer in facts and figures. Moscow, FLPH, 1958.    320p.

194  U.S.S.R. <u>Central Statistical Administration</u>. 1958 statistical yearbook
     on the national economy of the U.S.S.R. Washington, USGPO, 1960.  818p.

195  U.S.S.R. <u>Central Statistical Administration</u>. National economy of the
     U.S.S.R. in 1960:  statistical yearbook. Washington, USGPO, 1962. 937p.

196  Treml, V.G., Hardt, J.P.  Soviet economic statistics. Durham, Duke U.P.,
     1972.    457p.

197  Clarke, R.A.  Soviet economic facts, 1917-1970.  N.Y., Wiley;  L., Macmi-
     llan, 1972.    151p.

198  Yezhov, A. I.  Soviet statistics. Moscow, FLPH, 1957.    131p.

199  Clark, C.  A critique of Soviet statistics. L., Macmillan, 1939.  76p.

200  Marer, P.  Soviet and East European foreign trade, 1946-1969:  statisti-
     cal compendium and guide;  computer programs by G.J. Eubanks.  Bloomingt-
     on, Indiana U.P., 1972.    408p.

201  U.S.S.R. <u>Ministry of Foreign Trade</u>. Foreign trade of the U.S.S.R. in
     1961:  a statistical survey. Washingtom, USGPO, 1962.    230p.

202  Bergson, A. <u>and others</u>.  Soviet national income and product, 1928-48: re-
     vised data.  Santa Monica, Rand Corp., 1960.    155p.

203  Nimitz, A.E.  Soviet national income and product, 1956-1958.  Santa Moni-

ca, Rand Corp., 1962.    189p.

204  Becker, A.S.  Soviet national income and product, 1958—1962.  Santa Monica, Rand Corp., 1965—66.    2 vols.

205  Becker, A.S.  Soviet national income and product in 1965:  the goals of the seven year plan.  Santa Monica, Rand Corp., 1963.    250p.

206  Anderson, S.  Soviet national income, 1964—1966, in established prices.  Santa Monica, Rand Corp., 1968.    109p.

207  U.S.S.R.  Central Statistical Administration.  U.S.S.R. industry: a statistical compilation.  Moscow, State Statistical Publishing House,  1957.  434p.

208  Hodgman, D.R.  Soviet industrial production, 1928—1951.  Cambridge, Mass.  Harvard U.P., 1954.    241p.

209  Kaplan, N.M.  Capital investments in the Soviet Union, 1924—1951.  Santa Monica, Rand Corp., 1951.    218p.

210  Kaplan, N.M. and others.  A tentative input—output table for the U.S.S.R.  1941 plan, Santa Monica, Rand Corp., 1952.    153p.

211  Powell, R.P.  A materials—input index of Soviet construction, revised and extended.  Santa Monica, Rand Corp., 1959.    98p.

212  Kaplan, N.M. and others.  Indexes of Soviet industrial output.    Santa Monica, Rand Corp., 1960.    305p.

213  Holubnychy, V.  The industrial output of the Ukraine, 1913—1956:  a statistical analysis.  Munich, Institute for the Study of the U.S.S.R., 1957.  63p.

214  Gerschenkron, A.  A dollar index of Soviet machinery output, 1927—28  to  1937.  Santa Monica, Rand Corp., 1952.    210p.

215  Gerschenkron, A., Nimitz, A.E.  A dollar index of Soviet iron and steel output, 1927—28 to 1937.  Santa Monica, Rand Corp., 1953.    266p.

216  Nimitz, A.E.  A dollar index of Soviet coal output, 1927—28 to 1937.  Santa Monica, Rand Corp., 1953.    97p.

217  Gerschenkron, A.  A dollar index of Soviet electric—power output.  Santa Monica, Rand Corp., 1954.    104p.

218  Shimkin, D.B.  The Soviet mineral—fuels industries, 1928—1958:  a statistical survey.  Washington, USGPO, 1962.    183p.

219  Gerschenkron, A., Nimitz, A.E.  A dollar index of Soviet petroleum output, 1927—28 to 1937.  Santa Monica, Rand Corp., 1952.    210p.

220  Crosfield, Joseph, & Sons, Ltd.  Soviet crude oil production:  some statistics.  Warrington, 1963.    81p.

221   Grossman, G.   Soviet statistics of physical output of industrial commod-
      ities:   their compilation and quality.   Princeton, Princeton U.P., 1960.
      151p.

222   Bergson, A. and others.   Basic industrial prices in the U.S.S.R.,   1928-
      1950:   twenty-five branch series and their aggregation.   Santa Monica,
      Rand Corp., 1955.    129p.

223   Moorsteen, R.H.   Prices of prime movers, U.S.S.R., 1927-28 to 1949.   San-
      ta Monica, Rand Corp., 1954.    169p.

224   Turgeon, E.L. and others.   Prices of miscellaneous basic industrial prod-
      ucts, U.S.S.R., 1928-1950.   Santa Monica, Rand Corp., 1955.    147p.

225   Bergson, A., Turgeon, E.L.   Prices of ordinary rolled steel in the Soviet
      Union, 1928-1950.   Santa Monica, Rand Corp., 1952.   89p. & 67p. (Supp.).

226   Turgeon, E.L., Bergson, A.   Prices of non-ferrous metals in the Soviet
      Union, 1928-1950.   Santa Monica, Rand Corp., 1953.    96p.

227   Moorsteen, R.H.   Prices of tractors, trucks, and automobiles, U.S.S.R.,
      1928-1949.   Santa Monica, Rand Corp., 1953.    143p.

228   Turgeon, E.L.   Prices of coal and peat in the Soviet Union, 1928-1950.
      Santa Monica, Rand Corp., 1955.    82p.

229   Bernaut, R.   Prices of fuelwood and wood products in the U.S.S.R.,   1928-
      1950.   Santa Monica, Rand Corp., 1955.    90p.

230   Nimitz, A.E.   Prices of refined petroleum products in the U.S.S.R., 1928-
      1950.   Santa Monica, Rand Corp., 1955.    120p.

231   Bernaut, R., Bergson, A.   Prices of paints in the Soviet Union, 1928-1950.
      Santa Monica, Rand Corp., 1953.    83p.

232   Chapman, J.G.   Retail food prices in the U.S.S.R., 1937-1948.   Santa Mon-
      ica, Rand Corp., 1951.    117p.

233   Kaplan, N.M., White, W.L.   A comparison of 1950 wholesale prices in Sov-
      iet and American industry.   Santa Monica, Rand Corp., 1955.    356p.

234   Wainstein, E.S.   A comparison of Soviet and United States retail prices
      for manufactured goods and services in 1950.   Santa Monica, Rand Corp.,
      1956.    111p.

235   Becker, A.S.   Prices of producers' durables in the United States and the
      U.S.S.R. in 1955.   Santa Monica, Rand Corp., 1959.    304p.

236   Chapman, J.G.   Real wages in Soviet Russia since 1928.   Cambridge, Mass.,
      Harvard U.P., 1963.    395p.

237   Kushkina, R.I. Transport and communications in U.S.S.R., statistical han-
      dbook, U.S.S.R.   Washington, USGPO, 1968.    303p.

238  Nimitz, A.E.  Statistics of Soviet agriculture.  Santa Monica, Rand Corp. 1954.  96p.

239  U.S.A. Economic Research Service.  Agricultural statistics of Eastern Europe and Soviet Union, 1950-70.  Washington, USGPO, 1973.  106p.

240  Mickiewicz, E.  Handbook of Soviet social science data.  N.Y., Free Press, 1973.  225p.

241  Kantner, J.F., Kulchycka, L.W.  The U.S.S.R. population census of 1926: a partial evaluation.  Washington, USGPO, 1957.  142p.

242  Podiachikh, P.G.  The All-Union census of population of 1939.  Washington, USGPO, 1959.  257p.

243  Ullman, M.B.  The 1939 U.S.S.R. census of population:  organization and methodology with notes on plans for the 1959 census of population.  Washington, USGPO, 1959.  199p.

244  U.S.A.  Bureau of the Census.  Materials on the preparation and conduct . of the U.S.S.R.  All-Union population census of 1959.  Washington, USGPO, 1959.  131p.

245  Feshbach, M.  The Soviet statistical system:  labor force recordkeeping and reporting.  Washington, USGPO, 1960.  151p.

246  Eason, W.  The agricultural labor force and population of the U.S.S.R.: 1926-41.  Santa Monica, Rand Corp., 1954.  217p.

247  Sonin, M.I.  The reproduction of labor power in the U.S.S.R. and the balance of labor.  Washington, USGPO, 1960.  391p.

248  Weitzman, M.S., Elias, A.  The magnitude and distribution of civilian employment in the U.S.S.R., 1928-1959.  Washington, USGPO, 1961.  193p.

249  Smulevich, B.I.  Morbidity, mortality and the physical development of the populace: U.S.S.R.  Washington, USGPO, 1959.  140p.

II  GEOGRAPHY, DESCRIPTION AND TRAVEL ACCOUNTS

A  Atlases

250  Adams, A.E. and others. An atlas of Russian and East European history. L., Heinemann, 1967.  204p.

251  Chew, A.F.  An atlas of Russian history: eleven centuries of changing borders.  New Haven; L., Yale U.P., 1967.  113p.

252  Economist Intelligence Unit.  The U.S.S.R. and Eastern Europe.  L., Oxford U.P., 1956.  140p.

253  Fullard, H.  Soviet Union in maps.  Rev. ed.  L., Philip, 1972.  32p.

254  Horrabin, J.F., Gregory, J.S.  An atlas of the U.S.S.R.  N.Y.; West Drayton, Penguin Bks., 1945.  64p.

255  Kish, G.  Economic atlas of the Soviet Union.  2nd ed.  Ann Arbor, U. of Michigan P., 1971.  90p.

256  Nazaroff, A.I.  Picture map geography of the U.S.S.R.  Philadelphia, Lippincott, 1969.  165p.

257  Taaffe, R.N.  An atlas of Soviet affairs.  N.Y., Praeger; L., Methuen, 1965.  143p.


B  Geography

258  Borisov, A.A.  Climates of the U.S.S.R.  L., Oliver & Boyd, 1965. 270p.

259  Cressey, G.B.  Soviet potentials: a geographic appraisal.  Syracuse, Syracuse U.P., 1962.  232p.

260  Dewdney, J.C.  A geography of the Soviet Union.  2nd ed. N.Y.; Oxford, Pergamon, 1971.  169p.

261  Gregory, J.S., Shave, D.W.  The U.S.S.R.: a geographical survey. N.Y., Wiley, 1946.; L., Harrap, 1944.  636p.

262  Gregory, J.S.  Russian land, Soviet people: a geographical approach to the U.S.S.R.  L., Harrap, 1968.  947p.

263  Hooson, D.J.  A new Soviet heartland?  Princeton; L., Van Nostrand, 1964.  132p.

264  Hooson, D.J.  The Soviet Union: people and regions. Belmont, Wadsworth; L., U. of London P., 1966.  376p.

265  Jorre, G.  The Soviet Union: the land and its people.  3rd ed.  N.Y., Wiley; L., Longmans, 1967.  379p.

266    Kish, G.   Russia.   Garden City, N.Y., Doubleday, 1958.    63p.

267    Lydolph, P.E.   Geography of the U.S.S.R.   2nd ed.   N.Y., Wiley,    1970.
       683p.

268    Mellor, R.E.H.   Geography of the U.S.S.R.   L.,   Macmillan;   N.Y., St Mar-
       tin's P., 1964.    403p.

269    Mikhailov, N.N.   Soviet land and people:   a pocket geography of the USSR
       L., Soviet News, 1950.    118p.

270    Mirov, N.T.   Geography of Russia.   N.Y., Wiley;   L., Chapman & Hall, 1951
       362p.

271    Muraka, D.   The Soviet Union.   N.Y., Walker;   L., Thames & Hudson, 1971.
       240p.

272    Berg, L.S.   Natural regions of the U.S.S.R.:   ed. by J.A. Morrison, C.C.
       Nikiforoff.   N.Y., L., Macmillan, 1950.    436p.

273    Shabad, T.   The geography of the U.S.S.R.:   a regional survey.   N.Y., L.,
       Columbia U.P., 1951.    584p.

274    Balzak, S.S. and others.   Economic geography of the U.S.S.R.   N.Y.;    L.,
       Macmillan, 1949.    620p.

275    Baransky, N.N.   Economic geography of the U.S.S.R.   Moscow, FLPH,   1956.
       413p.

276    Cole, J.P., German, F.C.   A geography of the U.S.S.R.:   the background to
       a planned economy.   2nd ed.   L., Butterworths, 1970.    324p.

277    Mikhaylov, N.N.   Soviet geography:   the new industrial and economic dist-
       ributions of the U.S.S.R. 2nd ed.   L., Methuen, 1937.    229p.

278    Mikhailov, N.N.   Land of the Soviets:   a handbook of the U.S.S.R.   N.Y.,
       Furman, 1939.    351p.

279    Mikhailov, N.N. , Pokshinshevsky, V.V.   Soviet Russia:   the land and its
       people.   N.Y., Sheridan, 1948.    374p.

280    Mikhailov, N.N.   Glimpses of the U.S.S.R.:   its economy and geography.
       Moscow, FLPH, 1960.    297p.

281    Saushkin, I.G.   Economic geography of the Soviet Union.   Oslo, Akademisk
       Forlag, 1956.    150p.

282    Symons, L.   Russian agriculture:   a geographic survey.   N.Y.,   Wiley; L.,
       Bell, 1972.    348p.

283    Tseplyaev, V.P.   The forests of the U.S.S.R.   N.Y., Davey, 1966.   527p.

284    Kazakov, G.   Soviet peat resources:   a descriptive study.   N.Y., Research
       Program on the U.S.S.R., 1953.    201p.

285 Gerasimov, I.P. and others. Natural resources of the Soviet Union: their
use and renewal. San Francisco, Freeman, 1971.   349p.

286 Shabad, T.  Basic industrial resources of the U.S.S.R.  N.Y., Columbia U.
P., 1969.   393p.

287 Shimkin, D.B.  Minerals:  a key to Soviet power.  Cambridge, Mass., Harvard U.P., 1953.   452p.

288 Hodgkins, J.A.  Soviet power:  energy resources, production and potentials.  Englewood Cliffs; L., Prentice-Hall, 1961.   190p.

289 Hassman, H.  Oil in the Soviet Union:  history, geography, problems; with
the addition of much new information by A.M. Leeston.  Princeton, Princeton U.P., 1953.   173p.

290 Crosfield, Joseph, & Sons Ltd.  The location of Communist industry.  Warrington, Lancs., 1963.   109p.

291 Pryde, P.R.  Conservation in the Soviet Union.  Cambridge, Cambridge U.P.
1972.   301p.

292 Goldman, M.I.  The spoils of progress:  environmental pollution in the
Soviet Union.  Cambridge, Mass., M.I.T.P., 1972.   374p.

293 Izmerov, N.F.  Control of air pollution in the U.S.S.R.  Geneva, World H-
ealth Organization, 1973.   157p.

294 Fox, I.K.  Water resources law and policy in the Soviet Union.   Madison,
U. of Wisconsin P., 1971.   256p.


C   Picture books

295 Cartier-Bresson, H.  The people of Moscow.  N.Y., Simon & Schuster;  L.,
Thanes & Hudson, 1955.   163p.

296 Fichelle, A.  Russia in pictures:  from Moscow to Samarkand;   178 photographs.  N.Y., Studio;  L., Duckworth, 1956.   128p.

297 Hurlimann, M.  Moscow and Leningrad.  N.Y., Studio;  L., Thames & Hudson,
1958.   135p.

298 Kelly, M.N.  The Country Life picture book of Russia.  L., Country Life,
1952.   80p.

299 Klimenko, G.  Russia in pictures.  L., Oak Tree P., 1967.   64p.

300 Lensen, G.A.  April in Russia:  a photographic study.  Tallahassee, Diplomatic P., 1970.   208p.

301 Low, D., Martin, K.  Low's Russian sketchbook.  L., Gollancz, 1932. 141p.

302 Lukas, J.  Moscow:  a book of photographs.  L., Spring Books, 1964. 160p.

303  Neubert, K.  Portrait of Leningrad.  L., Hamlyn, 1966.  92p.

304  Vicky.  Meet the Russians.  L., Reinhardt, 1953.  60p.


D  Description and Travel Accounts

305  Ransome, A.  Russia in 1919.  N.Y., Huebach, 1919.  232p.;  Six weeks in
     Russia in 1919.  L., Allen & Unwin, 1919.  150p.

306  Goode, W.T.  Bolshevism at work.  L., Allen & Unwin, 1920.  142p.

307  Lansbury, G.  What I saw in Soviet Russia.  N.Y., Boni & Liveright;  L.,
     Parsons, 1920.  166p.

308  McBride, I.  "Barbarous Soviet Russia".  N.Y., Thomas Seltzer,  1920.
     155p.

309  Schwartz, A.  The voice of Russia.  N.Y., Dutton, 1920.  223p.

310  Snowden, E.A.  Through Bolshevik Russia.  L., Cassell, 1920.  188p.

311  Varney, J.C.  Sketches of Soviet Russia:  whole cloth and patches.  N.Y.,
     Nicholas Brown, 1920.  288p.

312  Malone, C.L.  The Russian Republic.  L., Allen & Unwin, 1920.  135p.

313  Brailsford, H.N.  The Russian workers republic.  N.Y., Harper, 1921. 274p
     L., Allen & Unwin, 1921.  206p.

314  Clarke, J.S.  Pen pictures of Russia under the 'Red Terror':  reminiscen-
     ces of a surreptitious journey to Russia to attend the 2nd Congress of t-
     he 3rd International.  Glasgow, National Workers Committees, 1921.  327p.

315  Englishwoman, An.  From a Russian diary, 1917-1920.  L., Murray,  1921.
     263p.

316  Harrison, M.E.  Marooned in Moscow:  the story of an American woman impr-
     isoned in Russia.  N.Y., Doran, 1921; L., Butterworth, 1922.  322p.

317  Pankhurst, S.  Soviet Russia as I saw it.  L., The Worker's Dreadnought,
     1921.  195p.

318  Ransome, A.  The crisis in Russia.  N.Y., Huebsch, 1921. 201p.; L., Allen
     & Unwin, 1921.  152p.

319  Roberts, C.E.B.  Through starving Russia:  being the record of a journey
     to Moscow and the Volga provinces in August and September 1921.  L., Met-
     huen, 1921.  165p.

320  Sheridan, C.C.  Mayfair to Moscow:  Clare Sheridan's diary.  N.Y., Boni
     & Liveright, 1921.  239p.;  Russian portraits.  L., Cape, 1921.  202p.

321  Terpenning, W.  To Russia and return.  No imprint.  120p.

322   Wells, H.G.   Russia in the shadows.   N.Y., Doran, 1921.   179p.; L., Hod-
      der & Stoughton, 1921.     154p.

323   Buxton, C.R.   In a Russian village.   L., Labour Publishing Co., 1922.96p.

324   Dukes, P.   Red dusk and the morrow:   adventures and investigations in red
      Russia.   Garden City, N.Y., Doubleday, 1922; L., Williams & Norgate,1922.
      312p.

325   Bryant, L.   Mirrors of Moscow.   N.Y., Thomas Seltzer, 1923.     209p.

326   Goldman, E.   My disillusionment in Russia.   Garden City, N.Y., Doubleday,
      1923.   242p.; L., Daniel, 1925.     263p.

327   Keun, O.   My adventures in Russia.   N.Y., Dodd; L., Lane, 1923.     320p.

328   Mackenzie, F.A.   Russia before dawn.   L., Fisher Unwin, 1923.     282p.

329   Maslov, S.S.   Russia after four years of revolution.   L., King,     1923.
      237p.

330   Goldman, E.   My further disillusionment in Russia.   Garden City,   N.Y.,
      Doubleday, 1924.     178p.

331   Marx, M.   The romance of a new Russia.   N.Y., Thomas Seltzer, 1924.   225p

332   Sarolea, C.   Impressions of Soviet Russia.   L., Nash & Grayson,1924. 276p

333   Strong, A.L.   The first time in history:   two years of Russia's new life
      (August 1921 to December 1923).   N.Y., Boni & Liveright;   L., Labour Pub-
      lishing Co., 1924.     249p.

334   Weidenfeld, K.   The remaking of Russia.   L., Labour Publishing Co., 1924.
      116p.

335   Berkman, A.   The Bolshevik myth:   diary, 1920-1922.   N.Y., Boni & Liveri-
      ght;   L., Hutchinson, 1925.     319p.

336   British trade union delegation to Russia and the Caucasus.   Russia.   L.,
      Trade Unions Congress, 1925.     234p.

337   Hullinger, E.W.   The reforging of Russia.   N.Y., Dutton, 1925.     390p.;
      L., Witherby, 1925.     402p.

338   Makeev, N., O'Hara, V.   Russia.   L., Benn, 1925.     346p.

339   Nichevo.   Burned bridges.   L., Grayson, 1925.     254p.

340   Shelley, G.   The blue steppes:   adventures among the Russians.   L., Hami-
      lton, 1925.     268p.

341   Shelley, G.   The speckled domes:   episodes of an Englishman's life in Ru-
      ssia.   L., Duckworth, 1925.     256p.

342 Sorokin, P. Leaves from a Russian diary. L., Hurst & Blackett, 1925. 310p.

343 Soviet eyewash: socialist whitewash; an examination of the official report of the B.T.U. delegation to Russia in November and December, 1924. Tiptree, The Anchor P., 1925. 124p.

344 Beraud, H. The truth about Moscow as seen by a French visitor. L., Faber & Gwyer, 1926. 261p.

345 Guest, L.H. The new Russia. L., Butterworth, 1926. 488p.

346 Nearing, S. Glimpses of the Soviet Union. N.Y., Social Science Publishers, 1926. 32p.

347 Porter, A. A Moscow diary. Chicago, Kerr, 1926. 153p.

348 American trade union delegation to the Soviet Union. Russia after ten years. N.Y., International Publishers, 1927. 96p.

349 Bury, H. Russia from within: personal experiences of many years, and especially since 1923, with opinions and convictions formed in consequence. L., Churchman, 1927. 226p.

350 Karlgren, A. Bolshevist Russia. N.Y., Macmillan; L., Allen & Unwin, 1927. 311p.

351 Lawton, L. The Russian revolution (1917-1926). L., Macmillan, 1927. 499p.

352 Lee, I. U.S.S.R. (Union of Soviet Socialist Republics): a world enigma. L., Benn, 1927. 192p.

353 McWilliams, R.F., McWilliams, M.S. Russia in nineteen twenty-six. N.Y., Dutton; L, Dent, 1927. 128p.

354 Rosenberg, J.N. On the steppes: a Russian diary. N.Y., Knopf, 1927. 215p.

355 Williams, A.R. The Russian land. N.Y., New Republic, 1927. 294p.

356 Brown, W.J. Three months in Russia. L., Labour Publishing Co., 1928. 189p.

357 Buxton, D.F. The challenge of Bolshevism: a new social ideal. L., Allen & Unwin, 1928. 95p.

358 Chase, S. and others. Soviet Russia in the second decade: a joint survey by the technical staff of the first American Trade Union Delegation. N.Y., John Day; L., Williams & Norgate, 1928. 364p.

359 Dreiser, T. Dreiser looks at Russia. N.Y., Liveright, 1928.; L., Cape, 1929. 264p.

360  Dykstra, G.O.  A belated rebuttal with Russia.  Allegan, Allegan P., 1928.
     196p.

361  Lee, I.L.  Present day Russia.  N.Y., Macmillan, 1928.    204p.

362  London, G.  Red Russia after ten years.  L., Methuen, 1928.    182p.

363  Newman, E.M.  Seeing Russia.  N.Y., Funk & Wagnalls, 1928.    382p.

364  Thompson, D.  The new Russia.  N.Y., Holt, 1928.    317p.; L., Cape, 1929.
     330p.

365  Ashmead-Bartlett, E.  The riddle of Russia.  L., Cassell, 1929.    266p.

366  Dewey, J.  Impressions of Soviet Russia and the revolutionary world- Mex-
     ico, China, Turkey.  N.Y., New Republic, 1929.    270p.

367  Dillon, E.J.  Russia today and tomorrow.  L., Dent, 1929.    325p.

368  Greenwall, H.J.  Mirrors of Moscow.  L., Harrap, 1929.    244p.

369  McCormick, A.O.  The hammer and the scythe:  Communist Russia enters the
     second decade.  N.Y., Knopf, 1929.;  Communist Russia:  the hammer and the
     scythe.  L., Williams & Norgate, 1929.    295p.

370  Tweedie, Mrs. A.  An adventurous journey:  Russia-Siberia-China.  Rev.ed.
     L., Butterworth, 1929.    286p.

371  Vidor, J.  Spying in Russia.  L., Lang, 1929.    284p.

372  Viollis, A.  A girl in Soviet Russia.  N.Y., Crowell, 1929.    347p.

373  Chamberlin, W.H.  Soviet Russia:  a living record and a history.  N.Y.,
     Chautauqua P.;  L., Duckworth, 1930.    425p.

374  De Chessin, S.  Darkness from the East.  L., Harrap, 1930.    252p.

375  Counts, G.S.  A Ford crosses Soviet Russia.  Boston, Mass.,    Stratford,
     1930.    233p.

376  Douillet, J.  Moscow unmasked:  a record of nine years' work and observa-
     tion in Soviet Russia.  L., Pilot P., 1930.    223p.

377  Edelhertz, B.  The Russian paradox:  a first-hand study of life under the
     Soviets.  N.Y., Walton Bk. Co., 1930.    152p.

378  Farson, N.  Seeing red:  today in Russia.  L., Eyre & Spottiswoode, 1930.
     275p.

379  Feiler, A.  The Russian experiment.  N.Y., Harcourt, 1930. 269p.;    The
     experiment of Bolshevism.  L., Allen & Unwin, 1930.    256p.

380  Foss, K.  Black bread and samovars:  an account of an unconventional jou-
     rney through Soviet Russia.  L., Arrowsmith, 1930.    247p.

381   Herrington, L.M.   A doctor diagnoses Russia. McKees Rocks, Penn., Herrington, 1930.   127p.

382   Rowan—Hamilton, N.   Under the red star.   L., Jenkins, 1930.   316p.

383   Barbusse, H.   One looks at Russia.   L., Dent, 1931.   206p.

384   Bourke—White, M.   Eyes on Russia.   N.Y., Simon & Schuster, 1931.   135p.

385   Brun, A.H.   Troublous times:   experiences in Bolshevik Russia and Turkestan.   L., Constable, 1931.   238p.

386   Chesterton, Mrs. C.   My Russian venture.   Philadelphia, Lippincott;   L.,
Harrap, 1931.   283p.

387   Counts, G.S.   The Soviet challenge to America.   N.Y., John Day, 1931. 339p

388   Eddy, J.S.   The challenge of Russia.   L., Jenkins, 1931.   278p.

389   Forman, A.   From Baltic to Black Sea:   impressions of Soviet Russia today.
L., Low, 1931.   240p.

390   Grady, E.G.   Seeing red:   behind the scenes in Russia today.   N.Y., Brew-
er, Warren & Putnam, 1931.   307p.

391   Hopper, B.   What Russia intends:   the peoples, plans and policy of Soviet
Russia.   L., Cape, 1931.   283p.

392   Istrait, P.   Russia unveiled.   L., Allen & Unwin, 1931.   262p.

393   Johnson, J.   Russia in the grip of Bolshevism:   a vivid story of a trip
to the land of the   Soviets.   N.Y., Revell, 1931.   160p.

394   Knickerbocker, H.R. and others.   The new Russia.   L., Faber, 1931. 126p.

395   Lipphard, W.B.   Communing with Communism:   a narrative of impressions of
Soviet Russia.   Philadelphia, Judson, 1931.   153p.

396   Loder, J. de V.   Bolshevism in perspective.   L., Allen & Unwin,   1931.
244p.

397   Long, R.   An editor looks at Russia:   one unprejudiced view of the land
of the Soviets.   N.Y., Long & Smith, 1931.; L., Constable, 1932.   114p.

398   Muldavin, A.   The red fog lifts.   N.Y., Appleton Century, 1931.   311p.

399   Noe, A.C.   Golden days of Soviet Russia.   Chicago, Rockwell, 1931   181p.

400   O'Flaherty, L.   I went to Russia.   L., Cape, 1931.   299p.

401   Polunin, N.   Russian waters.   L., Arnold, 1931.   306p.

402   Quisling, V.   Russia and ourselves.   L., Hodder & Stoughton, 1931.   284p.

403   Scheffer, P.   Seven years in Soviet Russia, with a retrospect.   N.Y., L.,

Putnam, 1931.    357p.

404  Sibley, R.  America's answer to the Russian challenge:  in which electric
     power, as a common denominator, is requisitioned to throw light on the R-
     ussian enigma and the challenge it presents to western civilization.  San
     Francisco, Farollan P., 1931.    171p.

405  Taylor, S.  Soviet and soul:  Russia through the eyes of youth.  L., Hou-
     ghton, 1931.    164p.

406  Toller, E.  Which world - which way?:  travel pictures from Russia and
     America.  L., Low, Marston, 1931.    178p.

407  Tweedie, O.  Russia at random.  L., Jarrolds, 1931.    192p.

408  White, W.C.  These Russians.  N.Y., Scribner's, 1931.    376p.

409  Acheson, J.  Young America looks at Russia.  N.Y., Stokes, 1932.    253p.

410  Burrell, G.A.  An American engineer looks at Russia.  Boston,  Mass.,
     Stratford, 1932.    324p.

411  Byron, R.  First Russia, then Tibet.  L., Macmillan, 1932.    328p.

412  Campbell, T.D.  Russia:  market or menace?  L., Longmans, 1932.    148p.

413  Craig-McKerrow, M.  The iron road to Samarcand.  L., De La Mare P., 1932.
     143p.

414  Crichton, C.F.A.M.-M.  Russian close-up.  L., Chatto & Windus, 1932.167p.

415  Darling, J.  Ding goes to Russia.  N.Y., McGraw-Hill, 1932.    195p.

416  Eckhardt, H. von.  Russia.  L., Cape, 1932.    711p.

417  Fischer, L.  Men and machines in Russia.  N.Y., Harrison Smith, 1932.283p

418  Frank, W.  Dawn in Russia:  the record of a journey.  N.Y.;  L., Scribne-
     r's, 1932.    272p.

419  Griffin, F.  Soviet scene:  a newspaperman's closeups of new Russia.  L.;
     Toronto, Macmillan, 1932.    279p.

420  Griffith, H.  Seeing Soviet Russia:  an informative account of the cheap-
     est trip in Europe.  L., Lane, 1932.    199p.

421  Hindus, M.G.  Humanity uprooted.  2nd ed.  Garden City, N.Y., Blue Ribbon
     Bks., 1932;  L., Cape, 1931.    370p.

422  Huxley J.  A scientist among the Soviets.  N.Y., Harper, 1932.  142p.; L.
     Chatto, 1932.    119p.

423  Jones, G.V.  Experiences in Russia - 1931:  a diary.  Pittsburg, Alton P.
     1932.

424  Mackiewicz, S.  Russian minds in fetters.  L., Allen & Unwin, 1932. 182p.

425  Monzie, A.de.  New Russia.  L., Allen & Unwin, 1932.    374p.

426  Nurenberg, T.  This new red freedom.  N.Y., Wadsworth, 1932.    327p.

427  Raiguel, G.E., Huff, W.K.  This is Russia.  Philadelphia, Penn Publishing Co., 1932.    423p.

428  Robinson, W.J.  Soviet Russia as I saw it;  its accomplishments, its crime and stupidities.  N.Y., International, 1932.    224p.

429  Rukeyser, W.A.  Working for the Soviets:  an American engineer in Russia.
N.Y., Covici-Friede;  L., Cape, 1932.    286p.

430  Seibert, T.  Red Russia.  N.Y., Century;  L., Allen & Unwin, 1932. 422p.

431  Walter, E.  Russia's decisive year.  N.Y., Putnam;  L., Hutchinson, 1932.
282p.

432  Wright, R.  One sixth of the world's surface.  Hammond, Ind., privately
printed, 1932.    145p.

433  Brown, E.T.  This Russian business.  L., Allen & Unwin, 1933.    256p.

434  Cole, M.I.  Twelve studies in Soviet Russia.  L., Gollancz, 1933. 282p.

435  Cummings, E.E.  Eimi (the journal of a trip to Russia).  N.Y., Covici-Friede, 1933.    432p.

436  Durant, W.  The lesson of Russia:  impressions from a brief visit.  N.Y.,
Simon & Schuster;  L., Putnam, 1933.    164p.

437  Hindus, M.G.  The great offensive.  N.Y., Smith and Haas;  L.,  Gollancz,
1933.    368p.

438  Hoyland, J.S.  The new Russia:  a Quaker visitor's impressions.  L., All-
enson, 1933.    94p.

439  Jarman, T.L.  Through Soviet Russia:  the diary of an English tourist. L.,
Houghton, 1933.    119p.

440  Lamont, C., Lamont, M.  Russia day by day:  a travel diary.  N.Y., Covici
-Friede, 1933.    260p.

441  Lockhart, J.G.  Babel revisited:  a churchman in Soviet Russia.  L., Cen-
tenary P., 1933.    128p.

442  Lyall, A.  Russian roundabout:  a non-political pilgrimage.  L., Harms-
worth, 1933.    207p.

443  Patrick, M.  Hammer and sickle.  L., Mathews & Marrot, 1933.    243p.

444  Purves-Stewart, J.  A physician's tour in Soviet Russia.  N.Y., Stokes;

L., Allen & Unwin, 1933.     176p.

445   Rowley, C.A.   Russia, a country up-side-down.   Painsville, Painsville
Telegraph Co., 1933.     196p.

446   Abbe, J.E.   I photograph Russia.   N.Y., McBride, 1934;   L., Harrap,   1935.
320p.

447   Duranty, W.   Duranty reports Russia;   ed. by G. Tuckerman.   N.Y., Viking,
1934.     351p.;   Russia reported.   L., Gollancz, 1934.     384p.

448   Durstine, R.S.   Red thunder.   N.Y.;   L., Scribner's 1934.     231p.

449   Eddy, S.   Russia today:   what we can learn from it.   N.Y., Farrar & Rinehart, 1934.     276p.

450   Elmhirst, L.K.   Trip to Russia.   N.Y., New Republic, 1934.     213p.

451   Grierson, J.   Through Russia by air.   L., Foulis, 1934.     174p.

452   Hamilton, C.M.   Modern Russia as seen by an English-woman.   N.Y., Dutton;
L., Dent, 1934.     235p.

453   Herriot, E.   Eastward from Paris.   L., Gollancz, 1934.     318p.

454   Muggeridge, M.   Winter in Moscow.   L., Eyre & Spottiswoode, 1934.     252p.

455   Rubin, J.H., Rubin, V.   I live to tell:   the Russian adventures of an American socialist.   Indianapolis, Bobbs-Merrill, 1934;   Moscow mirage.   L.,
Bles, 1935.     330p.

456   Skariatina, I.   First to go back:   an aristocrat in Soviet Russia.   L.,
Gollancz, 1934.     318p.

457   Smith, M.E.   From Broadway to Moscow.   N.Y., Macaulay, 1934.     317p.

458   Wells, C.   Kapoot:   the narrative of a journey from Leningrad to Mount
Ararat in search of Noah's Ark.   N.Y., McBride, 1934. 251p.;   L., Jarrolds, 1934.     285p.

459   Westgarth, J.R.   Russian engineer.   L., Archer, 1934.     193p.

460   Wicksteed, A.   My Russian neighbors;   recollections of ten years in Soviet Russia.   N.Y., Whittlesey House, 1934.     218p.

461   Fischer, L.   Soviet journey.   N.Y., Smith & Haas, 1935.     308p.

462   Franck, H.A.   A vagabond in Sovietland: America's perennial rambler goes
tourist.   N.Y., Stokes, 1935.     267p.

463   Gibson, W.J.   Wild career: my crowded years of adventure in Russia and
the Near East.   L., Harrap, 1935.     287p.

464   Griffith, H.F.   Playtime in Russia.   L., Methuen, 1935.     249p.

465  Lyons, E.  Modern Moscow.  L., Hurst & Blackett, 1935.    286p.

466  Maybury, H.  The land of Nichevo.  Liverpool, Daily Post Printer,  1935.
     161p.

467  Rolland, R.  I will not rest.  L., Selwyn & Blount, 1935.    320p.

468  Seymour, J.  In the Moscow manner.  L., Archer, 1935.    186p.

469  Strong, A.L.  I change worlds:  the remaking of an American.  N.Y., Holt;
     L., Routlege, 1935.    422p.

470  Waters, W.H.-H.  Russia then and now.  L., Murray, 1935.    296p.

471  Brown, J.  I saw for myself.  L., Selwyn & Blount, 1936.    276p.

472  Bullitt, N.  Three weeks in Russia.  Louisville, Ky., privately printed,
     1936.    105p.

473  Carr, B.  Black bread and cabbage soup.  Cincinnati, Powell & White, 1936.
     320p.

474  Christopher, M.  No soap and the Soviet.  Plainfield, Red Ram P.,    1936.
     101p.

475  Coates, W.P., Coates, Z.K.  Scenes from Soviet life.  L., Lawrence & Wish-
     art, 1936.    295p.

476  Miles, F.J.  Changing Russia.  L., Marshall, 1936.    144p.

477  Pares, B.  Moscow admits a critic.  L., Nelson, 1936.    94p.

478  Smith, A.  I was a Soviet worker.  N.Y., Dutton, 1936.  298p.;  L., Hale,
     1937.    286p.

479  Strom, A.  Uncle, give us bread.  L., Allen & Unwin, 1936.    357p.

480  Conolly, V.  Soviet tempo:  a journal of travel in Russia.  N.Y., Sheed
     & Ward, 1937;  L., Secker & Warburg, 1938.    189p.

481  Delafield, E.M.  I visit the Soviets.  N.Y., Harper, 1937.  344p.;  Straw
     without bricks:  I visit Soviet Russia.  L., Macmillan, 1937.    262p.

482  Duranty, W.  I write as I please.  N.Y., Simon & Schuster;  L., Hamilton,
     1935.    349p.

483  Feuchtwanger, L.  Moscow, 1937:  my visit described for my friends.  N.Y.
     Viking, 1937.  151p.;  Moscow, 1937.  L., Gollancz, 1937.    174p.

484  Gide, A.  Back from the U.S.S.R.  N.Y., Knopf;  L., Secker & Warburg,1937.
     121p.

485  Gould, M.  I visit the Soviets.  Toronto, Francis White Publications,1937.
     166p.

486  Hooper, A.S.  Through Soviet Russia, 1937.  No imprint, 1937.    126p.

487  Lee, H.  Twenty years after:  life in the U.S.S.R. today.  L., Lawrence
     & Wishart, 1937.    172p.

488  Littlepage, J.D., Bess, K.  In search of Soviet gold.  N.Y., Harcourt,
     1937.  310p.;  L., Harrap, 1939.    287p.

489  Lyons, E.  Assignment in Utopia.  N.Y., Harcourt, 1937.;  L., Harrap,1938.
     648p.

490  Mannin, E.  South to Samarkand.  N.Y., Dutton, 1937.;  L., Jarrolds, 1936.
     355p.

491  Marchant, H.S.  Scratch a Russian.  L., Drummond, 1937.    212p.

492  Stucley, P.  Russian spring.  L., Selwyn & Blount, 1937.    286p.

493  Terrell, R.  Soviet understanding.  L., Hutchinson, 1937.    284p.

494  P.T. (= Travers, P.L.)  Moscow excursion.  N.Y., Reynal & Hitchcock, 1937;
     L., Howe, 1934.    114p.

495  Williams, A.R.  The Soviets.  N.Y., Harcourt, 1937.    554p.

496  Allan, S.R.  Comrades and citizens.  L., Gollancz, 1938.    383p.

497  Bigland, E.  Laughing odyssey.  N.Y., Macmillan, 1938;  L., Hodder & Stou-
     ghton, 1937.    307p.

498  Chesterton, Mrs. C.  Sickle or swastika?  L., Paul, 1938.    268p.

499  Citrine, W.  I search for truth in Russia.  2nd ed. L., Routledge,  1938.
     420p.

500  Claudia.  Back to our own country, Russia:  land of the romantic past and
     the pregnant future.  L., Stockwell, 1938.    256p.

501  Dawson, P.M.  Soviet samples:  diary of an American physiologist.    Ann
     Arbor, Edward Brothers, 1938.    538p.

502  Gide, A.  Afterthoughts:  a sequel to "Back from the U.S.S.R." .    N.Y.,
     Dial P.;  L., Secker & Warburg, 1938.    142p.

503  Luck, S.I.  Observation in Russia.  L., Macmillan, 1938.    339p.

504  Newman, B.  Ride to Russia.  L., Jenkins, 1938.    332p.

505  Pope-Hennessy, U.B.  The closed city:  impressions of a visit to Leningrad.
     L., Hutchinson, 1938.    254p.

506  Silver, B.  The Russian workers' own story.  L., Allen & Unwin,    1938.
     251p.

507  Sloan, P.  Russia without illusions.  L., Muller, 1938.    268p.

508  The Soviet comes of age, by 28 of the foremost citizens of the U.S.S.R.;
     foreword by S. and B. Webb.  L., Hodge, 1938.    337p.

509  Francis, P.G.  I worked in a Soviet factory.  L., Jarrolds, 1939.  228p.

510  Timbres, H., Timbres, R.  We didn't ask Utopia:  a Quaker family in Russ-
     ia.  N.Y., Prentice-Hall, 1939.    290p.

511  Ciliga, A.  The Russian enigma.  L., Labour Bk. Service, 1940.    304p.

512  Johnson, H.  The Soviet power:  the socialist sixth of the world.  N.Y.,
     International Publishers, 1940.  346p.;  The Socialist sixth of the world.
     L., Gollancz, 1939.    384p.

513  Lansbury, V.  An Englishwoman in the U.S.S.R.  L., Putnam, 1940.    325p.

514  Trivanovitch, V.  Crankshafts or bread.  Ridgefield, Acorn Publishing Co.,
     1940.    236p.

515  Utley, F.  The dream we lost.  N.Y., John Day, 1940.    361p.

516  Cowles, V.  Looking for trouble.  L., Hamilton, 1941.    469p.

517  Hampel, E.  Yankee bride in Moscow.  N.Y., Liveright, 1941.    319p.

518  Pares, B.  Russia. 3rd ed.  L., Allan, 1941.    254p.

519  U.S.S.R. speaks for itself.  L., Lawrence & Wishart, 1941.    4 vols.

520  Barber, N.  Trans-Siberian.  L., Harrap, 1942.    180p.

521  Bigland, E.  The key to the Russian door.  L., Putnam, 1942.    254p.

522  Caldwell, E.  Moscow under fire:  a wartime diary, 1941.  L., Hutchinson,
     1942.    112p.

523  Chesterton, Mrs. C.  Salute the Soviet.  L., Chapman & Hall, 1942. 215p.

524  Citrine, W.  In Russia now.  L., Hale, 1942.    154p.

525  Duner, P.  A year and a day.  L., Drummond, 1942.    219p.

526  Edelman, M.  How Russia prepared:  U.S.S.R. beyond the Urals.  N.Y., Pen-
     guin, 1942.    127p.

527  Graebner, W.  Round trip to Russia.  Philadelphia, Lippincott,    1943.
     216p.

528  Hindus, M.  Russia fights on.  L., Collins, 1942.    255p.

529  Russian boy.  L., King, 1942.    139p.

530   Scott, J.   Behind the Urals:   an American worker in Russia's city of ste-
      el.   Boston, Mass., Houghton, 1942.    266p.

531   Werth, A.   Moscow '41.   L., Hamilton, 1942.    268p.

532   Borodin, G.   This Russian land.   L., Hutchinson,  1943.    184p.

533   Cassidy, H.C.   Moscow dateline, 1941-1943.   Boston, Mass., Houghton, 1943.
      367p.

534   Chamberlin, W.H.   The Russian enigma:   an interpretation.   N.Y., Scribner,
      1943.    321p.

535   Cole, M. and others.   Our Soviet ally.   L., Routledge, 1943.    194p.

536   Curie, E.   Journey among warriors.   L., Bell, 1943.    223p.

537   Dobb, M.H.   U.S.S.R.:   her life and her people.   L., U. of London P.,1943.
      138p.

538   Hindus, M.G.   Mother Russia.   N.Y., Garden City Publ. Co., 1943.    395p.;
      L., Collins, 1943.    512p.

539   Johnson, H.   The secret of Soviet strength.   N.Y., International Publis-
      hers, 1943.;   L., Muller, 1942.    154p.

540   Moore-Pataleewa, B.   I am a woman from Soviet Russia.    L.,   Gollancz,
      1943.    304p.

541   Sava, G.   Russia triumphant.   L., Faber, 1943.    216p.

542   Segal, L.   The real Russia.   L., Evans, 1943.    160p.

543   Strong, A.L.   The Russians are people.   L., Cobbett, 1943.    202p.

544   Tendulkar, D.G.   30 months in Russia.   Bombay, Karnatak, 1943.    96p.

545   Williams, A.R.   The Russians, the land, the people and why they fight.
      N.Y., Harcourt;   L., Harrap, 1943.    239p.

546   Dallin, D.J.   The real Soviet Russia.   New Haven, Yale U.P., 1944. 260p;
      L., Hollis & Carter, 1947.    298p.

547   Fischer, M.   My lives in Russia.   N.Y., Harper, 1944.    269p.

548   Loukomski, G.   The face of Russia.   L., Hitchinson, 1944.    108p.

549   Myles, N.W.   Behold Russia:   a vivid description of modern European Rus-
      sia.   Dallas, Mathis-Van-Hort, 1944.    258p.

550   Nazaroff, A.I.   The land of the Russian people.   Philadelphia, Lippincott,
      1944.    160p.

551   Pruszynski, X.   Russian year:   the notebook of an amateur diplomat. N.Y.,

Roy, 1944.     189p.

552   Street, L.  I married a Russian:  letters from Kharkov.  N.Y., Macmillan, 1944.     264p.;  L., Allen & Unwin, 1944.     288p.

553   Strong, A.L.  Peoples of the U.S.S.R.  N.Y., Macmillan, 1944.     246p.

554   Werth, A.  Leningrad.  N.Y., Knopf, 1944.     189p.

555   Buck, P.S.  Talk about Russia with Masha Scott.  N.Y., John Day,     1945. 128p.

556   Falkson, E.L.  A cockney among the reds.  L., Stockwell, 1945.     237p.

557   Lauterbach, R.E.  These are the Russians.  N.Y.;  L., Harper, 1945. 368p.

558   Snow, E.  People on our side.  Cleveland, World Publishing Co.,     1945. 324p.

559   Stevens, E.  Russia is no riddle.  N.Y., Greenberg, 1945.     300p.

560   Ward, H.F.  The Soviet spirit.  N.Y., International, 1945.     160p.

561   West, W., Mitchell, J.  Our good neighbors in Soviet Russia.  N.Y., Noble, 1945.     273p.

562   Wettlin, M.  Russian road:  three years of war in Russia as lived through by an American woman.  L., Hutchinson, 1945.     126p.

563   White, W.L.  Report on the Russians.  N.Y., Harcourt, 1945.     309p.; L., Eyre & Spottiswoode, 1945.     259p.

564   Winter, E.  I saw the Russian people.  Boston, Mass., Little, 1945. 299p.

565   Winterton, P.  Report on Russia.  L., Cresset P., 1945.     138p.

566   Ciliberti, C.  Backstairs mission in Moscow.  N.Y., Booktab P., 1946. 128p

567   Gibberd, K.  Soviet Russia:  an introduction.  New ed. L., RIIA,     1946. 124p.

568   Gregory, J.S.  Land of the Soviets.  L., Penguin, 1946.     284p.

569   Jacob, A.  A window in Moscow.  L., Collins, 1946.     320p.

570   King, B.  Introducing the U.S.S.R.  L., Pitman, 1946.     112p.

571   Lamont, C.  The peoples of the Soviet Union.  N.Y., Harcourt, 1946. 229p.

572   Lucas, W.O.  East of the Iron Curtain.  Chicago, Ziff-Davies, 1946. 361p.

573   Moorad, G.  Behind the curtain.  Philadelphia, Fireside P., 1946.     309p.

574   Salisbury, H.E.  Russia on the way.  N.Y., Macmillan, 1946.     414p.

575  Soloveytchik, G.  Russia in perspective.  L., Macdonald, 1946.    170p.

576  Ashby, E.  Scientist in Russia.  L., Penguin, 1947.    252p.

577  Atkinson, O.  Over at Uncle Joe's:  Moscow and me.  Indianapolis, Bobbs-
     Merrill, 1947.    325p.

578  Baczkowski, W.  Towards an understanding of Russia:  a study in policy
     and strategy.  Jerusalem, 1947.    215p.

579  Fischer, J.  Why they behave like Russians.  N.Y.; L., Harper, 1947. 262p

580  Fischer, J.  The scared men in the Kremlin.  L., Hamilton, 1947.    200p.

581  Gray, G.D.B.  Soviet land:  the country, its people and their work. L.,
     Black, 1947.    324p.

582  Jenkins, A.C.  Dear Olga.  L., Lane, 1947.    143p.

583  Johnson, H.  Soviet Russia since the war.  N.Y., Boni & Gaer, 1947. 270p.;
     L., Hutchinson, 1947.    292p.

584  King, F.  Footloose in the Soviet Union.  L., Valiant, 1947.    144p.

585  Kunitz, J.  Russia, the giant that came last.  N.Y., Dodd, 1947.    413p.

586  Lauterbach, R.E.  Through Russia's back door.  N.Y.; L., Harper,  1947.
     219p.

587  Lawrence, J.  Life in Russia.  L., Allen & Unwin, 1947.    239p.

588  Martel, G.  The Russian outlook.  L., Joseph, 1947.    187p.

589  Stern, B., Smith, S.  Understanding the Russians:  a study of Soviet life
     and culture.  N.Y., Barnes & Noble, 1947.    246p.

590  Street, L.  I married a Russian: letters from Kharkov.  N.Y., Emerson Bks.,
     1947.    331p.; L., Allen & Unwin, 1944.    288p.

591  Strohm, L.  Just tell the truth:  the uncensored story of how the common
     people live behind the Russian Iron Curtain.  N.Y., Scribner, 1947. 243p.

592  Bigland, E.  Understanding the Russians.  L., People's Universities  P.,
     1948.    119p.

593  Clifford, A., Nicholson, J.  The sickle and the stars.  L., Peter Davies,
     1948.    252p.

594  Crankshaw, E.  Russia and the Russians.  N.Y., Viking, 1948.    223p.; L.,
     Macmillan, 1947.    256p.

595  Gouzenko, I.  Iron curtain.  N.Y., Dutton, 1948.    280p.;  This was my
     choice.  L., Eyre & Spottiswoode, 1948.    324p.

596   Maloney, J.J.   Inside red Russia.   Pasadena, Perkins, 1948.        207p.;
      Sidney, Angus & Robertson, 1948.      198p.

597   Mikhailov, N., Pokshishevsky, V.   Soviet Russia:   the land and its people
      N.Y., Sheridan, 1948.      383p.

598   Overseas Press Club of America.   As we see Russia.   N.Y., Dutton,   1948.
      316p.

599   Price, M.P.   Russia, red or white:   a record of a visit to Russia after
      twenty-seven years.   L., Sampson, Low, 1948.      120p.

600   Smith, J.   People come first.   N.Y., International Publishers, 1948. 254p

601   Steinbeck. J.   A Russian journal.   N.Y., Viking, 1948.; L., Heinemann,
      1949.      220p.

602   Thomson, J.   Russia:   the old and the new.   L., Murray, 1948.        187p.

603   Utley, F.   Lost illusion.   Philadelphia, Fireside P., 1948.   188p.;   L.,
      Allen & Unwin, 1949.      237p.

604   Winterton, P.   Inquest on an ally.   L., Cresset P., 1948.      288p.

605   Alexander, J.A.   In the shadows:   three years in Moscow.   Melbourne, Her-
      ald and Weekly Times, 1949.      356p.

606   Emmens, R.G.   Guests of the Kremlin.   N.Y., Macmillan, 1949.      291p.

607   Hilton, R.   Military attache in Moscow.   Toronto, McClelland & Stewart,
      1949.      232p.

608   Kasenkina, O.   Leap to freedom.   Philadelphia, Lippincott, 1949.   295p.;
      L., Hurst & Blackett, 1950.      232p.

609   Magidoff, R.   In anger and pity:   a report on Russia.   Garden City, N.Y.,
      Doubleday, 1949.      269p.

610   Markham, T.   Russian child and Russian wife.   Toronto, Longmans,   1949.
      287p.

611   Mikhailov, N.N.   Across the map of the U.S.S.R.   N.Y., Four Continents,
      1949.      344p.

612   Parker, R.   Moscow correspondent.   L., Muller, 1949.      302p.;   Toronto,
      Saunders, 1949.      288p.

613   White, W.L.   Land of milk and honey.   N.Y., Harcourt, 1949.      312p.

614   British Workers' Delegation.   Russia with our own eyes:   the full report
      of the British Workers' Delegation to the Soviet Union, 1950.   L.,   1950.
      128p.

615   Davis, J.   Behind Soviet power:   Stalin and the Russians.   W. Haven, Conn.,

Readers P., 1950.    124p.

616  Garelik, J.   A Soviet city and its people.   N.Y., International Publish-
     ers, 1950.   96p.

617  Goodfriend, A.   If you were born in Russia.   N.Y., Farrar, 1950.   192p.

618  Hughes, W.R.   Those human Russians:  a collection of incidents related by
     Germans.   L., Gollancz, 1950.   128p.

619  Lindsay, J.   A world ahead:  journal of a Soviet journey.   L., Fore Publ-
     ications, 1950.   164p.

620  MacLean, F.   Escape to adventure.   Boston, Mass., Little, 1950.   419p.;
     Eastern approaches.   L., Cape, 1949.   544p.

621  Pirogov, P.   Why I escaped.   N.Y., Duell, 1950.   336p.;   L., Harvill, 1950.
     288p.

622  Smith, W.B.   My three years in Moscow.   Philadelphia, Lippincott,   1950.
     335p.

623  Stevens, E.   This is Russia, uncensored.   N.Y., Didier, 1950.   200p.

624  Wood, W.   Our ally:  the people of Russia, as told to M. Siere.   N.Y.,
     Scribner, 1950.   287p.

625  Carter, C., Carter D.   We saw socialism.   Toronto, Canadian-Soviet Frien-
     dship Society, 1951.   396p.

626  Crankshaw, E.   Cracks in the Kremlin wall.   N.Y., Viking, 1951.   279p.;
     Russia by daylight.   L., Joseph, 1951.   240p.

627  Hueck, C.de   My Russian yesterdays.   Milwaukee, Bruce, 1951.   132p.

628  Graham, S.   Summing up on Russia.   L., Benn, 1951.   224p.

629  Kravchenko, V.   I chose justice.   L., Hale, 1951.   418p.

630  Laycock, H.   Moscow close-up.   L., Yates, 1951.   224p.

631  National Union of Students.   British students visit the Soviet Union:  a
     report of a delegation of the National Union of Students, 1951.   L., K-H
     Services, 1951.   96p.

632  Marion, G.   All quiet in the Kremlin.   N.Y., Fairplay Publishers,   1951.
     183p.

633  Singh, I.   Report on Russia.   Bombay, Kutub Publications, 1951.   188p.

634  Thayer, C.W.   Bears in the caviar.   Philadelphia, Lippincott, 1951. 303p.

635  Czarnomski, F.B.   Can Russia survive?  an examination of the facts and
     figures of Soviet reality.   L., Melville P., 1952.   128p.

636  Dallas, D.  Dateline Moscow.  L., Heinemann, 1952.    260p.

637  Gonzalez, V.  (El Campesino).  El Campesino: life and death in Soviet R-
     ussia.  N.Y., Putnam, 1952.  218p.; Listen, comrades:  life and death in
     Soviet Russia.  L., Heinemann, 1952.    203p.

638  Gordey, M.  Visa to Moscow.  N.Y., Knopf; L., Gollancz, 1952.    419p.

639  Harding, S.M.  The Soviet Union today:  a scientist's impressions.   L.,
     Lawrence & Wishart, 1952.    132p.

640  Hardy, F.J.  Journey into the future.  Melbourne, Australian Bk. Society,
     1952.    336p.

641  Kelly, M.N.  Mirror to Russia.  L., Country Life, 1952.    242p.

642  Kirk, L.S.  Postmarked Moscow.  N.Y., Scribner, 1952.  278p.; L., Duck-
     worth, 1953.    240p.

643  Lonsdale, K.  Quakers visit Russia.  L., Friends House, 1952.    145p.

644  Manton, S.M.  The Soviet Union today:  a scientist's impressions.   L.,
     Lawrence & Wishart, 1952.    132p.

645  Rounds, F.  A window on Red Square.  Boston, Mass., Houghton, 1952. 304p.

646  Berman, H.J.  Russians in focus.  Boston, Mass., Little, 1953.    209p.

647  Einsiedel, H. von.  I joined the Russians:  a captured German flier's di-
     ary of the Communist temptation.  New Haven, Yale U.P., 1953.    295p.

648  Guirey, C.  Shadow of power.  Indianapolis, Bobbs-Merrill, 1953.   315p.

649  Kyaw Min.  Through the Iron Curtain via the back door.  L., Benn,  1953.
     287p.

650  Lamont, C.  Soviet civilization.  N.Y., Philosophical Library; L., Elek,
     1953.    433p.

651  Watkins, H.M.  The dove and the sickle.  L., Fore Publications,    1953.
     118p.

652  Lyons, E.  Our secret allies:  the peoples of Russia.  Boston, Mass., Li-
     ttle, 1953.; L., Arco, 1954.    376p.

653  Magidoff, R.  The Kremlin vs the People:  the story of the Cold Civil War
     in Stalin's Russia.  Garden City, N.Y., Doubleday, 1953.    288p.

654  Rounds, F.  A window on Red Square.  Boston, Mass., Houghton, 1953. 304p.
     L., Muller, 1953.    240p.

655  Sassoon, P.  Penelope in Moscow.  L., Weidenfeld & Nicolson, 1953.   157p.

656  Stevens, L.C.  Russian assignment.  Boston, Mass., Little, 1953.    552p.

Life in Russia. L., Longmans, 1954.    403p.

657  Gilmore, E.  Me and my Russian wife.  Garden City, N.Y., Doubleday,1954.
313p.;  L., Fireside P., 1956.    256p.

658  Hecht, R.S.  Dancing with the bear:  a capitalist's impressions of Soviet
Russia.  New Orleans, Publications P., 1954.    105p.

659  MacColl, R.  Just back from Russia:  77 days inside the Soviet Union.  L.,
Beaverbrook Newspapers, 1954.    224p.

660  Mahmuduzzafar, S.  Quest for life:  a record of five months in the Soviet
Union.  Bombay, People's Publishing House, 1954.    155p.

661  Maks, L.  Russia by the back door.  N.Y.;  L., Sheed & Ward, 1954.  264p.

662  Tortora, V.R.  Communist close-up:  a roving reporter behind the Iron Curtain.  N.Y., Exposition, 1954.    160p.

663  Borodin, N.M.  One man in his time.  L., Constable, 1955.    344p.

664  Chappelow, A.  Russian holiday.  L., Harrap, 1955.    190p.

665  Egginton, J.  Excursion to Russia.  L., Hutchinson, 1955.    164p.

666  Higgins, M.  Red plush and black bread.  Garden City, N.Y., Doubleday,
1955.    256p.

667  MacDuffie, M.  The red carpet:  10,000 miles through Russia on a visa from Krushchev.  N.Y., Norton, 1955. 319p.;  L., Cassell, 1955.    330p.

668  Miller, J.  Soviet Russia:  an introduction.  L., Hutchinson, 1955. 185p.

669  Peltier, M.  Soviet encounter.  L., Bles, 1955.    244p.

670  Salisbury, H.E.  Americans in Russia.  N.Y., Harper, 1955.    328p.;
Stalin's Russia and after.  L., Macmillan, 1955.    329p.

671  Sergeant, P.  Another road to Samarkand.  L., Hodder & Stoughton,  1955.
157p.

672  Stockwood, M.  I went to Moscow.  L., Epworth, P., 1955.    198p.

673  Strogov, S.  Escape from Moscow:  the diary of a Russian student.    L.,
Barker, 1955.    172p.

674  Van Paassen, P.  Visions rise and change.  N.Y., Dial, 1955.    400p.

675  Bissonnette, G.  Moscow was my parish.  N.Y., McGraw-Hill, 1956.    272p.

676  Bloomfield, A.  Russian roulette.  N.Y., Harcourt, 1956.    246p.

677  Capote, T.  The muses are heard.  N.Y., Random, 1956. 182p.; L., Heinemann, 1957.    178p.

678 Douglas, W.O. Russian journey. Garden City, N.Y., Doubleday,1956. 244p.

679 Houston, J.F. U.S.S.R. Edinburgh, Oliver & Boyd, 1956. 101p.

680 Johnstone, A. Ivan the not-so-Terrible. L., British Soviet Friendship Society, 1956. 164p.

681 Miller, M.S. Window on Russia: a doctor in the U.S.S.R. L., Lawrence & Wishart, 1956. 102p.

682 Petrov, V.M., Petrov, E. Empire of fear. N.Y., Praeger, 1956. 351p.

683 Sinha, S. Flight to Soviets. Bombay, Bharatiya Vidya Bhavan, 1956.

684 Sulzberger, C.L. The big thaw: a personal exploration of the 'new' Russia and the orbit countries. N.Y., Harper, 1956. 275p.

685 Evans, J.E. Through Soviet windows. N.Y., Dow Jones, 1957. 125p.

686 Fischer, L. Russia revisited: a new look at Russia and her satellites. Garden City, N.Y., Doubleday, 1957. 288p.; L., Cape, 1957. 260p.

687 Gunther, J. Inside Russia today. N.Y., Harper, 1957. 550p.; L., Hamilton, 1958. 591p.

688 The Land of the Soviets: the country and the people. Moscow, FLPH, 1957. 253p.

689 Metaxas, A. Russia against the Kremlin. Cleveland, World Publishing Co.; L., Cassell, 1957. 181p.

690 Belfrage, S. A room in Moscow. N.Y., Reynal; L., Deutsch, 1958. 190p.

691 Edmonds, R. Russian vistas: the record of a spring-time journey to Moscow, Leningrad, Kiev, Stalingrad, the Black Sea and the Caucasus. L., Phene P., 1958. 133p.

692 Jupp, G.A. A Canadian looks at the U.S.S.R. N.Y., Exposition P., 1958. 58p.

693 Kalb, M.L. Eastern exposure. N.Y., Farrar, 1958.; L., Gollancz, 1959. 332p.

694 Metlova, M. Black bread and caviar. N.Y., Vantage P., 1958. 315p.

695 Tucker, R.L. Impressions of Russia in 1958, a trip report, Santa Monica, Rand Corp., 1958. 195p.

696 Warp, H. Russia as I saw it. Chicago, Warp Bros., 1958.

697 Bell, R. By road to Moscow and Yalta. L., Redman, 1959. 292p.

698 Brown, J. Russia explored. L., Hodder & Stoughton, 1959. 222p.

699  Davidson-Houston, J.V.  Armed diplomat:  a military attache in Russia. L. Hale, 1959.    191p.

700  Dohrs, M.E.  Sketches of the Russian people.  Detroit, Garelick's Gallery 1959.

701  Dunsheath, J.  Guest of the Soviets:  Moscow and the Caucasus, 1957. L., Constable, 1959.    183p.

702  Ethridge, W.S.  Russian duet:  the story of a journey.  N.Y.,    Simon & Schuster, 1959.    313p.

703  Fleuchter, C.E., Potter, G.E.  The U.S.S.R.  Columbus, Merrill,    1959.

704  Godley, J.  (Lord Kilbracken).  Moscow gatecrash:  a peer behind the curtain.  Boston, Mass., Houghton, 1959.;  A peer behind the curtain.    L., Gollancz, 1959.    240p.

705  Groettrup, I.  Rocket wife.  L., Deutsch, 1959.    188p.

706  Hodges, L.H.  A Governor sees the Soviet:  letters from Luther H. Hodges of North Carolina. Raleigh, N.C., 1959.    100p.

707  Hughes, E.  Pilgrim's progress in Russia.  L., Housman's Publishers,1959. 167p.

708  James, F.C.  On understanding Russia.  Toronto, U. of Toronto P.,    1959. 63p.

709  Levine, I.R.  Main street, U.S.S.R.  Garden City, N.Y., Doubleday,    1959. 408p.;  The real Russia.  L., Allen, 1959.    384p.

710  Lyons, E.  The Soviet regime and the Russian people.  N.Y., American Committee for Liberation, 1959.

711  Newman, B.  Visa to Russia.  L., Jenkins, 1959.    244p.

712  Rama Rau, S.  My Russian journey.  N.Y., Harper;  L, Gollancz,1959. 300p.

713  Schakovsky, Z.  The privilege was mine:  a Russian princess returns to the Soviet Union.  N.Y., Putnam, 1959. 318p.;  L., Cape, 1959.    255p.

714  Scott, J.  The Soviet empire.  N.Y., 1959.    94p.

715  Stevenson, A.E.  Friends and enemies:  what I learned in Russia.  N.Y., Harper, 1959.;  L., Hart-Davies, 1958.    102p.

716  Bigland, E.  Russia has two faces.  L., Odhams P., 1960.    240p.

717  Charnock, J.  Russia:  the land and the people.  L., Bodley Head,  1960. 192p.

718  Clark, M.  Meeting Soviet man.  L., Angus & Robertson, 1960.    117p.

719  Conquest, R.  Common sense about Russia.  N.Y., Macmillan;  L., Gollancz,

1960.    175p.

720   Daiches, L.  Russians at law.  L., Joseph, 1960.    208p.

721   Deutscher, I.  Russia in transition.  Rev. ed. N.Y., Grove P., 1960. 265p.

722   Gouzenko, S.  Before Igor:  memories of my Soviet youth.  N.Y.,    Norton,
      1960.;  L., Cassell, 1961.    252p.

723   Harnwell, G.P.  Russian diary.  Philadelphia, Pennsylvania U.P.,    1960.
      125p.

724   Koslow, J.  The Kremlin:  symbol of Russia.  L., MacGibbon & Kee, 1960.
      222p.

725   Mair, G.B.  Destination Moscow.  L., Jenkins, 1960.    189p.

726   Nazaroff, A.I.  The land of the Russian people.  Rev. ed.  Philadelphia,
      Lippincott, 1960.;  L., Lutterworth P., 1960.    144p.

727   Hovak, J.  The future is ours, Comrade:  conversations with Russians. Ga-
      rden City, N.Y., Doubleday, 1960.    286p.  L., Bodley Head, 1960. 255p.

728   Salisbury, H.E.  To Moscow — and beyond:  a reporter's narrative.  N.Y.,
      Harper, 1960.    301p.

729   Tagore, R.  Letters from Russia.  Calcutta, Visva-Bharati, 1960.    222p.

730   Thayer, C.W., Editors of 'Life'.  Russia.  N.Y., Time Inc., 1960. 152p.,
      L., Sunday Times, 1962.    168p.

731   Whitney, T.P.  Has Russia changed?  N.Y., Foreign Policy Association,1960
      95p.

732   Armonas, B.  Leave your tears in Moscow, as told to A.L. Nasvytis.  Phil-
      adelphia, Lippincott, 1961.    222p.

733   Byford-Jones, W.  Uncensored witness.  L., Hale, 1961.    180p.

734   Hindus, M.G.  House without a roof:  Russia after forty-three years of
      revolution.  Garden City, N.Y., Doubleday, 1961.    550p.

735   Hingley, R.  Under Soviet skins:  an untourist's report.  L., Hamilton,
      1961.    224p.

736   Jacquet, E.  High heels in Red Square.  N.Y., Holt, 1961.    209p.

737   Keller, W.  Are the Russians ten feet tall?  L., Thames & Hudson,  1961.
      420p.

738   Lathe, H., Meierling, G.  Return to Russia.  L., The Galley P.,    1961.
      125p.

739   MacGregor-Hastie, R.  Don't send me to Omsk!:  a sort of travel book. L.,

MacDonald, 1961.    240p.

740  Miller, W.W.  Russians as people.  N.Y., Dutton, 1961.;  L., Phoenix House, 1960.    202p.

741  Neugebauer, K.  Russia as I saw it:  the journal of a tour in 1960.  N.Y., Exposition, 1961.    82p.

742  Norton, H.  Only in Russia.  Princeton;  L., Van Nostrand, 1961.  240p.

743  Pliever, H.  With my dogs in Russia.  L., Hammond, 1961.    190p.

744  Price, M.P.  Russia forty years on:  an account of a visit to Russia and Germany in the autumn of 1959;  with a chapter of impressions by Mrs E. Price.  L., Allen & Unwin, 1961.    133p.

745  Sejersted, F.  Moscow Diary.  L., Ampersand, 1961.    129p.

746  Eskelund, K.  Black caviar and red optimism:  travels in Russia.    L., Redman, 1962.    169p.

747  Fischer, B.  Reunion in Moscow:  a Russian revisits her country.  N.Y., Harper, 1962.    240p.

748  Gould, K.M., Gross, R.E.  The Soviet Union.  N.Y., Scholastic, 1962. 156p.

749  Gunther, J.  Inside Russia today.  Rev. ed.  N.Y., Harper; L., Hamilton, 1962.    604p.

750  Henderson, L.W.  A journey to Samarkand.  Toronto, Longmans, 1962. 153p.

751  Ispahani, M.A.H.  Leningrad to Samarkand.  Karachi, Forward Publications Trust, 1962.    151p.

752  Jones, M.  Big two:  life in America and Russia.  L., Cape, 1962.  316p.

753  McKnight, F.R.  The Russia I saw.  Dallas, Southwest Review, 1962. 129p.

754  Mahanta, K.C.  Three years in Soviet Russia.  Hyderabad, Seven Seas, 1962 140p.

755  Mehnert, K.  Soviet man and his world.  N.Y., Praeger, 1962.    310p.

756  Menon, K.P.S.  Russian panorama.  Bombay, Oxford U.P., 1962.    273p.

757  Mosby, A.  The view from No. 13 People's Street.  N.Y., Random,    1962. 308p.

758  Popescu, J.  The Volga.  L., Oxford U.P., 1962. 32p.

759  Royster, V.  Journey through the Soviet Union.  N.Y., Dow Jones,    1962. 89p.

760  Salisbury, H.E.  A new Russia.  N.Y., Harper, 1962.  143p.;  L., Secker

    & Warburg, 1963.   146p.

761   Schwartz, H.  The many faces of communism.  N.Y., Berkeley, 1962.  254p.

762   Whitney, T.P.  Russia in my life.  N.Y., Reynal, 1962.;  L., Harrap, 1963
      312p.

763   Belli, M.M., Jones, D.R.  Belli looks at life and law in Russia.  Indian-
      apolis, Bobbs, 1963.   381p.

764   East, W.G.  The Soviet Union.  Princeton, Van Nostrand, 1963.   136p.

765   Frolich, B.  How clear was my vodka:  the true story of an American Mod-
      el's experiences in the Soviet Union.  N.Y., Exposition, 1963.   154p.

766   Hope, B.  I owe Russia $1200.  Garden City, N.Y., Doubleday, 1963.  272p.

767   Menon, K.P.S.  The flying troika:  extracts from a diary of K.P.S. Menon,
      India's ambassador to Russia, 1952-1961.  L., Oxford U.P., 1963.   318p.

768   Reeve, F.D.  Robert Frost in Russia.  Boston, Mass., Little, 1963.  135p.

769   Ronchey, A.  Russia in the thaw.  N.Y., Norton, 1963.   249p.

770   Bower, H.M.  A short guide to Soviet life.  L., Phoenix House, 1964. 64p.

771   Constantini, O., Hubman, H.  Moscow.  Garden City, N.Y., Doubleday, 1964.
      68p.

772   Cusack, E.D.  Holidays among the Russians.  L., Heinemann, 1964.   281p.

773   Flambeau, V.  Tovarich:  more red letter days.  Boothbay Harbor, Boothbay
      Register, 1964.   198p.

774   Gilmore, E.  After the Cossacks burned down the "Y".  N.Y., Farrar, 1964.
      245p.;  The Cossacks burned down the Y.M.C.A.:  Russia revisited.  L.,
      Bodley Head, 1964.   208p.

775   Jackson, W.A.  Soviet Union.  Grand Rapids, Fideler, 1964.   192p.

776   Levine, I.D.  I rediscover Russia.  N.Y., Duell, 1964.   216p.

777   Mandel, W.  Russia re-examined:  the land, the people and how they live.
      N.Y., Hill & Wang, 1964.  244p.;  A new look at Russia:  the land, the p-
      eople and how they live.  L., Evans, 1965.   248p.

778   Petrovich, M.B.  The Soviet Union.  Boston, Mass., Ginn, 1964.   121p.

779   Pitcher, H.J.  Understanding the Russians.  L., Allen & Unwin,1964. 198p.

780   Scott, R.C.  Quakers in Russia.  L., Joseph, 1964.   302p.

781   Shaw, G.B.  The rationalization of Russia by Bernard Shaw;  ed. by H.M.
      Geduld.  Bloomington, Indiana U.P., 1964.   134p.

782  Sillitoe, A.  Road to Volgograd.  N.Y., Knopf, 1964.; L., Hogarth P.,
     1964.    176p.

783  Simpson, C.  Take me to Russia and Central Asian Republics of the Soviet
     Union.  Sydney, Angus & Robertson, 1964.  513p.;  This is Russia and Cen-
     tral Asian Republics of the Soviet Union.  L., Hodder & Stoughton, 1965.
     513p.

784  Smith, H.  Black man in Red Russia.  Chicago, Johnson, 1964.    221p.

785  Tschebotarioff, G.P.  Russia, my native land:  an U.S. engineer reminis-
     ces and looks at the present.  N.Y.; L., McGraw—Hill, 1964.    384p.

786  Van der Post, L.  A view of all the Russias.  N.Y., Morrow, 1964. 374p.;
     Journey into Russia.  L., Hogarth P., 1964.    307p.

787  Wigmans, J.H.  Ten years in Russia and Siberia.  L., Darton, Longman  &
     Todd, 1964.    234p.

788  Amar, A.R.  A student in Moscow.  Chester Springs, Dufour, 1965.    64p.

789  Basnett, F.  Travels of a capitalist lackey.  L., Allen & Unwin, 1965.
     224p.

790  Corsini, R.P.  Caviar for breakfast:  an American woman's adventures in
     Russia.  Indianapolis, Bobbs—Merrill, 1965.  288p.; L., Harvill P., 1967
     256p.

791  Folsom, F.  The Soviet Union:  a view from within.  N.Y., Nelson,  1965.
     225p.

792  French, R.A.  The U.S.S.R. and Eastern Europe.  N.Y., Oxford U.P., 1965.
     96p.

793  Gooding, J.  The catkin and the icicle:  aspects of Russia.  N.Y.,  Roy;
     L., Constable, 1965.    213p.

794  Hawkes, L.R.  Europe and the U.S.S.R.  Exeter, Wheaton, 1965.    126p.

795  Klein, W.  Moscow.  N.Y., Crown, 1965.    184p.

796  Kreusler, A.A.  A teacher's experiences in the Soviet Union.  Leyden, Br-
     ill, 1965.    194p.

797  Mihajlov, M.  Moscow summer.  N.Y., Farrar, 1965.; L., Sidgwick & Jackson
     1966.    220p.

798  Miller, W.W.  Russia:  a personal anthology.  L., Newnes, 1965.    192p.

799  Miller, W.  The U.S.S.R.  2nd ed. N.Y.; L., Oxford U.P. 1965.    126p.

800  Pietromarchi, L.  The Soviet world.  N.Y., Barnes;  L., Allen & Unwin,
     1965.    462p.

801   Pitcher, H.J.  Understanding the Russians.  New Rochelle, Soccer Associ-
      ates, 1965.;  L., Allen & Unwin, 1964.    197p.

802   Refregier, A.  An artist's journey.  N.Y., International Publishers,1965.
      96p.

803   Salisbury, H.E.  Russia.  N.Y., Macmillan;  L., Collier—Macmillan,  1965.
      138p.

804   Carnegie, S.  A dash of Russia.  L., P. Davies, 1966.    186p.

805   De Silva, C.C.  Out steppes the don:  the diary of a visit to the U.S.S.R
      by an Asian professor.  Colombo, M.D. Gunasena, 1966.    244p.

806   Latham, P.  Travel, business, study and art in the U.S.S.R.  L., Blackie,
      1966.    383p.

807   Rondiere, P.  Siberia.  L., Constable, 1966.    205p.

808   Soloukhin, V.  A walk in rural Russia.  N.Y., Dutton, 1966.;  L., Hodder
      & Stoughton, 1967.    254p.

809   Kalb, M.  The Volga:  a political journey through Russia.  N.Y., Macmill-
      an;  L., Collier—Macmillan, 1967.    196p.

810   Lensen, G.A.  The Soviet Union:  an introduction.  N.Y., Appleton, 1967.
      181p.

811   Newman, B.  To Russia and back.  L., Jenkins, 1967.    224p.

812   Roberts, E.A.  Russia today.  Silver Spring, The National Observer, 1967.
      205p.

813   Rosenfeld, S., Rosenfeld, B.  Return from Red Square.  Washington, Luce,
      1967.    236p.

814   Rothschild, P.  The irrational journey.  N.Y., Harcourt, 1967.; L., Hami-
      lton, 1968.    118p.

815   Van der Post, L.  A portrait of all the Russias.  N.Y., Morrow; L., Hog-
      arth, 1967.    175p.

816   Bailey, G.  The Great Britain—U.S.S.R. handbook.  L., Great Britain—U.S.-
      S.R. Association, 1968.    125p.

817   Blanch, L.  Journey into the mind's eye:  fragments of an autobiography.
      L., Collins, 1968.    376p.

818   Kirkup, J.  One man's Russia.  L., Pnoenix House, 1968.    161p.

819   Lawrence, J.  Soviet Russia.  N.Y., David White, 1968.; L., Benn,  1967.
      127p.

820   Red Russia after 50 years by the editors of 'Look' magazine.  N.Y., Cowl-

es Educational Corp., 1968.    158p.

821  Vladimirov, L.  The Russians.  N.Y., Praeger, 1968.    249p.

822  Jacob, A.  A Russian journey from Suzdal to Samarkand.  L., Cassell, 1969.
     160p.

823  Johnson, S.  The two faces of Russia.  L., Hale, 1969.    240p.

824  Kublin, H.  Russia:  selected readings.  N.Y., Houghton, 1969.    262p.

825  Kushner, M.D.  From Russia to America:  a modern Odyssey.  Philadelphia,
     Dorrance, 1969.    334p.

826  Message from Moscow by an observer.  N.Y., Knopf;  L., Cape, 1969.  288p.

827  Miller, J.  Life in Russia today.  N.Y., Putnam;  L., Batsford, 1969. 198p

828  Morath, I., Miller, A.  In Russia.  N.Y., Viking;  L., Secker & Warburg,
     1969.    240p.

829  Poe, H., Broad, M.  Never take nyet for an answer.  Old Tappan, Hewitt
     House, 1969.    159p.

830  Roberti, V.  Moscow under the skin.  L., Bles, 1969.    253p.

831  Robinson, J.M.  Americanski journalist:  ten thousand miles of Russia th-
     rough the eyes of an American observer.  Los Angeles, Western Cove P.,
     1969.    281p.

832  Settles, W.F.  Life under communism.  Chicago, Adams P., 1969.    186p.

833  Sherwood, D.  A redhead in Red Square.  N.Y., Dodd, 1969.    218p.

834  Shub, A.  The new Russian tradgedy.  N.Y., Norton, 1969.    128p.

835  Stewart, J.M.  Across the Russias.  Chicago, Rand McNally;  L., Harvill
     P., 1969.    256p.

836  Viser, F.J.  The U.S.S.R. in today's world.  Memphis, Memphis State U.P.,
     1969.    73p.

837  Waten, J.L.  From Odessa to Odessa:  the journey of an Australian writer.
     Melbourne, Cheshire, 1969.    198p.

838  Werth, A.  Russia:  hopes and fears.  N.Y., Simon & Schuster, 1969. 352p.
     Harmondsworth, Penguin, 1969.    391p.

839  The World and its people:  U.S.S.R.  N.Y., Greystone, 1969.    2 vols.

840  De Mauny, E.  Russian prospect:  notes of a Moscow correspondent.  N.Y.,
     Atheneum, 1970.;  L., Macmillan, 1969.    320p.

841  Kuhn, D., Kuhn, F.  Russia on our minds:  reflections on another mind.

Garden City, N.Y., Doubleday, 1970.    299p.

842   Mikhailov, N.  Discovering the Soviet Union.  2nd ed.  Moscow, Progress, 1970.    385p.

843   Miller, W.W.  Leningrad.  South Brunswick, Barnes;  L., Dent, 1970.  82p.

844   Tarsis, V.  Russia and the Russians.  L., Macdonald, 1970.    219p.

845   Tyrmand, L.  Kultural essays.  N.Y., Free P., 1970.    344p.

846   Koutaissoff, E.  The Soviet Union.  N.Y., Praeger;  L., Benn, 1971. 288p.

847   Lawrence, Sir J.  Russians observed.  Lincoln, U. of Nebraska P.,   1971; L., Hodder & Stoughton, 1969.    191p.

848   Menon, K.P.S.  Russia revisited.  Delhi, Vikas, 1971.    109p.

849   Miller, J.  Life in Russia today.  2nd ed.  L., Batsford, 1971.    198p.

850   Shulman, C.  We the Russians: voices from Russia.  N.Y., Praeger, 1971. 302p.

851   Dornberg, J.  The new tsars: Russia under Stalin's heirs.  Garden City, N.Y., Doubleday, 1972.    470p.

852   Jacoby, S.  Moscow conversations.  N.Y., Coward, 1972.  287p.; The friendship barrier: ten Russian encounters.  L., Bodley Head, 1972.    261p.

853   Popescu, J.  Let's visit the U.S.S.R. 2nd ed.  L., Burke, 1972.    96p.

854   Soloukhin, V.  Searching for icons in Russia.  N.Y., Harcourt, 1972.; L., Harvill P., 1971.    191p.

855   Bonavia, D.  Fat Sasha and the urban guerrilla: protest and conformism in the Soviet Union.  N.Y., Atheneum;  L., Hamilton, 1973.    193p.

856   Feifer, G.  Russia close-up.  L., Cape, 1973.    235p.

857   Parker, W.H.  The Russians, how they live and work.  N.Y., Praeger; Newton Abbot, David and Charles, 1973.    179p.

858   Pereira, M.  Across the Caucasus.  L., Bles, 1973.    272p.

859   Petrov, V.  Escape from the future: the incredible adventures of a young Russian.  Bloomington, Indiana U.P., 1973.    470p.

860   Rositzke, H.A.  The U.S.S.R. today.  N.Y., John Day;  Aylesbury, Abelard-Schumann, 1973.    114p.

861   Smith, J.  A family of peoples: the U.S.S.R. after fifty years.    N.Y., N.W.R. Publications, 1973.    160p.

E   Guidebooks

862  Guide to the Soviet Union. Moscow, State Publishing House, 1925.  354p.

863  Rado, A.  Guide-book to the Soviet Union.  Berlin, Society for Cultural
     Relations of the Soviet Union with Foreign Countries, 1928.    855p.

864  Intourist.  A pocket guide to the Soviet Union.  Moscow, Vneshtorgisdat,
     1932.    206p.

865  Holmes, B.  The traveller's Russia.  N.Y., Putnam, 1934.    246p.

866  Moen, L.  Are you going to Russia?  L., Chapman & Hall, 1934.    264p.

867  Mandel, W.  A guide to the Soviet Union.  N.Y., Dial P., 1946.    511p.

868  Nagel Publishers.  Moscow and environs;  Leningrad and environs.  Geneva,
     Nagel, 1958.    256p.

869  Taylor, K.  Going to Russia?:  a popular guide for tourists.  L., Lawrence
     & Wishart, 1958.    186p.

870  Levine, I.R.  Travel guide to Russia. Garden City, N.Y., Doubleday, 1960.
     416p.

871  Davidson-Houston, J.V.  Russia with your eyes open.  Chester Springs, Du-
     four, 1962.    123p.

872  Geis, D.  Let's travel in the Soviet Union.  Chicago, Travel P.,    1964.

873  Felber, J.E.  The American tourist's manual for the U.S.S.R.  Neward, Ptg
     Consultants, 1965.    192p.

874  Wraget, P.  U.S.S.R.  N.Y., McGraw-Hill, 1965.    831p.

875  Louis, V.E., Louis, J.M.  A motorist's guide to the Soviet Union. Oxford,
     Pergamon, 1967.    368p.

876  Whelpton, P.  Tourist's guide to Russia.  L., MacGibbon & Kee, 1967.
     183p.

877  Levin, D.  Moscow, Leningrad, Kiev:  a guide.  L., Collet's, 1973. 183p.

III   SOVIET SOCIETY


A     Social organization

(i)   General surveys

878   American Russian Institute.  The U.S.S.R. in reconstruction;  ed. by H.L.
      Moore.  N.Y., American Russian Institute, 1944.     160p.

879   Bauer, R. A. and others.  How the Soviet system works:  cultural, psycho-
      logical, and social themes.  Cambridge, Mass., Harvard U.P., 1956. 274p.

880   Bauer, R. A., Wasiolek, E.  Nine Soviet portraits.  2nd ed. Cambridge, M-
      ass., M.I.T.P.,  1965.     190p.

881   Berman, H.J.  The Russians in focus.  Boston, Mass., Little, 1953.  209p.

882   Binder, P.  Mischa and Mascha:  stories and drawings.  L., Gollancz, 1936
      315p.

883   Deal, R.L.  Lenin's master plan:  miracle or mirage?  Miracle for fourt-
      een million Communist party members, mirage for a hundred forty million
      adult non-party Russians.  N.Y., Vantage P., 1972.     188p.

884   Malnick, B.  Everyday life in Russia.  L., Harrap, 1938.     282p.

885   Fischer, G.  The Soviet system and modern society.  N.Y., Atherton, 1968.
      199p.

886   Hollander, P.  American and Soviet society:  a reader in comparative soc-
      iology and perception.  Englewood Cliff; Hemel Hempstead, Prentice-Hall,
      1969.     589p.

887   Hollander, P.  Soviet and American society:  a comparison.  N.Y.;   L.,
      Oxford, U.P., 1973.     476p.

888   Hendel, S., Braham, R.L.  The U.S.S.R. after 50 years:  promise and real-
      ity.  N.Y., Knopf, 1967.     299p.

889   Hoffman, G.W.  Recent Soviet trends.  Austin, U. of Texas P., 1956. 107p.

890   Inkeles, A., Bauer, R.A.  The Soviet citizen:  daily life in a totalitar-
      ian society.  Cambridge, Mass., Harvard U.P., 1959.     533p.

891   Inkeles, A.  Soviet society:  a book of readings.  Boston, Mass., Hought-
      on;  L., Constable, 1961.     703p.

892   Institute for the study of the history and culture of the U.S.S.R.  The
      U.S.S.R. today and tomorrow.  Munich, 1953.     205p.

893   Karpinsky, V.A.  The social and state structure of the U.S.S.R.  Moscow,
      FLPH, 1950.     238p.

894   Kassoff, A.   Prospects for Soviet society.   N.Y., Praeger, 1968.   586p.

895   Kosa, J.   Two generations of Soviet man:   a study in the psychology of
      Communism.   New Haven, College & U.P., 1964.   214p.

896   Laird, R.D.   The Soviet paradigm:   an experiment in creating a monohier-
      archical polity.   N.Y., Free P., 1970.   272p.

897   Lelchuk, V. and others.   A short history of Soviet society.   Moscow, Pro-
      gress, 1971.   445p.

898   Moorad, G.   Behind the iron curtain.   Philadelphia, Fireside P., 1946.
      309p.

899   Nogee, J.L.   Man, state and society in the Soviet Union.   N.Y., Praeger;
      L., Pall Mall, 1972.   599p.

900   Novak, J.   No third path.   Garden City, N.Y., Doubleday, 1962.   359p.

901   Osusky, S.   The way of the free.   N.Y., Dutton; L., Benn, 1952.   320p.

902   Pennar, J.   Report on the Soviet Union in 1956.   Munich, Institute for t-
      he study of the history and culture of the U.S.S.R., 1956.   218p.

903   Pomeroy, W.J.   Half a century of socialism:   Soviet life in the sixties.
      N.Y., International Publishers, 1967.   125p.

904   Rostow, W.W. and others.   The dynamics of Soviet society.   Rev. ed. N.Y.,
      Norton, 1967.   320p.

905   Runes, D.D.   Soviet impact on society:   a recollection.   N.Y., Philoso-
      phical Library, 1953.   202p.

906   Sorlin, P.   The Soviet people and their society from 1917 to the present.
      N.Y., Praeger; L., Pall Mall P., 1969.   293p.

907   Strauss, E.   Soviet Russia:   anatomy of a social history.   L., Lane, 1941.
      342p.

908   Strumilin, S.G.   Man, society and the future.   N.Y., Crosscurrents, 1964.
      111p.

909   Turin, S.P.   The US.S.R.:   an economic and social survey.   3rd. ed. Fore-
      st Hills, Transatlantic Arts, 1949.   274p.

910   Vakar, N.P.   The taproot of Soviet society.   N.Y., Harper, 1962.   204p.

911   Webb, S., Webb, B.   Soviet communism:   a new civilization.   3rd. ed. L.,
      Longmans, 1941.   1307p.

912   Zavalani, T.   How strong is Russia?   N.Y., Praeger, 1952; L., Hollis &
      Carter, 1951.   244p.

## (ii) Social structure and social change

913  Black, C.E.  The transformation of Russian society:  aspects of social change since 1861.  Cambridge, Mass., Harvard U.P., 1960.    695p.

914  Dowse, R.E.  Modernization in Ghana and the U.S.S.R.:  a comparative study.  N.Y., Humanities;  L., Routledge, 1969.    107p.

915  Hulicka, K., Hulicka, I.M.  Soviet institutions:  the individual and society.  Boston, Mass., Christopher Publishing House, 1967.    680p.

916  Inkeles, A.  Social change in Soviet Russia.  Cambridge, Mass., Harvard U.P., 1968.    475p.

917  Lodge, M.G.  Soviet elite attitudes since Stalin.  Columbus, Merrill, 1969.  135p.

918  Matthews, M.  Class and society in Soviet Russia.  L., Allen Lane, 1972.  366p.

919  Meissner, B.  Social change in the Soviet Union:  Russia's path towards an industrial society.  Notre Dame, U. of Notre Dame P., 1972.    247p.

920  Moore, B.  Terror and progress U.S.S.R.:  some sources of change and stability in the Soviet dictatorship.  Cambridge, Mass., Harvard U.P., 1954.  261p.

921  Vucinich, A.  Soviet economic institutions:  the social structure of production units.  Stanford, Stanford U.P., 1952.    150p.

922  Yanowitch, M., Fisher, W.A.  Social stratification and mobility in the U.S.S.R.;  with a commentary by S.M. Lipset.  White Plains, International Arts & Sciences P., 1973.    402p.

923  Ward, H.F.  In place of profit:  social incentives in the Soviet Union.  N.Y., Scribner's, 1933.    460p.

924  Armstrong, J.A.  The Soviet bureaucratic elite:  a case study of the Ukranian apparatus.  N.Y., Praeger;  L., Atlantic Bks., 1959.    174p.

925  Azrael, J.R.  Managerial power and Soviet politics.  Cambridge, Mass., Harvard U.P., 1966.    161p.

926  Berliner, J.S.  Factory and manager in the U.S.S.R.  Cambridge, Mass., Harvard U.P., 1957.    386p.

927  Bienstock, G. and others.  Management in Russian industry and agriculture.  N.Y.;  L., Oxford U.P., 1944.    198p.

928  De Witt, N.  Soviet professional manpower:  its education, training and supply.  Washington, National Science Foundation, 1955.    400p.

929  Granick, D.  The red executive:  a study of the organization man in Russian industry.  Garden City, N.Y., Doubleday;  L., Macmillan, 1960.  334p.

930  Richman, B.M.  Soviet management with significant American comparisons.

Englewood Cliffs; L., Prentice—Hall, 1965.    279p.

931   Strauss, E.   The ruling servants:   bureaucracy in Russia, France — and
      Britain?   L., Allen & Unwin, 1961.    308p.

932   Baikaloff, A.V.   In the land of Communist dictatorship:   labour and soc-
      ial conditions in Soviet Russia today.   L., Cape, 1929.    285p.

933   Broderson, A.   The Soviet worker:   labor and government in Soviet Society.
      N.Y., Random, 1966.    278p.

934   Brown, E.C.   Soviet trade unions and labor organizations.   Cambridge,
      Mass., Harvard U.P., 1966.    394p.

935   Conquest, R.   Industrial workers in the U.S.S.R.   L., Bodley Head, 1967.
      204p.

936   Deutscher, I.   Soviet trade unions:   their place in Soviet labour policy.
      L., R.I.I.A., 1950.    156p.

937   Dewar, M.   Labour policy in the U.S.S.R., 1917—1928.   L., R.I.I.A., 1956.
      286p.

938   Dunn, R.W.   Soviet trade unions.   N.Y., Vanguard P., 1928.    238p.

939   Freeman, J.   The Soviet worker:   an account of the economic, social and
      cultural status of labor in the U.S.S.R.   N.Y., Liveright, 1932.    344p.

940   Gliksman, J.G. and others.   The control of industrial labor in the Sov-
      iet Union.   Santa Monica, Rand Corp., 1960.    178p.

941   Gordon, M.   Workers before and after Lenin.   N.Y., Dutton, 1941.    524p.

942   Hammond, T.T.   Lenin on trade unions and revolution, 1893—1917.   N.Y.,
      Columbia U.P., 1957.    155p.

943   Hubbard, L.E.   Soviet labour and industry.   N.Y., Macmillan, 1943; L.,
      Macmillan, 1942.    314p.

944   International Labour Organization.   Industrial life in Soviet Russia. Ge-
      neva, I.L.O., 1924.  226p.   (I.L.O. Studies and Reports, Series B, No.14)

945   Kaplan, F.I.   Bolshevik ideology and the ethics of Soviet labor,   1917—
      1920, the formative years.   N.Y., Philosophical Library, 1968; L., Owen,
      1969.    521p.

946   Koerber, L. Life in a Soviet factory.   L., Lane, 1933.    280p.

947   International Labour Organization.   Labour conditions in Soviet Russia:
      systematic questionnaire and bibliography, prepared for the Mission of
      Enquiry to Russia.   L., Harrison, 1920.    438p.

948   Labour in the land of socialism:   stakhanovites in conference.   Moscow
      Co-operative Publishing Society of Foreign Workers, 1936.    240p.

949  Levine, I.R.  The new worker in Soviet Russia.  N.Y., Macmillan,  1973.
     191p.

950  Lozovsky, A.  Handbook on the Soviet trade unions for workers' delegat –
     tions.  Moscow, Co-operative Publishing Society of Foreign Workers, 1937.
     144p.

951  McAuley, M.  Labour disputes in Soviet Russia, 1957–1965.  Oxford, Clar-
     endon P., 1969.    269p.

952  Osipov, G.V.  Industry and labour in the U.S.S.R.  L., Tavistock,  1966.
     297p.

953  Pospielovsky, D.  Russian police trade unionism:  experiment or provoca-
     tion?  L., Weidenfeld & Nicolson, 1971.    189p.

954  Potichnyj, P.J.  Soviet agricultural trade unions.  Toronto, Toronto U.P.
     1972.    258p.

955  Price, G.M.  Labor protection in Soviet Russia.  L., Modern Bks.,  1929.
     128p.

956  Schwarz, S.M.  Labor in the Soviet Union.  N.Y., Praeger, 1952; L., Cres-
     set, 1953.    364p.

957  Silver, B.  The Russian worker's own story.  L., Allen & Unwin,  1938.
     251p.

958  Smith, A.  I was a Soviet worker.  L., Hale, 1937.    286p.

959  Sorenson, J.B.  The life and death of Soviet trade unionism, 1917–1928.
     N.Y., Atherton, 1969.    283p.

960  International Labour Organization.  The trade union movement in Soviet
     Russia.  Geneva, I.L.O., 1927. 287p.;  (I.L.O. Studies and Reports, Ser-
     ies A, No. 26).

(iii) Group structure

961  Alt, H., Alt, E.  The new Soviet man:  his upbringing and character dev-
     elopment.  N.Y., Bookman, 1964.    304p.

962  Gorer, G., Rickman, J.  The people of Great Russia:  a psychological stu-
     dy.  N.Y., Chanticleer P., 1950;  L., Cresset P., 1949.    235p.

963  Niemeyer, G., Reshetar, J.S.  An inquiry into Soviet mentality.  N.Y., P-
     raeger, 1956;  L., Atlantic P., 1957.    113p.

964  Radzinski, J.M.  Masks of Moscow:  a history of Russian behavior patterns
     Chicago, Regent House, 1960.    268p.

965  Binder, P.  Russian families.  L., Black, 1942.    134p.

966  Geiger, H.K.  The family in Soviet Russia.  Cambridge, Mass., Harvard U.P.

1968.    381p.

967  Mace, D.R., Mace, V.  The Soviet family.  Garden City, N.Y., Doubleday, 1963.  397p.;  L., Hutchinson, 1964.    335p.

968  Schlesinger, R.  Changing attitudes in Soviet Russia:  the family in the U.S.S.R.,  documents and readings.  L., Routlege, 1949.    408p.

969  Alt, H., Alt, E.  Russia's children:  a first report on child welfare in the Soviet Union.  N.Y., Bookman, 1959.    240p.

970  Bronfenbrenner, U.  Two worlds of childhood:  U.S. and U.S.S.R.    N.Y., Russell Sage Foundation, 1970.;  L., Allen & Unwin, 1971.    190p.

971  Chukovskii, K.I.  From two to five.  Berkeley, U. of California P., 1963. 168p.

972  Levin, D.  Children in Soviet Russia.  L., Faber, 1942.    151p.

973  Levin, D.  Leisure and pleasure of Soviet children.  L., MacGibbon, 1966. 131p.

974  Marcus, J.  Growing up in groups:  the Russian day care center and the Israeli kibbutz:  two manuals on early child care.  N.Y.;  L., Gordon & Breach, 1972.    295p.

975  Miller, F.  The wild children of the Urals.  L., Hodder & Stoughton, 1966 251p.

976  Vandivert, R.  Young Russia:  children of the U.S.S.R. at work and play. N.Y., Dodd, 1960.  60p.; Exeter, Wheaton, 1963.    70p.

977  Zenzinov, V.  Deserted:  the story of the children abandoned in Soviet Russia.  L., Joseph, 1931.    216p.

978  Fisher, R.T.  Pattern for Soviet youth:  a study of the congresses of the Komsomol, 1918—54.  N.Y., Columbia U.P., 1959.    452p.

979  Goure, L.  The military indoctrination of Soviet youth.  N.Y., National Strategy Information Center, 1973.    81p.

980  Kassof, A.  The Soviet youth program:  regimentation and rebellion. Cambridge, Mass., Harvard U.P., 1965.    206p.

981  Meek, D.L.  Soviet youth:  some achievements and problems:  excerpts from the Soviet press.  L., Routledge, 1957.    251p.

982  Mehnert, K.  Youth in Soviet Russia.  N.Y., Harcourt, 1933.    270p.

983  Taubman, W.  The view from Lenin Hills:  Soviet youth in ferment.    L., Hamilton, 1968.    249p.

984  Tyazhelnikov, Y.  Soviet youth.  Moscow, Novosti, 1972.    112p.

985    Brown, D.R.   The role and status of women in the Soviet Union.    N.Y.,
       Teachers College P., 1968.    139p.

986    Conus, E.   The protection of motherhood and childhood in the Soviet Un-
       ion .   Moscow, Medgiz, 1933.    117p.

987    Dodge, N.T.   Women in the Soviet economy:  their role in economic, scie-
       ntific and technical development.   Baltimore, Johns Hopkins P., 1966.
       349p.

988    Field, A.W.   The protection of women and children in Soviet Russia. L.,
       Gollancz, 1932.    263p.

989    Halle, F.W.   Woman in Soviet Russia.   L., Routledge, 1933.    409p.

990    Halle, F.W.   Woman in the Soviet East.   L., Secker & Warburg, 1938. 363p

991    Kingsbury,S.M., Fairchild, M.   Factory, family and women in the Soviet
       Union.   N.Y., Putnam, 1935.    334p.

992    St. George, G.   Our Soviet sister.   Washington, Luce, 1973.    256p.

993    Serebrennikov, G.N.   The position of women in the U.S.S.R. L., Gollancz,
       1937.    288p.

994    Smith, J.   Woman in Soviet Russia.   N.Y., Vanguard P., 1928.    216p.

995    Tchernavin, T.   We, Soviet women.   L., Hamilton, 1935.    304p.

996    Winter, E.   Red virtue:  human relationships in the new Russia.    N.Y.,
       Harcourt; L., Gollancz, 1933.    320p.

997    Churchward, L.G.   The Soviet intelligentsia:  an essay on the social st-
       ructure and roles of Soviet intellectuals during the 1960s.  Boston,
       Mass.,   L.,   Routledge, 1973.    204p.

998    Pipes, R.   The Russian intelligentsia.   N.Y., Columbia U.P.,    1961.
       234p.

999    Osborn, R.J.   Soviet social policies:  welfare, equality and community.
       Homewood, Dorsey, 1970.    294p.

1000   Connor, W.D.   Deviance in Soviet society:  crime, delinquency and alcoh-
       olism.   N.Y., Columbia.. U.P., 1972.    352p.

(iv)   Forced labour

1001   American Federation of Labor.   Slave labor in Russia:  the case presen-
       ted by the Federation to the United Nations.  Washington, 1949.  179p.

1002   Baldwin, R.N.   A new slavery:  forced labor;  the communist betrayal of
       human rights.   N.Y., Oceana, 1953.    158p.

1003   Bunyan, J.   The origin of forced labor in the Soviet state, 1917—1921:

documents and materials. Baltimore, Johns Hopkins P., 1967.    276p.

1004    Dallin, D., Nicolaevsky, B.  Forced labor in Soviet Russia.  New Haven,
        Yale U.P., 1947.;  L., Hollis & Carter, 1948.    331p.

1005    Herling, A.K.  The Soviet slave empire.  N.Y., Funk, 1951.    230p.

1006    International Confederation of Free Labor Unions.  Stalin's slavery cam-
        ps:  an indictment of modern slavery.  Boston, Mass., Beacon P., 1952.;
        Brussels, The Confederation.  1951.    105p.

1007    Murray, K.M., Duchess of Atholl.  The conscription of a people.    L.,
        Allan, 1931.    206p.

1008    Pim, A.W., Bateson, E.  Report on Russian timber camps.  L.,    Benn,
        1931.    132p.

1009    Gorky, M. and others.  Belomor:  an account of the construction of the
        new canal between the White Sea and the Baltic Sea.  N.Y., Smith and Ha-
        as, 1935.  344p.;  The White Sea canal:  being an account of the constr-
        uction of the new canal between the White Sea and the Baltic Sea.  L.,
        Lane, 1935.    356p.

1010    Ameel, J.  Red Hell:  twenty years in Soviet Russia.  L., Hale, 1941.
        316p.

1011    Becker, H.  Devil on my shoulder.  L., Jarrolds, 1955.    216p.

1012    Ciszek, W.J., Flaherty, D.L.  He leadeth me.  Garden City, N.Y., Double-
        day, 1973.    216p.

1013    Ciszek, W.J., Flaherty, D.L.  With God in Russia.  N.Y., McGraw—Hill,
        1964.    302p.

1014    Dark side of the moon;  preface by T.S. Eliot.  L., Faber, 1946.  232p.

1015    Ekart, A.  Vanished without trace:  the story of seven years in Soviet
        Russia.  L., Parrish, 1954.    320p.

1016    Fittkau, G.A.  My thirty—third year:  a priest's experience in a Russian
        work camp.  N.Y., Farrar, 1958.    263p.

1017    Gliksman, J.  Tell the West:  an account of his experiences as a slave
        laborer in the Union of Soviet Socialist Republics.  N.Y., Gresham, 1948
        358p.

1018    Gorbatov, A.V.  Black year.  L., Flegon, 1964.    176p.

1019    Herling, G.  A world apart.  N.Y., Roy; L., Heinemann, 1951.    262p.

1020    Krasnov, N.N.  The hidden Russia:  my ten years as a slave laborer. N.Y.
        Holt, 1960.    341p.

1021    Larsen, O.  Nightmare of the innocents.  N.Y., Philosophical Library,

1957.;  L., Melrose, 1955.    240p.

1022  Lias, G.  I survived.  N.Y., Day;  L., Evans, 1954.    224p.

1023  Noble, J.H., Everett, G.D.  I found God in Soviet Russia.  N.Y.,    St.
      Martin's P., 1959.;  L., Marshall, 1960.    192p.

1024  Noble, J.H.  I was a slave in Russia:  an American tells his story. N.Y.
      Devon–Adair, 1958.  182p.;  L., Brown, Watson, 1963.    160p.

1025  Out of the deep:  letters from Soviet timber camps;  preface by H.  Wal-
      pole.  L., Bles, 1933.    96p.

1026  Parvilahti, U.  Beria's gardens:  a slave laborer's experiences in the
      Soviet Union.  N.Y., Dutton, 1960.;  L., Hutchinson, 1959.    286p.

1027  Percow, A.  The Russians:  true stories of the slave–labor camps in Sov-
      iet–land, and of the brutalized men and women on both sides of the bar-
      bed wire.  N.Y., Greenwich Bk. Pubs., 1957.    119p.

1028  Petrov, V.  Soviet gold:  my life as a slave laborer in the Siberian mi-
      nes.  N.Y., Farrar, 1949.  426p.;  It happens in Russia:  seven years
      forced labour in the Siberian goldfields.  L., Eyre & Spottiswoode, 1951
      470p.  (See no. 860 for a reprint of this book).

1029  Rawicz, S.  The long walk.  L., Constable, 1956.    241p.

1030  Roeder, B.  Katorga:  an aspect of modern slavery.  L., Heinemann, 1958.
      271p.

1031  Rounault, J.  Nightmare.  N.Y., Crowell, 1952.  267p.;  My friend Vassia
      L., Hart–Davis, 1952.    280p.

1032  Rupert, R.  A hidden world.  L., Collins, 1963.    224p.

1033  Scholmer, J.  Vortuka.  N.Y., Holt;  L., Weidenfeld & Nicolson,    1954.
      264p.

1034  Silde, A.  The profits of slavery.  N.Y., American Latvian Youth Assoc-
      iation;  Stockholm, Latvian National Foundation in Scandinavia,    1958.
      302p.

1035  Wasilewska, E.  The silver Madonna;  or the odyssey of Eugenia Wasilew-
      ska.  L., Allen & Unwin, 1970.    216p.

1036  Wigmans, J.H.  Ten years in Russia and Siberia. L., Darton, Longman    &
      Todd, 1964.    234p.

1037  Wurmbrand, S.  The pastor's wife.  L., Hodder & Stoughton, 1970.    218p.

(v)   Collective behaviour , mass society and reform movements.

1038  Beckmann, P.  Whispered anecdotes:  humor from behind the Iron Curtain.
      Boulder, Gołem P., 1969.    143p.

1039   Mead, M.   Soviet attitudes toward authority:   an interdisciplinary app-
       roach to problems of Soviet character.   N.Y., McGraw-Hill, 1951.;   L.,
       Tavistock, 1955.   148p.

1040   Odom, W.E.   The Soviet volunteers:   modernization and bureaucracy in a
       public mass organization.   Princeton, Princeton U.P., 1973.   360p.

1041   Clews, J.C.   Communist propaganda techniques. N.Y., Praeger, 1964. 326p.

1042   Counts, G.S., Lodge, N.P.   Country of the blind:   the Soviet system   of
       mind control.   N.Y., Houghton, 1949.   378p.

1043   Hollander, G.D.   Soviet political indoctrination:   developments in mass
       media and propaganda since Stalin.   N.Y., Praeger, 1972.   244p.

1044   Inkeles, A.   Public opinion in Soviet Russia:   a study in mass product-
       ion.   Cambridge, Mass., Harvard U.P., 1950.   379p.

1045   Konstantinov, F.V.   The role of the socialist consciousness in the deve-
       lopment of Soviet society.   Moscow, FLPH, 1950.   113p.

1046   Reiners, W.O.   Soviet indoctrination of German war prisoners, 1941-1956.
       Cambridge, Mass., Center for International Studies, M.I.T., 1959.   80p.

1047   Springer, G.P.   Early Soviet theories in communication.   Cambridge, Mass.
       M.I.T., 1956.   91p.

1048   Zoul, L.   The Soviet inferno:   a validation of the Soviet manual of mat-
       erialistic bestiality, known in communist jargon as the manual on psych-
       o-political warfare.   N.Y., Public Opinion, 1966.   144p.

1049   Dewhirst, M., Farrell, R.   The Soviet censorship.   Metuchen, Scarecrow
       P., 1973.   170p.

1050   Hopkins, M.W.   Mass media in the Soviet Union.   N.Y., Pegasus,   1970.
       384p.

1051   Buzek, A.   How the Communist press works.   N.Y., Praeger, 1964.   287p.

1052   Kruglak, T.E.   The two faces of Tass.   Minneapolis, U. of Minnesota P.,
       1962.   263p.

1053   Brumberg, A.   In quest of justice:   protest and dissent in the Soviet
       Union today.   N.Y., Praeger; L., Pall Mall P., 1970.   477p.

1054   Gerstenmaier, C.   The voices of the silent.   N.Y., Hart, 1972.   587p.

1055   Gorbanevskaia, N.   Red square at noon.   N.Y., Holt; L., Deutsch,   1972.
       288p.

1056   Labedz, L., Hayward, M.   On trial:   the case of   Sinyavsky (Tertz) and
       Daniel (Arzhak).   L., Collins, 1967.   384p.

1057   Litvinov, P.   The demonstration in Pushkin Square. L., Collins, 1969.128p

1058  Litvinov, P.  The trial of the four:  a collection of materials on the
      case of Galanskov, Ginzburg, Dobrovolsky and Lashkova, 1967-68; English
      text edited and annotated by P. Reddaway.  N.Y., Viking; Harlow, Long –
      man, 1972.    432p.

1059  Medvedev, Z.A., Medvedev, R.A.   A question of madness.  N.Y., Knopf; L.,
      Macmillan, 1971.    223p.

1060  Nutter, G.W.  The strange world of Ivan Ivanov.  N.Y., World, 1969. 144p.

1061  Reddaway, P.  Uncensored Russia:  protest and dissent in the Soviet Uni-
      on;  the unofficial Moscow journal, a Chronicle of current events.  N.Y.
      American Heritage:  L., Cape, 1972.    499p.

1062  Reve, K van het.  Dear comrade:  Pavel Litvinov and the voices of Soviet
      citizens in dissent.  N.Y., Putnam, 1969.    199p.

1063  Rothberg, A.  The heirs of Stalin:  dissidence and the Svoiet regime,
      1953-1970.  Ithaca, Cornell U.P., 1972.    450p.

1064  Sadecky, P.  Octobriana and the Russian underground.  N.Y., Harper, 1971
      128p.;  L., Stacey, 1971.    176p.

1065  Sakharov, A.D.  Progress,coexistence, and intellectual freedom.  N.Y.,
      Norton, 1968.    158p.

(vi)  Population, urban and rural communities

1066  Milbank Memorial Fund.  Population trends in Eastern Europe, the U.S.S.R.
      and mainland China.  N.Y., 1960.    336p.

1067  Lorimer, F.  The population of the Soviet Union:  history and prospects.
      N.Y., Columbia U.P., 1946. 289p.;  L., Allen & Unwin, 1947.    303p.

1068  Osipov, G.V.  Town, country and people.  L., Tavistock;  N.Y.,    Barnes
      & Noble, 1969.    260p.

1069  Adams, A.E., Adams, J.S.  Men versus systems:  agriculture in the U.S.S.R.
      Poland and Czechoslovakia.  N.Y., Free P., 1971.    327p.

1070  Beauchamp, J.  Agriculture in Soviet Russia.  L., Gollancz, 1931.  126p.

1071  Belov, F.  The history of a Soviet collective farm.  N.Y., Praeger;  L.,
      Routledge, 1956.    237p.

1072  Benet, S.  The village of Viriatino:  an ethnographic study of a Russian
      village from before the revolution to the present.  Garden City,  N.Y.,
      Anchor Bks. 1970.    300p.

1073  Borders, K.  Village life under the Soviets.  N.Y., Vanguard P.,  1927.
      191p.

1074  Buchwald, N., Bishop, R.  From peasant to collective farmer.  N.Y., Int-
      ernational Publishers;  L., Lawrence, 1933.    101p.

- 58 -

1075  Conquest, R.  Agricultural workers in the U.S.S.R.  N.Y., Praeger;  L.,
      Bodley Head, 1968.    139p.

1076  Dunn, S.P., Dunn, E.  The peasants of Central Russia.  N.Y.; L., Holt,
      1967.    139p.

1077  Hindus, M.G.  Broken earth.  N.Y., Cape & Smith, 1931.; L.,    Unwin,
      1926.    288p.

1078  Hindus, M.G.  Red bread.  N.Y.; L., Cape, 1931.    372p.

1079  Laird, R.D.  Collective farming in Russia:  a political study of the Ru-
      ssian kolkhozy.  Lawrence, U. of Kansas P., 1958.    176p.

1080  Laird, R.D. and others.  The rise and fall of the MTS as an instrument
      of Soviet rule.  Lawrence, Governmental Research Center, U. of Kansas,
      1960.    97p.

1081  Laird, R.D.  Soviet agricultural and peasant affairs.  Lawrence, U. of
      Kansas P.;  L., Constable, 1964.    335p.

1082  Lewin, M.  Russian peasants and Soviet power:  a study of collectivizat-
      ion.  L., Allen & Unwin, 1968.    539p.

1083  Male, D.J.  Russian peasant organisation before collectivisation: a stu-
      dy of commune and gathering, 1925–1930.  Cambridge, Cambridge U.P., 1971.
      253p.

1084  Millar, J.R.  The Soviet rural community:  a symposium.  Urbana,  U. of
      Illinois P., 1971.    420p.

1085  Miller, R.F.  One hundred thousand tractors:  the MTS and the develop-
      ment of controls in Soviet agriculture.  Cmabridge, Mass., Harvard U.P.,
      1970.    423p.

1086  Shanin, T.  The awkward class:  political sociology of peasantry  in a
      developing society, Russia 1910–1925.  Oxford, Clarendon P., 1972. 253p.

1087  Smith, V.R.  In a collective farm village.  L., Friends of the Soviet
      Union, 1937.;  Moscow, Co-operative Publishing Society of Foreign Work-
      ers in the U.S.S.R., 1936.    229p.

1088  Strong, A.L.  The Soviets conquer wheat:  the drama of collective farm-
      ing.  N.Y., Holt, 1931.    288p.

1089  Stuart, R.C.  The collective farm in Soviet agriculture.  Lexington, Le-
      xington Bks., 1972.    254p.

(vii)  Social services

1090  Borodin, G.  Red surgeon.  L., Museum P., 1944.    224p.

1091  Clark, F.L., Brinton, L.N.  Men, medicine and food in the U.S.S.R.  L.,
      Lawrence & Wishart, 1936.    167p.

1092   Field, M.G.   Doctor and patient in Soviet Russia.   Cambridge, Mass., Harvard U.P. 1957.   266p.

1093   Field, M.G.   Soviet socialized medicine:   an introduction.   N.Y., Free P.;   L., Collier-Macmillan, 1967.   231p.

1094   Fridland, L.   The achievement of Soviet medicine.   N.Y., Twayne;   L., Vision, 1961.   352p.

1095   Fry, J.   Medicine in three societies:   a comparison of medical care in the U.S.S.R., U.S.A., and U.K. Aylesbury, MTP, 1969.   249p.

1096   Haines A.J.   Health work in Soviet Russia.   N.Y., Vanguard, 1928. 177p.

1097   Kingsbury, S.M., Fairchild, M.   Factory, family and woman in the Soviet Union.   N.Y., Putnam, 1935.   273p.

1098   Newsholme, A., Kingsbury, J.A.   Red medicine:   socialized health in Soviet Russia.   Garden City, N.Y., Doubleday, 1933.   312p.

1099   Pondoev, G.S.   Notes of a Soviet doctor,   2nd ed. N.Y., Consultants Bureau;   L., Chapman & Hall, 1959.   238p.

1100   Popov, G.A.   Principles of health planning in the U.S.S.R.   Geneva, World Health Organisation, 1971.   172p.

1101   Rokhlin, L.   Soviet medicine in the fight against mental diseases.   L., Lawrence & Wishart, 1959.   165p.

1102   Semashko, N.A.   Health protection in the U.S.S.R.   L., Gollancz,   1934. 176p.

1103   Sigerist, H.E.   Socialized medicine in the Soviet Union.   N.Y., Norton, 1937.   310p.

1104   Simon, B.   Psychology in the Soviet Union.   Stanford, Stanford U.P.,1957. 305p.

1105   Simon, B., Simon, J.   Educational psychology in the U.S.S.R.   Stanford, Stanford U.P., 1963.   283p.

1106   Sokoloff, B.   The white nights:   pages from a Russian doctor's notebook. N.Y., Devon-Adair, 1956.;   L., Holborn Publ., Co., 1959.   294p.

1107   Vinogradov, N.A.   Public health in the Soviet Union.   Moscow, FLPH, 1950. 144p.

1108   Williams, F.E.   Soviet Russia fights neurosis.   L., Routledge, 1934. 251p

B       The economy

(i)     General surveys

1109    Ames, E.  Soviet economic processes.  Homewood, Irwin, 1965.    257p.

1110    Asirvatham, A.  The U.S.S.R.:  its economic development.  2nd ed. Madras, Rochouse, 1961.    115p.

1111    Bandera, V.L., Melnyk, Z.L.  The Soviet economy in regional perspective. N.Y.;  L., Praeger, 1973.    352p.

1112    Bergson, A.  Soviet economic growth:  conditions and perspective.  Evanston, Row, Peterson, 1953.    376p.

1113    Bergson, A. and others.  Economic trends in the Soviet Union.  Cambridge, Mass., Harvard U.P., 1963.    392p.

1114    Bornstein, M., Fusfeld, D.R.  The Soviet economy:  a book of readings. 3rd ed.  Homewood, Irwin, 1970.    467p.

1115    Braverman, H.  The future of Russia.  N.Y., Macmillan, 1963.    175p.

1116    Brower, D.R.  The Soviet experience – success or failure?  N.Y.,  Holt, 1971.    129p.

1117    Campbell, R.W.  Soviet economic power:  its organization, growth and challenge.  2nd ed.  Boston, Mass., Houghton, 1966.; L., Macmillan, 1967. 184p.

1118    Chamberlin, W.H.  Russia's iron age.  Boston, Mass., Little, 1934. 389p.

1119    Cohn, S.H.  Economic development in the Soviet Union.  Lexington, Heath, 1970.    135p.

1120    Committee for Economic Development.  Soviet progress vs American enterprise.  N.Y., Doubleday, 1958.    126p.

1121    Congress for Cultural Freedom.  The Soviet economy:  a discussion.  L., Secker & Warburg, 1956.    158p.

1122    Czyrowski, N.L.  The economic factors in the growth of Russia:  an economic-historical analysis.  N.Y., Philosophical Library. 1957.    178p.

1123    Dellin, L.A.D., Gross, H.  Reforms in the Soviet and Eastern European economies.  Lexington, Lexington Bks., 1972.    175p.

1124    Dobb, M.  Soviet economic development since 1917.  6th ed.  N.Y., International Publishers;  L., Routledge, 1966.    515p.

1125    Dobbert, G.  Soviet economics.  L., Lane, 1933.    343p.

1126    Feiwel, G.R.  The Soviet quest for economic efficiency;  issues, controversies and reforms.  New ed. N.Y.;  L., Praeger, 1972.    790p.

1127    Friedman, E.M.  Russia in transition:  a business man's appraisal. N.Y., Viking;  L., Allen & Unwin, 1933.    614p.

1128    Garretson, R.C.  The abundant peace.  Cleveland, World, 1965.    255p.

1129  Glasser, E., Weiskopf, F.C.  The land without unemployment: three years
      of the five-year plan.  L., Lawrence, 1931.    215p.

1130  Gurevich, S.  The new economic upswing of the U.S.S.R. in the post-war
      Five-Year Plan period.  Moscow, FLPH, 1950.    256p.

1131  Goldman, M.I.  The Soviet economy:  myth and reality.  Englewood Cliffs,
      Prentice, 1968.    176p.

1132  Haensel, P.  The economic policy of Soviet Russia.  L., King, 1930. 190p

1133  Hoover, C.B.  The economic life of Soviet Russia.  N.Y., L., Macmillan,
      1931.    347p.

1134  Hutchings, R.  Soviet economic development.  N.Y., Barnes & Noble;  Oxf-
      ord, Blackwell, 1971.    314p.

1135  Jasny, N.  The Soviet economy during the Plan era.  Stanford, Stanford
      U.P., 1952.    116p.

1136  Kaplan, N.M.  The record of Soviet economic growth.  Santa Monica, Rand
      Corp., 1969.    245p.

1137  Kaser, M.C.  Soviet economics.  N.Y., McGraw-Hill;  L., Weidenfeld    &
      Nicolson, 1970.    256p.

1138  Katkoff, V.  Soviet economy 1940-1965.  Baltimore, Dangary, 1961. 559p.

1139  Katz, A.  The politics of economic reform in the Soviet Union.N.Y.; L.,
      Praeger, 1972.    230p.

1140  Kerner, R.J.  The U.S.S.R. economy and the war.  N.Y., Russian Economic
      Institute, 1943.    110p.

1141  Knickerbocker, H.R.  The red trade menace:  progress of the Soviet Five
      Year Plan.  N.Y., Dodd, 1931.    277p.

1142  Lawton, L.  Economic history of Soviet Russia.  L., Macmillan,    1932.
      2 vols.

1143  League of Nations.  Report on economic conditions in Russia, with spec-
      ial reference to the famine of 1921-22 and the state of agriculture. Ge-
      neva, 1922.    164p.

1144  Leason, J.W.The Russian economic threat.  N.Y., Gregory, 1958.    107p.

1145  Leites, K.  Recent economic developments in Russia.  L., Oxford  U.P.,
      1922.    240p.

1146  Lied, J.  Sidelights on the economic situation in Russia.  Moscow, Kush-
      nerev, 1922.    148p.

1147  Maddison, A.  Economic growth in Japan and the U.S.S.R.  L., Allen & Un-
      win, 1969.    174p.

1148  Maslov, E.P.  The Russian Federation.  Moscow, FLPH, 1960.    214p.

1149  Mavor, J.  The Russian Revolution.  L., Allen & Unwin, 1933.    470p.

1150  Mazour, A.G.  Soviet economic development:  operation outstrip, 1921-1965
      Princeton; L., Van Nostrand, 1967.    191p.

1151  Nansen, F.  Russia and peace.  L., Allen & Unwin, 1924.    162p.

1152  Nearing, S., Hardy, J.  The economic organization of the Soviet Union.
      N.Y., Vanguard P., 1927.    245p.

1153  Normano, J.F.  The spirit of Russian economics.  N.Y., Day, 1945. 170p.;
      L., Dobson, 1949.    130p.

1154  Nove, A.  Communist economic strategy:  Soviet growth and capabilities.
      Washingtom, National Planning Association, 1959.    83p.

1155  Nove, A.  An economic history of the U.S.S.R.  L., Allen Lane,    1969.
      416p.

1156  Nove, A.  The Soviet economy:  an introduction. 3rd ed.  N.Y., Praeger,
      1969.; L., Allen & Unwin, 1968.    373p.

1157  Nove, A.  Was Stalin really necessary?  Some problems of Soviet political
      economy.  L., Allen & Unwin, 1964.    317p.

1158  Perlo, V.  U.S.A. and U.S.S.R.:  the economic race.  N.Y., International
      Publishers, 1962.    127p.

1159  Peters, C.A.  American capitalism vs Russian communism.  N.Y.,  Wilson,
      1946.    305p.

1160  Prokopovitch, S.N.  The economic condition of Soviet Russia.  L., King,
      1924.    230p.

1161  Roberts, P.C.  Alienation and the Soviet economy:  towards a general th-
      eory of Marxian alienation, organizational principles and the Soviet ec-
      onomy.  Albuquerque, U. of New Mexico P., 1971.    121p.

1162  Schwartz, H.  An introduction to the Soviet economy.  Columbus, Merrill,
      1968.    168p.

1163  Schwartz, H.  Russia's Soviet economy. 2nd ed. N.Y., Prentice-Hall, 1954.
      682p.

1164  Schwartz, H.  The Soviet economy since Stalin.  Philadelphia, Lippincott;
      L.,  Gollancz, 1965.    259p.

1165  Scott, J.  Behind the Urals: an American worker in Russia's city of st-
      eel.  Boston, Mass.,  Houghton, 1942. 279p.;  L.,  Secker & Warburg,
      1943.    224p.

1166  Shaffer, H.G.  The Soviet economy:  a collection of Western and Soviet views. N.Y., Appleton; L., Methuen, 1964.    456p.

1167  Soviet economic reform:  progress and problems.  Moscow, Progress, 1972.
      246p.

1168  Soviet economy.  Moscow, Novosti, 1969.    104p.

1169  Spulber, N.  The Soviet economy:  structure, principles, problems.  Rev.
      ed. N.Y., Norton, 1969.    329p.

1170  Sutton, A.C.  Western technology and Soviet economic development,  1917
      to 1965.  Stanford, Hoover Institution P., 1968-73.    3 vols.

1171  Treml, V.G.  The development of the Soviet economy:  plans and perform-
      ance.  N.Y.;  L., Praeger, 1968.    298p.

1172  Treml, V.G. and others.  The structure of the Soviet economy:  analysis
      and reconstruction of the 1966 input-output table.  N.Y.;  L., Praeger,
      1972.    660p.

1173  U.S.S.R. Chamber of Commerce.  Economic conditions in the U.S.S.R.;  h-
      andbook for foreign economists, specialists and workers.  Moscow, Vnesh-
      torgizdat, 1931.    286p.

1174  U.S.A. Congress.  Joint Economic Committee.  Soviet economic prospects
      for the seventies.  Washington, USGPO, 1973.    776p.

1175  Voznesensky, N.  Economy of the U.S.S.R. during World War II.  Washing-
      ton, Public Affairs, 1948.    115p.

1176  Voznesensky, N.  Soviet economy during the Second World War.  N.Y., Int-
      ernational Publishers, 1949.    160p.

1177  Wilber, C.K.  The Soviet model and underdeveloped countries.  Chapel Hi-
      ll, U. of North Carolina P., 1969.    241p.

1178  Wiles, P.J.D.  The prediction of communist economic performance.  Camb-
      ridge, Cambridge U.P., 1971.    390p.

1179  Yugoff, A.  Economic trends in Soviet Russia.  L., Allen & Unwin,  1930.
      349p.

(ii)  Economic theory

1180  Bor, M.  Aims and methods of Soviet planning.  N.Y., International Pub-
      lishers;  L., Lawrence & Wishart, 1967.    255p.

1181  Bukharin, N.I.  The economic theory of the leisure class.  L., Lawrence,
      1927.    220p.

1182  Bukharin, N.I.  Economics of the transformation period:  with Lenin's c-
      ritical remarks.  N.Y., Bergman, 1971.    224p.

1183  Day, R.B.  Leon Trotsky and the politics of economic isolation.  Cambridge, Cambridge U.P., 1973.    221p.

1184  Dellenbrandt, J. A.  Reformists and traditionalists:  a study of Soviet
      discussions about economic reforms.  Uppsala, Political Science  Assoc-
      iation, 1972.    166p.

1185  Kantorovich, L.V.  The best use of economic resources.  Cambridge, Mass.
      Harvard U.P., 1965.    349p.

1186  Kaplan, N.M.  The choice among investment alternatives in Soviet theory.
      Santa Monica, Rand Corp., 1951.    95p.

1187  Liberman, E.G.  Economic methods and the effectiveness of production.
      White Plains, International Arts & Sciences P., 1972.    180p.

1188  Preobrazhensky, E.  The new economics.  Oxford, Clarendon P., 1965. 310p.

1189  Soviet views on the post-war world economy:  an official critique of Eu-
      gene Varga's "Changes in the economy of capitalism resulting from the
      Second World War";  ed. by L. Gruliow.  Washington, Public Affairs  P.,
      1948.    125p.

1190  Wilczynski, J.  The economics of socialism:  principles governing  the
      operation of the centrally planned economies in the U.S.S.R. and Eastern
      Europe under the new system.  Chicago, Aldine, 1971.; L., Allen & Unwin,
      1972.    233p.

1191  Wilcaynski, J.  Socialist economic development and reforms: from extens-
      ive to intensive growth under central planning in the U.S.S.R., Eastern
      Europe and Yugoslavia.  L., Macmillan, 1972.    350p.

1192  Yanowitch, M.  Contemporary Soviet economics:  a collection of readings
      from Soviet sources.  White Plains, International Arts & Sciences  P.,
      1969.  2 vols.

(iii)   The Soviet consumer

1193  Blanc, E.T.  The co-operative movement in Soviet Russia.  N.Y., Macmill-
      an, 1924.    324p.

1194  Hanson, P.  The consumer in the Soviet economy.  Evanston, Northwestern
      U.P.; L., Macmillan, 1968.    249p.

1195  International Labour Organization.  The co-operative movement in Soviet
      Russia.  Geneva, 1925.    362p.

1196  Miller, M.  The rise of the Russian consumer.  L., Institute of Economic
      Affairs, 1965.    254p.

1197  Paul, L.A.  Co-operation in the U.S.S.R.:  a study of the consumers' mo-
      vement.  L., Gollancz, 1934.    160p.

(iv)  Production and distribution

1198    Barker, G.R.  Some problems of incentives and labour productivity in So-
        viet industry.  Oxford, Blackwell, 1956.    129p.

1199    Blackman, J.H.  Transport development and locomotive technology in the
        Soviet Union.  Columbia, University of South Carolina, Bureau of Busin-
        ess Research, 1957.    64p.

1200    Clark, M.G.  The economics of Soviet steel.  Cambridge, Mass., Harvard
        U.P., 1955.    400p.

1201    Erlich, A.  The Soviet industrialization debate 1924-1928.  Cambridge,
        Mass., Harvard U.P., 1960.    214p.

1202    Galenson, W.  Labor productivity in Soviet and American industry.  N.Y.,
        Columbia U.P., 1954.    273p.

1203    Granick, D.  Soviet metal-fabricating and economic development: practice
        versus policy.  Madison, Wisconsin U.P., 1967.    367p.

1204    Hodgman, D.R.  Soviet industrial production, 1928-1951.  Cambridge, Mass.,
        Harvard U.P., 1954.    241p.

1205    Hunter, H.  Soviet transportation policy.  Cambridge, Mass., Harvard U.P.,
        1957.    416p.

1206    Hutchings, R.  Seasonal influences in Soviet industry.  L., Oxford U.P.,
        1971.    321p.

1207    Institute of Economic Affairs.  Communist economy under change:  studies
        in the theory and practice of markets and competition in Russia, Poland
        and Yugoslavia.  L., Deutsch, 1963.    272p.

1208    Jasny, N.  Soviet industrialization, 1928-1952.  Chicago, Chicago U.P.,
        1961.    467p.

1209    Melnyk, Z.L.  Soviet capital formation:  Ukraine, 1928/29-1932.  Munich,
        Ukrainian Free U.P., 1965.    182p.

1210    Moorstein, R., Powell, R.T.  The Soviet capital stock, 1928-1962.  Home-
        wood, Irwin, 1966.    672p.

1211    National Coal Board.  Technical Mission to the U.S.S.R.  The coal indus-
        try of the U.S.S.R.:  a report by the Technical Mission of the National
        Coal Board.  L., 1957.    107p.

1212    Ofer, G.  The service sector in Soviet economic growth:  a comparative
        study.  Cambridge, Mass., Harvard U.P., 1973.    202p.

1213    Rosovsky, H.  Industrialization in two systems:  essays in honor of  A.
        Gerschenkron.  N.Y., Wiley, 1966.    289p.

1214    Scott, J.  The Soviet world:  growth, disintegration and reform.  N.Y.,
        Time, 1966.    90p.

1215    Swianiewicz, S.    Forced labour and economic development:    an enquiry in-
        to the experience of Soviet industrialization.    L., Oxford U.P.,    1965.
        321p.

1216    Wellisz, S.H.    The economics of the Soviet bloc:    a study of decision m-
        aking and resource allocation.    N.Y.;    L., McGraw-Hill, 1964.        245p.

1217    Beauchamp, J.    Agriculture in Soviet Russia.    L., Gollancz, 1931. 126p.

1218    Burns, E.    Russia's productive system.    L., Gollancz, 1930.        288p.

1219    Campbell, T.D.    Russia, market or menace?    L., Longmans, 1932.        148p.

1220    Chayanov, A.V.    The theory of peasant economy.    South Holland,    Ill.,
        Irwin, 1966.    317p.

1221    Conklin, D.W.    An evaluation of the Soviet profit reforms with special
        reference to agriculture.    N.Y.;    L., Praeger, 1970.        193p.

1222    Hubbard, L.E.    The economics of Soviet agriculture.    L., Macmillan,1939.
        316p.

1223    Jasny, N.    Krushchev's crop policy.    Glasgow, Glasgow U., Institute of
        Russian and East European Studies, 1965.        243p.

1224    Jasny, N.    Socialized agriculture of the U.S.S.R.:    plans and perform-
        ance.    Stanford, Stanford U.P., 1949.        837p.

1225    Johnson, D.G., Kahan, A.    The Soviet agricultural program:    an evaluat-
        ion of the 1965 goals.    Santa Monica, Rand Corp., 1962.        122p.

1226    Karcz, J.F.    Soviet and East European agriculture.    Berkeley, California
        U.P., 1967.        445p.

1227    Karcz, J.F.    Soviet agricultural marketings and prices, 1928-1954. Santa
        Monica, Rand Corp., 1957.        513p.

1228    Kazakov, G.    The Soviet peat industry.    N.Y., Praeger, 1956.; L., Atlan-
        tic P., 1957.        245p.

1229    Laird, R.D., Crowley, E.L.    Soviet agriculture:    the permanent crisis.
        N.Y.;    L., Praeger, 1965.        209p.

1230    Laird, R.D., Laird, B.A.    Soviet communism and agrarian revolution, Har-
        mondsworth, Penguin, 1970.        158p.

1231    Nimitz, A.E.    Soviet agriculture since the September, 1953, reforms. Sa-
        nta Monica, Rand Corp., 1955.        191p.

1232    Nimitz, A.E.    Soviet government grain procurements, dispositions and st-
        ocks, 1940, 1945-1963.    Santa Monica, Rand Corp., 1964.        124p.

1233    Nimitz, A.E.    The new Soviet agricultural decrees (September Plenum,1953).
        Santa Monica, Rand Corp., 1954.        92p.

1234   Ploss, S.I.  Conflict and decision-making in Soviet Russia:  a case-study of agricultural policy, 1953-1963.  Princeton, Princeton U.P., 1965.  312p.

1235   Strauss, E.  Soviet agriculture in perspective:  a study of its successes and failures.  N.Y., Praeger;  L., Allen & Unwin, 1969.     328p.

1236   Timoshenko, V.P.  Agricultural Russia and the wheat problem.  Stanford, Food Research Institute & Hoover War Library, 1932.     571p.

1237   Volin, L.  A century of Russian agriculture:  from Alexander II to Khrushchev.  Cambridge, Mass., Harvard U.P., 1970.     644p.

1238   Wadekin, K-E.  The private sector in Soviet agriculture.  2nd ed.  Berkeley, U. of California P., 1973.     407p.

1239   Allen R.L.  Middle Eastern economic relations with the Soviet Union, Eastern Europe and mainland China.  Charlottesville, U. of Virginia, Woodrow Wilson Department of Foreign Affairs, 1958.     128p.

1240   Allen, R.L.  Soviet economic warfare.  Washington, Public Affairs  P., 1960.     293p.

1241   Allen, R.L.  Soviet influence in Latin America:  the role of economic relations.  Washington, Public Affairs P., 1959.     108p.

1242   Athay, R.E.  The economics of Soviet merchant-shipping policy.  Chapel Hill, U. of North Carolina P., 1971.     150p.

1243   Baykov, A.M.  Soviet foreign trade.  Princeton, Princeton U.P.,  1946.  140p.

1244   Berliner, J.S.  Soviet economic aid: the new aid and trade policy in underdeveloped countries.  N.Y., Harper, 1965.     232p.

1245   Brabant, J.M.P. van.  Bilateralism and structural bilateralism in inter-CMEA TRADE.  Rotterdam, Rotterdam U.P., 1973.     290p.

1246   Budish, J.M., Shipman, S.S.  Soviet foreign trade:  menace or promise.  L., Allen & Unwin, 1931.     236p.

1247   Business International S.A., Geneva.  Doing business with the  U.S.S.R.  Geneva, 1971.     199p.

1248   Butler, J.  The Soviet Union, Eastern Europe, and the world food markets.  N.Y.;  L., Praeger, 1964.     78p.

1249   Campbell, W.H. and others.  U.S.-Soviet trade:  facts for the businessman's appraisal;  structure, trends, procedures, experiences.  Cleveland, Trade Research Associates, 1960.     230p.

1250   Carter, J.R.  The net cost of Soviet foreign aid. N.Y.; L., Praeger, 1971.  134p.

1251   Cheng, C.  Economic relations between Peking and Moscow, 1949–63. N.Y.; L., Praeger, 1964.    119p.

1252   Condoide, M.V.  The Soviet financial system:  its development and relations with the western world.  Columbus, Ohio State U.P., 1951.    230p.

1253   Conolly, V.  Soviet economic policy in the East (Turkey, Persia, Afghanistan, Mongolia and Tana Tuva, Sin Kiang).  L., Oxford U.P., 1933. 168p.

1254   Conolly, V.  Soviet trade from the Pacific to the Levant;  with an economic study of the Soviet Far Eastern Region.  L., Oxford U.P., 1935. 238p.

1255   Crosfield, Joseph, & Sons Ltd.  Soviet trade in crude oil, oil products, and equivalent.  Warrington, 1964.    61p.

1256   Desai, P.  The Bokaro steel plant;  a study of Soviet economic assistance.  N.Y., American–Elsevier;  Amsterdam, North–Holland, 1972.  108p.

1257   Dewar, M. Soviet trade with Eastern Europe, 1945–1949.  L., RIIA, 1951. 123p.

1258   Flegon, A.  Soviet foreign trade techniques:  an inside guide to Soviet foreign trade.  L., Flegon, 1965.    148p.

1259   Freedman, R.O.  Economic warfare in the Communist bloc:  a study of Soviet economic pressure against Yugoslavia, Albania and Communist China. N.Y.;  L., Praeger, 1970.    192p.

1260   Giffen, J.H.  The legal and practical aspects of trade with the Soviet Union.  Rev. ed. N.Y.;  L., Praeger, 1971.    366p.

1261   Goldman, M.L.  Soviet foreign aid.  N.Y.;  L., Praeger, 1967.    265p.

1262   Greer, T.V.  Marketing in the Soviet Union.  N.Y.;  L., Praeger,  1973. 188p.

1263   Hammer, A.  The quest of the Romanoff treasure.  N.Y., Paisley P., 1936. 234p.

1264   Heymann, H.  We can do business with Russia.  N.Y., Ziff–Davies,  1945. 268p.

1265   Hubbard, L.E.  Soviet trade and distribution.  L., Macmillan, 1938. 381p.

1266   Ionescu, G.  The break–up of the Soviet empire in Eastern Europe.  Harmondsworth, Penguin, 1965.    169p.

1267   Kaser, M.  Comecon:  integration problems of the planned economies. N.Y.; L., Oxford U.P., 1965.    215p.

1268   Knickerbocker, H.R.  Soviet trade and the world depression.  L.,  Lane, 1931.    288p.

1269   Kohler, H.  Economic integration in the Soviet bloc.  N.Y.;  L., Praeger, 1965.    402p.

1270  Kovner, M.  The challenge of coexistence:  a study of Soviet economic diplomacy.  Washington, Public Affairs P., 1961.    130p.

1271  Lubell, H.  The Soviet oil offensive and inter-block economic competition.  Santa Monica, Rand Corp., 1961.    93p.

1272  Mellor, R.E.H.  Comecon:  challenge to the West.  N.Y.;  L., Van Nostrand, 1971.    152p.

1273  Mikesell, R., Berhman, J.  Financing free world trade with Sino-Soviet bloc.  Princeton, Princeton U., Department of Economics & Sociology,1958 109p.

1274  Nag, D.S.  Foreign economic policy of Soviet Russia.  Agra, Lakshmi Narain Agarwal, 1964.    111p.

1275  Neuberger, E.  The U.S.S.R. and the West as markets for primary products: stability, growth and size.  Santa Monica, Rand Corp., 1963.    150p.

1276  Nodel, W.  Supply and trade in the U.S.S.R.  L., Gollancz, 1934.  176p.

1277  Nove, A., Donnelly, D.  Trade with communist countries.  N.Y., Macmillan 1961.;  L., Hutchinson, 1960.    183p.

1278  Patolichev, N.    Foreign Trade.  Moscow, Novosti P. Agency, 1971. 179p.

1279  Pisar, S.  Coexistence and commerce:  guidelines for transactions between East and West.  L., Allen Lane, 1971.    558p.

1280  Rosefielde, S.  Soviet international trade in Heckscher-Ohlin perspective:  an input-output study.  Lexington;  L., Heath, 1973.    173p.

1281  Sawyer, C.A.  Communist trade with developing countries, 1964-5.  N.Y.; L., Praeger, 1966.    126p.

1282  Slusser, R.  Soviet economic policy in postwar Germany:  a collection of papers by former Soviet officials.  N.Y., Research Program on the U.S.S.R. 1953.    184p.

1283  Smith, G.A.  Soviet foreign trade:  organization, operation and policy, 1918-1971.  N.Y.;  L., Praeger, 1973.    370p.

1284  Stokke, B.R.  Soviet and eastern European trade and aid in Africa. N.Y.; L., Praeger, 1967.    326p.

1285  Tansky, L.  U.S. and U.S.S.R. aid to developing countries:  a comparative study of India, Turkey, U.A.R.  N.Y.;  L., Praeger, 1967.    192p.

1286  Vassiliev, V.  Policy in the Soviet bloc on aid to developing countries. Paris, OECD, 1969.    106p.

1287  Yanson, J.D.  Foreign trade in the U.S.S.R.  L., Gollancz, 1934.  176p.

1288    Zebot, C.A.   The economics of competitive coexistence:   convergence thr-
        ough growth.   N.Y.;   L., Praeger, 1964.     262p.

(v)    Wealth, income and finance

1289    Bergson, A.   The structure of Soviet wages:   a study in socialist econ-
        omics.   Cambridge, Mass., Harvard U.P., 1944.     255p.

1290    Bjork, L.   Wages, prices and social legislation in the Soviet Union. L.,
        Dobson, 1953.     199p.

1291    Chapman, J.G.   Wage variation in Soviet industry.   Santa Monica,   Rand
        Corp., 1970.     170p.

1292    Kaplan, N.M.   Earnings distribution in the U.S.S.R., Santa Monica, Rand
        Corp., 1969.     193p.

1293    Kirsch, L.J.   Soviet wages:   changes in structure and administration si-
        nce 1956.   Cambridge, Mass., MITP., 1972.     237p.

1294    Zagorsky, S.   Wages and regulation of conditions of labour in the U.S.S.R.
        L., King, 1930.     212p.

1295    Allakhverdan, D.A.   Soviet financial system.   Moscow, Progress, 1966.
        352p.

1296    Arnold, A.Z.   Banks, credit and money in Soviet Russia.   N.Y., Columbia
        U.P., 1937.     559p.

1297    Davies, R.W.   The development of the Soviet budgetary system. Cambridge,
        Cambridge U.P., 1958.     373p.

1298    Holzman, F.D.   Soviet taxation:   the fiscal and monetary problems of a
        planned economy.   Cambridge, Mass., Harvard U.P., 1955.     376p.

1299    Hubbard, L.E.   Soviet money and finance.   L., Macmillan, 1936.     339p.

1300    Jasny, N.   The Soviet price system.   Stanford, Stanford U.P., 1951. 179p.

1301    Katzenellenbaum, S.S.   Russian currency and banking.   L., King, 1925.
        198p.

1302    Reddaway, W.B.   The Russian financial system.   L., Macmillan, 1935. 106p.

1303    Sokolnikov, G.Y. and others.   Soviet policy in public finance, 1917-28.
        Stanford, Stanford U.P., 1931.     470p.

1304    Stec, G.   The local budget system of the U.S.S.R.:   its development and
        functions.   N.Y., Research Program on the U.S.S.R., 1955.     106p.

1305    Yurovsky, L.N.   Currency problems and policies of the Soviet Union. L.,
        Parsons, 1925.     152p.

(vi)  Economic planning

1306  Abouchar, A.  Soviet planning and spatial efficiency:  the pre-war cement industry.  Bloomington, Indiana U.P., 1971.  134p.

1307  Arakelian, A.  Industrial management in the U.S.S.R.  Washington, Public Affairs P., 1950.  168p.

1308  Balinsky, A. and others.  Planning and the market in the U.S.S.R.:  the 1960s.  New Brunswick, Rutgers U.P., 1967.  132p.

1309  Barker, G.R.  Some problems of incentives and labour productivity in Soviet industry:  a contribution to the study of the planning of labour in the U.S.S.R.  Oxford, Blackwell, 1956.  131p.

1310  Baykov, A.  The development of the Soviet economic system:  an essay on the experience of planning in the U.S.S.R.  N.Y., Macmillan;  Cambridge, Cambridge U.P., 1946.  514p.

1311  Bergson, A.  The economics of Soviet planning.  New Haven, Yale U.P., 1964.  394p.

1312  Bergson, A.  Planning and productivity under Soviet socialism.  Pittsburgh, Carnegie-Mellon U., 1968.  95p.

1313  Bernard, P.J.  Planning in the Soviet Union.  N.Y.; Oxford, Pergamon, 1966.  309p.

1314  Brutzkus, B.  Economic planning in Soviet Russia.  L., Routledge, 1935.  234p.

1315  Campbell, R.W.  Accounting in Soviet planning and management.  Cambridge, Mass., Harvard U.P., 1963.  318p.

1316  Conyngham, W.J.  Industrial management in the Soviet Union:  the role of the CPSU in industrial decision-making, 1917-1970.  Stanford, Hoover Institution P., 1973.  378p.

1317  Degras, J., Nove, A.  Soviet planning:  essays in honour of Naum Jasny.  N.Y., Praeger, 1965.; Oxford, Blackwell, 1964.  225p.

1318  Dobb, M.  Soviet planning and labor in peace and war:  four studies.  N.Y., International Publishers, 1944.; L., Routledge, 1942.  126p.

1319  Ellman, M.  Planning problems in the U.S.S.R.:  the contribution of mathematical economics to their solution, 1960-1971.  Cambridge, Cambridge U.P., 1973.  222p.

1320  Ellman, M.  Soviet planning today:  proposals for an optimally functioning economic system.  Cambridge, Cambridge U.P., 1971.  219p.

1321  Felker, J.L.  The Soviet economic controversies:  the emerging marketing concept and changes in planning, 1960-1965.  Cambridge, Mass., MITP, 1966.  172p.

1322  Granick, D.  Management of the industrial firm in the U.S.S.R.:  a study in Soviet economic planning. N.Y., Columbia U.P., 1954. 346p.

1323 Granick, D. Managerial comparisons of four developed countries—France, Britain, United States and Russia. Cambridge, Mass., MITP, 1972. 394p.

1324 Hirsch, H. Quantity planning and price planning in the Soviet Union. Philadelphia, U. of Pennsylvania P., 1961. 272p.

1325 Jasny, N. The Soviet economy during the plan era. Stanford, Stanford U.P., 1951. 116p.

1326 Kaplan, N.M. Capital investments in the Soviet Union, 1924—1951. Santa Monica, Rand Corp., 1952. 218p.

1327 Koropeckyj, I.S. Location problems in Soviet industry before World War II: the case of the Ukraine. Chapel Hill, U. of North Carolina P., 1971. 219p.

1328 Kursky, A. Planning of the national economy of the U.S.S.R. N.Y., Universal Distributors, 1949. 216p.

1329 Ronimois, H.E. Soviet planning and economic theory. Vancouver, U. of British Columbia P., 1950. 337p.

1330 Rothstein, A. Man and plan in Soviet economy. L., Muller, 1948. 300p.

1331 Samuel, M., Caplan, L. The great experiment: results of the five-year plans. L., Murray, 1935. 133p.

1332 Sharpe, M.E. Planning, profit and incentives in the U.S.S.R. White Plains, International Arts and Sciences P., 1966. 2 vols.

1333 Spulber, N. Socialist management and planning: topics in comparative socialist economics. Bloomington, Indiana U.P., 1971. 235p.

1334 Spulber, N. Foundations of Soviet strategy for economic growth: selected Soviet essays, 1924—1930. Bloomington, Indiana U.P., 1964. 530p.

1335 Spulber, N. Soviet strategy for economic growth. Bloomington, Indiana U.P., 1964. 175p.

1336 Treml, V.G. The development of the Soviet economy: plan and perform - ance. N.Y., Praeger, 1968. 298p.

1337 Yefimov, A. and others. Soviet planning: principles and techniques. Moscow, Progress, 1972. 193p.

1338 Yugow, A. Russia's economic front for war and peace: an appraisal of the three five-year plans. N.Y., Harper, 1942. 279p.; L., Watts, 1943. 292p.

1339 Zaleski, E. Planning reforms in the Soviet Union, 1962—1966: an analysis of recent trends in economic organization and management. Chapel

Hill, U. of North Carolina P., 1967.    203p.

1340  Zaleski, E.  Planning for economic growth in the Soviet Union,    1918-
      1932.  Chapel Hill, U. of North Carolina P., 1971.    425p.

1341  Zauberman, A.  Aspects of planometrics.  New Haven, Yale U.P.,    1967.
      318p.

1342  Chamberlin, W.H.  The Soviet planned economic order.  Boston,    Mass.,
      World Peace Foundation, 1931.    258p.

1343  Farbman, M.  Piatiletka:    Russia's five-year plan.  N.Y.,  New Repub -
      lic, 1931.    220p.

1344  From the first to the second five-year plan: a symposium.  Moscow  Co-
      operative Publishing Society of Foreign Workers, 1933.    490p.

1345  Grinko, G.F.  The five-year plan of the Soviet Union:  a political inte-
      rpretation. L., Lawrence, 1930.    340p.

1346  Knickerbocker, H.R.  The Soviet five-year plan and its effect on world
      trade.  L., Lane, 1931.    246p.

1347  Socialist planned economy in the Soviet Union.  L., Lawrence, 1932. 120p.

1348  The Soviet Union looks ahead:  the first five-year plan for economic co-
      nstruction.  L., Allen & Unwin, 1930.    275p.

1349  U.S.S.R. State Planning Commission.  Summary of the fulfilment of the
      first five-year plan:  report of the State Planning Commission. Moscow,
      Gosplan, 1933.    296p.

1350  Walter, E.  Russia's decisive year.  L., Hutchinson, 1932.    282p.

1351  Coates, W.P., Coates, Z.K.  The second five-year plan of development of
      the U.S.S.R.  L., Methuen, 1934.    129p.

1352  U.S.S.R. State Planning Commission.  The second five-year plan for the
      development of the national economy of the U.S.S.R. (1933-37);  ed. by
      I.B. Lasker and J. Swift.  L., Lawrence & Wishart, 1936.    671p.

1353  The Soviet seven year plan:  a study of economic progress and potential
      in the U.S.S.R.  L., Phoenix House, 1960.    126p.

1354  Soviet seven year plan, 1959-1965.  L., Todd Reference Bks., 1959. 248p.


C    Politics and government

(i)   General Surveys

1355  Amalrik, A.  Will the Soviet Union survive until 1984?;  with contrib-
      utions from H. Kamm and S. Monas and three additional letters from  A.
      Amalrik.  N.Y., Harper, 1970.  93p.;  L., Allen Lane, 1970.    124p.

1356   Antonelli, E.   Bolshevist Russia:   a philosophical survey.   L., Stanley
       Paul, 1920.   277p.

1357   Armstrong, J.A.   Ideology, politics and government in the Soviet Union:
       an introduction.   Rev. ed.   N.Y.; L., Praeger, 1967.   173p.

1358   Batsell, W.R.   Soviet rule in Russia.   N.Y., Macmillan, 1929.   857p.

1359   Braham, R.L.   Soviet politics and government: a reader.   N.Y.,   Knopf,
       1965.   615p.

1360   Brailsford, H.N.   How the Soviets work.   N.Y., Vanguard P., 1927.   169p.

1361   Brzezinski, Z.K.   Ideology and power in Soviet politics.   Rev. ed. N.Y.;
       L., Praeger, 1967.   291p.

1362   Brzezinski, Z.K.   The permanent purge:   politics in Soviet totalitarian-
       ism.   Cambridge, Mass., Harvard U.P., 1956.   256p.

1363   Carter, G.M.   The government of the Soviet Union.   2nd ed. N.Y.,   Har-
       court, 1967.   137p.

1364   Chamberlin, W.H.   Blueprint for world conquest:   the official Communist
       plan.   Chicago, Human Events, 1946.   263p.

1365   Churchward, L.G.   Contemporary Soviet government.   N.Y., American Else-
       vier; L., Routledge, 1968.   366p.

1366   Conquest, R.   The Soviet political system.   N.Y., Praeger; L., Bodley
       Head, 1968.   144p.

1367   Cornell, R.   The Soviet political system:   a book of readings.   Engle-
       wood Cliffs, Prentice, 1970.   392p.

1368   Ellsworth, R.   The Soviet state.   N.Y., Macmillan; L., Collier-Macmil-
       lan, 1968.   462p.

1369   Fainsod, M.   How Russia is ruled.   Rev. ed.   Cambridge, Mass., Harvard
       U.P., 1963.   686p.

1370   Florinsky, M.T.   Towards an understanding of the U.S.S.R.:   a study in
       government, politics and economic planning.   Rev. ed. N.Y., Macmillan,
       1951.   223p.

1371   Friedrich, C.J., Brezinzski, Z.K.   Totalitarian dictatorship and auto-
       cracy.   2nd ed. Cambridge, Mass., Harvard U.P., 1965.   439p.

1372   Gripp, R.C.   Patterns of Soviet politics.   Rev. ed. Homewood,   Dorsey,
       1967.   386p.

1373   Gurian, W.   Bolshevism:   theory and practice.   L., Sheed & Ward,   1932.
       402p.

1374   Gurian, W.   The Soviet Union:   background, ideology, reality:   a symposium. Notre Dame, U. of Notre Dame P., 1951.    216p.

1375  Harper, S.N., Thompson, R.  The government of the Soviet Union.  2nd ed.
      N.Y.; L., Van Nostrand, 1949.    369p.

1376  Hazard, J.N.  The Soviet system of government.  4th ed.  Chicago, U. of
      Chicago P., 1968.    275p.

1377  Hendel, S.  The Soviet crucible:  the Soviet system in theory and pract-
      ice.  4th ed.  North Scituate, Mass., Duxbury P., 1973.    436p.

1378  Hudson, G.F.  Fifty years of communism:  theory and practice 1917-1967.
      L., Watts, 1968.    234p.

1379  Huszar, G.B. de.  Soviet power and policy.  N.Y., Crowell, 1954.  598p.

1380  Juviler, P.H., Morton, H.W.  Soviet policy-making:  studies of communism
      in transition.  L., Pall Mall P., 1967.    274p.

1381  Kanet, R.E.  The behavioral revolution and communist studies:  applicat-
      ions of behaviorally oriented political research on the Soviet Union and
      Eastern Europe.  N.Y., Free P., 1971.    376p.

1382  Katare, S.L.  The government of the Soviet Union.  Jabalpur, Indian Bk.
      House, 1952.    235p.

1383  Kolarz, W.  How Russia is ruled.  L., Batchworth, 1953.    175p.

1384  Kulski, W.W.  The Soviet regime:  communism in practice.  4th ed.  Syra-
      cuse, Syracuse U.P., 1963.    444p.

1385  Lane, D.  Politics and society in the U.S.S.R.  N.Y., Random, 1971.; L.,
      Weidenfeld & Nicolson, 1970.    616p.

1386  Leites, N.  A study of Bolshevism.  Glencoe, Free P., 1953.    639p.

1387  McClosky, H., Turner, J.E.  The Soviet dictatorship.  N.Y.; L., McGraw-
      Hill, 1960.    657p.

1388  McNeal, R.H.  The Bolshevik tradition:  Lenin, Stalin, Khrushchev.  Eng-
      lewood Cliffs, Prentice, 1963.    181p.

1389  Maxwell, B.W.  The Soviet state:  a study of Bolshevik rule.  L., Selwyn
      & Blount, 1935.    384p.

1390  Meisel, J.H., Kozera, E.S.  Materials for the study of the Soviet system.
      Ann Arbor, Wahr Publishing Co., 1953.    613p.

1391  Meyer, A.G.  The Soviet political system:  an interpretation.  N.Y., Pr-
      aeger, 1965.    494p.

1392  Moore, B., Jr.  Soviet politics:  the dilemma of power, the role of ide-
      as in social change;  new epilogue by the author.  N.Y., Harper, 1965.
      504p.

1393   Moore, B., Jr.   Terror and progress, U.S.S.R.:   some sources of change and stability in the Soviet dictatorship.   Cambridge, Mass., Harvard U.P 1954.      261p.

1394   Raymond, E.L.   The Soviet state.   N.Y., Macmillan, 1968.      462p.

1395   Reshetar, J.S., Jr.   The Soviet polity:   government and politics in the U.S.S.R.   N.Y., Dodd, 1971.      412p.

1396   Rosenberg, A.   History of Bolshevism:   from Marx to the first five-year plan.   L., Oxford U.P., 1934.      250p.

1397   Schapiro, L.   The government and politics of the Soviet Union.   4th ed.   L., Hutchinson, 1970.      178p.

1398   Schuman, F.L.   Government in the Soviet Union.   2nd ed.   N.Y., Crowell, 1967.      266p.

1399   Schuman, F.L.   Soviet politics at home and abroad.   N.Y., Knopf,   1946.; L., Hale, 1948.      633p.

1400   Scott, D.J.R.   Russian political institutions.   3rd ed.   L., Allen & Unwin, 1965.      276p.

1401   Selznick, P.   The organizational weapon:   a study of Bolshevik strategy and tactics.   Glencoe, Free P., 1960.      350p.

1402   Shaffer, H.G.   The Soviet system in theory and practice.   N.Y., Appleton, 1965.      470p.

1403   Sloan, P.   How the Soviet state is run.   L., Lawrence & Wishart,   1941. 128p.

1404   Sloan, P.   Soviet democracy.   L., Gollancz, 1938.      288p.

1405   Snow, E.   The pattern of Soviet power.   N.Y., Random, 1945.      219p.

1406   Sternberg, F.   The end of a revolution:   Soviet Russia from revolution to reaction.   N.Y., John Day, 1953.      191p.

1407   Timasheff, N.S.   The great retreat:   the growth and decline of Communism in Russia.   N.Y., Dutton, 1946.      470p.

1408   Towster, J.   Political power in the U.S.S.R., 1917–1947.   N.Y.,   Oxford U.P., 1948.      443p.

1409   Wesson, R.G.   Soviet communism.   New Brunswick, Rutgers U.P., 1963. 275p.

1410   Wesson, R.G.   The Soviet Russian state.   N.Y.; L., Wiley, 1972.      404p.

1411   Wesson, R.G.   The Soviet state:   an aging revolution.   N.Y.; L., Wiley, 1972.      222p.

1412   Wilbur, W.H.   Russian communism:   a challenge and a   fraud.   Caldwell,

Caxton, 1964.   296p.

1413   Wolfe, B.D.   Communist totalitarianism:   Keys to the Soviet system.   Boston, Mass., Beacon, 1961.   328p.

(ii)   Political theory

1414   Bouscaren, A.T.   A textbook on communism.   Milwaukee, Bruce, 1965. 216p.

1415   Bukharin, N.   The ABC of communism.   Ann Arbor, U. of Michigan P., 1966. 422p.

1416   Cantril, H.   Soviet leaders and mastery over men.   New Brunswick, Rutgers U.P., 1960.   173p.

1417   Cliff, T.   Russia:   a marxist analysis.   L., International Socialism, 1964.   384p.

1418   Cliff, T.   Stalinist Russia:   a marxist analysis.   L., M. Kidron, 1955. 275p.

1419   De George, R.T.   The new marxism:   Soviet and East European marxism since 1956.   N.Y., Pegasus, 1968.   170p.

1420   Denno, T.   The Communist millenium:   the Soviet view.   The Hague, Nijhoff, 1964.   166p.

1421   Drachkovitch, M.M.   Fifty years of communism in Russia.   University Park Pa., Pennsylvania State U.P., 1968.   316p.

1422   Eissenstat, B.W.   Lenin and Leninism:   state, law and society.   Lexington, Heath, 1971.   322p.

1423   Goodman, E.R.   The Soviet design for a world state.   N.Y., Columbia U.P., 1960.   512p.

1424   Gurian, W.   Bolshevism:   an introduction to Soviet communism.   Notre Dame, U. of Notre Dame P., 1952.   **189p.**

1425   Jacobson, J.   Soviet communism and the socialist vision.   New Brunswick, Transaction Bks., 1972.   363p.

1426   Jaworskyj, M.   Soviet political thought:   an anthology.   Baltimore, Johns Hopkins P., 1967.   621p.

1427   Kalinin, M.I.   On communist ideology.   Moscow, FLPH, 1949.   479p.

1428   Kolarz, W.   Communism and colonialism.   N.Y., St Martin's P., 1964. 147p.

1429   Marcuse, H.   Soviet marxism:   a critical analysis.   N.Y., Columbia U.P.; L., Routledge, 1958.   271p.

1430   Meyer, A.G.   Leninism.   Cambridge, Mass., Harvard U.P., 1957.   324p.

1431    Plamenatz, J.P.   German marxism and Russian communism.   N.Y.,   Harper,
        1965.    356p.

1432    Postgate, R.W.   The Bolshevik theory.   L., Richards, 1920.    240p.

1433    Rieber, A.J.,Nelson, R.C.   The U.S.S.R. and communism:   source readings
        and interpretations.   Chicago, Scott, Foresman, 1964.    320p.

1434    Russell, B.   The theory of Bolshevism.   L., Allen & Unwin, 1921.   188p.

1435    Russia since 1917:   socialist views of Bolshevik policy.   L., Socialist
        Party of Great Britain, 1949.    114p.

1436    Spiro, G.   Marxism and the Bolshevik state.   Cooper Station, Red Star P.,
        1951.    107p.

1437    Tucker, R.C.   The Soviet political mind:   Stalinism and post-Stalin cha-
        nge.   Rev. ed. N.Y., Norton, 1971.;   L., Allen & Unwin, 1972.    304p.

1438    Ulam, A.B.   The new face of Soviet totalitarianism.   Cambridge, Mass.,
        Harvard U.P., 1963.    223p.

1439    Utechin, S.V.   Russian political thought:   a concise history.    N.Y.,
        Praeger;   L., Dent, 1964.    320p.

1440    Vigor, P.H.   A guide to Marxism and its effect on Soviet development.
        N.Y., Humanities P.; L., Faber, 1966.    253p.

1441    Wetter, G.A.   Soviet ideology today:   dialectical and historical mater-
        ialism.   N.Y., Praeger;   L., Heinemann, 1966.    334p.

(iii)   Political institutions

1442    Andrews, W.G., Scholz, F.D.   Soviet institutions and policies:   inside
        views.   Princeton;   L., Van Nostrand, 1966.    411p.

1443    Armstrong, J.A.   The politics of totalitarianism:   the Communist Party
        of the Soviet Union from 1934 to the present.   N.Y., Random House, 1961.
        458p.

1444    Avtorkhanov, A.   The Communist party apparatus.   Chicago, Regnery, 1966.
        422p.

1445    Avtorkhanov, A.   Stalin and the Soviet Communist Party:   a study in the
        technology of power.   N.Y., Praeger, 1959.;   L., Stevens, 1959.

1446    Barou, N.   Co-operation in the Soviet Union:   a survey prepared for the
        Fabian society.   L., Gollancz, 1946.    123p.

1447    Bernaut, E., Ruggles, M.J.   Soviet collective leadership.   Santa Monica,
        Rand Corp., 1956.    165p.

1448    Brailsford, H.N.   How the Soviets work.   N.Y., Vanguard,    1927.
        169p.

1449 Cantril, H. Soviet leaders and mastery over men. New Brunswick, Rutgers U.P., 1960. 173p.

1450 Deriabin, P. Watchdogs of terror: Russian bodyguards from the Tsars to the commissars. New Rochelle, Arlington House, 1972. 448p.

1451 Duranty, W. Stalin & Co., the Polittburo: the men who run Russia. N.Y. Sloane; L., Secker & Warburg, 1949. 252p.

1452 Farrell, R.B. Political leadership in Eastern Europe and the Soviet Union. Chicago, Aldine, 1970. 359p.

1453 Gehlen, M.P. The Communist Party of the Soviet Union: a functional analysis. Bloomington, Indiana U.P., 1969. 161p.

1454 Gibney, F. The K.hrushchev pattern. L., Prentice-Hall, 1961. 280p.

1455 Harper, S.N. Making Bolsheviks. Chicago, Chicago U.P., 1931. 167p.

1456 History of the Communist Party of the Soviet Union (Bolsheviks): short course; edited by a commission of the Central Committee of the CPSU. N.Y., International Publishers; Moscow, FLPH, 1939. 364p.

1457 History of the Communist Party of the Soviet Union. L., Cobbett, 1943. 345p.

1458 The History of the Communist Party of the Soviet Union. Moscow, FLPH, 1950. 447p.

1459 Hough, J.F. The Soviet prefects: the local party organs in industrial decision-making. Cambridge, Mass., Harvard U.P., 1969. 416p.

1460 Knorin, V.G. The Communist Party of the Soviet Union: a short history. Moscow, 1935. 516p.

1461 Leites, N. The operational code of the Politburo. N.Y.; L., McGraw-Hill, 1951. 100p.

1462 Leites, N. Kremlin moods. Santa Monica, Rand Corp., 1964. 309p.

1463 Meissner, B. The Communist Party of the Soviet Union: party leadership, organization and ideology; ed. and with a chapter on the Twentieth Party Congress by J.S. Reshetar. N.Y., Praeger; L., Atlantic P., 1957. 276p.

1464 Narkiewicz, O.A. The making of the Soviet state apparatus. Manchester, Manchester U.P., 1970. 238p.

1465 Norborg, C. Operation Moscow: psychological motives behind the Politburo and measures to contain Soviet imperialism. N.Y., Dutton, 1947.; L., Latimer House, 1948. 285p.

1466 Ponomarev, B.N. and others. History of the Communist Party of the Soviet Union. Moscow, FLPH, 1960. 765p.

1467 Popov, N. Outline history of the Communist Party of the Soviet Union. L., Lawrence, 1935. 2 vols.

1468 Reshetar, J.S. A concise history of the Communist Party of the Soviet Union. 2nd ed. N.Y., Praeger, 1964.; L., Pall Mall P., 1965. 372p.

1469 Rigby, T.H. Communist party membership in the U.S.S.R., 1917-1967. Princeton, Princeton U.P., 1968. 573p.

1470 Rothstein, A. The Soviet constitution. L., Labour Publ. Co., 1923. 142p.

1471 Schapiro, L. The Communist Party of the Soviet Union. 2nd ed. N.Y., Random; L., Eyre & Spottiswoode, 1970. 686p.

1472 Schapiro, L.B. The U.S.S.R. and the future: an analysis of the new program of the CPSU. N.Y., Praeger, 1963. 324p.

1473 Schueller, G.K. The Politburo. Stanford, Stanford U.P., 1951. 79p.

1474 Scott, D.J.R. Russian political institutions. 4th ed. L., Allen & Unwin, 1969. 270p.

1475 Strong, A.L. The new Soviet constitution: a study in socialist democracy. N.Y., Holt, 1937. 169p.

1476 Zinoviev, G. History of the Bolshevik party: a popular outline. L., New Park, 1973. 229p.

(iv) Political process

1477 Agabekov, G. Ogpu: the Russian secret terror. N.Y., Brentano, 1931. 277p.

1478 Amalrik, A. Involuntary journey to Siberia. N.Y., Harcourt, 1970. 297p L., Collins, 1970. 284p.

1479 Ameel, J. Red hell: twenty years in Soviet Russia. L., Hale, 1941. 316p.

1480 Azrael, J.R. Managerial power and Soviet politics. Cambridge, Mass., Harvard U.P., 1966. 258p.

1481 Baldwin, R.N. Liberty under the Soviets. N.Y., Vanguard P., 1928. 272p.

1482 Barghoorn, F.C. Politics in the U.S.S.R.: a country study. 2nd ed. Boston, Mass., Little, 1972. 360p.

1483 Beck, F., Godin, W. Russian purge and the extraction of confession. L., Hurst & Blackett, 1951. 232p.

1484 Bezsonov, Y. My twenty-six prisons and my escape from Solovetsky. L., Cape, 1929. 288p.

1485   Brzezinski, Z.K.   Dilemmas of change in Soviet politics.   N.Y., Columbia U.P., 1969.   163p.

1486   Brzezinski, Z.K., Huntingdon, S.P.   Political power:   U.S.A./U.S.S.R. N.Y., Viking P.; L., Chatto & Windus, 1964.   461p.

1487   Brunovsky, V.   The methods of the Ogpu.   L., Harper, 1931.   285p.

1488   Campbell, J.R.   Soviet policy and its critics.   L., Gollancz, 1938.   381p.

1489   Carson, G.B.   Electoral practices in the U.S.S.R.   N.Y., Praeger;   L., Thames & Hudson, 1956.   151p.

1490   Cattell, D.T.   Leningrad:   a case study of Soviet urban government.   N.Y.; L., Praeger, 1968.   173p.

1491   Cederholm, B.   In the clutches of the Tcheka.   L., Allen & Unwin, 1929. 349p.

1492   Chernavin, T.   Escape from the Soviets.   L., Hamilton, 1933.   320p.

1493   Ciliga, A.   The Russian enigma.   L., Routledge,1940.   304p.

1494   Conquest, R.   The politics of ideas in the U.S.S.R.   L.,   Bodley   Head, 1967.   176p.

1495   Conquest, R.   The Soviet police system.   L., Bodley Head, 1968.   103p.

1496   Conquest, R.   Power and policy in the U.S.S.R.: the study of Soviet dynastics.   N.Y., St Martin's P.;   L., Macmillan, 1961.   485p.

1497   Czapski, J.   The inhuman land.   L., Chatto & Windus, 1951.   301p.

1498   Dallin, A., Westin, A.F.   Politics in the Soviet Union:   seven cases.N.Y Harcourt, 1966.   296p.

1499   Daniels, R.V.   The conscience of the Revolution:   communist opposition in Soviet Russia.   Cambridge, Mass., Harvard U.P., 1960.   526p.

1500   Deacon, R.V.   A history of the Russian secret service. N.Y., Taplinger; L., Muller, 1972.   568p.

1501   De Beausobre, I.   The woman who could not die.   N.Y., Viking; L., Chatto & Windus, 1938.   301p.

1502   Deriabin, P., Gibney, F.   The secret world.   L., Barker, 1960.   334p.

1503   Dinerstein, H.S., Goure, L.   Communism and the Russian peasant;   Moscow in crisis:   two studies in Soviet control.   Glencoe, Free P., 1955. 254p.

1504   Dorosh, H.   Russian constitutionalism.   N.Y., Exposition P., 1944. 127p.

1505   Doubassof, I.   Ten months in a Bolshevik prison.   L., Blackwood,   1926. 308p.

506 Duranty, W. The Kremlin and the people. N.Y., Reynal & Hitchcock, 1941. 222p.; L., Hamilton, 1942. 176p.

507 Eaton, R. Under the red flag. N.Y., Brentamo, 1924. 262p.

508 'Essad Bey'. Secrets of the Ogpu: the plot against the world. L., Jarrolds, 1938. 301p.

509 Fainsod, M. Smolensk under Soviet rule. Cambridge, Mass., Harvard U.P. 1957.; L., Macmillan 1957. 484p.

510 Fischer, G. The Soviet system and modern society. N.Y., Atherton, 1968. 199p.

511 Galler, M., Marquess, H.E. Soviet prison camp speech: a survivor's glossary supplemented by terms from the work of A.I. Solzenicyn. Madison, U. of Wisconsin P., 1972. 216p.

512 Gaucher, R. Opposition in the U.S.S.R., 1917-1967. N.Y., Funk & Wagnalls, 1969. 547p.

513 Gilison, J. British and Soviet politics: legitimacy and convergence. Baltimore, Johns Hopkins P., 1972. 186p.

514 Gliksman, J. Tell the West. N.Y., Gresham, 1948. 358p.

515 Hadow, M. Paying guest in Siberia. L., Collins, 1959. 190p.

516 Hahn, W.G. The politics of Soviet agriculture, 1960-1970. Baltimore, Johns Hopkins P., 1972. 311p.

517 Harper, S.N. Civic training in Soviet Russia. Chicago, Chicago U.P., 1929. 401p.

518 Heilbrunn, O. The Soviet secret services. N.Y., Praeger; L., Allen & Unwin, 1956. 216p.

519 Hingley, R. The Russian secret police: Muscovite, Imperial Russian and Soviet political security operations, 1565-1970. N.Y., Simon & Schuster; L., Hutchinson, 1970. 305p.

520 Ionescu, G. Comparative communist politics. L., Macmillan, 1972. 64p.

521 Juviler, P.H., Morton, H.W. Soviet policy-making: studies of communism in transition. N.Y., Praeger, 1967. 274p.

522 Kindermann, K. In the toils of the O.G.P.U. L., Hurst & Blackett, 1933. 312p.

523 Kitchin, G. Prisoner of the Ogpu. L., Longmans, 1935. 333p.

524 Lermolo, E. Face of a victim. N.Y., Harper, 1955. 311p.

525 Letters from Russian prisons: consisting of reprints of documents by

polictcal prisoners in Soviet prisons, prison-camps and exile, and re - prints of affidavits concerning political persecution in Soviet Russia, official statements by Soviet authorities, excerpts from Soviet laws pertaining to civil liberties and other documents. L., Daniel, 1925. 317p.

1526  Levytsky, B.  The uses of terror:  the Soviet secret police, 1917-1970. N.Y., Coward;  L., Sidgwick & Jackson, 1972.   349p.

1527  Little, D.R.  Liberalization in the U.S.S.R.:  facade or reality?  Lexington, Heath, 1968.   135p.

1528  Malsagoff, S.A.  An island hell:  a Soviet prison in the far north. L., Philpot, 1926.   223p.

1529  Marchenko, A.  My testimony.  N.Y., Dutton;  L., Pall Mall P.,   1969. 415p.

1530  Maximoff, G.P.  The guillotine at work:  20 years of terror in Russia (data and documents).  Chicago, Chicago Section of the Alexander Berkman Fund, 1940.   627p.

1531  Mickiewicz, E.P.  Soviet political schools:  the Communist party adult instruction system.  New Haven, Yale U.P., 1967.   190p.

1532  Melgounov, S.P.  The red terror in Russia.  L., Dent, 1925.   271p.

1533  Mote, M.E.  Soviet local and republic elections:  a description of the 1963 elections in Leningrad based on official documents, press accounts, and private interviews.  Stanford, Hoover Institution P., 1965.   123p.

1534  Orloff, V.G.  The secret dossier:  my memoirs of Russia's political underworld.  L., Harrap, 1932.   274p.

1535  Parkins, M.F.  City planning in Russia.  Chicago, U. of Chicago P., 1953. 257p.

1536  Parry, A.  The new class divided:  science and technology versus Communism.  N.Y., Macmillan, 1966.   364p.

1537  Pethybridge, R.  A key to Soviet politics:  the crisis of the anti-party group.  N.Y., Praeger;  L., Allen & Unwin, 1962.   207p.

1538  Pidhainy, S.A.  Islands of death.  Toronto, Burns & MacEachern,   1953. 240p.

1539  Ploss, S.I.  The Soviet political process:  aims, techniques and exam - ples of analysis.  Waltham, Ginn, 1970.   304p.

1540  Popoff, G.  The Tcheka:  the red inquisition.  L., Philpot, 1925. 308p.

1541  Pritt, D.N.  Light on Moscow:  Soviet policy analysed.  Harmondsworth, Penguin, 1940.   223p.

1542  Prychodko, N.  One of the fifteen million.  Boston, Mass., Little, 1952.

236p.

1543 Rainer, H.  The baroque tower:  life in Russian prison camps.  N.Y., Vantage, 1971.   159p.

1544 Rawicz, S.  The long walk:  a gamble for life.  N.Y., Harper, 1956. 239p.

1545 Romanov, A.I.  Nights are longest there:  a memoir of the Soviet security service.  Boston, Mass., Little;  L., Hutchinson, 1972.   256p.

1546 Rush, M.  Political succession in the U.S.S.R.  2nd ed.  N.Y., Columbia U.P., 1968.   281p.

1547 Shachtman, M.  The bureaucratic revolution:  the rise of the Stalinist state.  N.Y., Donald P., 1962.   360p.

1548 Skilling, H.G., Griffiths, F.  Interest groups in Soviet politics.  Princeton, Princeton U.P., 1971.   435p.

1549 Solomon, M.  Magadan.  Princeton, Auerbach, 1971.   243p.

1550 Solonevich, I.  Russia in chains:  a record of unspeakable suffering.  L. Williams & Norgate, 1938.   312p.

1551 Solonevich, I.  Escape from Russian chains.  L., Williams & Norgate, 1938.   350p.

1552 Soviet Affairs Symposium, 4th, Garmisch-Partenkirchen, 1970.  The role and influence of Soviet pressure groups on CPSU policy.  Garmisch, U.S. Army Institute for Advanced Russian and East European studies, 1970. 156p

1553 Stewart, P.D.  Political power in the Soviet Union:  a study of decision -making in Stalingrad.  Indianapolis, Bobbs, 1968.   227p.

1554 Taubman, W.  Governing Soviet cities:  bureaucratic politics and urban development in the U.S.S.R.  N.Y.;  L., Praeger, 1973.   166p.

1555 Thompson, C.  Police state:  what you want to know about the Soviet Union.  N.Y., Dutton, 1950.   257p.

1556 Wittlin, T.  A reluctant traveller in Russia.  L., William Hodge, 1952. 237p.

1557 Wolin, S., Slusser, R.M.  The Soviet secret police.  N.Y., Praeger; L., Methuen, 1957.   408p.

v)  International Politics

(a)  International Law

1558 Baade, H.W.  The Soviet impact on international law.  Dobbs Ferry, Oceana, 1965.   174p.

1559 Erickson, R.J.  International law and the revolutionary state:  a case study of the Soviet Union and customary international law. Dobbs Ferry, Oceana, 1972. 254p.

1560 Grzybowski, K. Soviet private international law. Leyden, Sijthoff, 1965 179p.

1561 Ramundo, B.A. The Soviet socialist theory of international law. Washington, George Washington U.P., 1964. 110p.

1562 Taracouzio, T.A. The Soviet Union and international law: a study based on the legislation, treaties and foreign relations of the Union of Socialist Soviet Republics. N.Y., Macmillan, 1935. 530p.

1563 Slusser, R.M., Triska, J.F. A calendar of Soviet treaties, 1917–1957. Stanford, Stanford U.P., 1959. 530p.

1564 Shapiro, L. Soviet treaty series: a collection of bilateral treaties, agreements and conventions, etc., concluded between the Soviet Union and foreign powers. Washington, Georgetown U.P., 1950–55. 2 vols.

(b)    Disarmament

1565 Bloomfield, L.P. and others. Khrushchev and the arms race: Soviet interests in arms control and disarmement, 1954–1964. Cambridge, Mass., MITP., 1966. 338p.

1566 Clemens, W.C. The superpowers and arms control: from cold war to interdependence. Lexington Heath, 1973. 181p.

1567 Dallin, A. and others. The Soviet Union and disarmament: an appraisal of Soviet attitudes and intentions. N.Y.; L., Praeger, 1964. 282p.

1568 Halperin, N.H. Sino-Soviet reactions and arms control. Cambridge, Mass MITP., 1967. 342p.

1569 Larson, T.B. Disarmament and Soviet policy, 1964–1968. Englewood Cliffs, Prentice, 1969. 280p.

(c)    International organizations

1570 Dallin, A. The Soviet Union at the United Nations: an inquiry into Soviet motives and objectives. N.Y., Praeger; L., Methuen, 1962. 244p.

1571 Davis, K.W. The Soviets at Geneva: the U.S.S.R. at the League of Nations, 1919–1933. Geneva, Libraire Kundig, 1934. 315p.

1572 Fernbach, A.P. Soviet coexistence strategy: a case study of experience in the International Labor Organization. Washington, Public Affairs P., 1960. 63p.

1573 Jacobson, H.K. The U.S.S.R. and the U.N.'s economic and social activities. Notre Dame, U. of Notre Dame P., 1963. 309p.

1574 Mahaney, W.L. The Soviet Union, the League of Nations and disarmament,

1917-1935.  Philadelphia, 1940.    199p.

1575  Nogee, J.L.  Soviet policy towards international control of atomic energy.  Notre Dame, U. of Notre Dame P., 1961.    306p.

1576  Osakwe, C.  The participation of the Soviet Union in universal international organizations;  a political and legal analysis of Soviet strategies and aspirations inside ILO, UNESCO and WHO.  Leyden, Sijthoff, 1973.
194p.

1577  Rubinstein, A.Z.  The Soviets in international organizations:  changing
policy towards developing countries, 1953-1963.  Princeton, Princeton
U.P., 1964.    380p.

1578  Rubinstein, A.Z., Ginsburg, G.  Soviet and American policies in the United Nations:  a twenty-five year perspective.  N.Y., N.Y.U.P. 1971. 211p.

1579  Soviet spies in the shadow of the U.N.  Wavre, Ligue de la Liberte, Centre d'Information et de Documentation, 1969.    240p.

1580  Stoessinger, J.G., McKelvey, R.G.  The United Nations and the superpowers:
China, Russia & America.  3rd ed. N.Y., Random, 1973.    216p.

               (d)    Foreign policy and diplomacy

1581  Aspaturian, V.V.  The Union republics in Soviet diplomacy:  a study of
Soviet federalism in the service of Soviet foreign policy.  Geneva; Paris, Universite de Geneve.  Publications de l'Institut universitaire des
hautes etudes internationales, 1960.    228p.

1582  Barmine, A.  One who survived:  the life story of a Russian under the
Soviets.  Rev. ed.  N.Y., Putnam, 1945.  337p.;  Memoirs of a Soviet diplomat:  twenty years in the service of the U.S.S.R.  L., Dickson, 1938.
360p.

1583  Hague Conference on Russia, 1922.  Conference at the Hague:  1. Non-Russian Commission;  2. Russian Commission, June 26-July 20, 1922; minutes
and documents.  The Hague, 1922.    235p.

1584  Jamgotch, N.  Soviet-East European dialogues:  international relations
of a new type.  Stanford, Hoover Institution, 1968.    165p.

585  Jonas, A.M.  The Soviet Union and the atom:  peaceful sharing, 1954-1958.
Santa Monica, Rand Corp., 1958.    158p.

586  Kaznacheev, A.I.  Inside a Soviet embassy:  experiences of a Russian diplomat in Burma.  Philadelphia, Lippincott, 1962.  250p.;  L., Hale,1963.
187p.

587  Harper, S.N.  The Soviet Union and world problems.  Chicago, 1935. 254p.

588  Tornudd, K.  Soviet attitudes towards non-military regional co-operation.
2nd ed.  Helsingfors, 1963.    324p.

1589    Zimmerman, W.  Soviet perspectives on international relations.  Prince-
        ton, Princeton U.P., 1969.    336p.

                    (e)    Communist International

1590    Aspaturian, V.T.  The Soviet Union in the world communist system.  Stan-
        ford, Hoover Institution, 1966.    96p.

1591    Borkenau, F.  The Communist International.  L., Faber, 1938.    442p.

1592    Coates, W.P., Coates, Z.K.  World affairs and the U.S.S.R.  L ., Lawrence
        & Wishart, 1939.    251p.

1593    Columbia University.  Russian Institute  The anti-Stalin campaign and
        international communism:  a selection of documents.  N.Y., Columbia U.P.,
        1956.    338p.

1594    Cornell, R.  Youth and communism:  an historical analysis of internationa
        communist youth movements.  N.Y., Walker, 1965.    239p.

1595    Degras, J.  The Communist International, 1919-1943:  documents.  L., Ox-
        ford U.P., 1956-65.  3vols.

1596    Deutscher, I.  Ironies of history:  essays on contemporary communism.  L.,
        Oxford U.P., 1966.    278p.

1597    Dingle, R.J.  Russia's work in France.  L., Hale, 1938.    278p.

1598    Drachkovitch, M.M., Lazitch, B.  The Comintern:  historical highlights,
        essays, recollections, documents.  N.Y., Praeger;  L., Pall Mall P., 1966
        430p.

1599    Drachkovitch, M.M.  The revolutionary internationals, 1846-1943.  Stan-
        ford, Stanford U.P., 1966.    256p.

1600    Florinsky, M.T.  World revolution and the U.S.S.R.  L., Macmillan, 1933.
        264p.

1601    Footman, D.  International communism.  Carbondale, Southern Illinois U.P.
        L., Chatto & Windus, 1960.    151p.

1602    Gibbs, H.  The spectre of communism.  L., Selwyn & Blount, 1936.    287p.

1603    Gruber, H.  International communism in the era of Lenin:  a documentary
        study.  Garden City, N.Y., Anchor Bks., 1972.    426p.

1604    Grzybowski, K.  The socialist commonwealth of nations:  organizations and
        institutions.  New Haven, Yale U.P., 1964.    300p.

1605    International Conference on Sino-Soviet Bloc Affairs, 3d. Lake Kawaguchi
        1960.  Unity and contradiction;  ed by K. London.  N.Y., Praeger, 1962.
        464p.

1606    James, C.L.R.  World revolution, 1917-1936:  the rise and fall of the

                                    - 88 -

Communist International. L., Secker & Warburg, 1937. 429p.

1607 King-Hall, S. The communist conspiracy. N.Y., Macmillan; L., Constable, 1953. 293p.

1608 Kirkpatrick, E.M. Year of crisis: Communist propaganda activities in 1956. N.Y., Macmillan, 1957. 414p.

1609 Labedz, L. International communism after Khrushchev. Cambridge, Mass., MITP., 1965. 232p.

1610 Mackenzie, K.E. Comintern and world revolution, 1928-1943: the shaping of doctrine. N.Y., Columbia U.P., 1963. 368p.

1611 Miliukov, P. Bolshevism: an international danger: its doctrine and its practice through war and revolution. L., Allen & Unwin, 1920. 303p.

1612 Modelski, G. The Communist international system. Princeton, Princeton U.P., 1961. 78p.

1613 Murphy, J.T. New horizons. L., Lane, 1941. 352p.

1614 Nollau, G. International communism and world revolution: history and methods. N.Y., Praeger, 1961. 357p.

1615 Phelps-Fetherston, I. Soviet international front organization: a concise handbook. N.Y., Praeger,; L., Pall Mall P., 1965. 178p.

1616 Pritt, D.N. Light on Moscow: Soviet policy analysed. L., Penguin, 1939. 190p.

1617 Seton-Watson, H. From Lenin to Khrushchev: the history of world communism. N.Y., Praeger, 1960. 432p.

1618 Smal-Stocki, R., Sokolnicki, A.J. Russian and communist imperialism in action. Milwaukee, Slavic Institute of Marquette University, 1963. 205p.

1619 Thornton, R.C. The Comintern and the Chinese communists, 1928-1931. Seattle, U. of Washington P., 1969. 246p.

1620 Trotsky, L. The Third International after Lenin. N.Y., Pioneer, 1936. 357p.

1621 Walsh, E.A. Total empire: the roots and progress of world communism. Milwaukee, Bruce, 1951. 293p.

(f)    Espionage

1622 Accoce, P., Quet, P. The Lucy ring. L., Allen, 1967. 224p.

1623 Atholl, J. How Stalin knows: the story of the great atomic spy conspiracy. L., News of the World, 1951. 182p.

1624 Bailey, G. The conspirators: an extraordinary story of intrigue between Russia and Western Europe during the years before World War II. N.Y., Harper, 1960.; L., Gollancz, 1961.   306p.

1625   Bauermeister, A.   Spies break through:   memoirs of a German secret service officer. L., Constable, 1934.   185p.

1626   Bialoguski, M.   The case of Colonel Petrov:   how I weaned a high MVD official from Communism.   N.Y., McGraw-Hill, 1955.   238p.;   The Petrov story.   L., Heinemann, 1955.   247p.

1627   Blackstock, P.W.   The secret road to World War Two:   Soviet versus Western intelligence, 1921–1939.   Chicago, Quadrangle, 1969.   384p.

1628   Brown, W.J.   The Petrov conspiracy unmasked.   Sydney, Newsletter Printing, 1956.   360p.

1629   Bullock, J., Miller, H.   Spy ring:   the full story of the naval secrets case.   L., Secker & Warburg, 1961.   224p.

1630   Carpozi, G.   Red spies in Washington.   N.Y., Trident, 1968.   252p.

1631   Clarke, C.   The war within.   L., World Distributors, 1961.   190p.

1632   Cookridge, E.H.   The net that covers the world.   N.Y., Holt, 1955. 315p.;   Soviet spy net.   L., Muller, 1955.   256p.

1633   Cookridge, E.H.   Spy trade.   L., Hodder & Stoughton, 1971.   288p.

1634   Cookridge, E.H.   The third man:   the truth about 'Kim' Philby, double agent.   N.Y., Putnam;   L., Barker, 1968.   283p.

1635   Dallin, D.J.   Soviet espionage.   New Haven, Yale U.P., 1955.   558p.

1636   Deakin, F.W., Storry, G.R.   The case of Richard Sorge.   N.Y., Harper; L. Chatto & Windus, 1966.   373p.

1637   Deriabin, P., Gibney, F.   The secret world.   Garden City, N.Y., Doubleday, 1959.   334p.

1638   Dewar, H.   Assassins at large:   being a fully documented and hitherto unpublished account of the executions outside Russia ordered by the G.P.U Boston, Mass., Beacon P.;   L., Wingate, 1951.   203p.

1639   Donovan, J.B.   Stranger on a bridge:   the case of Colonel Abel.   N.Y., Popular Library, 1965.   384p.

1640   Foote, A.   Handbook for spies.   2nd ed.   L., Museum P., 1964.   192p.

1641   Granovsky, A.   I was an NKVD agent:   a top Soviet spy tells his story. N.Y., Devin, 1962. 343p.;   All pity choked:   the memoirs of a Soviet secret agent.   L., Kimber, 1955.   248p.

1642   Heilbrunn, O.   The Soviet secret service.   L., Allen & Unwin,   1956. 216p.

1643   Hirsch, R.   The Soviet spies:   the story of Russian espionage in North
       America.   N.Y., Kaye, 1947.   164p.

1644   Huminik, J.   Double agent.   L., Hale, 1968.   189p.

1645   Huss, P.J., Carpozi, G.   Red spies in the U.N.   N.Y., Coward, 1965. 287p.

1646   Hutton, J.B.   Danger from Moscow.   L., Spearman, 1960.   261p.

1647   Hutton, J.B.   School for spies:   the ABC of how Russia's secret service
       operates.   N.Y., Coward, 1962.;   L., Spearman, 1961.   222p.

1648   Hutton, J.B.   Struggle in the dark:   how Russian and other Iron Curtain
       spies operate.   L., Harrap, 1969.   208p.

1649   Johnson, C.   An instance of treason:   the story of the Tokio spy ring.
       Stanford, Stanford U.P., 1964.;   L., Heinemann, 1965.   278p.

1650   Kaledin, V.K.   The Moscow—Berlin secret services.   L., Hurst & Blackett,
       1940.   263p.

1651   Khokhlov, N.E.   In the name of conscience.   N.Y., McKay, 1959.   356p.;
       L., Muller, 1960.   356p.

1652   Kirkpatrick, L.B., Sargeant, H.H.   Soviet political warfare techniques;
       espionage and propaganda in the 1970s.   N.Y., National Strategy Inform-
       ation Center, 1972.   82p.

1653   Krivitsky, W.G.   I was Stalin's agent.   L., Hamilton, 1939.   297p.

1654   Lonsdale, G.   Spy:   twenty years of secret service:   memoirs of Gordon
       Lonsdale.   N.Y., Hawthorn;   L., Spearman, 1965.   218p.

1655   Lucas, N.   The great spy ring.   L., Barker, 1966.   284p.

1656   Meissner, H.O.   The man with three faces.   L., Evans, 1955.   192p.

1657   Monat, P.   Spy in the U.S.   L., Muller, 1964.   253p.

1658   Moorehead, A.   The traitors:   the double life of Fuchs, Pontecorvo and
       Nunn May.   L., Hamilton, 1952.   222p.

1659   Murray, N.   I spied for Stalin.   L., Odhams P., 1950.   256p.

1660   Newman, B.   The red spider web:   the story of Russian spying in Canada.
       L., Latimer House, 1947.   254p.

1661   Newman, B.   Soviet atomic spies.   L., Hale, 1952.   239p.

1662   Newman, J.   Famous Soviet spies:   the Kremlin's secret weapon.   Washing-
       ton, Bks. by U.S. News & World Report, 1973.   223p.

1663   Noel—Baker, F.   The spy—web:   a study of Communist espionage.   L., Batc-
       hworth, 1954.   203p.

1664   Page, B. and others. The Philby conspiracy. Garden City, N.Y., Double-
       day, 1968. 300p.; Philby: the spy who betrayed a generation. L., Deu-
       tsch, 1968.   296p.

1665   Penkovsky, O.V. The Penkovsky papers. Garden City, N.Y.,   Doubleday,
       1965. 411p.;  L., Collins, 1965.   349p.

1666   Philby, E. Kim Philby: the spy I married. N.Y., Ballantine,   1968.
       173p.;  Kim Philby: the spy I loved. L., Hamilton, 1968.   175p.

1667   Philby, K. My silent war: the Soviet master spy's own story. N.Y., G-
       rove;  L., MacGibbon, 1968.   159p.

1668   Pilat,O.R. The atom spies. N.Y., Putnam, 1952.   312p.

1669   Poretsky, E.K. Our own people: a memoir of 'Ignace Reiss' and his fri-
       ends. Ann Arbor, U. of Michigan P., 1970.;  L., Oxford U.P., 1969. 278p

1670   Powers, F.G. Operation overflight: the U-2 spy pilot tells his story
       for the first time. L., Hodder & Stoughton, 1971.   376p.

1671   Reinhardt, G. Crime without punishment: the secret Soviet terror again-
       st America. N.Y., Hermitage House, 1952.   322p.

1672   Ronbloom, H.K. The spy without a country. N.Y., Coward, 1965. Wenner-
       strom the spy. L., Hodder & Stoughton, 1966.   222p.

1673   Seale, P., McConville, M. Philby: the long road to Moscow. N.Y., Sim-
       on & Schuster;  L., Hamilton, 1973.   282p.

1674   Seth, R. The executioners: the story of Smersh. L., Cassell,   1967.
       199p.

1675   Seth, R. Unmasked!: the story of Soviet espionage. N.Y., Hawthorn,
       1965. 306p.; Forty years of Soviet spying. L., Cassell, 1965.   294p.

1676   Tietjen, A. Soviet spy ring. N.Y., Coward, 1961. 190p.;    L., Pan,
       1961.   153p.

1677   Trevor-Roper, H. The Philby affair: espionage, treason and secret ser-
       vice. L., Kimber. 1968.   126p.

1678   The trial of the U2: exclusive authorized account of the court proceed-
       ings of the case of Francis Gary Powers, heard before the Military Divi-
       sion of the Supreme Court of the U.S.S.R., Moscow, August 17,18,19, 1960
       introductory comment by H.J. Berman.   Chicago, Translation World, 1960.
       158p.

1679   Vidor, J. Spying in Russia. L., Long, 1929.   284p.

1680   White, J.B. The Soviet spy system. L., Falcon P., 1948.   133p.

1681   Whiteside, T. An agent in place: the Wennerstrom affair. N.Y., Viking,
       1966.   150p.

1682 Willoughby, C.A. Shanghai conspiracy: the Sorge spy ring – Moscow, Shanghai, Tokyo, San Francisco, New York. N.Y., Dutton, 1952. 315p.; Soviet master spy. L., Kimber, 1952. 256p.

1683 Wise, D., Ross, T.B. The U-2 affair. L., Cresset P., 1963. 276p.

1684 Wynne, G. Contact on Gorky Street. N.Y., Atheneum, 1968.; The man from Moscow: the story of Wynne and Penkovsky. L., Hutchinson, 1967. 222p.

(g)  Peace and war

1685 Akimov, N.I. Civil defense. Oak Ridge, Oak Ridge National Laboratory, 1971. 337p.

1686 Baldwin, H.W. The great arms race: a comparison of U.S. and Soviet power today. N.Y., Praeger, 1958. 116p.

1687 Barker, A.J., Walter, J. Russian infantry weapons of World War II. N.Y. Arco; L., Arms & Armour P., 1971. 80p.

1688 Basseches, N. The unknown army: the nature and history of the Russian military forces. N.Y., Viking, 1943. 239p.; L., Hutchinson, 1943. 164p.

1689 Becker, A.S. Soviet military outlays since 1955. Santa Monica, Rand Corp., 1964. 119p.

1690 Berchin, M., Ben-Horin, E. The red army. N.Y., Norton, 1942. 237p.; L., Allen & Unwin, 1943. 242p.

1691 Berman, H.J., Kerner, M. Documents on Soviet military law and administration. Cambridge, Mass., Harvard U.P., 1955. 164p.

1692 Berman, H.J., Kerner, M. Soviet military law and administration. Cambridge, Mass., Harvard U.P., 1955. 208p.

1693 Borisov, B. The Soviet army. Moscow, FLPH, 1960. 131p.

1694 Breyer, S. Guide to the Soviet navy. Annapolis, U.S. Naval Institute, 1970. 353p.

1695 Brzezinski, Z. Political controls in the Soviet army: a study based on reports by former Soviet officers. N.Y., Research Program on the U.S.S.R., 1954. 93p.

1696 Cain, C.W., Voaden, D.J. Military aircraft of the U.S.S.R. L., Jenkins, 1952. 72p.

1697 Cole, D.M. The Red Army. L., Rich, 1943. 156p.

1698 Crane, R.D., Onacewicz, W. Soviet materials on military strategy: inventory and analysis for 1963. Washington, Center for Strategic Studies, 1964. 139p.

1699   Dinerstein, H.S.   War and the Soviet Union:   nuclear weapons and the re-
       volution in Soviet military and political thinking.   Rev. ed. N.Y.;   L.,
       Praeger, 1962.    268p.

1700   Drum, K.   Airpower and Russian partisan warfare.   Maxwell Air Force Base,
       Air University, USAF Historical Division, 1962.    63p.

1701   Eliot, G.F.   If Russia strikes -.   N.Y., Bobbs, 1949.    252p.

1702   Eller, E.M.   The Soviet sea challenge.   Chicago, Cowles, 1971.    315p.

1703   Ely, L.B.   The Red Army today.   Harrisburg, Military Service, 1949. 256p.

1704   Erickson, J.   The Soviet high command:   a military-political history,
       1918-1941.   N.Y., St Martins P.,;   L., Macmillan, 1962.    889p.

1705   Erickson, J.   Soviet military power.   L., Royal United Services Instit-
       ute, 1971.    112p.

1706   Fairhall, D.   Russian sea power.   Boston, Mass., Gambit, 1971.    286p.;
       Russia looks to the sea - a study of the expansion of Soviet maritime p-
       ower.   L., Deutsch, 1971.    286p.

1707   Fomichenko, I.   The Red Army.   L., Hutchinson, 1945.    125p.

1708   Gallagher, M.P., Spielmann, K.F.   Soviet decision-making for defense: a
       critique of U.S. perspectives on the arms race.   N.Y.;   L.,    Praeger,
       1972.    102p.

1709   Garder, M.   A history of the Soviet army.   N.Y., Praeger;   L., Pall Mall
       P., 1966.    226p.

1710   Garthoff, R.L.   The Soviet image of future war.   Washington, Public Aff-
       airs P., 1959.    137p.

1711   Garthoff, R.L.   Soviet military doctrine.   Glencoe, Free P.,    1953.;
       How Russia makes war:   Soviet military doctrine.   L., Allen & Unwin,1954.
       587p.

1712   Garthoff, R.L.   Soviet military policy:   a historical analysis.    N.Y.,
       Praeger;   L., Faber, 1966.    276p.

1713   Garthoff, R.C.   Soviet strategy in the nuclear age.   Rev. ed. N.Y., Pra-
       eger, 1962.    301p.

1714   Goure, L.   Civil defense in the Soviet Union.   Berkeley, U. of Californ-
       ia P., 1962.    207p.

1715   Goure, L.   Soviet civil defense revisited, 1966-1969.   Santa Monica, Ra-
       nd Corp., 1969.    111p.

1716   Graham, G.   War and peace and the Soviet Union.   L., Gollancz, 1934. 287p.

1717   Guillaume, A.   Soviet arms and Soviet power:   the secrets of Russia's might. Washington, Infantry Journal P., 1949.   212p.

1718   Herrick, R.W.   Soviet naval strategy:   fifty years of theory and practice.   Annapolis, U.S.Naval Institute, 1968.   197p.

1719   Holst, J.J.   Comparative U.S. and Soviet deployments, doctrines and arms
limitations.   Chicago, U. of Chicago P., 1971.   60p.

1720   Horelick, A.L., Rush, M.   Strategic power and Soviet foreign policy. Chicago, U. of Chicago P., 1966.   225p.

1721   Jackson, R.   The red falcons:   the Soviet Air Force in action, 1919-1969.
Brighton, Clifton Bks., 1970.   236p.

1722   Jacobsen, C.G.   Soviet strategy - Soviet foreign policy:   military considerations affecting Soviet policy-making.   Glasgow, Robert Maclehose,
1972.   236p.

1723   Kalashnik, M.   Safeguarding peaceful labour.   Moscow, Novosti  Agency,
1969.   103p.

1724   Kerr, W.   The Russian army:   its men, its leaders and its battles. N.Y.,
Knopf, 1944.   250p.;   L., Gollancz, 1944.   140p.

1725   Khmel, A.   Education of the Soviet soldier:   party-political work in the
Soviet armed forces.   Moscow, Progress, 1972.   217p.

1726   Kilmarx, R.A.   A history of Soviet air power.   N.Y., Praeger; L., Faber,
1962.   359p.

1727   Kolkowicz, R.   The Soviet army and the communist party:   institutions in
conflict.   Santa Monica, Rand Corp., 1966.   715p.

1728   Koriakov, M.   I'll never go back:   a Red Army officer talks.   L., Harrap,
1948.   216p.

1729   Kournakoff, S.N.   Russia's fighting forces.   N.Y., Duell, 1942.   258p.

1730   Krylov, I.N.   Soviet staff officer.   N.Y., Philosophical Library;   L.,
Falcon, 1951.   298p.

1731   Lee, A.   The Soviet air force.   3rd ed. N.Y., Day, 1962.; L., Duckworth,
1961.   288p.

1732   Lee, A.   The Soviet air and rocket forces.   N.Y., Praeger;   L., Weidenfeld & Nicolson, 1959.   311p.

1733   Liddell Hart, B.H.   The Red Army:   the Red Army, 1918-1945;   the Soviet
Army, 1946 to the present.   N.Y., Harcourt, 1956.;   The Soviet army. L.,
Weidenfeld & Nicolson, 1956.   480p.

1734   MccGwire, M.   Soviet naval developments:   capability and context; papers
relating to Russia's maritime interests.   N.Y.; L., Praeger, 1973. 554p.

1735   Mackintosh, M.   Juggernaut:   a history of the Soviet armed forces.   L.,
       Secker & Warburg, 1967.     320p.

1736   Meister, J.   The Soviet navy.   Garden City, N.Y., Doubleday;   L., Macdon-
       ald, 1972.     2 vols.

1737   Meretskov, K.A.   Serving the people.   Moscow, Progress, 1971.     377p.

1738   Milson, J.   Russian tanks, 1900-1970:   the complete illustrated history
       of Soviet armoured theory and design.   Harrisburg, Stackpole, 1971.192p.

1739   Minz, I.   The Red army.   N.Y., International Publishers, 1943.     160p.;
       Moscow, 1942.     172p.

1740   Munro, C.   Soviet air forces:   fighters and bombers.   N.Y., Sports Car
       P., 1972.     121p.

1741   Nansen, F.   Russia and peace.   N.Y., Macmillan, 1924.     162p.

1742   Nowarra, H.J., Duval, G.R.   Russian civil and military aircraft, 1884-
       1969.   L., Fountain P., 1971.     288p.

1743   O'Ballance, E.   The Red army.   L., Faber, 1964.     237p.

1744   Orgill, D.   T-34:   Russian armour.   L., Macdonald, 1971.     160p.

1745   Parry, A.   Russia's rockets and missiles.   Garden City, N.Y., Doubleday;
       L., Macmillan, 1960.     382p.

1746   Perrett, B.   Fighting vehicles of the Red Army.   N.Y., Arco, 1970.   104p.

1747   Pokrovsky, G.I.   Science and technology in contemporary war.   N.Y., Pra-
       eger, 1959.;   L., Stevens, 1960.     180p.

1748   Polmar, N.   Soviet naval power:   challenge for the 1970s.   N.Y., Nation-
       al Strategy Information Center, 1972.     106p.

1749   Remington, R.A.   The Warsaw pact:   case studies in Communist conflict r-
       esolution.   Cambridge, Mass., MITP, 1971.     268p.

1750   Saunders, G.M.   The Soviet navy.   N.Y., Praeger;   L., Weidenfeld & Nico-
       lson, 1958.     340p.

1751   Sokolovsky, V.D.   Military strategy:   Soviet doctrines and concepts.   L.,
       Pall Mall P., 1963.     396p.

1752   Soloviev, M.   My nine lives in the Red Army.   N.Y., McKay;   L., Thames &
       Hudson, 1955.     308p.

1753   The Soviet army.   Moscow, Progress, 1971.     350p.

1754   Soviet seapower.   Washington, Georgetown U., Center for Strategic   and
       International Studies, 1969.     134p.

1755 The Soviet Union and peace: the most important of the documents issued by the government of the USSR concerning peace and disarmament from 1917 to 1929. N.Y., International; L., Lawrence, 1929. 292p.

1756 Stockwell, R.E. Soviet airpower. N.Y., Pageant P., 1956. 238p.

1757 Stoiko, M. Soviet rocketry: past, present and future. N.Y., Holt, 1970.; Newton Abbot, David & Charles, 1971. 272p.

1758 Taracouzio, T.A. War and peace in Soviet diplomacy. N.Y., Macmillan, 1940. 354p.

1759 Theberge, J.D. Soviet seapower in the Caribbean: political and strategic implications. N.Y.; L., Praeger, 1972. 175p.

1760 Tokaev, G.A. Soviet imperialism. N.Y., Philosophical Library, 1956; L., Duckworth, 1954. 73p.

1761 U.S.A. Air Force Department Soviet military thought series, 1. The offensive (Soviet view) by A.A. Sidorenko. Washington, USGPO, 1973. 228p.

1762 Virski, F. My life in the Red Army. N.Y., Macmillan, 1949. 260p.

1763 White, D.F. The growth of the Red Army. Princeton, Princeton U.P., 1944. 486p.

1764 Wolfe, T.W. The Soviet military scene: institutional and defense policy considerations. Santa Monica, Rand Corp., 1966. 195p.

1765 Wolfe, T.W. Soviet power and Europe: the evolution of a political-military posture, 1945-1964. Santa Monica, Rand Corp., 1968. 483p.

1766 Wolfe, T.W. Soviet power and Europe: 1965-1969. Santa Monica, Rand Corp., 1969. 581p.

1767 Wolfe, T.W. Soviet strategy at the crossroads. Cambridge, Mass., Harvard U.P., 1964. 342p.

1768 Wolfe, T.W. Trends in Soviet thinking on theater warfare, conventional operations, and limited war. Santa Monica, Rand Corp., 1964. 119p.

1769 Wollenberg, E. The red army: a study of the growth of Soviet imperialism. 2nd ed. N.Y., Transatlantic, 1941. 400p.

1770 Woodward, D. The Russians at sea. N.Y., International Publications; L. Kimber, 1965. 254p.

1771 Zile, Z.L. and others. The Soviet legal system and arms inspection: a case study in policy implementation. N.Y., Praeger, 1972. 394p.

D     Law

1772   Archer, P.  Communism and the law.  L., Bodley Head, 1963.     112p.

1773   Association of American Law Schools.  The law of U.S.—U.S.S.R. trade:
       papers prepared for conference of American and Soviet legal scholars,
       June 1965.  Washington, 1965.     163p.

1774   Association of American Law Schools.  Soviet legal philosophy.  Cambr-
       idge, Mass., Harvard U.P., 1951.     465p.

1775   Barry, D.D.  Governmental tort liability in the Soviet Union.   Czecho-
       slovakia, Hungary, Poland, Roumania and Yugoslavia.  Leyden, Sijthoff,
       1970.     327p.

1776   Berman, H.J.  Justice in the U.S.S.R.: an interpretation of Soviet law.
       Rev. ed.  Cambridge, Mass., Harvard U.P., 1963.     454p.

1777   Berman, H.J.  Soviet criminal law and procedure:  the RSFSR codes.  2nd
       ed. Cambridge, Mass., Harvard U.P., 1972.     399p.

1778   Berman, H.J., Quigley, J.B.  Basic laws on the structure of the Soviet
       state.  Cambridge, Mass., Harvard U.P., 1969.     325p.

1779   Boim, L. and others.  Legal controls in the Soviet Union.  Leyden, Sij-
       thoff, 1966.     339p.

1780   Butler, W.E.  The law of Soviet territorial waters:  a case study of
       Maritime legislation and practice.  N.Y.; L.,Praeger, 1967.  192p.

1781   Butler, W.E.  The Soviet Union and the law of the sea.  Baltimore, Johns
       Hopkins P., 1971.     245p.

1782   Civil code of the Russian Soviet Federated Socialist Republic:  an Engl-
       ish translation.  Ann Arbor, U. of Michigan Law School, 1965.     150p.

1783   The civil code and the code of civil procedure of the R.S.F.S.R.  1964.
       Leyden, Sijthoff, 1966.     312p.

1784   Conquest, R.  Justice and the legal system in the U.S.S.R.  L., Bodley
       Head, 1968.     152p.

1785   Constitution (fundamental law) of the Union of Soviet Socialist Repub-
       lics, as amended and added to the fifth session of the Supreme Soviet of
       the U.S.S.R.  Fourth Convocation.  Moscow, FLPH, 1957.     115p.

1786   Denisov, A., Kirichenko, M.  Soviet state law.  Moscow, FLPH, 1960. 460p.

1787   Efron, A.  The new Russian empire:  a theory of the Soviet state concei-
       ved in terms of a dynamic interpretation of law.  New Haven, Tuttle,
       1941.     130p.

1788   The federal criminal code of the Soviet Union.  Leyden, Sijthoff, 1959.
       157p.

1789   Feifer, G.  Justice in Moscow.  N.Y., Simon & Schuster;  L., Bodley Head,

1964.    353p.

1790  Feldbrugge, F.J.M.  Encyclopedia of Soviet law.  Dobbs Ferry, Oceana, 1973.  2 vols.

1791  Feldbrugge, F.J.M.  Soviet criminal law:  Gereral part.  Leyden, Sijthoff, 1964.    291p.

1792  Ginsburgs, G.  Soviet citizenship law.  Leyden, Sijthoff, 1968.    270p.

1793  Gray, W.  Soviet civil legislation.  Ann Arbor, U. of Michigan Law School, 1965.  1 vol. (loose-leaf).

1794  Grigoryan, L., Dolgopolov, Y.  Fundamentals of Soviet state law.  Moscow, Progress, 1971.    328p.

1795  Grzybowski, K.G.  Soviet legal institutions:  doctrines and social functions.  Ann Arbor, U. of Michigan P., 1962.    300p.

1796  Gsovski, V., Grzybowski, K.  Government, law and courts in the Soviet Union and Eastern Europe.  N.Y., Praeger; L., Stevens, 1959.    2 vols.

1797  Hazard, J.N.  Settling disputes in Soviet society:  the formative years of legal institutions.  N.Y., Columbia U.P., 1960.    534p.

1798  Hazard, J.N. and others.  The Soviet legal system:  contemporary documetation and historical commentary.  Rev. ed.  Dobbs Ferry, Oceana, 1969.  667p.

1799  Hazard, J.N., Weisberg, M.L.  Cases and readings on Soviet law.  N.Y., Columbia Law Review, 1950.    431p.

1800  Hearn, C.V.  Russian assignment:  a policeman looks at crime in the U.S.S.R.  L., Hale, 1962.    192p.

1801  Johnson, E.L.  An introduction to the Soviet legal system.  L., Methuen, 1969.    248p.

1802  Kelsen, H.  The communist theory of law.  N.Y., Praeger; L., Stevens, 1955.    203p.

1803  Koerber, L.v.  Soviet Russia fights crime.  N.Y., Dutton, 1935.;  L., Routledge, 1934.    240p.

1804  Konstantinovsky, B.A.  Soviet law in action:  the recollected cases of a Soviet lawyer.  Cambridge, Mass., Harvard U.P., 1953.    77p.

1805  Kucherov, S.  The organs of Soviet administration of justice:  their history and operation.  Leyden, Brill, 1970.    754p.

1806  La Fave, W.R.  Law in the Soviet society.  Urbana, U. of Illinois P., 1965.    297p.

1807  Lapenna, I.  Soviet penal policy.  Chester Springs, Dufour;  L., Bodley

Head, 1968.    148p.

1808    Lapenna, I.  State and law:  Soviet and Yugoslav theory.  New Haven, Yale U.P.;  L., Athlone P., 1964.    135p.

1809    Levitsky, S.L.  Introduction to Soviet copyright laws.  Leyden, Sijthoff,
1964.    303p.

1810    The merchant shipping code of the Soviet Union.  Leyden, Sijthoff, 1960.
151p.

1811    The merchant shipping code of the U.S.S.R. (1968).  Baltimore, Johns Hopkins P., 1970.    169p.

1812    Morgan, G.G.  Soviet administrative legality:  the role of the Attorney
General.  Stanford, Stanford U.P., 1962.    281p.

1813    Nagorski, Z.  Legal problems under Soviet domination.  N.Y., Association
of Polish Lawyers in exile in the United States, 1956.    132p.

1814    Petrazhitsky, L.I.  Law and morality.  Cambridge, Mass., Harvard U.P.,
1955.    335p.

1815    Romashkin, P.S.  Fundamentals of Soviet law.  Moscow, FLPH, 1961. 517p.

1816    Rudden, B.  Soviet insurance law.  Leyden, Sijthoff, 1966.    219p.

1817    Schlesinger, R.  Soviet legal theory:  its social background and development.  N.Y., Oxford U.P.;  L., Routledge, 1945.    299p.

1818    Sedugin, P.  New Soviet legislation on marriage and the family.    Moscow,
Progress, 1973.    127p.

1819    Sheinin, L.R.  The People's Courts in the U.S.S.R.  Moscow, Progress,
1957.    111p.

1820    Soviet legislation series.  Fundamentals of civil legislation of the U.S.
S.R. and the Union Republics;  Fundamentals of civil procedure of the U.
S.S.R. and the Union Republics:  official texts.  Moscow, Progress, 1968.
131p.

1821    Terebilov, V.  The Soviet court.  Moscow, Progress, 1973.    181p.

1822    Thompson, C.  The police state:  what you want to know about the Soviet
Union.  N.Y., Dutton, 1950.    248p.

1823    Voinov, K.  Outlaw:  the autobiography of a Soviet waif.  N.Y., Pantheon,
1955. 291p.;  L., Harvill P., 1955.    243p.

1824    Vyshinsky, A.Y.  The law of the Soviet state.  N.Y.;  L., Macmillan, 1948
749p.

1825    Yaresh, L.A.  Arbitration in the Soviet Union.  N.Y., Research Program
on the U.S.S.R, 1954.    149p.

1826 Zelitch, J. Soviet administration of criminal law. Philadelphia, U. of
Pennsylvania P., 1931. 405p.


E   Education

1827 Ablin, F. Contemporary Soviet education: a collection of readings from
Soviet journals. White Plains, International Arts & Sciences P., 1969.
295p.

1828 Ablin, F. Education in the U.S.S.R.: a collection of readings from Soviet journals. N.Y., International Arts & Sciences P., 1963. 2 vols.

1829 Academy of Pedagogical Sciences of the R.S.F.S.R. Soviet preschool education. N.Y.; L., Holt, 1969. 182p.

1830 Amar, A. A student in Moscow. L., Ampersand, 1961. 64p.

1831 Bartley, D.E. Soviet approaches to bilingual education. Philadelphia,
Center for Curriculum Development, 1971. 281p.

1832 Benton, W. The teachers and the taught in the U.S.S.R. N.Y., Atheneum,
1966. 167p.

1833 Benton, W. This is the challenge: the Benton reports of 1956-58 on the
nature of the Soviet threat. N.Y., Associated College P., 1958. 254p.

1834 Bereday, G.Z.F. Comparative method in education. N.Y., Holt, 1964. 302p.

1835 Bereday, G.Z.F., Pennar J. The politics of Soviet education. N.Y., Praeger; L., Atlantic P., 1960. 218p.

1836 Bereday, G.Z.F. and others. The changing Soviet school: the Comparative Education Society field study in the U.S.S.R. Boston, Mass., Houghton;
L., Constable, 1960. 514p.

1837 Bowen, J.E. Soviet education: Anton Makarenko and the years of experiment. Madison, U. of Wisconsin P., 1962. 232p.

1838 College of Preceptors. Delegation to the U.S.S.R., May 1961. Education
in the Soviet Union: report of a College of Preceptors delegation, May
1961. L., 1962. 111p.

1839 Counts, G.S., Lodge, N.P. The challenge of Soviet education. N.Y.; L.,
McGraw-Hill, 1957. 330p.

1840 Crowther, J.G. Industry and education in the Soviet Union. L., Heinemann, 1932. 94p.

1841 Deineko, M.M. Forty years of public education in the U.S.S.R.: facts
and figures. Moscow, FLPH, 1957. 117p.

1842 Derthick, L.G. Soviet commitment to education: report of first official United States mission to the U.S.S.R. Washington, USGPO, 1959.116p.

1843   Esipov, B.P., Goncharov, N.K.   I want to be like Stalin.   N.Y., Day; L.,
       Gollancz, 1947.   150p.

1844   Fediaevsky, V., Hill, P.S.   Nursery schools and parent education in Sov-
       iet Russia.   L., Kegan Paul, 1936.   265p.

1845   Fitzpatrick, S.   The Commissariat of Englightenment:   Soviet organizat-
       ion of education and the arts under Lunacharsky, October 1917-1921. Cam-
       bridge, Cambridge U.P., 1970.   380p.

1846   Goodman, W.L.   Anton Simeonovitch Makarenko:   Russian teacher.   L., Rou-
       tledge, 1949.   146p.

1847   Grant, D.   The humanities in Soviet higher education.   Toronto, U. of T-
       oronto P., 1960.   96p.

1848   Grant, N.   Soviet education.   3rd ed.   Harmondsworth, Penguin,   1972.
       190p.

1849   Hans, N. Hessen, S.   Educational policy in Soviet Russia.   L., King,1930.
       236p.

1850   Hechinger, F.M.   The big red schoolhouse.   Garden City, N.Y., Doubleday,
       1959.   240p.

1851   James, F.C.   On understanding Russia.   Toronto, Toronto U.P., 1960. 63p.

1852   Johnson, W.H.   Russia's educational heritage;   new introduction by G.S.
       Counts.   N.Y., Octagon, 1969.   351p.

1853   Katterle, Z.B.   Schools in the Soviet.   Washington, American Association
       of School Administrators, 1965.   72p.

1854   King, B.   Changing man:   the education system of the U.S.S.R. L., Goll-
       ancz,   1936.   265p.

1855   King, B.   Russia goes to school:   a guide to Soviet education. L., Hein-
       emann, 1948.   185p.

1856   King, E.J.   Communist education.   L., Methuen, 1963.      309p.

1857   Kline, G.L.   Soviet education.   N.Y., Columbia U.P.; L., Routledge, 1957.
       192p.

1858   Korol, A.G.   Soviet education for science and technology.   N.Y., Wiley
       & Cambridge, Mass., MITP.;   L., Chapman & Hall, 1957.      513p.

1859   Kreusler, A.A.   A teacher's experience in the Soviet Union.   Leyden, Br-
       ill, 1965.      194p.

1860   Kreusler, A.A.   The teaching of modern foreign languages in the Soviet
       Union.   Leydin, Brill, 1963.      130p.

1861   Levin, D.   Soviet education today.   2nd ed.   N.Y., Monthly P.; L., Mac-

Gibbon & Kee, 1963.    179p.

1862   Makarenko, A., Makarenko, G.S.   A book for parents.   Moscow, FLPH, 1954.
       409p.

1863   Makarenko, A.   The road to life:   an epic of education.   Moscow, Goslit-
       izdat, 1954.    3 vols.

1864   Makarenko, A.   The story of the Gorky colony.   L., Nott, 1936.    288p.

1865   Massachusetts Institute of Technology.   Center for International Studies.
       Documentary and reference material on education in the Soviet Union.   C-
       ambridge, MITP., 1956.    2 vols.

1866   Moos, E.   Education in the Soviet Union.   N.Y., National Council of Amer-
       ican-Soviet Friendship, 1963.    111p.

1867   Morton, M.   The arts and the Soviet child:   the esthetic education of c-
       hildren in the U.S.S.R.   N.Y., Free P.;   L., Collier-Macmillan, 1972.
       454p.

1868   Nearing, S.   Education in Soviet Russia.   N.Y., International Publishers,
       1926.    159p.

1869   Noah, H.J.   Economics of education in the U.S.S.R.   N.Y., Praeger, 1969.
       227p.

1870   Noah, H.J.   Financing Soviet schools.   N.Y., Teachers College P.,   1966.
       294p.

1871   Pennar, J. and others.   Modernization and diversity in Soviet education
       with special reference to nationality groups.   N.Y.;   L., Praeger, 1971.
       395p.

1872   Pinkevich, A.   The new education in the Soviet Republic.   L., Williams
       & Norgate, 1930.    403p.

1873   Pinkevich, A.   Science and education in the U.S.S.R.   L., Gollancz,1935.
       176p.

1874   Poignant, R.   Education and development in Western Europe, the United S-
       tates, and the U.S.S.R.:   a comparative study.   N.Y., Teachers College
       P., 1969.    329p.

1875   Prokofiev, M.A. and others.   Higher education in the U.S.S.R.   Paris,
       UNESCO, 1961.    59p.

1876   Redl, H.B.   Soviet educators on Soviet education.   N.Y., Free P., 1964.
       252p.

1877   Rosen, S.M.   Education and modernization in the U.S.S.R.   Reading, Mass.,
       Addison, 1971.    234p.

1878   Rosen, S.M.   Part-time education in the U.S.S.R.:   evening and correspondence study.  Washington, USGPO, 1965.    141p.

1879  Rudman, H.C.  The school and state in the U.S.S.R.  N.Y., Macmillan; L.,
      Collier—Macmillan. 1967.    286p.

1880  Sejersted, F.  Moscow diary.  L., Ampersand, 1961.    129p.

1881  Shakhnazarov, G.K. and others.  Social science:  text book for the grad-
      uating class of secondary schools and secondary educational institutions.
      Lexington, Heath, 1973.    290p.

1882  Shapovalenko, S.G.  Polytechnical education in the U.S.S.R.  Paris,UNES-
      CO, 1963.    433p.

1883  Shih, Cheng—chih.  The status of science and education in Communist Chi-
      na and a comparison with that in the U.S.S.R.  Hong Kong, Union,  1962.
      76p.

1884  Shneidman, N.N.  Literature and ideology in Soviet education.  Lexington,
      Heath, 1973.    207p.

1885  Shore, M.J.  Soviet education:  its psychology and philosophy.  N.Y., P-.
      hilosophical Library, 1947.    346p.

1886  Shumilin, I.N.  Soviet higher education.  Munich, Institute for the Stu-
      dy of the U.S.S.R., 1962.    178p.

1887  Soviet preschool education.  N.Y., Holt, 1969.    2 vols.

1888  Tomiak, J.J.  The Soviet Union.  Newton Abbot, David and Charles, 1972.
      144p.

1889  U.S.A.  Dept. of Health, Education and Welfare.  Education in the U.S.S-
      R.  Washington, USGPO, 1957.    226p.

1890  U.S.S.R.  Ministry of Higher Education.  Soviet technological curricula.
      N.Y., Pitman, 1964.    391p.

1891  Vigdorova, F.A.  Diary of a Russian schoolteacher.  N.Y., Grove P.,1960.
      256p.

1892  Weaver, K.D.  Lenin's grandchildren:  preschool education in the Soviet
      Union.  N.Y., Simon & Schuster, 1971.    254p.

1893  Willis, H.R.  Sovietized education:  a study of Soviet education and some
      of its effects.  N.Y., Exposition, 1965.    90p.

1894  Wilson, L.W.  The new schools in new Russia.  N.Y., Vanguard, 1928. 216p

1895  Woody, T.  New minds:  new men?:  the emergence of the Soviet citizen.
      N.Y., Macmillan, 1932.    482p.

1896  Yelyutin, V.  Higher education in the U.S.S.R.  N.Y., International Arts
      & Sciences P., 1959.    55p.

1897　Zinoviev, M.A.　Soviet methods of teaching history.　Ann Arbor, Edwards, 1952.　163p.

F　Leisure and sport

1898　Lipovsky, A.　The Soviet circus:　a collection of articles.　Moscow, Progress, 1967.　283p.

1899　Louis, V., Louis, J.　Sport in the Soviet Union.　N.Y., Macmillan;　Oxford, Pergamon, 1964.　69p.

1900　Morton, H.W.　Soviet sport:　mirror of Soviet society.　N.Y., Collier; L., Collier-Macmillan, 1963.　221p.

1901　Alexander, C.H.O'D.　Fischer v. Spassky — Reykjavik 1972, with a report from Reykjavik by F. Wyndham.　L., Wildwood, 1972.　144p.

1902　Botvinnik, M.　Botvinnik's best games, 1947-70.　L., Batsford,　1972. 237p.

1903　Botvinnik, M.　Championship chess:　match tournament for the absolute chess championship of the U.S.S.R., Leningrad-Moscow 1941.　L., MacGibbon & Kee, 1950.　186p.

1904　Botvinnik, M.　Computers, chess and long-range planning.　N.Y., Springer 1970.　89p.

1905　Botvinnik, M.　One hundred selected games, 1925-1946.　L., MacGibbon & Kee, 1951.　272p.

1906　Cafferty, B.　Spassky's 100 best games.　N.Y., Macmillan;　L., Batsford, 1972.　254p.

1907　Candidates matches 1968.　Nottingham, Chess Player, 1970.　245p.

1908　Chernev, I.　The Russians play chess:　fifty-six master games.　N.Y., Dover, 1964.　215p.

1909　Clarke, P.H.　100 Soviet chess miniatures.　N.Y., Scribners, 1964.; L., Bell, 1963.　174p.

1910　Clarke, P.H.　24th U.S.S.R. chess championship, Moscow, January-February 1957.　L., British Chess Magazine, 1959.　116p.

1911　Geller, Y.P.　Grandmaster Geller at the chessboard.　Nottingham, Chess Player, 1969.　181p.

1912　Gligoric, S.　Fischer vs. Spassky:　the world chess championship match 1972.　N.Y., Simon & Schuster.;　L., Collins, 1972.　127p.

1913　Golombek, H.　Fischer v. Spassky:　the world chess championship match, 1972.　L., Barrie & Jenkins, 1973.　138p.

1914   Hartson, W.R.   Modern chess opening theory as surveyed in 36th U.S.S.R.
       Championship 1969, complete with all the games.   Nottingham, Chess Play-
       er, 1969.   70p.

1915   Horton, M.H.   Modern opening chess theory as surveyed in 37th U.S.S.R.
       Championship 1969.   Nottingham, Chess Player, 1970.   176p.

1916   Kotov, A., Yudovich, M.   The Soviet school of chess.   Moscow, FLPH,1958.
       390p.

1917   Levy, D.N.L.   The match of the century:   U.S.S.R. v The rest of the wor-
       ld, Belgrade, March 29th to April 5th 1970.   Nottingham, Chess Player,
       1970.   109p.

1918   Reshevsky, S.   Chess — the Fischer—Spassky games for the world champion-
       ship:   the complete match with analysis.   Edinburgh, Bartholomew, 1972.
       128p.

1919   Richards, D.J.   Soviet chess:   chess and communism in the U.S.S.R.   Oxf-
       ord, Clarendon P., 1965.   201p.

1920   Smyslov, V.V.   My best games of chess 1935—1957.   N.Y., Dover;   L., Rou-
       tledge, 1958.   154p.

1921   Soltis, A.   The best chess games of Boris Spassky.   N.Y., MacKay, 1973.
       288p.

1922   Steiner, G.   The sporting scene:   white knights at Reykjavik.   L., Faber ,
       1973.   67p.

1923   Wade, R.G.   Soviet chess.   N.Y., MacKay;   L., Spearman, 1968.   288p.

1924   Wade, R.G.   The world chess championship, 1963:   M.M. Botvinnik v Tigran
       Petrosian.   L., Spearman, 1963.   218p.

IV    ART

A    General

1925  Freeman, J. and others. Voices of October: art and literature in Sov-
      iet Russia. N.Y., Vanguard P., 1928.    317p.

1926  Fulop-Miller, R. The mind and face of Bolshevism: an examination of c-
      ultural live in Soviet Russia. Rev. ed. N.Y., Harper, 1965.    350p.

1927  Griffith, H. Playtime in Russia. L., Methuen, 1935.    249p.

1928  Johnson, P., Labedz, L. Khrushchev and the arts: the politics of Sov-
      iet culture, 1962-1964. Cambridge, Mass., MITP., 1965.    200p.

1929  Laqueur, W.Z., Lichtheim, G. The Soviet cultural scene, 1956-1957. N.Y.
      Praeger; L., Stevens, 1958.    300p.

1930  London, K. The seven Soviet arts. New Haven, Yale U.P., 1938.;    L.,
      Faber, 1937.    381p.

1931  Zhdanov, A.A. Essays on literature, philosophy and music. N.Y., Inter-
      national Publications, 1950. 96p.; On literature, music and philosophy
      L., Lawrence & Wishart, 1950.    112p.

1932  Zvorykin, A.A. and others. Cultural policies in the Union of Soviet So-
      cialist Republics. Paris, UNESCO, 1970.    68p.


B    Literature

(i)   Literature in general

1933  Alexandrova, V. A history of Soviet literature. Garden City, N.Y., Do-
      ubleday, 1963.    369p.

1934  Bann, S., Bowlt, J.E. Russian formalism: a collection of articles and
      texts in translation. Edinburgh, Scottish Academic P., 1973.    178p.

1935  Blake, P., Hayward, M. Dissonant voices in Soviet literature. N.Y., P-
      antheon; L., Allen & Unwin, 1964.    308p.

1936  Blake, P., Hayward, M. Half-way to the moon: new writings from Russia.
      N.Y., Holt; L., Weidenfeld & Nicolson, 1964.    276p.

1937  Borland, H. Soviet literary theory and practice during the first Five-
      Year Plan, 1928-32. N.Y., Columbia U.P., 1950.    256p.

1938  Brown, E.J. Major Soviet writers: essays in criticism. N.Y., L., Ox-
      ford U.P., 1973.    439p.

1939  Brown, E.J. The proletarian episode in Russian literature, 1928-1932.
      N.Y., Columbia U.P., 1953.    311p.

1940  Brown, E.J. Russian literature since the Revolution. Rev. ed. N.Y., C-
      ollier, 1969.    367p.

1941  Carlisle, O.A. Voices in the snow: encounters with Russian writers. N.
      Y., Random, 1962.    224p.

1942  Davis-Poynter, R.G. For freedom, theirs and ours: an anthology of Rus-
      sian writing; introductory essay by M. Foot. N.Y., Stein & Day, 1969.
      199p.; L., MacGibbon & Kee, 1968.    175p.

1943　Eastman, M.　Artists in uniform:　a study of literature and bureaucracy.
　　　　N.Y., Knopf; L., Allen & Unwin, 1934.　261p.

1944　Erlich, V.　Russian formalism:　history, doctrine.　N.Y., Lounz,　1955.
　　　　276p.

1945　Ermolaev, H.　Soviet literary theories, 1917-1934:　the genesis of soci-
　　　　alist realism.　Berkeley, U. of California P., 1963.　261p.

1946　Field, A.　Pages from Tarusa:　new voices in Russian writing.　Boston,
　　　　Little, 1963.; L., Chapman & Hall, 1965.　367p.

1947　Friedburg, M.　Russian classics in Soviet jackets.　N.Y., Columbia U.P.,
　　　　1962.　228p.

1948　Gibian, G.　Interval of freedom:　Soviet literature during the thaw,1954
　　　　-1957.　Minneapolis, U. of Minnesota P., 1960.　180p.

1949　Glenny, M.　"Novy Mir":　a selection, 1925-67.　L., Cape, 1972.　415p.

1950　Guerney, B.G.　An anthology of Russian literature in the Soviet period
　　　　from Gorki to Pasternak.　N.Y., Random, 1960.　452p.

1951　Hare, R.　Russian literature from Pushkin to the present day.　L., Meth-
　　　　uen, 1947.　258p.

1952　Hayward, M., Labedz, L.　Literature and revolution in Soviet Russia, 1917
　　　　-62:　a symposium.　N.Y.; L., Oxford U.P., 1963.　235p.

1953　Hayward, M., Crowley, E.L.　Soviet literature in the sixties:　an inter-
　　　　national symposium.　N.Y., Praeger, 1964.; L., Methuen, 1965.　221p.

1954　Holthusen, J.　Twentieth-century Russian literature:　a critical study;
　　　　supplement by E. Markstein on censorship, samizdat and new trends. N.Y.,
　　　　Ungar, 1972.　320p.

1955　Kunitz, J.　Russian literature since the revolution.　N.Y., Boni-Gaer,
　　　　1948.　932p.

1956　Lemon, L.T., Ries, M.J.　Russian formalist criticism:　four essays. Lin-
　　　　coln, U. of Nebraska P., 1965.　143p.

1957　McLean, H., Vickery, W.N.　The year of protest, 1956:　an anthology of
　　　　Soviet literary materials.　N.Y., Random, 1961.　269p.

1958　Maguire, R.A.　Red virgin soil:　Soviet literature in the 1920s.　Prin-
　　　　ceton, Princeton U.P., 1968.　482p.

1959　Markov, V.　Russian futurism:　a history.　Berkeley, U. of California P.,
　　　　1968.　467p.

1960　Mendelson, M.　Soviet interpretation of contemporary American literature
　　　　Washington, Public Affairs P., 1948.　125p.

1961　Mihajlov, M.　Russian themes.　N.Y., Farrar; L., Macdonald, 1968. 373p.

1962　Muchnic, H.L.　From Gorky to Pasternak:　six writers in Soviet Russia.
　　　　N.Y., Random, 1961.; L., Methuen, 1963.　438p.

1963　Dulanoff, H.　The Serapion Brothers:　theory and practice.　The Hague,
　　　　Mouton, 1966.　186p.

1964　Problems of Soviet literature:　report and speeches at the first Soviet

Writers Congress. N.Y., International Publishers; L., Lawrence, 1935. 279p.

1965 Proffer, C.R. Soviet criticism of American literature in the sixties: an anthology. Ann Arbor, Ardis, 1972. 213p.

1966 Reavey, G. Soviet literature today. New Haven, Yale U.P., 1947. 187p.; L., Drummond, 1942. 190p.

1967 Reavey, G., Slonim, M.L. Soviet literature. N.Y., Covici-Friede, 1934. L., Wishart, 1933. 430p.

1968 Reilly, A.P. America in contemporary Soviet literature. N.Y., N.Y.U.P., 1971. 217p.

1969 Roberts, S.E. Essays in Russian literature: the conservative view; Leontiev, Rozanov, Shestov. Athens, Ohio U.P., 1968. 392p.

1970 Scammell, M. Russia's other writers. Harlow, Longman, 1970. 216p.

1971 Simmons, E.J. An outline of modern Russian literature (1880-1940). Ithaca, Cornell U.P., 1943. 93p.

1972 Simmons, E.J. Through the glass of Soviet literature: views of Russian society. N.Y., Columbia U.P., 1953. 301p.

1973 Slonim, M.L. Soviet Russian literature: writers and problems. N.Y.; L., Oxford U.P., 1964. 365p.

1974 Steinberg, J. Verdict of three decades: from the literature of individual revolt against Soviet Communism, 1917-1950. N.Y., Duell, 1950. 634p

1975 Struve, G. Russian literature under Lenin and Stalin, 1917-1953. Norman, U. of Oklahoma P., 1971.; L., Routledge, 1972. 454p.

1976 Swayze, H. Political control of literature in the U.S.S.R., 1946-1959. Cambridge, Mass., Harvard U.P., 1962. 301p.

1977 Thomson, B. The premature revolution: Russian literature and society, 1917-1946. L., Weidenfeld & Nicolson, 1972. 325p.

1978 Thompson, E.M. Russian formalism and Anglo-American new criticism: a comparative study. The Hague, Mouton, 1971. 162p.

1979 Vickery, W.N. The cult of optimism: political and ideological problems of recent Soviet literature. Bloomington, Indiana U.P., 1963. 189p.

1980 Whitney, T.P. The new writing in Russia. Ann Arbor, U. of Michigan P., 1964. 412p.

1981 Yarmolinsky, A. Literature under communism: the literary policy of the Communist Party of the Soviet Union from the end of World War II to the death of Stalin. Bloomington, Indiana U., Russian & East European Institute, 1960. 165p.

1982  Zavalishin, V.  Early Soviet writers.  N.Y., Praeger, 1958.     394p.

(ii)  Prose literature

1983  Bearne, C.G.  Modern Russian short stories.  L., MacGibbon & Kee, 1968-
69.  2 vols.

1984  Cournos, J.  Short stories out of Soviet Russia.  N.Y., Dutton;  L., Dent,
1929.    206p.

1985  Fen, E.  Modern Russian stories.  L., Methuen, 1943.     243p.

1986  Fen, E.  Soviet stories of the last decade.  Forest Hills, Transatlantic
Arts;  L., Methuen, 1945.     223p.

1987  Flying Osip:  stories of new Russia;  tr. by L.S. Friedland and J.R. Piroshnikoff.  Freeport, Bks. for Libraries, 1970.     318p.

1988  Friedburg, M.  A bilingual collection of Russian short stories.  N.Y.,
Random, 1964-65.  2 vols.

1989  Gibian, G., Samilov, M.  Modern Russian short stories.  N.Y., Harper,19-
65.    380p.

1990  Ginsburg, M.  The fatal eggs, and other Soviet satire.  N.Y., Macmillan;
L., Collier-Macmillan, 1965.     305p.

1991  Gorodetsky, N., Coulson, J.S.  Russian short stories:  20th century.  N.Y.;
L., Oxford U.P., 1965.     232p.

1992  Guerney, B.G.  New Russian stories.  N.Y., Directions;  L., P. Owen,1953.
240p.

1993  Harper, K. and others.  New voices:  contemporary Soviet short stories.
N.Y., Harcourt, 1966.     201p.

1994  Henry. P.  Classics of Soviet satire.  L., Collett's, 1972.     235p.

1995  Kapp, Y.  Short stories of Russia today;  tr by T. Shebunina.  Boston,
Mass., Houghton, 1959.     250p.

1996  Konovalov, S.  Bonfire:  stories out of Soviet Russia;  an anthology of
contemporary Russian literature.  L., Benn, 1932.     320p.

1997  Kunitz, J.  Azure cities:  stories of new Russia;  tr. by J. Robbins. N.-
Y., International Publishers;  L., Modern Bks., 1929.     320p.

1998  Loaf sugar, and other Soviet stories.  L., Lawrence & Wishart, 1957. 240p.

1999  Newnham, R.  Soviet short stories:  Sovetskie rasskazy.  L., Dobson,1963.
224p.

2000  Orga, M.  The house on the Fontanka:  modern Soviet short stories.  L.,
Kimber, 1970.     216p.

2001   Pomorska, K.  Fifty years of Russian prose:  from Pasternak to Solzhen-
       itsyn.  Cambridge, Mass., MITP., 1971.    2 vols.

2002   Reavey, G.  Fourteen great short stories by Soviet authors.  N.Y., Avon,
       1959.    224p.

2003   Reeve, F.D.  Great Soviet short stories.  N.Y., Dell, 1962.    480p.

2004   Road to victory:  twelve tales of the Red Army.  L., Hutchinson,  1945.
       174p.

2005   Rodker, J.  Soviet anthology:  short stories by Soviet writers;  tr. by
       A. Brown and others.  L., Cape, 1943.    231p.

2006   Short stories of the war;  tr. by E. Donnelly.  Moscow, FLPH, 1942. 71p.

2007   Soviet short stories.  L., Pilot P., 1944.    152p.

2008   Soviet short stories.  Moscow, FLPH, 1947.    471p.

2009   Stronger than death:  short stories of the Russian at war.  San Francis-
       co, American Russian Institute, 1944.    81p.

2010   Such a simple thing:  a short collection of stories by Gorky, A. Tolstoy,
       Andrei Merkulov, Yurii Kazakov.  Moscow, Mezhdunarodnaya Kniga,   1959.
       260p.

2011   25 stories from the Soviet Republic.  Moscow, FLPH, 1961.    487p.

2012   Van Doren, M.  The night of the summer solstice, and other stories of t-
       he Russian war.  N.Y., Holt, 1943.    245p.

2013   We carry on:  tales of the war;  tr. by D. Fromberg.  Moscow, FLPH, 1942.
       171p.

2014   Yarmolinsky, A.  Soviet short stories.  N.Y., Doubleday, 1960.    301p.

2015   Bearne, C.G.  Vortex:  new Soviet science fiction.  L., MacGibbon & Kee,
       1970.    224p.

2016   Dutt, V.L.  Soviet science fiction.  N.Y., Collier, 1962. 189p.; A vis-
       itor from outer space:  science fiction stories by Soviet writers.  Mos-
       cow, FLPH, 1962.    201p.

2017   Ginsburg, M.  Last door to Aiya:  a selection of the best new science f-
       iction from the Soviet Union.  N.Y., S.G. Phillips, 1968.    192p.

2018   Magidoff, R.  Russian science fiction;  tr. by D. Johnson.  L., Allen &
       Unwin, 1964.    272p.

2019   Magidoff, R.  Russian science fiction, 1968:  an anthology;  tr. by  H.
       Jacobson.  N.Y., N.Y.U.P., 1968.    211p.

2020   Path into the unknown:  the best of Soviet science fiction;  intro. by

J. Merril. N.Y., Delacote, 1968.; L., MacGibbon & Kee, 1966.    191p.

2021    Prokofeva, R.    More Soviet science fiction.   N.Y., Collier, 1962. 190p.

2022    Gasiorowska, X.   Women in Soviet fiction, 1917-1964.   Madison, U. of Wisconsin, P., 1968.    288p.

2023    Rogers, T.F.   Superfluous men and the post-Stalin thaw:   the alienated hero in Soviet prose during the decade 1953-1963.   The Hague, Mouton, 1972.    410p.

2024    Simmons, E.J.   Russian fiction and Soviet ideology:   introduction to Fedin, Leonov and Sholokhov.   N.Y., Columbia U.P., 1958.    267p.

2025    Yershov, P.   Science fiction and utopian fantasy in Soviet literature. N.Y., Research Program on the U.S.S.R., 1954.    66p.

(iii)  Poetry

2026    Binyon, T.J.   A Soviet verse reader.   L., Allen & Unwin, 1964.    165p.

2027    Bosley, K.   Russia's underground poets.   N.Y., Praeger, 1968.;   Russia's other poets.   Harlow, Longman, 1968.    92p.

2028    Hollo, A.   Red cats.   San Francisco, City Lights Bks.;   Northwood, Scorpion P., 1962.    64p.

2029    Lindsay, J.   Modern Russian poetry.   L., Vista Bks., 1960.    48p.

2030    Lindsay, J.   Russian poetry 1917-1955.   L., Bodley Head, 1957.    156p.

2031    Markov, V.   Modern Russian poetry.    Indianapolis, Bobbs, 1967.    842p.

2032    Massie, S.   The living mirror:   five young people from Leningrad;   tr. by M. Hayward and others.   Garden City, N.Y., Doubleday;   L., Gollancz, 1972.    344p.

2033    Milner-Gulland, R.   Soviet Russian verse:   an anthology.   N.Y., Macmillan 1964.    254p.

2034    Ognyev, V.   Vo ves golos:   Soviet poetry.   Moscow, Progress, 1966. 451p.

2035    Poetry from the Russian underground:   a bilingual anthology;   tr. by J. Langland and others.   N.Y., Harper, 1973.    249p.

2036    Reavey, G.   The new Russian poets 1953-1968:   an anthology.   L., Calder, 1968.    292p.

2037    Shelley, G.   Modern poems from Russia.   L., Allen & Unwin, 1942.    93p.

2038    Kaun, A.   Soviet poets and poetry.   Berkeley U. of California P., 1943. 208p.

2039    Matejka, L., Pomorska, K.   Readings in Russian poetics:   formalist and structuralist views.  Cambridge, Mass., MITP., 1971.   306p.

2040  Patrick, G.Z.  Popular poetry in Soviet Russia.  Berkeley, U. of California P., 1929.   289p.

2041  Poggioli, R.  The poets of Russia, 1890-1930.  Cambridge, Mass., Harvard U.P., 1960.   383p.

2042  Strakhovsky, L.I.  Craftsmen of the word:  three poets of modern Russia; Gumilyov, Aklinatova, Mandelstam.  Cambridge, Mass., Harvard U.P., 1949.  114p.

(iv)  Drama

2043  Bakshy, A., Nathan, P.  Soviet scene:  six plays of Russian life.  New Haven, Yale U.P., 1946.   348p.

2044  Dana, H.W.L.  Seven Soviet plays.  N.Y., Macmillan, 1946.   520p.

2045  Glenny, M.  Three Soviet plays.  Baltimore;  Harmondsworth, Penguin, 19-66.   218p.

2046  MacAndrew, A.R.  Four Soviet masterpieces.  N.Y., Bantam, 1965.   248p.

2047  Marshall, H.  Soviet one-act plays:  eleven one-acters.  Forest Hills, Transatlantic Arts, 1945.   106p.

2048  Roberts, S.R.  Soviet historical drama:  its role in the development of a national mythology.  The Hague, Nijhoff, 1965.   218p.

2049  Wiener, L.  The contemporary drama of Russia.  Boston, Mass., Little,19-24.   276p.

(v)  Individual writers.

Abdanath, J.Y.

2050  A tale of hate and pity.  L., Phoenix, 1951.   254p.

Abramov, F.

2051  The dodgers;  tr. by D. Floyd.  L., Flegon with Bond, 1963.   174p.

Afinogenov, A.N.

2052  Distant point:  a play;  tr. by H. Griffith, songs freely adapted by G. Parsons.  L., Pushkin, P., 1941.   95p.

2053  Fear;  tr. by N. Strelsky and others.  Ploughskeepie, Theater of Vassar College, 1934.   67p.

2054  Listen Professor! :  a play in three acts.  N.Y., French, 1944.   78p.

Agapov, B.

2055  After the battle.  L., Hutchinson, 1943.    78p.

Agranovski, A.

2056  Air strike:  heroes of the war in the air by A. Agranovski and V. Galaktionov;  tr. by D. Ogden.  Moscow, FLPH, 1958.    114p.

Aitmatov, C.

2057  Farwell Gul'sary;  tr. by J. French.  L., Hodder & Stoughton, 1970.  191p

2058  The white steamship.  L., Hodder & Stoughton, 1972.    188p.

Akhmadulina, B.

2059  Fever & other new poems;  intro. by Y. Yevtushenko, tr. by G. Dutton and
I. Mezhakoff-Koriakin.  N.Y., Morrow, 1969.;  L., Owen, 1970.    66p.

Akhmatova, A.

2060  Forty-seven love poems;  tr. by N. Duddington.  L., Cape, 1927.    64p.

2061  A poem without a hero;  tr. by C. Proffer and A. Humesky.  Ann Arbor, A-
rdis, 1973.    54p.

2062  Poems of Akhmatova;  tr. by S. Kunitz and M. Hayward.  Boston, Little,
1973.    173p.

2063  Selected poems;  tr. by R. McKane and an essay by A. Sinyavsky.  L., Oxford U.P., 1969.    111p.

2064  Verheul, K.  The theme of time in the poetry of Anna Axmatova.  The Hague, Mouton, 1971.    233p.

Aksenov, V.

2065  Colleagues;  tr. by A. Brown.  L., Putnam, 1962.    240p.

2066  It's time, my love, it's time;  tr. by O. Stevens.  Nashville, Aurora P-
ublications;  L., Macmillan, 1969.    223p.

2067  A starry ticket;  tr. by A. Brown.  L., Putnam, 1962.    224p.

Aleksander, I.Y.

2068  The running tide;  tr. by B. Guerney.  N.Y., Duell, 1943.    264p.

A·malrik, A.

2069  Nose! Nose? No-se! and other plays;  tr. by D. Weissbort.  N.Y., Harcourt, 1973.    228p.

Amosoff, N.

2070    Notes from the future;    tr. by G. StGeorge.    L., Cape, 1971.    384p.

    Andronikov, I.L.

2071    The last days of Pushkin;    tr. by L Litvinova.    Moscow, FLPH,1957. 174p.

    Antonov, S.P.

2072    It happened in Penkovo.    Moscow, Mezhdunarodnaya Kniga, 1959.    209p.

    Aramilev, I.A.

2073    On the trail:    stories of a hunter;    tr. by G. and J. Kittell.    Moscow,
        FLPH, 1956.    345p.

    Arbuzov, A.

2074    Confession at night.    L., Davis-Poynter, 1971.    88p.

2075    An Irkutsk story.    N.Y., Pitman, 1963.    111p.

2076    The promise;    tr. by A. Nicolaieff.    L., Oxford U.P., 1967.    76p.

    Arsenyev, V.K.

2077    Dersu the trapper:    a hunter's life in Ussuria;    tr. by M. Burr.    N.Y.,
        Dutton, 1941.;    L., Secker & Warburg, 1939.    352p.

    Avdeyenko, A.Y.

2078    In love;    tr. by A. Wixley.    N.Y., International Publications;    L., Law-
        rence, 1935.    283p.

    Avdeyev, V.F.

2079    The new proof-reader (a story);    tr. by O. Shartse.    Moscow, FLPH, 1955.
        141p.

    Azhaev, V.

2080    Far from Moscow.    Moscow, FLPH, 1950.    3 vols.

    Babayevsky, S.

2081    Cavalier of the gold star;    tr. by R. Kisch.    L., Lawrence & Wishart,19-
        56.    628p.

    Babel, I.

2082    Benya Krik the gangster, and other stories.    N.Y., Schocken, 1948. 122p.

2083    The collected stories;    tr. by W. Morison, intro. by L. Trilling.    N.Y.,
        Criterion, 1955.;    L., Methuen, 1957.    381p.

2084    Lyubka the Cossack and other stories;   tr. by A.B. MacAndrew.   N.Y., New
        American Library, 1963.    285p.

2085    You must know everything:  stories 1915-1937;   tr. by M. Hayward, ed. by
        N. Babel.   N.Y., Farrar, 1969.;   L., Cape, 1970.    283p.

2086    Benia Krik;   tr. by I Montagu and S. Nolbandov.   L., Collet, 1935.    95p

2087    Red cavalry;   tr. by N. Helstein,   N.Y., Knopf, 1929.    213p.

2088    Isaac Babel:  the lonely years, 1925-1939;   ed. by N. Babel.   N.Y., Far-
        rar, 1964.    402p.

2089    Carden, P.   The art of Isaac Babel.   Ithaca, Cornell U.P., 1972.   223p.

2090    Hallett, R.   Isaac Babel.   N.Y., Ungar, 1973.   118p.;   Letchworth,  Bra-
        dda, 1972.    147p.

        Badigin, K.S.

2091    Men of the ice-breaker Sedov;   tr. by F. Smitham.   L., Hutchinson, 1945.
        95p.

        Baklanov, G.I.

2092    The foothold;   tr. by R. Ainsztein. Chester Springs, Dufour, 1965.; L.,
        Chapman & Hall, 1962.    221p.

2093    South of the main offensive.   Chester Springs, Dufour, 1965.;   L., Chap-
        man & Hall, 1963.    192p.

        Balabanova, A.

2094    Tears.   N.Y., Laub, 1943.    157p.

        Balter, B.

2095    Goodbye boys;   tr. by F. Ashbee.   L., Collins, 1967.    285p.

        Bazhov, P.

2096    The malachite casket:  tales from the Urals;   tr. by A. Williams.   L.,
        Hutchinson, 1944.    192p.

        Bek, A.

2097    And not to die.   N.Y.,   SRT,   1949.    242p.

2098    Berezhkov:  the story of an invention;   tr. by B. Isaacs.   Moscow, FLPH,
        1957.    519p.

2099    On the forward fringe:  a novel of General Panfilov's division.   L., Hut
        chinson, 1945.    236p.

2100  Volokolamsk Highway.  Moscow, FLPH, 1958.    330p.

Belyayev, A.R.

2101  The amphibian.  Moscow, Mezhdunarodnaya Kniga, 1959.    180p.

2102  The old fortress:  a trilogy;  tr. by R. Daglish.  Moscow, FLPH,  1955.
853p.

Bill-Belozerkovsky, V.

2103  Life is calling:  a play in four acts;  tr. by A. Wixley.  N.Y., International Publishers, 1939.    88p.

Blok, A.

2104  The spirit of music.  N.Y., Transatlantic Arts, 1949.    70p.

2105  The twelve, and other poems;  tr. by J. Stallworthy and P. France.  L.,
Eyre & Spottiswoode, 1970.    181p.

2106  Kemball, R.  Alexander Blok:  a study in rhythm and metre.  The Hague,
Mouton, 1965.    539p.

2107  Kisch, C.  Alexander Blok, prophet of revolution:  a study of his life
and work illustrated by translations from his poems and other writings.
N.Y., Roy;  L., Weidenfeld & Nicolson, 1960.    202p.

2108  Reeve, F.D.  Aleksandr Blok:  between image and idea.  N.Y., Columbia U.
P., 1962.    268p.

2109  Vogel, L.E.  Aleksandr Blok:  the journey to Italy with English translations of the poems and prose sketches on Italy.  Ithaca, Cornell  U.P.,
1973.    279p.

Bondarev, I.

2110  Silence:  a novel of post-war Russia;  tr. by E. Fen.  L., Chapman & Hall, 1965.    255p.

Borodin, N.M.

2111  One man in his time.  L., Constable, 1955.    343p.

Borodin, S.

2112  Dmitri Donskoi;  tr. by E. and C. Paul.  L., Hutchinson, 1944.    304p.

Bragin, M.G.

2113  Field Marshall Kutuzov;  tr. by J. Fineberg.  N.Y., Four Continents,1946
132p.

Brodsky, J.

2114   Selected poems;   foreword by W.H. Auden.   N.Y., Harper;   Harmondsworth,
       Penguin, 1973.   168p.

       Bubennov, M.

2115   The white birch-tree;   tr. by R. Parker.   Moscow, FLPH, 1954.   2 vols.

2116   The white birch-tree;   tr. by L. Stoklitsky.   Moscow, FLPH, 1949.   577p.

       Bulgakov, M.

2117   Diaboliad, and other stories;   tr. by E. and C.R. Proffer.   Bloomington,
       Indiana U.P., 1972.   236p.

2118   The early plays of M. Bulgakov;   tr. by E. and C.R. Proffer.   Blooming-
       ton, Indiana U.P., 1972.   418p.

2119   Black snow:   a theatrical novel;   tr. by M. Glenny.   L., Hodder & Stoug-
       hton, 1967.   224p.

2120   Flights:   a play in eight dreams & four acts;   tr. by M. Ginsburg. N.Y.,
       Grove, 1969.   107p.

2121   The heart of a dog;   tr. by M. Glenny.   L., Collins, 1968.   128p.

2122   The Master and Margarita;   tr. by M. Glenny.   N.Y., Grove;   L., Collins,
       1967.   402p.

2123   On the run;   a play in eight dreams.   L., Ginn, 1972.   112p.

2124   The White Guard;   tr. by M. Glenny.   L., Collins, 1971.   320p.

       Bykov, V.U.

2125   The ordeal.   L., Bodley Head, 1972.   170p.

       Chapygin, A.

2126   Stepan Razin;   tr. by C. Paul.   L., Hutchinson, 1946.   480p.

       Chukovskaia, L.

2127   The deserted house;   tr. by A.B. Werth.   L., Barrie & Rockliff, 1967.
       128p.

2128   Going under.   L., Barrie & Jenkins, 1972.   144p.

       Chukovski, K.I.

2129   Baltic skies;   tr. by R. Daglish.   Moscow, FLPH, 1957.   632p.

       Chumandrin, M.F.

2130   White stone.   N.Y., International Publishers;   L., Lawrence, 1933. 80p.

Daniel, Y.

2131  The man from M.I.S.P.;  tr. by M.V. Nesterov.  L., Flegon P., 1967. 48p.

2132  Prison poems;  tr. by D. Burg and A. Boyars.  Chicago, O'Hara, 1972.; L., Calder, 1971.   77p.

2133  This is Moscow speaking, and other stories;  tr. by S. Hood and others. L., Collins, 1968.   159p.

2134  Dalton, M.  Andrei Siniavski and Julii Daniel: two Soviet 'heretical' writers.  Wurzburg, Jal-Verlag, 1973.   190p.

2135  Hayward, M.  On trial:  the Soviet state versus 'Abram Tertz' and 'Nikolai Arzhak'.  N.Y., Harper, 1966.   183p.

Dikovski, S.V.

2136  The commandant of Bird Island;  tr. by N. Kaye.  Moscow, FLPH, 1947. 327p.

Dombrovskii, I.

2137  The keeper of antiquities;  tr. by M. Glenny.  Harlow, Longman, 1969. 273p.

Dudintsev, V.

2138  A new year's tale;  tr. by G. Azrael.  N.Y., Dutton;  L., Hutchinson, 1960.   48p.

2139  Not by bread alone;  tr. by E. Bone.  N.Y., Dutton, 1957.   512p.;  L., Hutchinson, 1957.   447p.

Durov, V.

2140  My circus animals;  tr. by J. Cournos.  Boston, Mass., Houghton, 1936. 122p.

Efremov, I.A.

2141  A meeting over Tuscarova, and other adventure stories;  tr. by M. and N. Nicholas.  L., Hutchinson, 1946.   124p.

2142  Stories;  tr. by O. Gorchakov.  Moscow, FLPH, 1954.   259p.

2143  Andromeda:  a space-age tale.  Moscow, Mezhdunarodnaya Kniga, 1959. 290p.

Ehrenburg, I.

2144  Chekov, Stendhal and other essays.  L., MacGibbon & Kee, 1962.   232p.

2145  European crossroads:  a Soviet journalist in the Balkans;  tr. by A. Markov.  N.Y., Knopf, 1947.   176p.

2146 The extraordinary adventures of Julio Jurenito and his disciples; tr. by U. Vanzler. N.Y., Covici-Friede, 1930. 399p.

2147 The fall of Paris; tr. by G. Shelley. N.Y., Knopf, 1943.; L., Hutchinson, 1942. 529p.

2148 Julio Jurenito; tr. by A. Bostock, Y. Kapp. N.Y., Covici-Friede, 1930.; L., MacGibbon & Kee, 1958. 317p.

2149 The love of Jeanne Ney; tr. by H. Matheson. Garden City, N.Y., Doubleday, 1930. 388p.; L., Davies, 1929. 356p.

2150 Memoirs, tr. by T. Shebunina, Y. Kapp.

People and life: memoirs of 1891-1917. N.Y., Knopf, 1962. 453p.; L., MacGibbon & Kee, 1961. 240p.

Memoirs, 1921-1941. Cleveland, World, 1964. 543p.

Men, years, life: the war, 1941-45. Cleveland, World, 1965. 198p.

Post-war years, 1945-54. Cleveland, World, 1967. 349p.

People and life:
Vol.2. First years of revolution. 1918-21.
Vol.3. Truce, 1921-23.
Vol.4. Eve of war, 1933-41.

Men, years-life:
Vol.5. The war.
Vol.6. Post-war years, 1945-54.
L., MacGibbon & Kee, 1962-66. 5 vols.

2151 The ninth wave; tr. by T. Shebunina, J. Castle. L., Lawrence & Wishart, 1954. 895p.

2152 Out of chaos; tr. by A. Bakshy. N.Y., Holt, 1934. 399p.

2153 Russia at war; tr. by G. Shelley. L., Hamilton, 1943. 277p.

2154 The spring. L., MacGibbon & Kee, 1961. 208p.

2155 The storm; tr. by J. Fineberg. N.Y., Gaer, 1949. 508p.

2156 The storm; tr. by E. Hartley, T. Shebunina. L., Hutchinson, 1949. 800p.

2157 The stormy life of Lazik Roitschwantz; tr. by L. Borochowicz, G. Flor. N.Y., Polyglot Library, 1960. 311p.; L., Elek, 1965. 269p.

2158 A street in Moscow; tr. by S. Volochova. N.Y., Covici-Friede, 1932. 278p.; L., Grayson, 1933. 284p.

2159 The thaw; tr. by M. Harari. Chicago, Regnery; L., Collins, 1954. 230p.

Esenin, S.

2160 Confessions of a hooligan: fifty poems. Cheadle, Carcanet, 1973. 107p.

2161 Graaff, F.de. Sergej Esenin: a biographical sketch. The Hague, Mouton, 1966. 178p.

Esenin-Volpin, A.S.

2162 A leaf of spring: with the text appearing in both the original Russian and an English translation by G. Reavey. N.Y., Praeger; L., Thames & Hudson, 1961. 173p.

Evtushenko, E.

2163 Kazan University, and other new poems; tr. by E. Jacka, G. Dutton. Melbourne, Sun Bks, 1973. 112p.

2164 Poems chosen by the author; tr. by P. Levi and R. Milner-Gulland. N.Y., Hill & Wang; L., Collins, 1966. 96p.

2165 The poetry of Yevgeny Yevtushenko; tr. by G. Reavey. Rev. ed. L., Calder, 1969. 274p.

2166 Selected poems; tr. by P. Levi, R. Milner-Gulland. N.Y., Dutton; Harmondsworth, Penguin, 1962. 92p.

2167 Stolen apples: poetry; English adaptations by J. Dickey and others. Garden City, N.Y., Doubleday, 1971.; L., W.H. Allen, 1972. 328p.

2168 Winter station; tr. by O.J. Frederickson. N.Y., Lounz, 1965. 77p.

2169 Yevtushenko poems; tr. by H. Marshall. N.Y., Dutton, 1966. 190p.

2170 A precocious autobiography; tr. by A.B. MacAndrew. N.Y., Dutton, 1964.; Harmondsworth, Penguin, 1965. 137p.

Fadeyev, A.

2171 Leningrad in the days of the blockade; tr. by R. Charques. L., Hutchinson, 1945. 104p.

2172 The nineteen; tr. by R. Charques. N.Y., International Publishers; L., Lawrence, 1929. 293p.

2173 The rout; tr. by O. Gorchakov. Moscow, FLPH, 1955. 208p.

2174 The young guard. Moscow, FLPH, 195?. 715p.

Fedin, K.

2175 Early joys; tr. by H. Kazanina. N.Y., Vintage, 1960.; Moscow, FLPH, 1948. 503p.

2176  No ordinary summer;  tr. by M. Wettlin.  Moscow, FLPH, 1950.    2 vols.

Fedorova, N.

2177  The children.  Boston, Mass., Little, 1942.    386p.

2178  The family.  Boston, Mass., Little, 1940.    346p.

Fedoseyev, G.A.

2179  Mountain trails;  tr. by G. Hanna.  Moscow, FLPH, 1958.    493p.

Fialko, N.M.

2180  The new city.  N.Y., Margent P., 1937.    153p.

Forsh, O.

2181  Palace and prison;  tr. by F. Solasko.  Moscow, FLPH, 1958.    261p.

2182  Pioneers of freedom.  Moscow, FLPH, 1954.    392p.

Furmanov, D.

2183  Chapayev;  tr. by G. and J. Kittell.  Moscow, FLPH, 1956.    383p.

Garshin, V.M.

2184  The scarlet flower;  tr. by B. Isaacs.  Moscow, FLPH, 1961.    280p.

Gazdanov, G.

2185  Buddha's return;  tr. by N. Wreden.  N.Y, Dutton, 1951.    224p.

2186  The specter of Alexander Wolf;  tr. by N. Wreden.  N.Y., Dutton, 1950.
      223p.;  L., Cape, 1950.    189p.

Gladkov, F.

2187  Cement;  tr. by A. Arthur, C. Ashleigh.  N.Y., International Publishers;
      L., Lawrence, 1929.    311p.

Golubov, S.

2188  No easy victories:  a novel of General Bagration and the campaign of 1812;
      tr. by J. Fineberg.  L., Hutchinson, 1945.  256p.;  Bagrattion:  the hon-
      our and glory of 1812.  Moscow, FLPH, 1945.    263p.

Gorbatov, B.

2189  Donbas;  tr. by B. Isaacs.  Moscow, FLPH, 1953.    406p.

2190  Taras' family;  tr. by E. Donnelly.  N.Y., Cattell, 1946.  215p.;  L.,
      Hutchinson, 1944.    132p.

Gorbanevskaya, N.

2191  Selected poems, with transcript of her trial and papers relating to her detention in a prison psychiatric hospital; ed. by D. Weissbort. Oxford, Carcanet P., 1972.   156p.

Gorky, M.

2192  Articles and pamphlets. Moscow, FLPH, 1950.   407p.

2193  Best short stories. N.Y., Grayson; L., Cape, 1939.   403p.

2194  Five plays; tr. by N. Wettlin. Moscow, FLPH, 1956.   524p.

2195  Literature and life: a selection from the writings of Gorki; tr. by E. Bone. L., Hutchinson, 1946.   157p.

2196  On literature: selected articles. Moscow, FLPH, 1960.   398p.

2197  Selected works. Moscow, FLPH, 1948.   2 vols.

2198  Seven plays; tr. by A. Bakshy, P. Nathan. New Haven, Yale U.P., 1945.   396p.

2199  The story of a novel, and other stories; tr. by M. Zakrevsky. N.Y., MacVeagh; L., Jarrolds, 1925.   273p.

2200  Tales of Italy. Moscow, FLPH, 195?.   293p.

2201  Through Russia: a book of stories; tr. by C. Hogarth. N.Y., Dutton; L., Dent, 1932.   276p.

2202  Unrequited love, and other stories, tr. by M. Budberg. N.Y., Ravin; L., Weidenfeld & Nicolson, 1949.   204p.

2203  Untimely thoughts: essays on revolution, culture and the Bolsheviks, 1917-1918. N.Y., Erickson, 1968.   320p.

2204  At the bottom; tr. by W. Laurence. N.Y., French, 1930.   133p.

2205  Autobiography: My childhood, In the world, My universities; tr. by I. Schneider. N.Y., Citadel P.; L., Elek, 1953.   616p.

2206  Bystander; tr. by B. Guerney. N.Y., Cape-Smith; L., Cape, 1930. 729p.

2207  Childhood; tr. by M.Wettlin. N.Y.; L., Oxford U.P., 1961. 330p.; Moscow, FLPH, 1954.   397p.

2208  The children of the sun; tr. by M. Budberg. L., Davis-Poynter, 1973.   119p.

2209  The courageous one; adapted by M. Goldina, H . Chout. N.Y., French,1958 85p.

2210  Culture and the people. N.Y., International Publishers;  L., Lawrence, 1940.  224p.

2211  Decadence;  tr. by V. Dewey.  N.Y., MacBride, 1927.  357p.

2212  Decadence;  tr. by V. Scott-Gatty.  L., Cassell, 1927.  323p.

2213  Enemies;  tr. by K. Hunter-Blair, J. Brooks.  N.Y., Viking;  L., Eyre Methuen, 1972.  90p.

2214  Foma Gordeyev;  tr. by M. Wettlin.  L., Lawrence & Wishart, 1956. 264p.; Moscow, FLPH, 1955.  361p.

2215  Fragments from my diary. Rev. ed. L., Allen Lane, 1972.  265p.

2216  The judge;  tr. by M. Zakrevsky, B. Clark.  N.Y., McBride, 1924.  105p.

2217  The life of Matvei Kozhemyakin;  tr. by M. Wettlin.  Moscow, FLPH, 1961. 604p.

2218  The life of a useless man.  L., Deutsch, 1972.  284p.

2219  Literary portraits;  tr. by I. Litvinov.  Moscow, FLPH, 1955.  310p.

2220  Lower depths;  tr. by M. Budberg.  L., Weidenfeld & Nicolson, 1959. 124p

2221  The lower depths:  scenes from Russian life;  tr. by E. Hopkins.  Boston Mass., International Pocket Library, 1965.  108p.

2222  The lower depths.  L., Eyre Methuen, 1973.  90p.

2223  The magnet;  tr. by A. Bakshy.  N.Y., Cape-Smith;  L., Cape, 1931. 839p.

2224  Mother;  tr. by M. Wettlin.  Moscow, FLPH, 1954.  416p.

2225  My apprenticeship;  tr. by M. Wettlin.  Moscow, FLPH, 1957.  608p.

2226  My childhood;  tr. by I. Schneider.  L., Elek, 1960.  190p.

2227  My childhood;  N.Y., Appleton, 1937.  374p.

2228  My childhood;  tr. by R. Wilks.  Baltimore;  Harmondsworth, Penguin,1966 234p.

2229  My universities;  tr. by H. Altschuler.  Moscow, FLPH, 1954.  268p.

2230  My university days.  N.Y., Boni-Liveright, 1923.  327p.

2231  On guard for the Soviet Union.  N.Y., International Publishers;  L., Lawrence, 1933.  172p.

2232  Orphan Paul;  tr. by L. Turner, M. Strever.  N.Y., Boni-Gaer;  Toronto, Progress, 1946.  270p.

2233  Other fires; tr. by A. Bakshy. N.Y., Appleton, 1933.  506p.

2234  The petty bourgeois; tr. by I Kosin. Seattle, Washington State U.P.,
1972.  86p.

2235  Reminiscences; intro. by M. Van Doren. N.Y., Dover, 1946.  215p.

2236  Reminiscences of my youth; tr. by V. Dewey. L., Heinemann, 1924. 334p.

2237  Reminiscences of Tolstoy, Chekov and Andreyev tr. by K. Mansfield and
others. L., Hogarth, 1934.; Toronto, Longmans, 1949.  191p.

2238  A sky-blue life. N.Y., New American Library, 1964.  254p.

2239  The spectre; tr. by A. Bakshy. N.Y., Appleton, 1938.  679p.

2240  The three; tr. by M. Wettlin. Moscow, FLPH, 1958.  471p.

2241  Through Russia; tr. by L.J. Hogarth. N.Y., Dutton; L., Dent, 1959.
276p.

2242  Borras, F.M. Maxim Gorky the writer: an interpretation. Oxford, Clarendon P., 1967.  195p.

2243  Letters; tr. by V. Dutt. Moscow, Progress, 1966.  199p.

2244  Gourfinkel, N. Gorky. N.Y., Grove; L., Evergreen, 1960.  192p.

2245  Habermann, G. Maksim Gorky. N.Y., Ungar, 1971.  105p.

2246  Hare, R. Maxim Gorky: romantic realist and conservative revolutionary.
N.Y.; L., Oxford U.P., 1962.  156p.

2247  Kaun. A.S. Maxim Gorky and his Russia. L., Cape, 1932.  620p.

2248  Levin, D. Stormy petrel: the life and work of Maxim Gorky. N.Y., Appleton, 1965.; L., Muller, 1967.  332p.

2249  Roskin, A. From the banks of the Volga: the life of Maxim Gorky. N.Y.,
Philosophical Library. 1946.  126p.

2250  Weil, I. Gorky: his literary development and influence on Soviet intellectual life. N.Y., Random, 1966.  240p.

2251  Wolfe, B.D. The bridge and the abyss: the troubled friendship of Maxim
Gorky and V.I. Lenin. N.Y., Praeger; L., Pall Mall P., 1967.  180p.

Granin, D.

2252  Those who seek; tr. by R. Daglish. Moscow, FLPH, 1955.  538p.

Green, E.

2253  Wind from the south. Moscow, FLPH, 1950.  291p.

Gribachev, N.

2254 August stars; tr. by R. Bobrova and others. Moscow, FLPH, 1956. 74p.

Grin, A.

2255 Luker, N.J.L. Alexander Grin. Letchworth, Bradda, 1973. 125p.

Grossman, L.

2256 Death of a poet: a novel of the last years of Alexander Pushkin. L., Hutchinson, 1945. 256p.

Grossman, V.

2257 Forever flowing. L., Deutsch, 1973. 247p.

2258 The inferno of Treblinka. Shanghai, Epoch, 1945. 64p.

2259 Kolchugin's youth; tr. by R. Edmonds. L., Hutchinson, 1946. 190p.

2260 No beautiful nights. N.Y., Messner, 1944. 223p.

2261 People immortal; tr. by E. Donnelly. N.Y., Four Continents, 1945.; L., Hutchinson; Moscow, FLPH, 1943. 135p.

2262 Stalingrad hits back; tr. by A. Fineberg, D. Fromberg. Moscow, FLPH, 1942. 27p.

2263 The years of war (1941-1945); tr. by E. Donnelly, R. Prokofieva. Moscow, FLPH, 1946. 451p.

Gubski, N.

2264 Bitter bread. N.Y., Holt, 1934. 297p.

2265 City of white night. N.Y., Norton, 1931. 353p.

2266 Foreign bodies. L., Mathews-Marrot, 1932. 338p.

2267 The gladiator. L., Elkin-Matthews-Marrot, 1930. 378p.

Gulia, G.

2268 Springtime in Moscow. Moscow, FLPH, 1952. 239p.

Gumilevski, L.

2269 Dog lane; tr. by N. Wreden. N.Y., Vanguard, 1930. 296p.

Guzenko, I.

2270 The fall of a Titan; tr. by M. Black. N.Y., Norton; L., Cassell, 1953. 680p.

Herman, Y.

2271 Alexei the gangster; tr. by S. Garry. L., Routledge, 1940. 288p.

2272 Antonina; tr. by S.Garry. L., Routledge, 1937. 470p.

2273 Happy landing (from M. Lakhonina's diary). Moscow, FLPH, 1942, 83p.

2274 Tonia. N.Y., Knopf, 1938. 470p.

Hippius, Z.

2275 Selected works of Zinaida Hippius; tr. by T. Pachmuss. Urbana, U. of Illinois P., 1972. 315p.

2276 The green ring; tr. by S. Koteliansky. L., Daniel, 1920. 104p.

2277 Matich, O. Paradox in the religious poetry of Zinaida Gippius. Munich, Fink, 1972. 127p.

2278 Pachmuss, T. Zinaida Hippius: an intellectual profile. Carbondale, Southern Illinois U.P., 1971. 491p.

Ignatov, P.K.

2279 Partisans of the Kuban; tr. by J. Fineberg. L., Hutchinson, 1945. 212p.

Ilf, I.A. & Petrov, Y.P.

2280 Diamonds to sit on. Bombay, Kutub, 1947. 227p.

2281 The golden calf; tr. by J.H.C. Richardson. L., Muller, 1964. 340p.

2282 Little golden America: two famous Soviet humorists survey the United States. N.Y., Farrar, 1937. 387p.; L., Routledge, 1944. 296p.

2283 The little golden calf!; tr. by C. Malamuth N.Y., Farrar; L., Grayson, 1932. 402p.

2284 A Russian comedy of errors; tr. by E. Hill and D. Mudie. N.Y., Harper; L., Methuen, 1930. 280p.

2285 The twelve chairs; tr. by J. Richardson. L., Muller, 1965. 322p.

Ivanov, V.

2286 The adventures of a fakir. N.Y., Vanguard, 1935. 300p.; I live a queer life: an extraordinary autobiography. L., Lovat Dickson, 1935. 316p.

2287 Armoured train 14-69; tr. by Gibson-Cowan, and A. Grant. N.Y., International Publishers; L., Lawrence, 1933. 67p.

2288 West, J.D. Russian symbolism: a study of Vyacheslav Ivanov and the Russian symbolist aesthetic. L., Methuen, 1970. 250p.

Kalinin, A.

2289　In the south;　tr. by S. Garry.　L., Hutchinson, 1946.　192p.

Kallinikov, I.F.

2290　The land of bondage;　tr. by P. Kirwan.　L., Grayson, 1933.　128p.

2291　Women and monks;　tr. by P. Kirwan.　N.Y., Harcourt;　L., Secker, 1930.
876p.

Karazin, N.

2292　Cranes flying south;　tr. by M. Pokrovsky.　L., Routledge, 1936.　235p.

Kassil, L.A.

2293　Early dawn;　tr. by S. Rosenberg.　Moscow, FLPH, 1956.　361p.

2294　The hero's brother.　Moscow, FLPH, 1957.　79p.

2295　The land of Shvambriana;　tr. by S. Glass, N. Guterman.　N.Y., Viking,
1935.　289p.

Katayev, V.P.

2296　The cottage in the steppe;　tr. by F. Solasko, E. Manning.　Moscow, FLPH
1956.　379p.

2297　The embezzlers;　tr. by L. Zarin.　N.Y., MacVeagh, 1929.　300p.;　L.,
Black, 1929.　254p.

2298　Forward, Oh time!;　tr. by C. Malamuth.　L., Gollancz, 1934.　432p.

2299　The grass of oblivion;　tr. by R. Daglish.　L., Macmillan, 1969.　222p.

2300　The holy well;　tr. by M. Hayward, H. Shukman.　L., Collins, 1967.　160p.

2301　Peace is where the tempests blows;　tr. by C. Malamuth.　N.Y., Farrar.;
Lonely white sail, or peace is where the tempest blows.　L., Allen & Unwin, 1937.　341p.

2302　Semyon Kotko;　tr. by B. Kagan.　Moscow, Mezhdunarodnaya Kniga,　1941.
62p.

2303　The small farm in the steppe;　tr. by A. Bostock.　L., Lawrence & Wishart, 1958.　286p.

2304　Squaring the circle: a play in three acts;　tr. by C. Malamuth, E.　Lyons.　N.Y., French, 1936.　118p.

2305　Squaring the circle: a comedy in three acts;　tr. by N. Goold-Verschoyle.　L., Wishart, 1934.　110p.

2306  Time forward; tr. by C. Malamuth. N.Y., Farrar, 1933.    345p.

2307  The white sail gleams; tr. by L. Stcklitsky. Moscow, FLPH, 1954. 294p.

2308  The wife; tr. by G. and C. Portnoff. L., Hutchinson, 1946.    96p.

      Kaverin, V.

2309  The larger view; tr. by E.Swan. N.Y., Stackpole; L., Collins, 1938.
      432p.

2310  Open book; tr. by B. Pearce. L., Lawrence & Wishart; Moscow, FLPH,
      1955.    743p.

2311  Two captains; tr. by E. Swan. N.Y., Modern Age, 1942. 442p.; L., Cass-
      ell, 1938.    484p.

2312  Two captains; tr. by B. Pearce. L., Lawrence & Wishart, 1957.    674p.

2313  Piper, D.G.B. V.A. Kaverin: a Soviet writer's response to the problem
      of commitment: the relationship of Skandalist and Khuzhodnik neizvesten
      to the development of Soviet literature in the late nineteen-twenties.
      Pittsburgh, Duquesne U.P., 1970.    180p.

      Kazakevich, E.G.

2314  Heart of a friend: a story; tr. by R. Dixon. Moscow, FLPH, 1955. 247p.

2315  Spring on the Oder; tr. by R. Daglish. Moscow, FLPH, 1953.    549p.

2316  Star; tr. by L. Stoklitsky. L., Collet; Moscow, FLPH, 1950.    143p.

      Kazakov, I.P.

2317  Going to town and other stories. Boston, Mass., Houghton, 1964.    196p.

2318  The smell of bread, and other stories; tr. by M. Harari, A. Thomson. L.,
      Harvill P., 1965.    256p.

      Ketlinskaya, V.

2319  Days of our life; tr. by A. Bostock. L., Lawrence & Wishart,1955. 831p.

      Kharms, D.

2320  Russia's lost literature of the absurd: a literary discovery; selected
      works ofDaniil Kharms and Alexander Vvedensky; ed. and tr. by G. Gibian.
      Ithaca, Cornell U.P., 1971.    209p.

      Kirshon, V.M.

2321  Red rust, by V.M. Kirshon and A.V. Uspenski; tr. by V. and F. Vernon.
      N.Y., Coward, 1930.    182p.

Kluchanskaya, A M.

2322  Commissar Krilenko.  N.Y., Liveright, 1939.    407p.

Knorre, F.

2323  Stories;  tr. by E. Felgenhauer, L.Navrozov.  Moscow, FLPH, 1955.  143p.

Kollontai, A.

2324  Free love;  tr. by C. Hogarth.  L., Dent, 1932.    279p.

2325  A great love;  tr. by L. Love.  N.Y., Vanguard, 1929.    243p.

2326  Red love.  N.Y., Seven Arts, 1927.    286p.

Koptyayeva, A.D.

2327  Ivan Ivanovitch;  tr. by M. Wettlin.  Moscow, FLPH, 1952.    547p.

Kosmodemyanskaya, L.T.

2328  The story of Zoya and Shura;  original text ed. by F. Vigdorova;  tr. by
      R. Daglish.  Moscow, FLPH, 1953.    284p.

Kozhevnikov, V.

2329  Entr'acte;  tr. by D. Oglander.  L., Cobden-Sanderson, 1936.    190p.

2330  Living water;  tr. by B. Isaacs.  Moscow, FLPH, 1954.    604p.

2331  Tales of the war;  tr. by D. Fromberg.  Moscow, FLPH, 1942.    67p.

Kriger, Y.G.

2332  From Moscow to the Prussian frontier.  L., Hutchinson, 1945.    136p.

Krymov, V.P.

2333  End of the imp;  tr. by M. Burr.  L., Allen & Unwin, 1937.    335p.

2334  Fienka.  tr. by M. Burr.  L., Allen & Unwin. 1949.    300p.

2335  He's got a million;  tr. by M. Burr.  L., Allen & Unwin, 1936.    328p.

2336  The impenitent midge;  tr. by A. Brown.  L., Lane, 1953.    200p.

2337  Out for a million;  tr. by M. Burr.  L., Allen & Unwin, 1935.    347p.

2338  The tanker ' Derbent';  tr. by R. Dixon.  Moscow, FLPH, 1954.    239p.

2339  The tanker 'Derbent';  tr. by J. Spink.  Harmondsworth, Penguin, 1944.
      190p.

Kushchevsky, I.

2340  Nikolai Negorov, or, the successful Russian; tr. by D.P. and B. Costello. L., Calder, 1967.    368p.

Kuznetsov, A.

2341  Babi Yar: a documentary novel, tr. by J. Guralsky. L., MacGibbon & Kee, 1967.    399p.

2342  Babi Yar: a document in the form of a novel by A. Anatoli; tr. by D. Floyd. N.Y., Farrar; L., Cape, 1970.    477p.

2343  Sequel to a legend. Moscow, Mezhdunarodnaya Kniga, 1959.    130p.

Lann, Y.L.

2344  Extraordinary adventures of Karik and Volga; tr. by J. Mandeville. L., Hutchinson, 1946.    302p.

2345  Old England; tr. by G. Shelley. L., Hutchinson, 1945.    352p.

Lavrenev, B.A.

2346  Stout heart, and other stories; tr. by D. Fromberg. Moscow, FLPH, 1943. 55p.

2347  The forty first; tr. by M. Wettlin, N. Jochel. Moscow, FLPH, 1961. 190p

2348  Story of a simple thing, tr. by S. Bertensson. n.p., 1934.    92p.

2349  White death; tr. by S. Bertensson, Hollywood, 193?. 81p.

Lazarevski, V.A.

2350  Under the Bolshevik uniform; tr. by U. Troubridge. L., Butterworth, 1936.    320p.

Lebedev, I.I.

2351  Legion of dishonor. N.Y., Liveright, 1940.    314p.

Leberekht, G.

2352  Light in Koordi: a novel by Hans Leberecht. Moscow, FLPH, 1951. 400p.

Leonov, L.

2353  The badgers; tr. by H. Kazanina. L., Hutchinson, 1947.    336p.

2354  Chariot of wrath; tr. by N. Guterman. N.Y., Fisher, 1946.    193p.

2355  Road to the ocean; tr. by N. Guterman. N.Y., Fisher, 1944.    510p.

2356   Skutarevsky;  tr. by A. Brown.  N.Y., Harcourt;  L., Dickson, 1936. 444p.

2357   Soviet river;  tr. by I. Montagu, S. Nalbandov.  N.Y., Dial, 1932.; Sot.
       L., Putnam, 1933.    390p.

2358   The thief;  tr. by H. Butler.  N.Y., Dial;  L., Secker, 1931.    566p.

2359   Tuatamur;  tr. by I. Montagu, S. Nalbandov.  L., Collet, 1935.    50p.

       Lidin, V.

2360   The apostate;  tr. by H. Matheson.  L., Cape, 1931.    336p.

2361   The price of life;  tr. by H. Matheson.  N.Y., Harper, 1932.    336p.

       Lukash, I.

2362   The flames of Moscow;  tr. by N. Duddington.  N.Y., Macmillan, 1930.475p.

       Luknitzki, P.

2363   Nisso;  tr. by M. Wettlin.  Moscow, FLPH, 1949.    482p.

       Lunacharsky, A.

2364   Three plays;  tr. by L Magnus, K. Walter.  N.Y., Dutton;  L., Routledge,
       1923.    299p.

       Lunz, L.

2365   The city of truth;  tr. by J. O'Silver.  L., O'Dempsey, 1929.    52p.

       Maksimov, S.

2366   The restless heart;  tr. by H. Reigart.  N.Y., Scribner, 1951.    349p.

       Mandelstam, O.

2367   The complete poems of Osip Emilevich Mandelstam;  tr. by B. Raffel, A.
       Burago.  Albany, State U. of N.Y. P., 1973.    353p.

2368   The prose of Mandelstam:  The noise of time;  Theodosia;  The Egyptian
       stamp;  tr. by C. Brown.  Princeton, Princeton U.P., 1965.    209p.

2369   Selected poems;  tr. by C. Brown, W.S. Merwin.  L., Oxford U.P., 1973 .
       100p.

2370   Selected poems;  tr. by D. McDuff.  Cambridge, Rivers P., 1973.    182p.

2371   Brown, C.  Mandelstam.  Cambridge, Cambridge U.P., 1973.    320p.

2372   Mandelstam, N.  Hope against hope:  a memoir, tr. by M. Hayward.  L., C-
       ollins, 1971.    432p.

2373  Mandelstam, N.   Chapter 42, and The goldfinch and other poems by O. Man-
      delstam;   tr. by D.Rayfield.   L., The Menard P., 1973.     39p.

      Marienhof, A.

2374  Cynics;   tr. by V. Bell, L. Coleman.   N.Y., Boni, 1930.    237p.

      Matveyev, V.

2375  Bitter draught;   tr. by D. Flower.   L., Collins, 1935.    297p.

2376  Commissar of the gold express:   an episode in the Civil War.  N.Y., Int-
      ernational Publishers;   L., Lawrence, 1933.     212p.

      Mayakovsky, V.

2377  The bedbug, and selected poetry;   tr. by M. Hayward, G. Reavey.    N.Y.,
      Meridian Bks., 1960.;   L., Weidenfeld & Nicolson, 1961.     317p.

2378  The complete plays of Vladimir Mayakovsky;   tr. by G. Daniels.  N.Y., W-
      ashington Sq., 1968.    274p.

2379  Mayakovsky;   tr. by M. Marshall.   N.Y., Hill & Wang;   L., Dobson, 1965.
      432p.

2380  Wi the haill voice:   25 poems translated into Scots.   Oxford, Carcanet
      P., 1972.    93p.

2381  Brown, E.J.  Mayakovsky:  a poet in the revolution.  Princeton, Prince-
      ton U.P., 1973.    386p.

2382  Humesky, A.  Majakovskij and his neologisms.  N.Y., Rausen, 1964.    270p

2383  Ikonnikov, A.A.  Mayakovsky:  his life and work.  N.Y., Philosophical L-
      ibrary, 1946.    162p.

2384  Marshall, H.  Mayakovsky and his poetry.  N.Y., Transatlantic Arts; L.,
      Pilot P., 1945.    157p.

2385  Shklovsky, V.  Mayakovsky and his circle.  N.Y., Dodd, 1972.    259p.

2386  Stahlberger, L.L.  The symbolic system of Mayakovsky.  The Hague, Mouton
      1964.    151p.

2387  Woroszylski, W.  The life of Mayakovsky.  N.Y., Orion P., 1970.; L., Go-
      llancz, 1972.    559p.

      Matislavski, S.

2388  Rook — herald of spring:  a story about N. Bouman;  tr. by D. Skvirsky.
      Moscow, FLPH, 1954.    417p.

      Musatov, A.

2389   Stozhari village;   tr. by R. Dixon.  Moscow, FLPH, 1954.     231p.

Nagibin, Y.

2390   Dreams.  Stories.  Moscow, Mezhdunarodnaya Kniga, 1959.     161p.

2391   Each for all.  L., Hutchinson, 1945.     68p.

2392   The pipe:  stories;   tr. by V. Shneerson.  Moscow, FLPH, 1954.     112p.

Narokov, N.

2393   The chains of fear;   tr. by C. Bird.  Chicago, Regnery, 1958.     282p.

Nazorov, P.

2394   Moved on!:  from Kashgar to Kashmir;   tr. by M. Burr.  L., Allen, 1935.
       317p.

Nekrasov, V.P.

2395   Both sides of the ocean:  a Russian writer's travels in Italy and the U-
       nited States.  N.Y., Holt, 1964.     191p.

2396   Front-line Stalingrad;   tr. by D. Floyd.  L., Collins, 1962.     320p.

2397   Kira;   tr. by M. Budberg.  L., Cresset P., 1963.     165p.

2398   Kira Georgievna;   tr. by W.N. Vickery.  N.Y., Pantheon, 1962.     183p.

Nikolayeva, G.

2399   Harvest.  N.Y., Four Continents, 1953.;   Moscow, FLPH, 1952.     655p.

2400   The newcomer:  the manager of an MTS and the chief agronomist;   tr. by
       D. Skvirsky.  Moscow, FLPH, 1955.     168p.

Nilin, P.

2401   Comrade Venka.  N.Y., Simon & Schuster, 1959.  246p.;   L., Hutchinson,
       1959.     304p.

2402   Cruelty;   tr. by J. Guralsky.  Moscow, FLPH, 1958.     254p.

Nizovoi, P.

2403   Into the Arctic night;   tr. by J. Bimstone.  L., Hutchinson, 1947. 236p.

2404   The ocean;   tr. by J. Cournos.  N.Y., Harper;   L., Hamilton, 1936. 421p.

Novikov-Priboi, A.

2405   The Captain;   tr. by C. Paul.  L., Allen & Unwin, 1936.     144p.

2406    The sea beckons: short novels and stories; tr. by B. Isaacs. Moscow,
        FLPH, 1956.    458p.

2407    Tsushima; tr. by E. and C. Paul. N.Y., Knopf, 1937. 446p.; L., Allen
        & Unwin, 1936.    407p.

        Obruchev, V.A.

2408    Kukushkin: a geographer's tales; tr. by V. Bowen. L., Constable, 1962.
        228p.

2409    Plutonia; tr. by F. Solasko. Moscow, FLPH, 1956.    327p.

2410    Sannikov land; tr. by D. Skvirsky. Moscow, FLPH, 1956.    372p.

        Odoyevtzeva, I.

2411    All hope abandon; tr. by F. Reed. N.Y., Pantheon, 1949.    281p.

2412    Out of childhood; tr. by D. Nachsen. N.Y., Scott, 1930.; L., Constab-
        le, 1934.    260p.

        Odulok, T.

2413    Snow people: Chukchee. New Haven, Human Relations Area Files,    1954.
        73p.

        Ogniov, N.

2414    Diary of a communist schoolboy; tr. by A. Werth. N.Y., Payson—Clarke;
        L., Gollancz, 1928.    288p.

2415    Diary of a communist undergraduate; tr. by A. Werth. N.Y., Payson—Cla-
        rke; L., Gollancz, 1929.    288p.

        Okudzhava, B.

2416    The extraordinary adventures of secret agent Shipov in pursuit of Count
        Leo Tolstoy in the year 1862. Aylesbury, Abelard—Schuman, 1973.    214p.

        Olesha, Y.

2417    Envy and other works; tr. by A.B. MacAndrew. Garden City, N.Y., Doubl-
        eday, 1967.    288p.

2418    Envy; tr. by A. Wolfe. L., Hogarth, 1936.    275p.

2419    Love, and other stories; tr. by R. Payne. N.Y., Washington Square,1967.
        230p.

2420    The three fat men; tr. by F. Glagoleva. Moscow, FLPH, 1964.    187p.

2421    The wayward comrade and the commissars. N.Y., New American Library,1960.
        143p.

2422 Beaujour, E.K.  The inevitable land:  a study of the artistic imaginat-
     ion of Iurii Olesha.  N.Y., Columbia U.P., 1970.    222p.

Osipov, K.

2423 Alexander Suvorov;  tr. by E. Bone.  L., Hutchinson, 1944.    207p.

Osipov, V.

2424 Siberian diamonds;  tr. by X. Danko.  Moscow, FLPH, 1958.    74p.

Ossorgin, M.

2425 My sister's story;  tr. by N Helstein, G. Harris.  N.Y., MacVeagh, 1931.;
     L., Secker, 1932.    235p.

2426 Quiet street.  N.Y., MacVeagh;  L., Secker. 1930.    344p.

Ostrovsky, N.

2427 Born of the storm;  tr. by L. Hiler.  N.Y., Critics Group P., 1939.251p.

2428 Hail, life!:  articles, speeches, letters;  tr. by H. Altschuler.  Mos-
     cow, FLPH, 1954.    190p.

2429 How steel was tempered;  tr. by R. Prokofieva.  Moscow, FLPH, 1952. 2vols

2430 The making of a hero;  tr. by A. Brown.  N.Y., Dutton;  L., Secker & Wa-
     rburg, 1937.    440p.

Panfiorov, F.

2431 And then the harvest;  tr. by S. Garry.  L., Putnam, 1939.    457p.

2432 Brusski:  a story of peasant life in Soviet Russia;  tr. by Z. Mitrov,
     J. Tabrisky.  N.Y., International Publications;  L., Lawrence, 1930.300p.

2433 With their own eyes.  Moscow, FLPH, 1942.    98p.

Panova, V.

2434 The factory;  tr. by M. Budberg.  L., Putnam, 1949.    261p.

2435 Looking ahead;  tr. by D. Skvirsky.  Moscow, FLPH, 1955.    295p.

2436 Span of the year;  tr. by V. Traill.  L., Collins, 1956.    282p.

2437 A summer to remember.  N.Y., Yoseloff, 1962.    177p.

2438 Time walked.  N.Y., Taplinger, 1959.;  L., Collins, 1957.    177p.

2439 The train;  tr. by E. Manning, M. Budberg.  N.Y., Knopf, 1949.    281p.;
     L., Putnam, 1948.    252p.

Parkhomov, M.

2440 I speak from the grave. Moscow, Mezhdunarodnaya Kniga, 1959. 169p.

Pasternak, B.

2441 Fifty poems; tr. by L.P. Slater. N.Y., Barnes; L., Allen & Unwin, 1963. 92p.

2442 In the interlude: poems, 1945–1960; tr. by H. Kamen. N.Y.; L., Oxford U.P., 1962. 250p.

2443 Poems; tr. by E.M. Kayden. 2nd ed. Yellow Springs, Antioch P., 1964. 312p.

2444 Poems; tr. by L.P. Slater. 2nd ed. Fairwarp, Uckfield, P. Russell, 1959. 37p.

2445 The poems of Dr. Zhivago; tr. by D. Davie. N.Y., Barnes; Manchester, U. of Manchester P., 1965. 204p.

2446 The poems of Dr. Zhivago; tr. by E.M. Kayden. Kansas City, Hallmark, 1967. 61p.

2447 The poetry of Boris Pasternak, 1917–1959; tr. by G. Reavey. N.Y., Putnam, 1959. 257p.

2448 Prose and poems; tr. by S. Schimanski. Rev. ed. L., Benn, 1959. 312p.

2449 Safe conduct: an early autobiogrpahy and other works; tr. by A. Brown (and) Five lyric poems, tr. by L.P. Slater. N.Y., New Directions; L, Elek, 1959. 304p.

2450 The adolescence of Zhenya Lubers; tr. by T. Langnas. N.Y., Philosophical Library, 1961. 87p.

2451 The blind beauty: a play; tr. by M. Hayward, M. Harari. N.Y., Pantheon; L., Collins, 1969. 128p.

2452 Doctor Zhivago; tr. by M. Hayward, M. Harari. N.Y., Pantheon; L., Collins, 1958. 558p.

2453 An essay in autobiography; tr. by M. Harari. L., Collins, 1959. 160p.

2454 I remember: sketches for an autobiography; tr. by D. Magarshack (and) Translating Shakespeare; tr. by M. Harari. N.Y., Pantheon, 1959. 191p.

2455 The last summer; tr. by G. Reavey. L., Owen, 1959. 143p.

2456 Letters to Georgian friends; tr. by D. Magarshack. N.Y., Harcourt; L., Secker & Warburg, 1968. 190p.

2457 Sister my life: summer 1917; tr. by P.C. Flayderman. N.Y., Washington Sq., 1967. 170p.

2458   Conquest, R.  The Pasternak affair:  courage of genius;  a documentary
       report.  Philadelphia, Lippincott, 1962.  192p.;  Courage of genius: the
       Pasternak affair;  a documentary report on its literary and political s-
       ignificance.  L., Collins, 1961.   191p.

2459   Davie, D., Livingstone, A.  Pasternak.  L., Macmillan, 1969.   277p.

2460   Payne, P.S.R.  The three worlds of Boris Pasternak.  N.Y., Coward, 1961.
       220p.;  L., Hale, 1962.   191p.

2461   Plank, D.L.  Pasternak's lyric:  a study of sound and imagery.  The Hag-
       ue, Mouton, 1966.   123p.

2462   Rowland, M.F. Rowland, P.  Pasternak's Doctor Zhivago.  Carbondale, Sou-
       thern Illinois U.P., 1967.   216p.

2463   Ruge, G.  Pasternak:  a pictorial biography.  N.Y., McGraw—Hill; L., Th-
       ames & Hudson, 1959.   143p.

       Paustovsky, K.

2464   The black gulf;  tr. by E. Schimanskaya.  L., Hutchinson, 1946.   124p.

2465   The flight of time:  new stories;  tr. by L. Navrozov.  Moscow,   FLPH,
       1955.   99p.

2466   The golden rose:  literature in the making;  tr. by S. Rosenberg.  Mos-
       cow, FLPH, 1957.   238p.

2467   The story of a life;  tr. by J. Barnes and others.  N.Y., Pantheon; L.,
       Collins, 1964—69.  5 vols.
       Vol.1.  Childhood and schooldays.
       Vol.2.  Slow approach of thunder.
       Vol.3.  In that dawn.
       Vol.4.  Years of hope.
       Vol.5.  Southern adventure.

       Pavlenko, P.

2468   Flames of vengeance.  Moscow, FLPH, 1942.   108p.

2469   The forest guerrillas:  a story of the partisans of Lake Ilmen.  L., La-
       bour Bk. Service, 1944.   114p.

2470   Happiness;  tr. by J. Fineberg.  L., Collet;  Moscow, FLPH, 1950.  595p.

2471   Red planes fly east;  tr. by S. Garry.  N.Y., International Publishers;
       L., Routledge, 1938.   523p.

       Perventzev, A.

2472   Cossack commander;  tr. by S. Garry.  L., Routledge, 1939.   313p.

2473   The ordeal.  N.Y., Harper, 1944.  262p.;  The test.  L., Hutchinson,1944

252p.

Pilnyak, B.

2474 Tales of the wilderness;  tr. by F. O'Dempsey.  N.Y., Knopf;  L., Routledge, 1925.    223p.

2475 Ivan Moscow;  tr. by A. Schwartzmann.  N.Y., Christopher, 1935.    92p.

2476 Mother Earth, and other stories;  tr. by V.T. Reck, M. Green.  N.Y., Praeger, 1968.;  L., Deutsch, 1969.    290p.

2477 The naked year;  tr. by A. Brown.  N.Y., Payson-Clarke;  L., Putnam,1928.
305p.

2478 The Volga falls to the Caspian Sea;  tr. by C. Malamuth.  N.Y., Farrar,
1931.    353p.;  L., Davies, 1932.    322p.

Pismensky, A.

2479 One thousand souls;  tr. by I. Litvinov.  N.Y., Grove P., 1959.    473p.;
Moscow, FLPH, 1958.    572p.

2480 The simpleton.  Moscow, Mezhdunarodnaya Kniga, 1959.    160p.

Platonov, A.P.

2481 The fierce and beautiful world;  tr. by J. Barnes.  L., Hodder & Stoughton, 1971.    252p.

2482 Jordan, M.  Andrei Platonov.  Letchworth, Bradda, 1973.    119p.

Polevoi, B.

2483 Shores of a new sea:  short stories;  tr. by I. Zhelezhova.  Moscow,FLPH
1954.    143p.

2484 We are Soviet people.  Moscow, FLPH, 1949.    589p.

2485 From Belgorod to Carpathians.  N.Y., Universal, 1947.    164p.

2486 From a Soviet war correspondent's notebook.  L., Hutchinson, 1945. 164p.

2487 A story about a real man;  tr. by J. Fineberg.  Moscow, FLPH, 1949. 559p.

2488 To the last breath.  L., Hutchinson, 1945.    79p.

Polyakov, A.

2489 Russians don't surrender;  tr. by N. Guterman.  N.Y., Dutton, 1942. 191p.

2490 Westbound tanks.  L., Hutchinson, 1943.    100p.

2491 With a Soviet unit through Nazi lines.  L., Hutchinson, 1941.    40p.

Popov, I.

2492    While waiting for dawn.  Moscow, FLPH, 1944.    99p.

2493    Steel and slag;  tr. by H. Altschuler.  Moscow, FLPH, 1951.    647p.

Pravdin, M.

2494    Double eagle;  tr. by K. Kirkness.  L., Selwyn-Blount, 1934.    416p.

Prishvin, M.

2495    The black Arab, and other stories;  tr. by D. Magarshack.  L., Hutchinso
        1947.    286p.

2496    The sun's storehouse:  short stories;  tr. by I. Litvinov.  Moscow, FLPH
        1955.    158p.

2497    Jen Sheng:  the root of life;  tr. by G. Walton, P. Gibbons.  N.Y., Put-
        nam;  L., Melrose, 1936.    177p.

2498    The lake and the wood;  or nature's calendar;  tr. by W. L. Goodman. N.Y
        Pantheon, 1952.;  L., Routledge, 1951.    258p.

2499    Nature's diary;  tr. by L. Navrozov.  Moscow, FLPH, 1958.    363p.

2500    Ship-timber grove;  tr. by D. Fry.  L., Lawrence & Wishart, 1957.    192p.

2501    The treasure trove of the sun;  tr. by T. Balkoff-Downe.  N.Y., Viking,
        1952.    79p.

Ptashkina, N.

2502    The diary;  tr. by P. de Chary.  L., Cape, 1923.    316p.

Rakhmanova, A.

2503    Flight from terror;  tr. by I. Zeitlin.  N.Y., Day, 1933.    342p.

2504    Restless old age:  the troubled past.  L., Soviet Weekly, 1958.    38p.

Rozov, V.

2505    In search of happiness.  L., Evans, 1961.    72p.

Rybakov, A.

2506    The bronze bird.  Moscow, FLPH, 195?    292p.

2507    The dirk;  tr. by D. Skvirsky.  Moscow, FLPH, 1954.    287p.

2508    Kortik.  Moscow, FLPH, 1953.    214p.

Ryss, Y.

2509   Before the shadows fell.  L., Hutchinson, 1946.    160p.

Semenov, I.S.

2510   Petrovka 38;  tr. by M. Scammell.  L., MacGibbon & Kee, 1965.    205p.

Serafimovich, A.

2511   The iron flood.  N.Y., International Publishers, 1935.  246p.; Moscow, FLPH, 196?    207p.

2512   Sand and other stories;  tr. by G.H. Hanna.  Moscow, FLPH, 1958. 301p.

Serge, V.

2513   The case of Comrade Tulayev;  tr. by W. Trask.  L., Hamilton, 1951. 328p.

Sergeyev-Tzenski, S.

2514   Brusilov's break-through: a novel of the First World War, tr. by H. Altschuler.  L., Hutchinson, 1945.    336p.

2515   Transfiguration;  tr. by M. Budberg.  N.Y., McBride, 1926.    300p.

Sharov, A.

2516   Life triumphs: a story of heroes of science;  tr. by V. Dutt.  Moscow, FLPH, 1954.    249p.

Shiryayev, P.

2517   Flattery's foal;  tr. by A. Freemantle.  N.Y., Knopf, 1938.    294p.

Shishkov, V.

2518   Children of darkness.  L., Gollancz, 1931.    288p.

Shklovsky, V.B.

2519   Zoo: or letters not about love, tr. by R. Sheldon.  Ithaca, Cornell U.P., 1971.    164p.

Shmelev, I.

2520   Inexhaustible cup;  tr. by T.D. France.  N.Y., Dutton, 1928.    147p.

2521   The story of a love;  tr. by N. Tsytovitch.  N.Y., Dutton, 1931. 323p.

2522   The sun of the dead;  tr. by C.J. Hogarth.  N.Y., Dutton;  L., Dent,1927. 297p.

Sholokhov, M.

2523   Hate.  Moscow, FLPH, 1942.    55p.

2524  Fierce and gentle warriors;  tr. by M. Morton.  L., Heinemann, 1969. 86p.

2525  One man's destiny:  and other stories, articles and sketches, 1923-1963;
      Tr. by H.C. Stevens.  N.Y., Knopf;  L., Putnam, 1967.    271p.

2526  And quiet flows the Don;  tr. by S. Garry, rev. by R. Daglish.  Moscow,
      FLPH, 1960.    4 vols.

2527  And quiet flows the Don;  tr. by S. Garry.  N.Y., Knopf;  L., Putnam,19-
      34.    755p.

2528  The Don flows home to the sea;  tr. by S. Garry.  N.Y., Knopf,    1941.
      777p.;  L., Putnam, 1940.    861p.

2529  The fate of a man;  tr. by R. Daglish.  Moscow, FLPH, 1958.    67p.

2530  Harvest on the Don;  tr. by H.C. Stevens.  N.Y., Knopf, 1961. 367p.;  L.,
      Putnam, 1960.    399p.

2531  Seeds of tomorrow;  tr. by S. Garry.  N.Y., Knopf, 1935. 404p.;  Virg-
      in soil upturned.  L., Putnam, 1935.    496p.

2532  Tales from the Don;  tr. by H.C. Stevens.  L., Putnam, 1961.    285p.

2533  Bearne, C.G.  Sholokhov.  Edinburgh, Oliver & Boyd, 1969.    113p.

2534  Klimenko, M.  The world of young Sholokhov:  vision of violence.  North
      Quincy, Christopher, 1972.    287p.

2535  Price, R.F.  Mixail Soloxov in Yugoslavia:  reception and literary impa-
      ct.  Boulder, East European Quarterly, 1973.    180p.

2536  Stewart, D.H.  Mikhail Sholokhov:  a critical introduction.  Ann Arbor,
      U. of Michigan P., 1967.    250p.

      Shvarts, E.L.

2537  The dragon;  tr. by E.R. Hapgood.  N.Y., Theatre Arts Bks., 1963.  78p.
      L., Heinemann, 1969.    108p.

      Simonov, K.

2538  Friends and foes;  tr. by I. Zukhovitskaya.  Moscow, FLPH, 1952.   78p.

2539  Days and nights;  tr. by J. Fineberg.  L., Hutchinson;  Toronto, Progr-
      ess, 1945.    244p.

2540  Days and nights;  tr. by J. Barnes.  N.Y., Simon & Schuster;  Toronto,
      Musson, 1945.    422p.

2541  Days and nights.  Shanghai, Epoch, 1945.    400p.

2542  The living and the dead;  tr. by R. Ainsztein.  N.Y., Doubleday,  1962.;
      Victims and heroes.  L., Hutchinson, 1963.    558p.

2543    No quarter on Russia's fighting lines. N.Y., Fisher, 1943.    231p.

2544    The whole world over, adapted from "And so it will be": a comedy in two
        acts; tr. by T. Schnee. N.Y., Dramatists Play Service, 1947.    86p.

        'Tertz, A.' = Sinyavsky, A.

2545    The icicle and other stories; tr. by M. Hayward, R. Hingley. L., Coll-
        ins, 1963.    191p.

2546    The Makepeace experiment; tr. by M. Harari. L., Collins, 1965. 192p.

2547    On socialist realism. N.Y. Pantheon, 1961.    95p.

2548    The trial begins; tr. by M. Hayward. L., Collins, 1960.    128p.

2549    For freedom of imagination, by A. Sinyavsky: tr. by L. Tibos, M. Pepp-
        ard. N.Y., Holt, 1971.    212p.

2550    Unguarded thoughts, by A. Sinyavsky. L., Collins, 1972.    95p.

        Siomushkin, T.

2551    Alitet goes to the hills; tr. by B. Isaacs. Moscow, FLPH, 1948. 301p.

2552    Children of the Soviet Arctic. L., Hutchinson, 1944.    256p.

        Skrebitzki, G.

2553    White birds island; tr. by Z. Voynow. N.Y., Knopf, 1948.    84p.

        Smirnov, V.G.

2554    The Lopotkin inheritance, adapted by L. du G. Peach. L., French, 1963.
        68p.

2555    Sons; tr. by N. Yohel. Garden City, N.Y., Doubleday, 1947.    305p.

        Smirnova, N.

2556    Marfa: a Siberian novel; tr. by M. Burr. L., Boriswood, 1936.    246p.

        Sobko, V.

2557    Guarantee of peace. Moscow, FLPH, 1951.    543p.

        Sobol, A.

2558    Freak show; tr. by J. Covan. N.Y., Kendall, 1930.    416p.

        Sobolev, L.

2559    The green light; tr. by R. Parker, V. Scott. Moscow, FLPH, 1955. 223p.

2560  One desire.  Moscow, FLPH, 1942.    118p.

2561  Romanoff;  tr. by A. Fremantle.  N.Y., Longmans, 1935.    311p.

2562  Soul of the sea;  tr. by N. Orloff.  Philadelphia, Lippincott,    1946.
      352p.;  L., Hutchinson, 1945.    191p.

2563  Storm warning;  tr. by A. Fremantle.  L., Dickson, 1935.    321p.

      Sokolnikova, G.

2564  Nine women;  tr. by H. Stevens.  N.Y., Cape, 1932.    287p.

      Sokolov, B.

2565  The crime of Doctor Garine.  N.Y., Covici, 1928.    144p.

      Soloviov, L.

2566  Adventures in Bukhara;  tr. by T. Shebunina.  L., Lawrence & Wishart,
      1955.    256p.

2567  Black sea sailor.  Moscow, FLPH, 1944.    98p.

2568  The enchanted prince.  Moscow, Mezhdunarodnaya Kniga, 1959.    449p.

      Solzhenitsyn, A.

2569  August 1914, tr. by M. Glenny.  N.Y., Farrar, 1972.  622p.;  L., Bodley
      Head, 1972.    645p.

2570  Cancer ward;  tr. by N. Bethell, D. Burg.  N.Y., Farrar, 1969.    560p.;
      L., Bodley Head, 1970.    619p.

2571  The cancer ward;  tr. by R. Frank.  N.Y., Dial, 1968.    616p.

2572  Candle in the wind;  tr. by K. Armes, A. Hudgins.  Minneapolis, U. of M-
      innesota P.,;  L., Bodley Head, 1973.    141p.

2573  The first circle;  tr. by M. Guybon.  L., Collins, 1968.    581p.

2574  The first circle;  tr. by T.P. Whitney.  N.Y., Harper, 1968.    580p.

2575  For the good of the cause;  tr. by D. Floyd, M. Hayward.  N.Y., Praeger;
      L., Pall Mall P., 1964.    134p.

2576  The love-girl and the innocent;  tr. by N. Bethell, D. Burg.  N.Y., Far-
      rar;  L., Bodley Head, 1969.    131p.

2577  One day in the life of Ivan Denisovich;  tr. by G. Aitken.  Rev. ed. N.Y
      Farrar;  L., Bodley Head, 1971.    174p.

2578  One day in the life of Ivan Denisovich;  tr. by M. Hayward, R. Hingley.
      N.Y., Praeger;  L., Pall Mall P., 1963.    210p.

2579    One day in the life of Ivan Denisovich;   tr. by R. Parker.   N.Y., Dutton;
        L., Gollancz, 1963.    160p.

2580    One word of truth:   the Nobel speech on literature, 1970.   L., Bodley H-
        ead, 1972.    27p.

2581    Lecture (Nobel prize lecture).   L., Stenvalley P., 1973.    55p.

2582    Stories and prose poems;   tr. by M. Glenny.   N.Y., Farrar, 1971.   267p.;
        L., Bodley Head, 1971.    242p.

2583    We never make mistakes!:   two short novels;   tr. by P.W. Blackstock. 2nd
        ed.   Columbia, U. of South Carolina P., 1971.   110p.;   L., Sphere, 1972.
        138p.

2584    Fiene, D.M.   Alexander Solzhenitsyn:   an international bibliography of
        writings by and about him.   Ann Arbor, Ardis, 1973.    148p.

2585    Bjorkegren, H.   Aleksandr Solzhenitsyn:   a biography.   N.Y., Third P.,
        1972.   186p.;   Henley-on-Thames, Aidan Ellis, 1973.    205p.

2586    Burg, D., Feifer, G.   Solzhenitsyn:   a biography.   N.Y., Stein & Day; L.,
        Hodder & Stoughton, 1972.    371p.

2587    Grazzini, G.   Solzhenitsyn.   L., Joseph, 1973.    256p.

2588    Labedz, L.   Solzhenitsyn:   a documentary record.   N.Y., Harper,1971.229p.
        Harmondsworth, Penguin, 1972.    264p.

2589    Lukacs, G.   Solzhenitsyn.   Cambridge, Mass., MITP., 1971.    88p.

2590    Medvedev, Z.   Ten years after Ivan Denisovich.   L., Macmillan, 1973.202p.

2591    Moody, C.   Solzhenitsyn.   N.Y., Barnes & Noble;   Edinburgh, Oliver & Bo-
        yd, 1973.    184p.

2592    Rothberg, A.   Aleksandr Solzhenitsyn:   the major novels.   Ithaca, Corne-
        ll U.P., 1971.    215p.

        Stanislavsky, K.

2593    Maximka:   sea stories;   tr. by B. Isaacs.   Moscow, FLPH, 1956.    240p.

        Stepanov, A.

2594    Port Arthur:   a historical narrative;   tr. by J. Fineberg.   Moscow, FLPH,
        1947.    784p.

        Surguchiov, I.

2595    Autumn;   tr. by D. Modell.   N.Y., Appleton, 1924.    86p.

2596    Autumn;   adapted by M. Kennedy, G. Ratoff.   L., Nelson, 1939.    104p.

Svirski, A.

2597　Ginger.　Moscow, Mezhdunarodnaya Kniga, 1959.　364p.

Syomin, V.

2598　Seven in one house;　tr. by M. Glenny.　L., Joseph, 1968.　188p.

Tarsis, V.

2599　The gay life;　tr. by D. Parker.　L., Collins, 1968.　224p.

2600　The pleasure factory;　tr. by M. Glenny.　L., Collins, 1967.　224p.

2601　A thousand illusions;　tr. by M. le Masque.　L., Collins, 1969.　191p.

2602　Ward 7:　an autobiographical novel;　tr. by K. Brown.　N.Y., Dutton; L., Collins, 1965.　159p.

Teleshov, N.

2603　A writer remembers;　tr. by L. Britton.　L., Hutchinson, 1946.　173p.

Tendryakov, V.

2604　Son-in-law;　tr. by Y. Rebrov.　Moscow, FLPH, 1956.　163p.

2605　Three, seven, ace & other stories;　tr. by D. Alger and others.　N.Y., Harper; L., Collins, 1973.　252p.

Tenin, V.

2606　Moscow nights:　sleep soundly, dear comrade;　tr. by M. le Masque.　L., Olympia P., 1971.　288p.

Teveliov, M.

2607　Hotel in Snegovets;　tr. by O. Shartse.　Moscow, FLPH, 1956.　176p.

2608　Verkhovina:　our land so dear;　tr. by S. Rosenberg.　Moscow, FLPH, 1955.　528p.

Tikhonov, V.

2609　The mountains and the stars.　Boston, Mass., Little;　L., Heinemann,1938.　426p.

Tolstoy, A.N.

2610　Daredevils and other stories;　tr. by D. Fromberg.　Moscow, FLPH, 1942.　76p.

2611　Russian tales for children;　tr. by E. Shimanskaya.　N.Y., Dutton, 1947.　194p.

612   Selected stories. Moscow, FLPH, 1949.   639p.

613   A week in Turnevo and other stories. N.Y., Grove, 1958.   187p.

614   Bread;  tr. by S. Garry. L., Gollancz, 1937.   447p.

615   Darkness and dawn;  tr. by E. Bone, E. Burns. N.Y., Longmans; L., Gollancz, 1936.   570p.

616   The death box;  tr. by B. Guerney. L., Methuen, 1936.   357p.

617   The Garin death ray;  tr. by G. Hanna. Moscow, FLPH, 1957.   343p.

618   The golden key or the adventures of Buratino;  tr. by E. Hartley. N.Y., Universal; L., Hutchinson, 1947.   148p.

619   Imperial majesty;  tr. by H. Matheson. L., Matthews Marrot, 1932. 444p.

620   The lame prince: a story. Moscow, FLPH, 1958.   170p.

621   Little cock-feather frock;  tr. by E. Felgenhauer. Moscow, FLPH, 1955. 16p.

622   The making of Russia. L., Hutchinson, 1945.   104p.

623   My country: articles and stories of the Great Patriotic War of the Soviet Union;  tr. by D. Fromberg. L., Hutchinson, 1943.   117p.

624   Nikita's childhood;  tr. by V. Lansbury-Dutt. L., Hutchinson, 1945.128p.

625   Ordeal: a trilogy;  tr. by I. and T. Litvinov. Moscow, FLPH, 1953.3vols

626   Peter the First;  tr. by T. Shebunina. N.Y., Macmillan, 1959. 768p.; L., Lawrence & Wishart, 1956.   795p.

627   Peter the Great;  tr. by E. Bone, E. Burns. L., Gollancz, 1936.   463p.

628   Peter the Great;  tr. by H. Matheson. N.Y., Covici-Friede, 1932.   387p.

629   Road to Calvary;  tr. by E. Bone. L., Hutchinson; Toronto, Ryerson P., 1945.   680p.

630   Road to Calvary;  tr. by R. Townsend. N.Y., Boni-Liveright, 1923. 451p.

Treniov, K.

631   In a Cossack village and other stories;  tr. by J. Atkinson. L., Hutchinson, 1946.   335p.

Tretyakov, S.

632   Chinese testament: the autobiography of Tan-Shih-Hua as told to Tretyakov. L., Gollancz, 1934.   383p.

2633   Roar China: an episode in nine scenes; tr. by F. Polianovskaya, B. Nixon. N.Y., International Publishers, 1932. 89p.; L., Lawrence, 1931. 87p.

Trifonov, Y.

2634   Students; tr. by I. Litvinova, M. Wettlin. Moscow, FLPH, 1953. 497p.

Tsvetayeva, M.

2635   Selected poems; tr. by E. Feinstein. N.Y.,; L., Oxford U.P., 1971. 103p.

2636   Karlinsky, S. Marina Cvetaeva: her art and life. Berkeley, U. of California P., 1966. 317p.

Tsiolkovsky, K.

2637   Beyond the planet earth; tr. by K. Syers. N.Y.; Oxford, Pergamon,1960. 190p.

Tynyanov, Y.

2638   Death and diplomacy in Persia; tr. by A. Brown. L., Boriswood, 1938. 357p.

2639   Stradivari: the violin-maker; tr. by C. Angoff. N.Y., Knopf,1940. 99p.

Uspenskaya, Y.

2640   One summer; tr. by I. Litvinova, M. Wettlin. Moscow, FLPH, 1954. 362p.

Uspenski, P.

2641   Strange life of Ivan Osokin. N.Y., Hermitage House, 1954. 166p.

Valeriy, I.

2642   The bluebottle; tr. by T. Jones and, Red and black; tr. by D. Alger. L., Collins, 1962. 188p.

Volodin, A.

2643   Five evenings; tr. by A. Nicolaeff. Minneapolis, Minnesota U.P., in association with the Minnesota Theater Company. 1966. 101p.

Vigdorova, F.

2644   Diary of a school-teacher; tr. by R. Prokofieva. Moscow, FLPH, 1954. 343p.

Vinogradov, A.

2645   The black consul; tr. by E. Burns. N.Y., Viking; L., Gollancz, 1935. 438p

2646    The condemnation of Paganini;    tr. by S. Garry.    L., Hutchinson,    1945.
        288p.

2647    Three colours of time:    a novel of Stendhal;    tr. by G. Shelley.    L., H-
        utchinson, 1946.    340p.

        Voronkova, L.F.

2648    Little girl from the city;    tr. by J. Berger.    Boston, Mass., Little,
        1948.    165p.

        Voronski, A.

2649    Waters of life and death;    tr. by L. Zarine.    L., Allen & Unwin, 1936.
        343p.

        Voznesensky, A.

2650    Antiworlds and the fifth ace:    poems;    tr. by W. H. Auden.    N.Y., Basic,
        1966.    120p.;    L., Oxford U.P., 1968.    296p.

2651    Dogalypse:    San Francisco poetry reading.    San Francisco, City Lights
        Bks., 1972.    48p.

2652    Selected poems;    tr. by H. Marshall.    N.Y., Hill & Wang;    L., Methuen,
        1966.    129p.

2653    Selected poems;    tr. by A. Hollo.    N.Y., Grove, 1964.    107p.

        Yan, V.

2654    Batu-Khan:    a tale of the thirteenth century;    tr. by L. Britton.    L.,
        Hutchinson, 1945.    320p.

2655    Jenghiz Khan:    a tale of thirteenth century Asia;    tr. by L. Britton. L.,
        Hutchinson;    Toronto, Ryerson, 1945.    272p.

        Yanovsky, V.S.

2656    No man's time;    tr. by I Levitin, R.N. Parris.    L., Chatto & Windus,1967.
        224p.

        Yugov, A.

2657    Immortality;    tr. by D. Magarshack.    L., Hutchinson, 1945.    304p.

        Yurasov, V.

2658    Parallax;    tr. by T.B. Drowne.    N.Y., Norton, 1966.    628p.

        Zabolotsky, N.A.

2659    Scrolls:    selected poems;    tr. by D. Weissbort.    L., Cape, 1971.    95p.

Zaitzev, B.

2660  Anna.  L., Allen & Unwin, 1937.    148p.

Zakrutkin, V.

2661  Floating stanitza;  tr. by B. Isaacs.  Moscow, FLPH, 1954.    369p.

Zamyatin, E.

2662  The dragon:  fifteen stories;  tr. by M. Ginsburg.  N.Y., Random, 1966;
L., Gollancz, 1972.    291p.

2663  A Soviet heretic:  essays;  tr. by M. Ginsburg.  Chicago, U. of Chicago
P., 1970.    322p.

2664  We;  tr. by B. Guerney.  N.Y., Viking, 1972.;  L., Cape, 1970.    285p.

2665  We;  tr. by G. Zilboorg.  N.Y., Dutton, 1924.    286p.

2666  Richards, D.J.  Zamyatin:  a Soviet heretic.  N.Y., Hillary, 1963;  L.,
Bowes, 1962.    112p.

2667  Shane, A.M.  The life and works of Evgenij Zamjatin.  Berkeley, U. of C-
alifornia.P., 1968.    302p.

Zhigalova, O.

2668  Across the green past;  tr. by T. Drowne. Chicago, Regnery, 1952. 214p.

Zlotovski, K.

2669  Deep sea divers;  tr. by B. Kinkead.  Philadelphia, Lippincott,    1938.
212p.

Zoshchenko, M.

2670  Nervous people and other satires;  tr. by M. Gordon, H. McLean.  L., Gollancz, 1963.    450p.

2671  Scenes from the bathhouse, and other stories of communist Russia;  tr.
by S. Monas.  Ann Arbor, U. of Michigan P., 1961.    245p.

2672  Russia laughs;  tr. by H. Clayton.  Boston, Mass., Lothrop-Lee-Shephard;
Toronto, Longmans, 1935.    352p.

2673  The woman who could not read, and other tales;  tr. by E. Fen.  L., Methuen, 1940.    153p.

2674  The wonderful dog and other tales;  tr. by E. Fen.  2nd ed.  L., Methuen,
1942.    179p.

C     Theatre

2675   Balukhatuy, S.D.   'The seagull', produced by Stanislavsky: 'The seagull'
       by Anton Chekov, production score for the Moscow Arts Theatre by K.S.
       Stanislavsky.   N.Y., Theatre Arts; L., Dobson, 1952.   292p.

2676   Bowers, F.   Broadway, U.S.S.R.: ballet, theater and entertainment in
       Russia today.   N.Y., Nelson, 1959.   215p.; Entertainment in Russia; ba-
       llet, theatre and entertainment in Russia today.   Edinburgh, Nelson,
       1959.   227p.

2677   Bradshaw, M.   Soviet theaters, 1917-1941.   N.Y., Research Program on the
       U.S.S.R., 1954.   317p.

2678   Carter, H.   The new spirit in the Russian theatre, 1917-1928.   L., Bren-
       tano, 1929.   348p.

2679   Carter, H.   The new theatre and cinema of Soviet Russia.   L., Chapman &
       Dodd, 1924.   278p.

2680   Edwards, C.   The Stanislavsky heritage: its contribution to the Russian
       and American theaters.   N.Y., N.Y.U.P.; L., Owen, 1966.   345p.

2681   Freed, D.   Freud and Stanislavsky: new directions in the performing
       arts.   N.Y., Vantage, 1964.   128p.

2682   Fulop-Miller, R., Gregor, J.   The Russian theatre: its character and
       history, with special reference to the revolutionary period.   L., Harrap,
       1930.   136p.

2683   Gorchakov, N.M.   Stanislavsky directs.   N.Y., Funk & Wagnall, 1954. 402p.

2684   Gorchakov, N.M.   The theater in Soviet Russia.   N.Y., Columbia U.P.,1957.
       480p.

2685   Gorchakov, N.M.   The Vakhtangov school of stage art.   Moscow, FLPH, 1960.
       205p.

2686   Gyseghem, A.van.   The theatre in Soviet Russia.   L., Faber, 1943.   220p.

2687   Houghton, N.   Moscow rehearsals: an account of methods of production in
       the Soviet theater.   N.Y., Harcourt, 1936.   265p.;   L., Allen & Unwin,
       1938.   313p.

2688   Houghton, N.   Return engagement: a postscript to Moscow rehearsals.   N.Y.
       Holt, 1962.   205p.

2689   Macleod, J.   Actors cross the Volga: a study of the 19th century Russi-
       an theatre and of Soviet theatres in war.   L., Allen & Unwin, 1946. 359p.

2690   Macleod, J.   The new Soviet theatre.   L., Allen & Unwin, 1943.   242p.

2691   Macleod, J. A Soviet theatre sketch book.   L., Allen & Unwin, 1951.   168p.

2692   Magarshack, D.   Stanislavsky: a life.   L., MacGibbon & Kee, 1950.   414p.

2693   Markov, P.A.   The Soviet theatre.   L., Gollancz, 1934.   176p.

2694   Meyerhold, V.E.   Meyerhold on theatre;   ed. by E. Braun.   N.Y., Hill &
       Wang, 1969.   336p.

2695   Moore, S.   The Stanislavski system:   the professional training of an ac-
       tor.   Rev. ed. N.Y., Viking, 1965.;   L., Gollancz, 1966.   112p.

2696   Nemirovich-Danchenko, V.   My life in the Russian theatre.   Boston, Mass.
       Little, 1936.;   L., Bles, 1968.   365p.

2697   Obraztov, S.   My profession.   Moscow, FLPH, 1957.   255p.   (Puppetry).

2698   Sayler, O.M.   Inside the Moscow Art Theatre.   N.Y., Brentano, 1925. 240p

2699   Stanislavsky, K.   An actor prepares.   N.Y., Theater Arts, 1930.   295p.

2700   Stanislavsky, K.   Building a character.   N.Y., Theater Arts, 1949. 312p.
       L., Reinhardt & Evans, 1950.   300p.

2701   Stanislavsky, K.   My life in art.   Boston, Little, 1924.;   L., Bles,1962.
       586p.

2702   Stanislavsky, K.   Stanislavsky on the art of the stage.   2nd ed.   N.Y.,
       Hill & Wang;   L., Faber, 1961.   311p.

2703   Stanislavsky, K.   Stanislavsky   produces Othello.   L., Bles, 1948. 243p.

2704   Stanislavsky, K.   Stanislavski's legacy:   comments on some aspects of an
       actor's art and life.   L., Reinhardt, 1959.   157p.

2705   Symons, J.M.   Meyerhold's theatre of the grotesque:   the post-revolutio-
       nary productions, 1920-1932.   Cambridge,   Rivers P., 1973.   230p.

2706   Tairov, A.   Notes of a director.   Coral Gables, U. of Miami P.,   1959.
       153p.

2707   Washburn, J.N.   Soviet theater:   its distortion of America's image,1921-
       1973.   Chicago, American Bar Association, 1973.   63p.

2708   Yershov, P.   Comedy in the Soviet theatre.   N.Y., Praeger, 1956.;   L.,
       Atlantic P., 1957.   280p.


D   Films

2709   Arossev, A.   Soviet cinema.   Moscow, VOKS, 1935.   312p.

2710   Babitsky, P., Lutich, M.   The Soviet movie industry:   two studies.   N.Y.
       Research Program on the U.S.S.R., 1953.   83p.

2711   Babitsky, P., Rimberg, J.   The Soviet film industry.   N.Y., Praeger,1955.
       377p.

- 152 -

2712  Barna, Y.  Eisenstein.  L., Secker & Warburg, 1973.    287p.

2713  Bryher.  Film problems of Soviet Russia.  L.; Territet, Pool, 1929. 139p.

2714  Dickinson, T., Roche, C. de la.  Soviet cinema.  L., Falcon P.,    1948. 136p.

2715  Dovzhenko, A.  The poet as filmaker:  selected writings.  Cambridge, Mass., MITP., 1973.    323p.

2716  Eisenstein, S.  Film essays and a lecture.  N.Y., Praeger, 1970.  220p.

2717  Eisenstein, S.  Film form:  essays in film theory.  N.Y., Harcourt,1949.; L., Dobson, 1951.    279p.

2718  Eisenstein, S.  The film sense.  N.Y., Harcourt, 1942.;  L., Faber,1943. 279p.

2719  Eisenstein, S.  Ivan the Terrible:  a film.  L., Lorrimer, 1970.  264p.

2720  Eisenstein, S.  Ivan the Terrible:  a screen play.  N.Y., Simon & Schuster, 1962.;  L., Secker & Warburg, 1963.    319p.

2721  Eisenstein, S., Sinclair, U.  The making and unmaking of 'Que viva Mexico'.  Bloomington, Indiana U.P.;  L., Thames & Hudson, 1970.    449p.

2722  Eisenstein, S.  Mexican drawings — Sergei Eisenstein.  Moscow, Sovetskii Khudozhnik, 1969.    156p.

2723  Eisenstein, S.  Notes of a film director.  Rev trans.  N.Y., Dover,1970. 207p.

2724  Eisenstein, S.  Potemkin:  a film.  N.Y., Simon & Schuster, 1968.  100p.; The battleship Potemkin.  L., Lorrimer, 1968.    104p.

2725  Eisenstein, S.  Que viva Mexico!  Rev. ed.  L., Vision P., 1972.    93p.

2726  Leyda, J.  Kino:  a history of the Russian and Soviet film.  N.Y., Macmillan;  L., Allen & Unwin, 1960.    493p.

2727  Montagu, I.  With Eisenstein in Hollywood:  a chapter of autobiography by I. Montagu, including the scenarios of Sutter's Gold and American Tragedy.  N.Y., International Publications, 1969.;  Berlin, Seven Seas Bks., 1967.    356p.

2728  Moussinac, L.  Sergei Eisenstein.  N.Y., Crown, 1970.    226p.

2729  Nilsen, V.  The cinema as a graphic art:  on a theory of representation in the cinema;  with an appreciation by S. Eisenstein. `L., Nisbet,1937. 227p.

2730  Nizhny, V.B.  Lessons with Eisenstein.  L., Allen & Unwin, 1962.; Moscow, Iskusstvo, 1958.    182p.

2731 Pudovkin, V.I. Film technique, and, Film acting: memorial ed. with portrait and a revised and completed record of the author's film work. L., Vision P., 1958. 388p.

2732 Pudovkin, V.I., Dovzhenko, A. Mother: a film by V.I. Pudovkin; Earth; a film by A. Dovzhenko. N.Y., Simon & Schuster; L., Lorrimer, 1973. 102p.

2733 Rimberg, J.D. The motion picutre in the Soviet Union, 1918-1952: a sociological analysis. N.Y., Arno P., 1973. 238p.

2734 Schnitzer, L. and others. Cinema in revolution: the heroic age of the Soviet film. N.Y., Hill & Wang; L., Secker & Warburg, 1973. 208p.

2735 Seton, M. Sergei M. Eisenstein: a biography. L., Lane, 1952. 533p.

2736 The Soviet cinematography. Bombay, People's Publishing House, 1950. 244p.

2737 Vronskaya, J. Young Soviet film-makers. L., Allen & Unwin, 1972. 127p.


E    Music

2738 Abraham, G. Eight Soviet composers. L., Oxford U.P., 1943. 102p.

2739 Bakst, J. A history of Russian-Soviet music. N.Y., Dodd, 1966. 416p.

2740 Boelza, I. Handbook of Soviet musicians. Forest Hills, Transatlantic Arts, 1945.; L., Pilot P., 1943. 115p.

2741 Hanson, L., Hanson, E.M. Prokofiev: a biography in three movements. N.Y., Random, 1964. 368p.; Prokofiev: the prodigal son: an introduction to his life and work in three movements. L., Cassell, 1964. 243p.

2742 Ikonnikov, A.A. Myaskovsky: his life and work. N.Y., Philosophical Library, 1946. 162p.

2743 Kay, N. Shostakovich. L., Oxford U.P., 1971. 80p.

2744 Krebs, S.D. Soviet composers and the development of Soviet music. N.Y., Norton; L., Allen & Unwin, 1970. 364p.

2745 Malko, N. A certain art. N.Y., Morrow, 1966. 235p.

2746 Martynov, I. Dmitri Shostakovich. N.Y., Philosophical Library, 1947. 197p.

2747 Moisenko, R. Realist music: 25 Soviet composers. L., Meridian, 1949. 277p.; Supplement. L., Fore, 1951. 32p.

2748 Nestyev, I.V. Prokofiev. Stanford, Stanford. U.P., 1961. 528p.

2749 Nestyev, I.V. Sergei Prokofiev: his musical life. N.Y., Knopf, 1946. 193p.

2750  Olkhovsky, A.V.  Music under the Soviets:  the agony of an art.  N.Y., Praeger;  L., Routledge, 1955.  427p.

2751  Piatigorsky, G.  Cellist.  Garden City, N.Y., Doubleday, 1965.  273p.

2752  Polyakova, L.V.  Soviet music.  L., Central Bks.;  Moscow, FLPH, . 1961.  184p.

2753  Prokofiev, S.  Autobiography, articles, reminiscences.  Moscow, FLPH, 1960.  334p.

2754  Rabinovich, D.  Dmitry Shostakovich.  L., Lawrence & Wishart, 1959. 166p.

2755  Samuel, C.  Prokofiev.  N.Y., Grossman;  L., Calder, 1971.  191p.

2756  Schwarz, B.  Music and musical life in Soviet Russia.  N.Y., Norton; L., Barrie & Jenkins, 1972.  550p.

2757  Seroff, V.I., Galli-Shohat, N.  Dimitri Shostakovich:  the life and background of a Soviet composer.  N.Y., Knopf, 1943.  260p.

2758  Shneerson, G.  Aram Khachaturyan.  Moscow, FLPH, 1959.  103p.

2759  Unger, H., Walford, N.  Hammer, sickle and baton:  the Soviet memoirs of a musician.  L., Cresset P., 1939.  275p.

2760  Werth, A.  Musical uproar in Moscow.  L., Turnstile P., 1949.  103p.


F  Dance

2761  Bellew, H.  Ballet in Moscow today.  N.Y., Graphic;  L., Thames & Hudson, 1956.  203p.

2762  Bocharnikova, E., Gabovich, M.  Ballet school of the Bolshoi Theatre. Moscow, FLPH, n.d.  92p.

2763  Bogdanov-Berezovsky, V.M.  Ulanova and the development of the Soviet ballet.  L., MacGibbon & Kee, 1952.  147p.

2764  Chudnovsky, M.  Folk Dance Company of the U.S.S.R.  Igor Moiseyev art director.  Moscow, FLPH, 1959.  104p.

2765  Duncan, I., Macdougall, A.R.  Isadora Duncan's Russian days, and her last years in France.  N.Y., Covici-Friede;  L., Gollancz, 1929.  384p.

2766  Grey, B.  Red curtain up.  N.Y., Dodd, 1960.;  L., Secker & Warburg,1958. 84p.

2767  Kahn, A.E.  Days with Ulanova.  L., Collins, 1962.  236p.

2768  Nikitina, A.  Nikitina, by herself.  L., Wingate, 1959.  124p.

2769  Roslavleva, N.  The 'Beryozka' State Dance Company.  Moscow, FLPH, 1960.

104p.

2770  Roslavleva, N.  Era of the Russian ballet.  N.Y., Dutton, 1966.    320p.

2771  Schwezoff, I.  Borzoi.  L., Hodder & Stoughton, 1935.    441p.

2772  Shneider, I.I.  Isadora Duncan:  the Russian years.  N.Y., Harcourt,1968.
      221p.

2773  Sizova, M.I.  Ulanova:  her childhood and schooldays.  L., Black,  1962.
      176p.

2774  Slonimsky, J.  The Bolshoi Theatre Ballet notes.  Moscow, FLPH,  1956.
      96p.

2775  Slonimsky, J. and others.  Soviet ballet.  N.Y., Philosophical Library,
      1947.    285p.


G    Architecture

2776  Kopp, A.  Town and revolution:  Soviet architecture and city planning,
      1917–1935.  N.Y., Braziller;  L., Thames & Hudson, 1970.    274p.

2777  Lissitzky, E.  El Lissitzky:  life, letters, texts.  N.Y., Graphic Arts;
      L., Thames & Hudson, 1968.    407p.

2778  Lissitzky, E.  Russia:  an architecture for world revolution.  Cambridge
      Mass., MITP.;  L., Lund Humphries, 1970.    239p.

2779  Shvidkovsky, O.A.  Building in the U.S.S.R., 1917–1932.  N.Y., Praeger;
      L., Studio Vista, 1971.    144p.

2780  Voyce, A.  Russian architecture:  Trends in nationalism and modernism.
      N.Y., Philosophical Library, 1948.    306p.


H    Sculpture, Painting, Drawing.

2781  Arts Council of Great Britain.  Art in revolution:  Soviet art and desi-
      gn since 1917.  L., Arts Council, 1971.    113p.

2782  Berger, J.  Art and revolution:  Ernst Neizvestny and the role of the a-
      rtist in the U.S.S.R.  N.Y., Pantheon;  L., Weidenfeld & Nicolson, 1969.
      191p.

2783  Bojko, S.  New graphic design in revolutionary Russia.  L., Lund Humph-
      ries, 1972.    156p.

2784  Chen, J.  Soviet art and artists.  L., Pilot P., 1944.    106p.

2785  Conway, W.M.  Art treasures in Soviet Russia.  L., Arnold, 1925.    278p.

2786  Crocodile album of Soviet humour;  ed. by I. Montagu, H. Marshall.  L.,

Pilot P., 1943.    96p.

2787  Fahey, J.A.  A cartoon view of Russia.  N.Y., Vantage, 1968.    88p.

2788  Gray, C.  The great experiment:  modern Russian art.  N.Y., Abrams; L.,
      Thames & Hudson, 1962.    326p.

2789  Loukomsky, G.  History of modern Russian painting, 1840-1940.  L., Hutc-
      hinson, 1945.    184p.

2790  Malevich, K.S.  Essays on art, 1915-1933.  Chester Springs, Dufour;  L.,
      Rapp & Whiting, 1969.    2 vols.

2791  Milenkovitch, M.M.  The view from Red Square:  a critique of cartoons f-
      rom Pravda and Izvestia, 1947-1964.  N.Y., Hobbs, 1966.    162p.

2792  Nelson, W.  Out of the Crocodile's mouth:  Russian cartoons about the U-
      nited States from "Krokodil", Moscow's humour magazine.  Washington, Pu-
      blic Affairs, 1949.    116p.

2793  Soviet fine arts.  Moscow, Progress, 1970.    258p.

2794  Swearingen, R.  What's so funny, comrade?:  152 cartoons from "Krokodil"
      1958-1961 (the official Soviet humor magazine), stories from the humor-
      underground and scholarly commentary.  N.Y., Praeger, 1961.    156p.

V    TECHNOLOGY


A    General

2795  The training, placement and utilization of engineers and technicians in
      the Soviet Union.  N.Y., Engineers Joint Council, United States Exchange
      Mission to the U.S.S.R., 1961.    101p.


B    Agriculture

2796  Galton, D.  Survey of a thousand years of beekeeping in Russia.  Chalfont
      St Peter, Bee Research Association, 1971.    90p.


C    Industry

2797  American Steel and Iron Ore Delegation.  Steel in the Soviet Union:  the
      report of the American Steel and Iron Ore Delegation's visit to the Sov-
      iet Union, May and June 1958;  compiled by E.L. Ryerson.  N.Y., American
      Iron and Steel Institute, 1959.    376p.

2798  Bashkirov, S.I.  Hard metals production technology and research in the
      U.S.S.R.  N.Y., Macmillan, 1964.    351p.

2799  Hemy, G.W.  The Soviet chemical industry.  N.Y., Barnes & Noble; L., Hi-
      ll, 1971.    382p.

2800  Kaufman, A.  Small-scale industry in the Soviet Union.  N.Y., National
      Bureau of Economic Research, 1962.    95p.

2801  Hodgkins, J.A.  Soviet power:  energy resources, production and potenti-
      als.  Englewood Cliffs, Prentice, 1961.    190p.

2802  Kramish, A.  Atomic energy in the Soviet Union.  Stanford, Stanford U.P.,
      1959.    232p.

2803  Weitz, B.I.  Electric power development in the U.S.S.R.:  a collective
      study.  L., Lawrence & Wishart, 1937.    496p.


D    Building

2804  Kaganovich, L.M.  The socialist reconstruction of Moscow and other citi-
      es of the U.S.S.R.  Moscow, Co-operative Publishing Society of Foreign
      Workers, 1931.    125p.

2805  Simon, E.D. and others.  Moscow in the making.  L., Longmans, 1937. 253p

2806  U.S.S.R.  Council of Ministers.  State Committee on Planning.  Regulations
      and standards for the planning and development of towns, approved by Go-
      sstroi, on the authority of the U.S.S.R. Soviet of Ministers, 1st Decem-
      ber 1958; ed. by K. Watts and R. Hardbottle.  Boston Spa, National Lend-

ing Library for Science and Technology, 1962.    101p.

E    Transportation

2807    Garbutt, P.E.    Russian railways.    N.Y., Macdonald, 1949.    96p.

2808    Le Fleming, H.M., Price, J.H.    Russian steam locomotives.    L., Marshbank, 1960.    112p.

2809    Soviet merchant ships 1945-1968.    Havant, K. Mason, 1969.    280p.

2810    Stroud, J.    Soviet transport aircraft since 1945.    L., Pitman, 1968.318p

2811    Trilling, L.    Soviet education in aeronautics.    Cambridge, Mass., MIT Center for International Studies, 1956.    112p.

2812    Tverskoi, K.N.    The unified transport system of the U.S.S.R.    L., Gollancz, 1935.    176p.

2813    Westwood, J.N.    Soviet railways today.    N.Y., Citadel, 1964.; L., Allan, 1963.    192p.

2814    Williams, E.W. and others.    Freight transportation in the Soviet Union including comparisons with the United States.    Princeton, Princeton U.P., 1962.    221p.

2815    Yakovlev, A.    Notes of an aircraft designer.    Moscow, FLPH, 1961.    275p.

F    Land exploration

2816    Armstrong, T.    The northern sea route: Soviet exploration of the North East Passage.    Cambridge, Cambridge U.P., 1952.    162p.

2817    Armstrong, T.    The Russians of the Arctic: aspects of Soviet exploration and exploitation of the Far North, 1937-57.    N.Y., Essential; L., Methuen, 1958.    182p.

2818    Bardukov, G.    Over the North Pole.    L., Harrap, 1938.    110p.

2819    Bergman, S.    Through Kamchatka by dog-sled and skis: a vivid description of adventurous journeys among the interesting and almost unknown peoples of the most inaccessible parts of the remote Siberian peninsula.    L., Seeley Service, 1927.    284p.

2820    Brontman, L.K.    On top of the world: the Soviet expedition to the North Pole, 1937.    N.Y., Covici-Friede, 1938.    343p.; L., Gollancz,1938. 287p.

2821    Fame of the falcon: life stories of nine famous Soviet air aces.    L., Hutchinson, 1946.    104p.

2822    Giudici, D.    The tragedy of the 'Italia': with the rescuers to the Red Tent.    L., Benn, 1928.    216p.

2823   Gruber, R.   I went to the Soviet Arctic.   Rev. ed.   N.Y., Viking,   1944.
       320p.

2824   Hunt, Sir J., Brasher, C.   The red snows:   an account of the British Ca-
       ucasus Expedition.   L., Hutchinson, 1960.      175p.

2825   Khvat, L.K.B., Khvat, L.   The heroic flight of the Rodina.   Moscow, FLPH,
       1938.      107p.

2826   Matters, L.   Through the Kara Sea:   the narrative of a voyage in a tramp
       steamer through Arctic waters to the Yenisei River.   L., Skeffington,
       1932.      284p.

2827   Mogilevska, S.   The camp on the icefield.   L., Routledge, 1938.      232p.

2828   Papanin, I.D.   Life on an ice floe:   diary of Ivan Papanin.   N.Y., Mess-
       ner, 1939.   300p.;   L., Hutchinson, 1947.      240p.

2829   Parijanine, M.   The Krassin.   N.Y., Macaulay, 1928.      218p.

2830   Romm, M.   The ascent of Mt. Stalin.   L., Lawrence & Wishart, 1936. 270p.

2831   Slesser, M.   Red peak:   a personal account of the British-Soviet Pamir
       expedition.   N.Y., Coward;   L., Hodder & Stoughton, 1964.      256p.

2832   Smolka, H.P.   40,000 against the Arctic:   Russia's polar empire.   L.,
       Hutchinson, 1937.      288p.

2833   Soviet Antarctic Expedition:   information bulletin.   Amsterdam, Elsevier,
       1964.      2 vols.

2834   Soviet heroes;   ed. by I Montagu and H. Marshall.   L., Pilot P.,   1942.
       137p.

2835   Stefansson, V.   Unsolved mysteries of the Arctic.   L., Harrap,      1939.
       352p.

2836   Taracouzio, T.A.   Soviets in the Arctic:   an historical, economic and po-
       litical study of the Soviet advance into the Arctic.   N.Y., Macmillan,
       1938.      565p.

2837   Tolmachev, I.P.   Siberian passage:   an explorer's search into the Russi-
       an Arctic.   New Brunswick, Rutgers U.P., 1949.      238p.

2838   Unishevsky, V.   Red pilot:   memoirs of a Soviet airman.   L., Hurst & Bl-
       ackett, 1939.      260p.

2839   The voyage of the 'Chelyushkin' by members of the expedition.   L., Chat-
       to & Windus, 1935.      325p.


G      Space exploration

2840   Abbas, K.A.   Till we reach the stars:   the story of Yuri Gagarin.   L.,

Asia Publishing House, 1962.    145p.

2841  Bergaust, E.   The Russians in space.  N.Y., Putnam, 1969.    95p.

2842  Burchett, W., Purdy, A.   Gherman Titov's flight into space.  L., Hamilton, 1962.    156p.

2843  Burchett, W., Purdy, A.   Cosmonaut Yuri Gagarin:  first man in space.  L.,
Gibbs & Phillips, 1961.    187p.

2844  Caidin, M.   Red star in space.  N.Y., Crowell, 1963.    280p.

2845  Caidin, M.   War for the moon.  N.Y., Dutton, 1959.    258p.

2846  Gagarin, Y., Lebedev, V.   Survival in space.  N.Y., Praeger, 1969. 166p.

2847  Gatland, W.K.   Spacecraft and boosters:  the first comprehensive analysis of more than seventy U.S. and Soviet space launchings, 1961.    Los
Angeles, Aero Publishers;  L., Iliffe, 1964.    296p.

2848  Krieger, F.J.   Behind the sputniks:  a survey of Soviet space science.
Washington, Public Affairs P., 1958.    380p.

2849  Parry, A.   Russia's rockets and missiles.  L., Macmillan, 1960.    382p.

2850  Petrovich, G.V.   The Soviet encyclopedia of space flight.  Moscow, Mir
Publishers, 1969.    619p.

2851  Pikelner, S.B.   Soviet science of interstellar space.  N.Y., Philosophical Library, 1963.    230p.

2852  Riabchikov, E.   Russians in space.  Garden City, N.Y., Doubleday, 1971.;
L., Weidenfeld & Nicolson, 1972.    300p.

2853  Smolders, P.L.   Soviets in space:  the story of the Salyut and the Soviet approach to present and future space travel.  Rev. ed. Guildford, L-
utterworth, 1973.    285p.

2854  Sharpe, M.R.   Yuri Gagarin:  first man in space.  Huntsville, Strode,19-
69.    119p.

2855  Sheldon, C.S.   Review of the Soviet space program with comparative United States data.  N.Y., McGraw-Hill, 1968.    152p.

2856  Shelton, W.   Soviet space exploration:  the first decade.  L., Barker,
1969.    341p.

2857  Shternfield, A.   Soviet space science.  L., Hutchinson, 1959.    361p.

2858  Titov, G.S., Caidin, M.   I am eagle!  Indianapolis, Bobbs, 1962. 212p.

2859  Titov, G.S.   Gherman Titov, first man to spend a day in space:  the Soviet cosmonaut's autobiography as told to Pavel Barashev and Yuri Dokuchayev.  N.Y., Crosscurrents, 1962.    112p.

2860   Vassiliev, M.   Sputnik into space.   N.Y., Dial, 1958.   181p.;   L., Souv-
       enir, 1958.   147p.

2861   Vladimirov, L.   The Russian space bluff.   L., Tom Stacey, 1971.   192p.

2862   Wukelic, G.E.   Handbook of Soviet space-science research;   written by t-
       he staff and consultants of Battelle Memorial Institute, Columbus Labor-
       atories.   N.Y.;   L., Gordon & Breach, 1968.   505p.

2863   Zaehringer, A.J.   Soviet space technology.   N.Y., Harper, 1961.   179p.

VI    RELIGION

A    General

2864    Bach, M.   God and the Soviets. N.Y., Crowell, 1958.    214p.

2865    Benningsen, G.   Religion in Russia. L., Burns Oates, 1940.    110p.

2866    Casey, R.P.   Religion in Russia. N.Y., Harper, 1946.    198p.

2867    Conference in defence of peace of all churches and religious associat-
        ions in the U.S.S.R., held in Troitse-Sergiyeva Monastery, Zagorsk, on
        May 9-12, 1952. Moscow, Moscow Patriarchate, 1952.    286p.

2868    Conquest R.   Religion in the U.S.S.R.   N.Y., Praeger;   L., Bodley Head,
        1968.    135p.

2869    Cooke, R.J.   Religion in Russia under the Soviets. N.Y., Abingdon P.,
        1924.    311p.

2870    Emhardt, W.C.   Religion in Soviet Russia. L., Mowbray, 1929.    387p.

2871    Fletcher, W.C., Strover, A.J.   Religion and the search for new ideals in
        the U.S.S.R.   N.Y., Praeger, 1967.    135p.

2872    Grunwald, C de.   God and the Soviets. L., Hutchinson, 1961.    255p.

2873    Hayward, M., Fletcher, W.C.   Religion and the Soviet state:  a dilemma
        of power. L., Pall Mall P., 1969.    200p.

2874    Hecker, J.F.   Religion and communism:  a study of religion and atheism
        in Soviet Russia. L., Chapman & Hall, 1933.    303p.

2875    Hecker, J.F.   Religion under the Soviets. N.Y., Vanguard, 1927.    207p.

2876    Kline, G.   Religious and anti-religious thought in Russia. Chicago, U.
        of Chicago P., 1968.    179p.

2877    Kolarz, W.   Religion in the Soviet Union. N.Y., St. Martin's P.;   L.,
        Macmillan, 1961.    518p.

2878    MacEoin, G.   The communist war on religion. N.Y., Devon-Adair,    1951.
        264p.

2879    Marshall, R.H.   Aspects of religion in the Soviet Union, 1917-1967. Chi-
        cago, U. of Chicago P., 1971.    489p.

2880    Shuster, G.N.   Religion behind the Iron Curtain. N.Y., Macmillan, 1954.
        281p.

2881    Szczesniak, B.   The Russian revolution and religion:  a collection of do-
        cuments concerning the suppression of religion by the Communists    1917-
        1925. Notre Dame, U. of Notre Dame P., 1959.    289p.

2882  Timasheff, N.S.  Religion in Soviet Russia, 1917–1942.  N.Y.; L., Sheed & Ward, 1943.  171p.

2883  Valentinov, A.A.  The assault of heaven.  L., Boswell, 1925.  266p.

2884  Weiant, E.T.  Sources of modern mass atheism in Russia.  College Park, Md., The Author, 1953.  142p.


B  Christianity

2885  Almedingen, M.E.  The Catholic Church in Russia today.  L., Burns Oates, 1923.  132p.

2886  Anderson, P.B.  People, church and state in modern Russia.  N.Y., Macmillan, 1944.  240p.; L., Students' Christian Movement, 1944.  160p.

2887  Bales, J.D.  Two worlds: Christianity and Communism; study course for youth and adults.  Cincinnati, Standard, 1965.  128p.

2888  Bolshakoff, S.  Russian non–conformity: the story of "unofficial" religion in Russia.  Philadelphia, Westminster P., 1950.  192p.

2889  Bourdeaux, M.  Faith on trial in Russia.  N.Y., Harper, 1971.  192p.

2890  Bourdeaux, M.  Opium of the people: the Christian religion in the U.S.-S.R.  L., Faber, 1965.  233p.

2891  Bourdeaux, M.  Patriarch and prophets: persecution of the Russian Orthodox Church today.  N.Y., Praeger, 1970.; L., Macmillan, 1969.  359p.

2892  Cianfarra, C.M.  The Vatican and the Kremlin.  N.Y., Dutton, 1950. 258p.

2893  Ciszek, W.J., Flaherty, D.L.  With God in Russia.  N.Y., McGraw–Hill,1964.; L., P. Davies, 1965.  302p.

2894  Curtiss, J.S.  The Russian Church and the Soviet State, 1917–1950.  Boston, Mass., Little, 1953.  387p.

2895  Derrick, M.  Eastern Catholics under Soviet rule.  L., Sword of the Spirit, 1946.  62p.

2896  Durasoff, S.  The Russian Protestants: evangelicals in the Soviet Union 1944–1964.  Rutherford, Fairleigh Dickinson U.P., 1969.  312p.

2897  Evans, S.  Churches in the U.S.S.R.  L., Cobbett P., 1944.  160p.

2898  Father George.  God's underground; as told to Gretta Palmer.  N.Y., Appleton, 1949.  296p.; Through God's underground.  L., Hollis & Carter, 1949.  226p.

2899  Fedotoff, G.P.  The Russian church since the Revolution.  L., S.P.C.K., 1928.  96p.

2900   Fireside, H.   Icon and swastika:   the Russian Orthodox Church under Nazi and Soviet control.   Cambridge, Mass., Harvard U.P., 1971.   242p.

2901   Fletcher, W.C.   The Russian Orthodox Church underground, 1917-1970. N.Y.; L., Oxford U.P., 1971.   314p.

2902   Fletcher, W.C.   A study in survival:   the church in Russia, 1927-1943. N.Y., Macmillan; L., S.P.C.K., 1965.   169p.

2903   Grunwald, C.de.   The churches and the Soviet Union.   N.Y., Macmillan, 1962.   225p.

2904   Harris, R., Howard-Johnston, X.   Christian appeals from Russia.   L., Hodder & Stoughton, 1969.   159p.

2905   Harris, T.L.   Unholy pilgrimage.   N.Y., Round Table P.;   Edinburgh, Clark, 1937.   185p.

2906   Howard-Johnston, X., Bourdeaux, M.   Aida of Leningrad:   the story of Aida Skripnikova.   Reading, Gateway Outreach, 1972.   121p.

2907   Jackson, J.H.   Eternal flame:   the story of a preaching mission to Russia.   Philadelphia, Christian Education P., 1956.   125p.

2908   Johnston, J.   God's secret armies within the Soviet Empire.   N.Y., Putnam, 1954.   268p.;   God's secret armies.   L., Museum P., 1956.   221p.

2909   Kourdakov, S.   Sergei.   L., Oliphants, 1973.   205p.

2910   McCullagh, F.   The Bolshevik persecution of Christianity.   L., Murray, 1924.   329p.

2911   Mackenzie, F.A.   The Russian crucifixion:   the full story of the persecution of religion under Bolshevism.   L., Jarrolds, 1930.   140p.

2912   Parsons, H.L.   Christianity in Soviet Russia.   N.Y., American Institute for Marxist Studies, 1972.   72p.

2913   Pollock, J.C.   The faith of the Russian Evangelicals.   N.Y., McGraw-Hill, 1964.;   The Christians from Siberia.   L., Hodder & Stoughton, 1964. 190p.

2914   Russian Orthodox Church in the fight for peace.   Moscow, The Moscow Patriarchate, 1950.   129p.

2915   Simon, G.   Church, state and opposition in the U.S.S.R.   L., Hurst,1973.   248p.

2916   Spinka, M.   The church and the Russian Revolution.   N.Y., Macmillan,1927.   320p.

2917   Spinka, M.   The church in Soviet Russia.   N.Y.;   L., Oxford U.P., 1956.   179p.

2918   Stroyen, W.B.   Communist Russia and the Russian Orthodox Church   1943-

1962. Washington, Catholic U. of America, 1967.     161p.

2919 Strube, W.P.  The star over the Kremlin.  Grand Rapids, Baker Bks., 1962.
     108p.

2920 Struve, N.  Christians in contemporary Russia.  2nd ed.  N.Y., Scribners,
     1967.; L., Collins, 1966.     464p.

2921 Telepun, L.M.  The bloody footsteps.  N.Y., Vantage, 1954.     145p.

2922 The truth about religion in Russia; issued by the Moscow Patriarchate.
     L., Hutchinson, 1944.     175p.

2923 Wurmbrand, R.  Underground saints.  Old Tappan, Revell, 1969.  207p.;The
     Soviet saints.  L., Hodder & Stoughton, 1968.     189p.

2924 Zatko, J.J.  Descent into darkness:  the destruction of the Roman Catho-
     lic Church in Russia, 1917-1923.  Notre Dame, U. of Notre Dame P., 1965.
     232p.

2925 Zernov, N.  The Russian religious renaissance of the twentieth century.
     N.Y., Harper, 1964.; L., Darton, 1963.     410p.


C    Islam

2926 Benningsen, A., Lemercier-Quelquejay, C.  Islam in the Soviet Union. N.Y.,
     Praeger; L., Pall Mall P., 1967.     272p.

2927 Central Asian Research Centre and Oxford University.  St Antony's Colle-
     ge.  Soviet Affairs Study Group. Islam and Russia:  a detailed analysis
     of "An outline of the history of Islamic studies in the U.S.S.R." by N.
     A. Smirnov, with an introduction by A.K.S. Lambton.  L., Luzac,   1956.
     87p.

2928 Hakim, K.A.  Islam and communism.  2nd ed.  Lahore, Institute of Islamic
     Culture, 1962.     263p.

2929 Institute for the study of the U.S.S.R.  Islam and communism:  a confer-
     ence.  Munich, 1960.     72p.

2930 Spector, I.  The Soviet Union and the Muslim world, 1917-1956.  Seattle,
     U. of Washington P., 1956.     151p.

2931 Vakhabov, A.  Islam in the U.S.S.R.  Moscow, Novosti P.  Agency Publish-
     ing House, 1972.     138p.

2932 Zenkovsky, S.A.  Pan-Turkism and Islam in Russia.  Cambridge, Mass., Ha-
     rvard U.P., 1960.     345p.


D    Judaism

2933 Baron, S.W.  The Russian Jew under Tsars and Soviets.  N.Y., Macmillan;

L., Collier—Macmillan, 1964.    427p.

2934   Cang, J.   The silent millions:   a history of the Jews in the Soviet Union.  L., Rapp & Whiting, 1969.    246p.

2935   Cohen, R.   Let my people go!:   today's documentary story of Soviet Jewr-
y's struggle to be free.  N.Y., Popular Library, 1971.    286p.

2936   Dennen, L.   Where the ghetto ends:   Jews in Soviet Russia.  N.Y., King,
1934.    254p.

2937   Eliav, A.L.   Between hammer and sickle.  Rev. ed.  N.Y., New American L-
ibrary, 1969.    237p.

2938   Gilboa, Y.A.   The black years of Soviet Jewry, 1939—1953.  Boston, Mass.
Little, 1971.    418p.

2939   Gitelman, Z.Y.   Jewish nationality and Soviet politics:   the Jewish sections of the C.P.S.U., 1917—1930.  Princeton, Princeton U.P., 1972. 573p

2940   Goldberg, B.Z.   The Jewish problem in the Soviet Union:   analysis and s-
olution.  N.Y., Crown, 1961.    374p.

2941   Goldberg, D.   Sussman sees it through:   a reappraisal of the Jewish position under the Soviets.  N.Y., Bloch, 1935.    244p.

2942   Goldman, G.G.   Zionism under Soviet rule, 1917—1928.  N.Y., Herzl  P.,
1960.    136p.

2943   Greenbaum, A.A.   Jewish scholarship in Soviet Russia, 1918—1941.  Boston,
Mass., The Author, 1959.    148p.

2944   Heifetz, E.   The slaughter of the Jews in the Ukraine in 1919.  N.Y., S-
eltzer, 1921.    408p.

2945   Kochan, L.   The Jews in Soviet Russia since 1917.  2nd ed.  N.Y.;   L.,
Oxford U.P., 1972.    377p.

2946   Rothenberg, J.   The Jewish religion in the Soviet Union.  N.Y., Ktav,
1972.    242p.

2947   Rubin, R.I.   The unredeemed:   anti—Semitism in the Soviet Union.  Chicago, Quadrangle, 1968.    316p.

2948   Rusinek, A.   Like a song, like a dream:   a Soviet girl's quest for freedom.  N.Y., Scribner, 1973.    267p.

2949   Schectman, J.B.   Star in eclipse:   Russian Jewry revisited.  N.Y.;  L.,
Yoseloff, 1962.    255p.

2950   Schulman, E.   A history of Jewish education in the Soviet Union.  N.Y.,
Ktav, 1971.    184p.

2951   Schwarz, S.N.   The Jews in the Soviet Union.  Syracuse, Syracuse U.P.,

1951.    380p.

2952   Skoczylas, E.   The realities of Soviet anti-semitism.   Philadelphia, U.
       of Pennsylvania, Foreign Policy Research Institute, 1964.    72p.

2953   Smolar, B.   Soviet Jewry today and tomorrow.   N.Y., Macmillan,    1971.
       228p.

2954   Wiesel, E.   The Jews of silence.   2nd ed. L., Vallentine, Mitchell, 1973.
       141p.

2955   Zander, W.   Soviet Jewry, Palestine and the West.   L., Gollancz,   1947.
       109p.

A    General

2956   Abramovitch, R.R.   The Soviet revolution 1917, 1939.   N.Y., International Universities P.;   L., Allen & Unwin, 1962.    473p.

2957   Andics, H.   Rule of terror.   N.Y., Holt;   L., Constable, 1969.    208p.

2958   Aragon, L.   A history of the U.S.S.R: from Lenin to Khrushchev.   N.Y., McKay;   L., Weidenfeld & Nicolson, 1964.    684p.

2959   Basily, N. de.   Russia under Soviet rule: twenty years of Bolshevik experiment.   L., Allen & Unwin, 1938.    508p.

2960   Best, H.   The Soviet experiment.   N.Y., R.R. Smith, 1941.    120p.

2961   Carr, E.H.   A history of Soviet Russia.   N.Y., Macmillan;   L., Macmillan, 1950-    Vol.1-
       Vol. 1.   The Bolshevik revolution, 1917-1923.   3 vols.
       Vol. 2.   The Interregnum, 1923-1924.
       Vol. 3.   Socialism in one country, 1924-1926.   3 vols.
       Vol. 4.   (with R.W. Davies) Foundations of a planned economy, 1926-1929.
                 2 vols.

2962   Chamberlin, W.H.   Soviet Russia: a living record and a history.   L., Duckworth, 1930.    453p.

2963   Coates, W.P. Coates, Z.K.   From Tsardom to the Soviet constitution.   L., Allen & Unwin, 1938.    320p.

2964   Dallin, D.J.   From purge to coexistence: essays on Stalin's & Khrushchev's Russia.   Chicago, Regnery, 1964.    289p.

2965   Daniels, R.V.   The conscience of the revolution: Communist opposition in Soviet Russia.   Cambridge, Mass., Harvard U.P., 1960.    526p.

2966   Deutscher, I.   Heretics and renegades, and other essays;   with a new introduction by E.H. Carr.   L., Cape, 1969.    228p.

2967   Deutscher, I.   The unfinished revolution: Russia 1917-1967.   N.Y.; L., Oxford U.P., 1967.    115p.

2968   Dmytryshyn, B.   U.S.S.R.: a concise history.   N.Y., Scribner's, 1965.    620p.

2969   Duranty, W.   The U.S.S.R.: the story of Soviet Russia.   Philadelphia, Lippincott;   L., Hamilton, 1944.    293p.

2970   Drachkovitch, M.M.   Fifty years of communism in Russia.   University Park, Pennsylvania State U.P., 1968.    316p.

2971   East, W.G.   The Soviet Union.   Princeton, Van Nostrand, 1963.    136p.

2972  Fischer, L.  Men and politics.  L., Cape, 1941.   639p.

2973  Goldston, R.C.  The Soviets:  a pictorial history of Communist Russia.
N.Y., Bantam, 1967.   252p.

2974  Grey, I.  The first fifty years:  Soviet Russia, 1917-1967.  N.Y., Coward;  L., Hodder & Stoughton, 1967.   558p.

2975  Guins, G.C.  Communism on the decline.  L., Batsford, 1957.   287p.

2976  Hindus, M.  House without roof:  Russia after forty-three years of revolution.  Carden City, N.Y., Doubleday, 1961.;  L., Gollancz,1962. 562p.

2977  Hindus, M.  The Kremlin's human dilemma:  Russia after half a century of
revolution.  Carden City, N.Y., Doubleday, 1967.   395p.

2978  Hird, J.W.  Under Czar and Soviet:  my thirty years in Russia.  L., Hurst & Blackett, 1932.   287p.

2979  Holt, R.T., Turner, J.E.  Soviet Union:  paradox and change.  N.Y., Holt,
1962.   204p.

2980  Huberman, L. and others.  50 years of Soviet power.  N.Y.;  L., Monthly
Review P., 1967.   94p.

2981  Hudson, G.F.  Fifty years of communism:  theory and practice, 1917-1967.
Harmondsworth, Penguin, 1971.   229p.

2982  Hyde, N.V., Hyde, F.  Russia then and always.  N.Y., Coward, 1944. 331p.

2983  Ielita-Wilczkovski, C.  Before and after Stalin.  L., Selwyn & Blount,
1939.   251p.

2984  International Conference on World Politics, 6th, Berlin, 1967.  The Soviet Union:  a half century of communism;  ed. by K. London.  Baltimore,
Johns Hopkins P., 1968.   493p.

2985  Kanet, R., Volgyes, I.  On the road to communism:  essays on Soviet domestic and foreign policies.  Lawrence, U.P. of Kansas, 1972.   212p.

2986  Katkov, G., Shukman, H.  Lenin's path to power:  Bolshevism and the destiny of Russia.  L., BPC Unit 75, 1971.   128p.

2987  Kautsky, K.  Bolshevism at a deadlock.  L., Allen & Unwin, 1931.   193p.

2988  Kieser, G.  Why is Russia so strong?:  the foundations of Russia's strength.  Bienne, Chaseral, 1945.   264p.

2989  Lamont, C.  Soviet civilization.  N.Y., Philosophical Library, 1952. 433p.

2990  Liberman, S.  Building Lenin's Russia.  Chicago, U. of Chicago P., 1945.
288p.

2991  Lin Yutang.  The secret name:  the Soviet record 1917-1958.  L., Heinemann, 1959.    234p.

2992  Lyons, E.  Workers' paradise lost:  fifty years of Soviet communism;  a
balance sheet.  N.Y., Funk & Wagnalls, 1967.    387p.

2993  McNeal, R.H.  The Russian revolution:  why did the Bolsheviks win?  N.Y.,
Rinehart, 1959.    62p.

2994  Miller, W.  The U.S.S.R.  N.Y.;  L., Oxford U.P., 1963.    126p.

2995  Monkhouse, A.  Moscow, 1911-1933:  being the memoirs of Allan Monkhouse.
L., Gollancz, 1933.    349p.

2996  Nenarokov, A.P.  Russia in the twentieth century:  the view of a Russian
history.  N.Y., Morrow, 1968.    309p.

2997  Nettl, J.P.  The Soviet achievement.  N.Y., Harcourt;  L., Thames & Hudson, 1967.    288p.

2998  Nicolaevsky, B.I.  Power and the Soviet elite:  "The letter of an old B-
olshevik" and other essays;  ed. by J.D.Zagoria.  Stanford, Hoover Institution;  N.Y., Praeger, 1965.    275p.

2999  Pankratova, A.M.  A history of the U.S.S.R.  Moscow, FLPH, 1948.  3 vols.

3000  Pethybridge, R.W.  A history of postwar Russia.  N.Y., New American Library;  L., Allen & Unwin, 1966.    263p.

3001  Rauch, G. von.  A history of Soviet Russia.  6th ed. N.Y., Praeger;  L.,
Pall Mall P., 1972.    541p.

3002  Rieber, A.J., Nelson, R.C.  A study of the U.S.S.R. and Communism:    an
historical approach.  Chicago, Scott Foresman, 1962.    256p.

3003  Riha, T.  Readings in Russian civilization.  2nd ed.  Vol.3:  Soviet Russia, 1917-present.  Chicago, U. of Chicago P., 1969.    501-844p.

3004  Rothstein, A.  A history of the U.S.S.R.  Harmondsworth, Penguin, 1950.
384p.

3005  Salisbury, H.E,  The Soviet Union:  the fifty years.  N.Y., Harcourt,
1967.; Anatomy of the Soviet Union.  L., Nelson, 1967.    484p.

3006  Schuman, F.L.  Russia since 1917:  four decades of Soviet politics. N.Y.,
Knopf, 1957.    508p.

3007  Schwartz, H.  The red phoenix:  Russia since World War II.  N.Y., Praeger, 1961.    427p.

3008  Serge, V.  From Lenin to Stalin.  2nd ed.  N.Y., Monad P., 1973.    160p.

3009  Smirnov, I.I. and others.  A short history of the U.S.S.R.  N.Y., Universal Distributors, 1965.    334p.

3010   Sternberg, F.   The end of a revolution:   Soviet Russia from revolution
       to reaction.   L., Gollancz, 1953.      191p.

3011   Tokaev, G.A.   Betrayal of an ideal.   L., Collins, 1954.      298p.

3012   Treadgold, D.W.   The development of the U.S.S.R.:   an exchange of views.
       Seattle, U. of Washington P., 1964.      399p.

3013   Treadgold, D.W.   Twentieth century Russia.   3rd ed.   Chicago, Rand McNal-
       ly, 1971.      563p.

3014   Ulam, A.B.   The Bolsheviks:   the intellectual and political history of
       the triumph of Communism in Russia.   N.Y., Macmillan, 1965.; Lenin and
       the Bolsheviks:   the intellectual and political history of the triumph
       of Communism in Russia.   L., Secker & Warburg, 1966.      598p.

3015   Von Laue, T.M.   Why Lenin?   Why Stalin?   A reappraisal of the Russian r-
       evolution, 1900-1930.   Philadelphia, Lippincott, 1964.;   L., Weidenfeld
       & Nicolson, 1966.      242p.

3016   Werth, A.   Russia:   the post-war years;   epilogue by H.E. Salisbury.  N.-
       Y., Taplinger;   L., Hale, 1971.      446p.

3017   Westwood, J.N.   Russia 1917-1964.   N.Y., Harper;   L., Batsford, 1966.
       208p.

3018   Wolfe, B.D.   An ideology in power:   reflections on the Russian revolut-
       ion.   N.Y., Stein;   L., Allen & Unwin, 1969.      406p.

3019   Wood, S.H.   Russia in the early twentieth century:   1904-1924.   Bath, B-
       rodie, 1965.      100p.


B      The October Revolution

(i)    General

3020   Adams, A.E.   The Russian Revolution and Bolshevik victory:   causes and
       processes.   2nd ed.   Lexington, Heath, 1972.      196p.

3021   Astrov, E. and others.   Illustrated history of the Russian Revolution.
       L., Lawrence, 1928.      2 vols

3022   Beatty, B.   The red heart of Russia.   N.Y.;   L., Century, 1918.      480p.

3023   Berdyaev, N.   The Russian Revolution.   Ann Arbor, U. of Michigan P.,1961.
       91p.

3024   Best, H.   The Soviet state and its inception.   N.Y., Philosophical Libr-
       ary, 1951.      448p.

3025   Beury, C.E.   Russia after the Revolution.   Philadelphia, Jacobs,   1918.
       138p.

3026  Brinton, C.  The anatomy of revolution.  Rev. ed.  N.Y., Random, 1965.
310p.

3027  Bunyan, J.  Fisher, H.H.  The Bolshevik Revolution, 1917-1918:  docum —
ents and materials.  Stanford, Stanford U.P., 1934.    735p.

3028  Bykov, P.M.  The last days of Tsardom.  L., Lawrence, 1937.    90p.

3029  Carmichael, J.  A short history of the Russian Revolution.  N.Y., Basic,
1964.;  L., Nelson, 1965.    256p.

3030  Carr, E.H.  The October Revolution:  before and after.  N.Y., Knopf,1969.;
1917:  before and after.  L., Macmillan, 1969.    178p.

3031  Cash, A.  The Russian Revolution.  Carden City, N.Y., Doubleday,1969.; L.,
Benn, 1967.    145p.

3032  Chamberlin, W.H.  The Russian Revolution, 1917-1927.  N.Y.;  L., Macmillan, 1935.    2 vols.

3033  Curtiss, J.S.  The Russian Revolution of 1917.  Princeton, Van Nostrand;
L., Macmillan, 1957.    191p.

3034  Daniels, R.V.  Red October:  the Bolshevik Revolution  of 1917.  N.Y.,
Scribners;  L., Secker & Warburg, 1968.    269p.

3035  Daniels, R.V.  The Russian Revolution.  Englewood Cliffs, Prentice-Hall,
1972.    184p.

3036  Dorr, R.L.C.  Inside the Russian Revolution.  N.Y., Macmillan,1917.243p.

3037  Dziewanowski, M.K.  The Russian Revolution:  an anthology.  N.Y., Crowell, 1970.    222p.

3038  Fisher, J.  The true book about the Russian Revolution.  L., Muller, 19-
60.    144p.

3039  Footman, D.  The Russian revolutions.  N.Y., Putnam, 1964.;  L., Faber,
1962.    140p.

3040  Goldston, R.  The Russian Revolution.  Indianapolis, Bobbs, 1966.;  L.,
Phoenix, 1967.    224p.

3041  Halliday, E.M.  Russia in revolution by the editors of 'Horizon' magazine.
L., Cassell, 1968.    153p.

3042  Hingley, R.  Russian Revolution.  L., Bodley Head, 1970.    128p.

3043  Kochan, L.  Russia in revolution, 1890-1918.  N.Y., New American Library,
1966.    365p.

3044  Kochan, L.  The Russian Revolution.  L., Wayland, 1971.    128p.

3045  Lecar, H.  The Russian Revolution:  a concise history and interpretation.

N.Y., Ardmore, 1967.    149p.

3046  Liebman, M.  The Russian Revolution:  the origins, phases and meaning of
      the Bolshevik victory.  N.Y., Random;  L., Cape, 1970.    389p.

3047  Luxemburg, R.  The Russian Revolution, and Leninism or Marxism?;  new i-
      ntro. by B.D. Wolfe.  Ann Arbor, U. of Michigan P., 1961.    189p.

3048  Melgunov, S.P.  The Bolshevik seizure of power;  ed. by S.G. Pushkarev
      and B.S. Pushkarev.  Santa Barbara, American Bibliographical Center-Clio
      P.;  Oxford, European Bibliographical Center—Clio P., 1972.    260p.

3049  Meyendorff, A., Baron.  The background of the Russian Revolution.  L.,
      Bell, 1929.    193p.

3050  Moorehead, A.  Russian Revolution.  N.Y., Harper;  L., Collins, 1958.
      310p.

3051  Pearlstein, E.W.  Revolution in Russia!:  as reported by the 'New York
      Tribune' and the 'New York Herald', 1894—1921.  N.Y., Viking,1967. 297p.

3052  Peck, I.  The Russian Revolution.  N.Y., Scholastic, 1967.    126p.

3053  Pethybridge, R.  The spread of the Russian Revolution:  essays on 1917.
      N.Y., St Martin's P.;  L., Macmillan, 1972.    238p.

3054  Pethybridge, R.  Witnesses to the Russian Revolution.  N.Y., Citadel,
      1968.;  L., Allen & Unwin, 1964.    308p.

3055  Petrunkevitch, A. and others.  The Russian Revolution.  Cambridge, Mass.,
      Harvard U.P., 1918.    109p.

3056  Pipes, R.  The formation of the Soviet Union:  communism and nationalism,
      1917—1923.  Rev. ed. Cambridge, Mass., Harvard U.P., 1964.    365p.

3057  Pipes, R.  Revolutionary Russia.  Cambridge, Mass., Harvard U.P., 1968.
      365p.

3058  Reed, J.  Ten days that shook the world.  N.Y., Boni & Liveright, 1919.
      371p.

3059  Roy, M.N.  Russian Revolution.  Calcutta, Renaissance, 1949.    632p.

3060  Rossif, F., Chapsal, M.  Portrait of a revolution;  Russia, 1896—1924.
      Boston, Little, 1969.    160p.

3061  Serge, V.  Year one of the Russian Revolution.  Chicago, Holt;  L., All-
      en Lane, 1972.    436p.

3062  Shukman, H.  Lenin and the Russian Revolution.  L., Batsford, 1966. 224p.

3063  Sorokin, P.A.  The sociology of revolution.  N.Y., Lippincott,1925. 428p

3064  Stepun, F.  The Russian soul and revolution.  N.Y., Scribner's, 1936.

184p.

3065  Trotsky, L.  From October to Brest-Litovsk.  N.Y., The Socialist Public-
      ation Society, 1919.  100p.;  History of the Russian Revolution to Brest
      -Litovsk, L., Allen & Unwin, 1919.    149p.

3066  Trotsky, L.  The history of the Russian Revolution.  N.Y., Simon & Schu-
      ster, 1932.;  L., Gollancz, 1932-33.    3 vols.

3067  Tyrkova-Williams, A.  From liberty to Brest-Litovsk.  L., Macmillan,1919.
      526p.

3068  Vandervelde, E.  Three aspects of the Russian Revolution.  N.Y., Scribn-
      er's;  L., Allen & Unwin, 1918.    241p.

3069  Voline.(= Eichenbaum, V.M.)  Nineteen-Seventeen:  the Russian Revolution
      betrayed.  N.Y., Libertarian Bk. Club;  L., Freedom P., 1954.    269p.

3070  Von Mohrenschildt, D.S.  The Russian Revolution of 1917:  contemporary
      accounts.  N.Y.;  L., Oxford U.P., 1971.    320p.

3071  Von York, T.  Russia's road to revolution:  a social, cultural and inte-
      llectual history of the Russian Revolution of 1917.  Boston, Mass., Chr-
      istopher Pub., 1963.    200p.

3072  Walsh, E.A.  The fall of the Russian Empire.  L., Williams & Norgate,
      1928.    357p.

3073  Werstein, I.  Ten days in November:  the Russian Revolution.  Philadel-
      phia, Macrae, 1967.    191p.

3074  Wolfe, B.D.  Three who made a revolution:  a biographical history. 4th
      ed.  N.Y., Dial, 1964.    661p.

(ii)  Special aspects

3075  Andreyev, A.  The Soviets of Workers' and Soldiers' deputies on the eve
      of the October Revolution, March-October, 1971.  Moscow, Progress, 1971.
      356p.

3076  Avrich, P.  The anarchists in the Russian Revolution.  Ithaca, Cornell
      U.P.;  L., Thames & Hudson, 1973.    179p.

3077  Bashkiroff, Z.  Nights are longest there.  N.Y., Holt, 1961.  286p.; The
      sickle and the harvest.  L., Spearman, 1960.    224p.

3078  Hindus, M.G.  The Russian peasant and the Revolution.  N.Y., Holt, 1920.
      323p.

3079  Owen, L.O.  The Russian peasant movement, 1906-1917.  L., King,  1937.
      267p.

3080  Poole, E.  'The dark people':  Russia's crisis.  N.Y., Macmillan, 1919.
      226p.

3081   Poole, E.  The village:  Russian impressions.  N.Y., Macmillan,   1919.
       234p.

3082   Radkey, O.H.  The agrarian foes of Bolshevism:  promise  and default of
       the Russian socialist revolutionaries, February to October, 1917.  N.Y.,
       Columbia U.P., 1958.    521p.

3083   Radkey, O.H.  The election to the Russian Constituent Assembly of 1917.
       Cambridge, Mass., Harvard U.P., 1950.    89p.

3084   Radkey, O.H.  The sickle under the hammer:  the Russian Socialist Revol-
       utionaries in the early months of Soviet rule.  N.Y., Columbia U.P.,1963
       525p.

3085   Worth, R.D.  The allies and the Russian Revolution:  from the fall of t-
       he monarchy to the Peace of Brest-Litovsk.  Durham, N.C., Duke U.P.1954.
       294p.

(iii)  Personal accounts

3086   Boleslawski, R., Woodward, H.  Lances down.  L., Grayson, 1933.    296p.

3087   Botchkareva, M.  Yashka:  my life as peasant, exile and soldier.  L., C-
       onstable, 1919.    339p.

3088   Bryant, L.  Six red months in Russia:  an observer's account of Russia
       before and during the proletarian dictatorship.  L., Heinemann,   1919.
       299p.

3089   Buchanan, M.  Petrograd:  the city of trouble, 1914-1918.  L., Collins,
       1918.    282p.

3090   Buchanan, Sir G.  My mission to Russia, and other diplomatic memories.
       L., Cassell, 1923.    2 vols.

3091   Cantacuzene, Princess.  Revolutionary days:  recollections of Romanoffs
       and Bolsheviki, 1914-1917.  L., Chapman & Hall, 1920.    411p.

3092   Crosley, P.S.  Intimate letters from Petrograd.  N.Y., Dutton,   1920.
       305p.

3093   Dosch-Fleurot, A.  Through war to revolution:  being the experiences of
       a newspaper correspondent in war and revolution, 1914-1920.  L.,  Lane,
       1931.    242p.

3094   Eastman, M.  Love and revolution:  my journey through an epoch.  N.Y.,
       Random, 1965.    665p.

3095   Francis, D.R.  Russia from the American embassy, April 1916-November 19-
       18.  N.Y., Scribner's,1922.    349p.

3096   Hard, W.  Raymond Robins' own story.  N.Y., Harper, 1920.    248p.

3097   Harper, F.M.  Runaway Russia.  N.Y., Century, 1918.    321p.

3098    Heald, E.T.  Witness to revolution:  letters from Russia, 1916-1919. Kent, Kent State U.P., 1972.    367p.

3099    Hoare, S.J.G.  The fourth seal:  the end of a Russian chapter.  L., Heinemann, 1930.    377p.

3100    Houghteling, J.L.  A diary of the Russian Revolution.  N.Y., Dodd, 1918.  195p.

3101    Ilyin-Genevsky, A.F.  From the February Revolution to the October Revolution, 1917.  L., Modern Bks, 1931.    122p.

3102    Jones, S.  Russia in revolution:  being the experiences of an Englishman in Petrograd during the upheaval.  L., Herbert Jenkins, 1917.    279p.

3103    Keeling, H.V.  Bolshevism:  Mr. Keeling's five years in Russia.  L., Hodder & Stoughton, 1919.    212p.

3104    Kehler, H.  The red garden.  N.Y., Knopf, 1922.    204p.

3105    Lockhart, R.H.B.  Memoirs of a British agent.  L., Putnam, 1932.  355p.

3106    Lockhart, R.H.B.  The two revolutions:  an eye-witness study of Russia, 1917.  L., Phoenix, 1957.    116p.

3107    Loukomsky, A.  Memoirs of the Russian Revolution.  L., Fisher Unwin,1922.  256p.

3108    Meyendorff, Baroness S.Z.  Through terror to freedom:  the dramatic story of an Englishwoman's life and adventures in Russia before, during and after the Revolution.  L., Hutchinson, 1929.    288p.

3109    Mikhelson, A.L.  A schoolboy caught in the Russian Revolution:  the record of a nightmare adolescence.  L., Putnam, 1935.    218p.

3110    Pollock, J.  The Bolshevik adventure.  L., Constable, 1919.    279p.

3111    Pollock, J.  War and revolution in Russia:  sketches and studies.  L., Constable, 1918.    280p.

3112    Ponafidine, E.C.  Russia:  my home;  an intimate record of personal experiences before, during and after the Bolshevik Revolution.  N.Y., Blue Ribbon Bks., 1931.    312p.

3113    Power, R.  Under the Bolshevik reign of terror.  N.Y., McBride,  1919.  279p.

3114    Price, M.P.  My reminiscences of the Russian Revolution.  L., Allen & Unwin, 1921.    388p.

3115    Riis, S.M.  Yankee Komisar.  N.Y., Speller, 1935.    236p.

3116    Ross, E.A.  Russia in upheaval.  N.Y., Century, 1919.    349p.

3117    Robien, L., <u>Comte de</u>. The diary of a diplomat in Russia, 1917–1918.  N.
        Y., Praeger, 1970.;  L., Joseph, 1969.    318p.

3118    Sayler, O.M.  Russia: white or red.  Boston, Mass., Little, 1919. 303p.

3119    Sisson, E.G.  One hundred red days, 25 Nov. 1917–4 March 1918:  a person-
        al chronicle of the Bolshevik Revolution.  New Haven, Yale U.P.,   1931.
        502p.

3120    Skariatina, I.  A world can end.  L., Cape, 1931.    351p.

3121    Stebbing, E.P.  From Czar to Bolshevik.  L., Lane, 1918.    322p.

3122    Steinberg, I.N.  In the workshop of the revolution.  N.Y., Rinehart,1953.
        L., Gollancz, 1955.    306p.

3123    Sukhanov, N.N.  The Russian Revolution 1917: a personal record;  ed. by
        J. Carmichael.  N.Y.;  L., Oxford U.P., 1955.    691p.

3124    Wightman, O.S.  The diary of an American physician in the Russian Revol-
        ution, 1917.  N.Y., Brooklyn Daily Eagle, 1928.    230p.

3125    Wilcox, E.H.  Russia's ruin.  L., Chapman & Hall, 1919.    316p.

3126    Williams, A.R.  Journey into revolution: Petrograd, 1917–1918.  Chicago,
        Quadrangle, 1969.    346p.

3127    Williams, A.R.  Through the Russian Revolution.  N.Y., Boni & Liveright,
        1921.  286p.;  L., Labour Publishing Co., 1923.    311p.

3128    Wilton, R.  Russia's agony.  L., Arnold, 1918.    356p.

3129    Woytinsky, E.  Two lives in one.  N.Y., Praeger, 1965.    324p.

3130    Yarkovsky, J.M.  It happened in Moscow.  N.Y., Vantage, 1961.    301p.


C    War communism, and the New Economic Policy

(i)    General

3131    Avrich, P.  Kronstadt, 1921.  Princeton, Princeton U.P., 1970.    271p.

3132    Brailsford, H.N.  The Russian workers' republic.  L., Allen & Unwin,1921
        206p.

3133    British Labour Delegation to Russia, 1920.  Report.  L., Labour Party,
        1921.    151p.

3134    Bulygin, P.  The murder of the Romanovs.  L., Hutchinson, 1935.    286p.

3135    Bunyan, J.  Intervention, civil war and communism in Russia, April–Dece-
        mber 1918:  documents and materials.  Baltimore, Johns Hopkins P., 1936.
        594p.

3136  Fisher, H.H.  The famine in Soviet Russia, 1919–1923:  the operations of the American Relief Administration.  N.Y., Macmillan, 1927.  609p.

3137  Fry, A.R.  A Quaker adventure:  the story of nine years' relief and administration.  L., Nisbet, 1926.  389p.

3138  Godden, G.M.  Russia under the red flag:  a record of socialism in our time.  L., Burns Oates, 1929.  194p.

3139  Golder, F.A., Hutchinson, L.  On the trail of the Russian famine.  Stanford, Stanford U.P., 1927.  319p.

3140  Goode, W.T.  Bolshevism at work.  L., Allen & Unwin, 1920.  142p.

3141  Gorky, M. **and others.**  History of the Civil War in the U.S.S.R.  L., Lawrence & Wishart, 1937–47.  2 vols.

3142  Hiebert, P.C., Miller, O.O.  Feeding the hungry:  Russian famine, 1919–1925;  American Mennonite relief operations under the auspicies of Mennonite Central Committee.  Scottdale, Mennonite Central Committee, 1929.  465p.

3143  Lawton, L.  The Russian revolution, 1917–1926.  L., Macmillan,  1926.  524p.

3144  Lewin, M.  Lenin's last struggle.  N.Y., Pantheon, 1968.;  L., Faber, 1969.  193p.

3145  Miliukov, P.N.  Russia today and tomorrow.  L., Macmillan, 1922.  392p.

3146  Miller, F.  The wild children of the Urals.  N.Y., Dutton, 1965.  751p.

3147  O'Conor, J.F.  The Sokolov investigation of the alleged murder of the Russian Imperial Family:  a translation of sections of Nicholas A. Sokolov 'The murder of the Imperial Family'.  N.Y., Speller, 1971.  257p.;  L., Souvenir P., 1972.  271p.

3148  Pipes, R.E.  The formation of the Soviet Union:  communism and nationalism, 1917–1923.  Cambridge, Mass., Harvard U.P., 1954.  355p.

3149  Pollack, E.  The Kronstadt rebellion:  the first armed rebellion against the Soviets.  N.Y., Philosophical Library, 1959.  98p.

3150  Ransome, A.M.  The crisis in Russia.  L., Allen & Unwin, 1921.  152p.

3151  The restoration of culture in the famine areas of Russia:  being the interim report of the State Economic Planning Commission of the Council for Labour and Defence of the R.S.F.S.R.  L., Labour Publishing Co.,  1922.  167p.

3152  Rosmer, A.  Moscow under Lenin.  N.Y., Monthly Review P., 1972.;  Lenin's Moscow.  L., Pluto P., 1971.  253p.

3153  Ross, E.A.  The Russian Soviet Republic.  L., Allen & Unwin, 1923.  405p.

3154  Step, E.S.  The Kronstadt thesis for a free Russian government.  N.Y.,
      Speller, 1964.    134p.

3155  Voline.(=Eichenbaum, V.M.)  The unknown revolution (Kronstadt 1921, Uk-
      raine 1918-21)  N.Y., Libertarian Bk. Club, 1956.;  L., Freedom P.,1955.
      270p.

3156  Willis, E.F.  Herbert Hoover and the Russian prisoners of World War I: a
      study in diplomacy and relief, 1918-1919.  Stanford, Stanford    U.P.,
      1951.    67p.

(ii)  The Civil War and Intervention

3157  Ackerman, C.W.  Trailing the Bolsheviks:  twelve thousand miles with the
      Allies in Siberia.  N.Y., Scribner's, 1919.    308p.

3158  Albertson, R.  Fighting without a war:  an account of military interven-
      tion in North Russia.  N.Y., Harcourt, 1920.    138p.

3159  Aleksandrov, G.F. and others.  History of the Civil War in the U.S.S.R.
      N.Y., Universal  Distributors, 1946.    2 vols.

3160  Aten, M., Orrmont, A.  Last train over Rostov bridge.  N.Y., Messner,
      1961.;  L., Cassell, 1962.    340p.

3161  Baerlein, H.P.B.  The march of the seventy thousand.  L., Parsons, 1926.
      287p.

3162  Becvar, G.  The lost legion:  a Caechoslovakian epic.  L., Stanley,1939.
      256p.

3163  Bennett, G.  Cowan's war:  the story of British naval operations in the
      Baltic, 1918-1920.  L., Collins, 1964.    254p.

3164  Blair, D., Dand, C.H.  Russian hazard:  the adventures of a British Sec-
      ret Service Agent in Russia.  L., Hale, 1937.    288p.

3165  Bradley, J.  Allied intervention in Russia.  L., Weidenfeld & Nicolson,
      1968.    251p.

3166  Brinkley, G.A.  The Volunteer Army and allied intervention in South Rus-
      sia, 1917-1921:  a study in the politics and diplomacy of the Russian ci-
      vil war.  Notre Dame, Notre Dame U.P., 1966.    446p.

3167  Coates, W.P., Coates, Z.K.  Armed intervention in Russia, 1918-1922.  L.,
      Gollancz, 1935.    400p.

3168  Coleman, F.A.  Japan or Germany:  the inside story of the struggle in S-
      iberia.  N.Y., Doran, 1918.  232p.;  Japan moves north.  L., Cassell,
      1918.    177p.

3169  A Chronicler. (=Cudahy, J.)  Archangel:  the American war with Russia.
      Chicago, McClurg, 1924.    216p.

- 180 -

3170  D'Abernon, <u>Viscount</u>. The eighteenth decisive battle of the world:  Warsaw, 1920. L., Hodder & Stoughton, 1931.    178p.

3171  Denikin, A.I.  The White Army.  L., Cape, 1930.    368p.

3172  Donohoe, M.H.  With the Persian Expedition.  L., Arnold, 1919.    276p.

3173  Dukes, <u>Sir</u> P.  Red dusk and the morrow:  adventures and investigations in Red Russia.  L., Williams & Norgate, 1922.    312p.

3174  Dukes, <u>Sir</u> P.  The story of ST 25:  adventure and reomance in the Secret Intelligence Service in Red Russia.  L., Cassell, 1938.    380p.

3175  Dunsterville, L.C.  The adventures of Dunsterville.  L., Arnold,  1920.  323p.

3176  Dupuy, R.E.  Perish by the sword:  the Czechoslovakian anabasis and our supporting campaigns in North Russia and Siberia 1918-1920.  Harrisburg, Military Service, 1939.    302p.

3177  Dwinger, E.E.  The army behind barbed wire:  a Siberian diary.  L., Allen & Unwin, 1930.    341p.

3178  Dwinger, E.E.  Between White and Red.  N.Y., Scribner's, 1932.    492p.

3179  Ellis, C.M.  The British 'intervention' in Transcaspia, 1918-1919.  Berkeley, U. of California P., 1963.;  The Transcaspian episode, 1918-1919.  L., Hutchinson, 1963.    176p.

3180  Fleming, P.  The fate of Admiral Kolchak.  N.Y., Harcourt;  L., Hart-Davies, 1963.    253p.

3181  Footman, D.  Civil war in Russia.  N.Y., Praeger, 1962.;  L., Faber, 1961.    328p.

3182  Gordon, A.G.  Russian civil war.  L., Cassell, 1937.    280p.

3183  Graves, W.S.  America's Siberian adventure.  N.Y., Smith, 1931.    363p.

3184  Halliday, E.M.  The ignorant armies.  N.Y., Harper, 1960.    232p.

3185  Hill, G.A.  Dreaded hour.  L., Cassell;  Toronto, McClelland, 1936. 280p.

3186  Hodges, P.  Britmis:  a great adventure of the war:  being an account of allied intervention in Siberia and of an escape across the Gobi to Peking.  L., Cape, 1931.    364p.

3187  Hodgson, J.E.  With Denikin's armies:  being a description of the Cossack counter-revolution in South Russia, 1918-1920.  L., Lincoln Williams, 1932.    195p.

3188  Ironside, W.E.  Archangel, 1918-1919.  L., Constable, 1953.    201p.

3189  Jackson, R.  At war with the Bolsheviks:  the allied intervention into

Russia, 1917-1920.  L., Stacey, 1972.    251p.

3190  Kenez, P.  Civil war in South Russia, 1918:  the first year of the Volunteer Army.  Berkeley, U. of California P., 1971.    351p.

3191  Kindall, S.G.  American soldiers in Siberia.  N.Y., R.R. Smith,  1945.  251p.

3192  Luckett, R.  The White Generals:  an account of the White movement and the Russian Civil War.  N.Y., Viking;  Harlow, Longman, 1971.    413p.

3193  McCullagh, F.  A prisoner of the reds:  the story of a British officer captured in Siberia.  L., Murray, 1921.    310p.

3194  Magnus, B.  Smell of smoke.  L., Duckworth, 1936.    314p.

3195  Manning, C.A.  The Siberian fiasco.  N.Y., Library Publishers, 1952.210p

3196  Maynard, C.C.M.  The Murmansk adventure.  L., Hodder & Stoughton, 1928.  311p.

3197  Moore, J.R. and others.  The history of the American expedition fighting the Bolsheviks:  campaigning in North Russia, 1918-19.  Detroit, Polar Bear Pub. Co., 1920.    303p.

3198  Morley, J.W.  The Japanese thrust into Siberia, 1918.  N.Y., Columbia U. P., 1957.    395p.

3199  Palen, L.S.  The white devil of the Black Sea.  L., Lane, 1924.    297p.

3200  Palen, L.S.  The white devil's mate.  L., Lane, 1927.    275p.

3201  Polovtsoff, P.A.  Glory and downfall:  reminiscences of a Russian General Staff Officer.  L., Bell, 1935.    363p.

3202  Roberts, C.E.B.  In Denikin's Russia and the Caucasus, 1919-20: being the record of a journey to South Russia, the Crimea, Armenia, Georgia and Baku in 1919 and 1920.  L., Collins, 1921.    324p.

3203  Rosenberg, W.G.  A.I. Denikin and the anti-Bolshevik movement in South Russia.  Amherst, Amherst College P., 1961.    80p.

3204  Silverlight, J.  The victors' dilemma:  Allied intervention in the Russian Civil War.  N.Y., Weybright & Talley, 1971.;  L., Barrie & Jenkins, 1970.    392p.

3205  Singleton-Gates, G.R.  Bolos and Barishynas:  being an account of the doings of the Sadleir-Jackson Brigade, and Altham Flotilla, on North Dvina during the summer, 1919.  Aldershot, 1920.    194p.

3206  Soutar, A.  With Ironside in North Russia.  L., Hutchinson, 1940.    250p

3207  Special Delegation of the Far Eastern Republic to the Washington Conference, 1922.  Japanese intervention in the Russian Far East.  Washington,

1922.    165p.

3208    Stewart, G.  The white armies of Russia:  a chronicle of counter-revol-
        ution and allied intervention.  N.Y.; L., Macmillan, 1933.    469p.

3209    Strakhovsky, L.I.  Intervention at Archangel:  the story of allied inter-
        vention and Russian counter-revolution in North Russia, 1918-1920.  Prin-
        ceton, Princeton U.P., 1944.    336p.

3210    Strakhovsky, L.I.  The origins of American intervention in North Russia
        (1918).  Princeton, Princeton U.P., 1937.    140p.

3211    Strod, I.  Civil war in the Taiga:  a story of guerilla warfare in the
        forests of Eastern Siberia.  L., Modern Bks., 1933.    152p.

3212    Swettenham, J.A.  Allied intervention in Russia, 1918-1919 and the part
        played by Canada.  L., Allen & Unwin, 1967.    315p.

3213    Unterberger, B.M.  American intervention in the Russian civil war.  Lex-
        ington, Heath, 1969.    113p.

3214    Unterberger, B.M.  America's Siberian expedition, 1918-1920:  a study of
        national policy.  Durham, N.C., Duke U.P., 1956.    271p.

3215    Varneck, E., Fisher, H.H.  The testimony of Kolchak, and other Siberian
        materials.  Stanford, Stanford U.P., 1935.    466p.

3216    Ward, J.  With the 'Die-Hards' in Siberia.  L., Cassell, 1920.    272p.

3217    White, J.A.  The Siberian intervention.  Princeton, Princeton U.P., 1950.
        471p.

3218    Wild, M.  Secret service on the Russian Front.  L., Bles, 1932.    324p.

3219    Williamson, H.N.H.  Farwell to the Don:  the Russian Revolution in the
        journals of Brigadier H.N.H. Williamson.  N.Y., Day, 1971.; L., Collins,
        1970.    288p.

3220    Wrangel, P.N.  The memoirs of General Wrangel.  N.Y., Duffield, 1930.;
        Always with honor.  N.Y., Speller, 1957.; Memoirs.  L., Williams & Nor-
        gate, 1929.    356p.

iii)    Personal accounts

3221    Balabanoff, A.  My life as a rebel.  L., Hamilton, 1938.    358p.

3222    Bechhofer, C.E.  Through starving Russia:  being the record of a journey
        to Moscow and the Volga provinces in August and September 1921.  L., Me-
        thuen, 1921.    165p.

3223    Borodin, N.N.  One man in his time.  N.Y., Macmillan; L., Constable,
        1955.    344p.

3224    Brown, W.A.  The groping giant:  Revolutionary Russia as seen by an American democrat. New Haven, Yale U.P., 1920.    199p.

3225  Buxhoevden, _Baroness_ S. Left behind. L., Williams & Norgate,    1929.
      182p.

3226  Castellane, _Count_ B.V.de. One crowded hour: an autobiography. L., Al-
      len & Unwin, 1934.    285p.

3227  Clarke, J.S. Pen pictures of Russia under the 'Red Terror': reminiscen-
      ces of a surreptitious journey to Russia to attend the Second Congress of
      the Third International. Glasgow, National Workers' Committee,    1921.
      327p.

3228  Colquhoun, J. Adventures in Red Russia from the Black Sea to the White
      Sea. L., Murray, 1926.    193p.

3229  Dyboski, R. Seven years in Russia and Siberia, 1914-1921. Cheshire, C-
      onu., Cherry Hill Bks., 1971.    177p.

3230  Eaton, R. Under the red flag. L., Brentano, 1924.    262p.

3231  Fen, E. Remember Russia. L., Hamilton, 1973.    346p.

3232  Gibbs, P. Since then. L., Hutchinson, 1930.    414p.

3233  Harding, S. The underworld of state. L., Allen & Unwin, 1925.    256p.

3234  Harrison, M.E. Marooned in Moscow: the story of an American woman imp-
      risoned in Russia. L., Butterworth, 1922.    322p.

3235  Keeling, E.H. Adventures in Turkey and Russia. L., Murray, 1924. 240p

3236  Keeling, H.V. Bolshevism: Mr. Keeling's five years in Russia. L., Ho-
      dder & Stoughton, 1919.    212p.

3237  Keun, O. My adventures in Bolshevik Russia. L., Lane, 1923.    320p.

3238  Koudrey, V. Once a commissar. L., Hamilton, 1938.    319p.

3239  Lansbury, G. What I saw in Russia. L., Parsons, 1920.    172p.

3240  Markov, S.V. How we tried to save the Tsaritsa. L., Putnam, 1929. 288p.

3241  Meck, G. von. As I remember them. L., Dobson, 1973.    448p.

3242  Nadejda. Once I had a home: the diary and narrative of Nadejda, lady
      of honour to their Imperial Majesties the late Empress Alexandra Fedor-
      ovna and the Empress Marie Fedorovna of Russia. L., Duckworth,    1926.
      320p.

3243  Payne, M.A. Plague, pestilence and famine. L., Nisbet, 1923.    146p.

3244  Power, R. Under Cossack and Bolshevik. L., Methuen, 1919.    279p.

- 184 -

3245  Price, H.T.  Boche and Bolshevik:  experiences of an Englishman in the
German Army and in Russian prisons.  L., Murray, 1919.  247p.

3246  Ptaschkina, N.  The diary of Nelly Ptaschinka.  L., Cape, 1923.  316p.

3247  Rachmanova, A.  Flight from terror:  an autobiography.  L., Sheed & Ward
1933.  318p.

3248  Ransome, A.M.  Six weeks in Russia in 1919.  L., Allen & Unwin,  1919.
150p.

3249  Reswick, W.  I dreamt revolution.  Chicago, Regnery, 1952.  328p.

3250  Rubin, J.  Moscow mirage.  L., Bles, 1935.  320p.

3251  Sheridan, C.  Russian portraits.  L., Cape, 1921.  202p.

3252  Shklovskii, V.  A sentimental journey:  memoirs, 1917-1922.  Ithaca, Cornell U.P., 1970.  304p.

3253  Sokoloff, B.  On the banks of the River Neva.  Ilfracombe, Stockwell,
1973.  336p.

3254  Sorokin, P.A.  Leaves from a Russian diary, and thirty years after.  Rev.
ed.  Boston, Mass., Beacon P., 1950.  346p.

3255  Tchernoff, O.  New horizons:  reminiscences of the Russian Revolution.
L., Hutchinson, 1936.  287p.

3256  Urch, R.O.G.  'We generally shoot Englishmen':  an English schoolmaster
's five years of mild adventure in Moscow (1915-1920).  L., Allen & Unwin, 1936.  300p.

3257  Vining, L.E.  Held by the Bolsheviks:  the diary of a British officer in
Russia, 1919-1920.  L., St Catherine's P., 1924.  280p.

3258  Viroubova, A.  Memories of the Russian court.  L., Macmillan, 1923. 400p

3259  White, D.F.  Survival through war and revolution in Russia.  L., Oxford
U.P., 1939.  395p.

3260  Wilton, R.  The last days of the Romanovs, from 15th March 1917.  L., B-
utterworth, 1920.  320p.

3261  Wolkonsky, Prince S.  My reminiscences.  L., Hutchinson, 1925.  2 vols.

3262  Wolkonsky, Princess P.  The way of bitterness:  Soviet Russia, 1920. L.,
Methuen, 1931.  212p.

3263  Woman under fire:  six months in the Red Army;  a woman's diary and experiences of revolutionary Russia.  L., Hutchinson, 1930.  286p.

3264  Wonlar-Larsky, N.  The Russia that I loved.  L., MacSwinney, 1937. 205p.

3265  Woronoff, O.  Upheaval.  L., Hutchinson, 1932.  226p.

3266  Yourievsky, Princess C.  My book: some pages from my life.  L., Nash & Grayson, 1924.  120p.

3267  Yurlova, M.  Cossack girl.  L., Cassell, 1934.  312p.

D  The Stalin era

(i)  General

3268  Ammende, E.  Human life in Russia.  L., Allen & Unwin, 1936.  319p.

3269  Chamberlin, W.H.  Russia's iron age.  L., Duckworth, 1935.  400p.

3270  Dallin, D.J.  The new Soviet empire.  New Haven, Yale U.P.;  L., Hollis & Carter, 1951.  218p.

3271  Daniels, R.V.  The Stalin revolution: foundations of Soviet totalitarianism.  2nd ed. Lexington, Heath, 1972.  233p.

3272  Davis, J.  Behind Soviet power: Stalin and the Russians.  N.Y., Readers P., 1946.  120p.

3273  Eastman, M.  Since Lenin died.  L., Labour Publishing Co., 1925.  158p.

3274  Eastman, M.  Stalin's Russia and the crisis in socialism.  N.Y., Norton; L., Allen & Unwin, 1940.  284p.

3275  Farbman, M.S.  Bolshevism in retreat.  L., Collins, 1923.  312p.

3276  Farbman, M.S.  After Lenin: the new phase in Russia.  L., Parsons, 1924. 280p.

3277  Fineberg, A.  Soviet Union 1936.  L., Lawrence & Wishart, 1936.  752p.

3278  Gibson, M.  Russia under Stalin.  L., Wayland, 1972.  128p.

3279  Hutton, J.B.  The great illusion.  L., David Bruce & Watson, 1970.  271p

3280  Khrushchev, N.S.  The anatomy of terror: Khrushchev's revelations about Stalin's regime.  Washington, Public Affairs P., 1956.  73p.

3281  Khrushchev, N.S.  The crimes of the Stalin era: special report to the 20th Congress of the Communist Party of the Soviet Union;  annotated by B.I. Nicolaevsky.  N.Y., The New Leader, 1956.  67p.

3282  Khrushchev, N.S.  Report of the Central Committee, C.P.S.U., to the XXth Congress of the Communist Party of the Soviet Union.  N.Y., New Century, 1956.  125p.

3283  Kravchenko, V.A.  I chose freedom.  N.Y., Scribner, 1946.;  L., Hale,1947.  496p.

3284   Kravchenko, V.A.   I chose justice.   N.Y., Scribner;   L., Hale, 1950.
       458p.

3285   Kravchenko versus Moscow:   the report of the famous Paris case;   intro.
       by T.Humphreys.   L., Wingate, 1950.      253p.

3286   Labin, S.   Stalin's Russia.   L., Gollancz, 1949.      492p.

3287   Lazarevski, V.   Under the Bolshevik uniform.   L., Butterworth, 1936.
       320p.

3288   Leonhard, W.   Child of the Revolution.   Chicago, Regnery;   L., Collins,
       1957.      447p.

3289   Medvedev, R.A.   Let history judge:   the origins and consequences of Sta-
       linism.   N.Y., Knopf, 1971.;   L., Macmillan, 1972.      566p.

3290   Randall, F.B.   Stalin's Russia:   an historical reconsideration.   N.Y.,
       Free P.;   L., Collier-Macmillan, 1965.      328p.

3291   Rigby, T.H.   The Stalin dictatorship:   Khrushchev's 'Secret Speech' and
       other documents.   L., Methuen;   Sydney, Sydney U.P., 1968.      128p.

3292   Serge, V.   From Lenin to Stalin.   N.Y., Pioneer, 1937.   112p.;   L., Seck-
       er & Warburg,  1937.      230p.

3293   Serge, V.   Russia twenty years after.   N.Y., Hillman-Curl, 1937.   298p.;
       L., Jarrolds, 1937.      287p.

3294   Strong, A.L.   The Stalin era.   N.Y., Mainstream, 1956.      128p.

3295   Those who built Stalingrad, as told by themselves;   foreword by M. Gorky.
       N.Y., International Publishers, 1934.      268p.

3296   Tobenkin, E.   Stalin's ladder:   war and peace in the Soviet Union.   N.Y.,
       Minton, Balch, 1933.      294p.

3297   Tokaev, G.A.   Comrade X.   L., Harvill P., 1956.      370p.

3298   Tokaev, G.A.   Stalin means war.   L., Weidenfeld & Nicolson, 1951.   214p.

3299   Uralov, A.   The reign of Stalin.   L., Lane, 1953.      256p.

3300   White, J.B.   Red Russia arms.   Burrup, Mathieson, 1932.      144p.

3301   Winterton, P.   Inquest on an ally.   L., Cresset;   Toronto, Collins, 1948.
       288p.

3302   Wolfe, B.D.   Khrushchev and Stalin's ghost:   text, background and meani-
       ng of Khrushchev's secret report to the Twentieth Congress on the night
       of February 24-25, 1956.   N.Y., Praeger, 1956.;   L., Atlantic P., 1957.
       322p.

(ii)   The purges

3303   Alexandrov, V.   The Tukhachevsky affair.   Englewood Cliffs, Prentice,
       1964.;   L., Macdonald, 1963.     201p.

3304   Avinov, M.   Marie Avinov:   pilgrimage through hell;   an autobiography
       told by P. Chavchavadze.   Englewood Cliffs, Prentice, 1968.     275p.

3305   Beck, F., Godin, W.   The Russia purge and the extraction of confession.
       N.Y., Viking, 1951.     277p.

3306   Berger, J.   Nothing but the truth.   N.Y., Day, 1971.   286p.;   Shipwreck
       of a generation:   The memoirs of Joseph Berger.   L., Harvill P., 1971.
       286p.

3307   Buber, M.   Under two dictators.   L., Gollancz;   Toronto, Longmans,1949.
       381p.

3308   Callcott, M.S.   Russian justice.   N.Y., Macmillan, 1935.     265p.

3309   The case of Leon Trotsky:   report of hearings on the charges made again-
       st him in the Moscow trials;   by the preliminary commission of inquiry,
       J. Dewey (Chairman) and others.   L., Secker & Warburg, 1937.     617p.

3310   Coates, W.P.   The Moscow trial (April 1933).   L., Anglo-Russian Parliam-
       entary Committee, 1933.     165p.

3311   Coates, W.P., Coates, Z.K.   The Moscow trial (January 1937), and two sp-
       eeches by Joseph Stalin.   L., Anglo-Russian Parliamentary Committee,
       1937.     281p.

3312   Collard, D.   Soviet justice, and the trial of Radek and others.   L., Go-
       llancz, 1937.     208p.

3313   Conquest, R.   The great terror:   Stalin's purges of the thirties.   Rev.
       ed. N.Y.;   L., Macmillan, 1973.     844p.

3314   Cummings, A.J.   The Moscow trial.   L., Gollancz, 1933.     287p.

3315   Edelman, M.   GPU Justice.   L., Allen & Unwin, 1938.     231p.

3316   Katkov, G.   The trial of Bukharin.   N.Y., Stein & Day;   L., Batsford,
       1969.     255p.

3317   Keeton, G.W.   The problem of the Moscow trial.   L., Black, 1933.   143p.

3318   Kleist, P.   G.P.U. Justice.   L., Allen & Unwin, 1938.     207p.

3319   Leites, N., Bernaut, E.   Ritual of liquidation:   the case of the Moscow
       trials.   Glencoe, Free P.;   L., Spearman, 1954.     515p.

3320   The Moscow trials:   an anthology.   L., New Park Publications, 1967. 150p.

3321   Orlov, A.   The secret history of Stalin's crimes.   L., Jarrolds, 1954.
       368p.

3322   Ponomarev, B.  The plot against the Soviet Union and world peace;  facts
       and documents;  compiled from the verbatim report of the court proceed-
       ings in the case of the anti-Soviet "Bloc of Rights and Trotskyists". L.,
       Lawrence & Wishart, 1938.    187p.

3323   Prychodko, N.  One of the fifteen million.  L., Dent, 1952.    170p.

3324   Rothstein, A.  Wreckers on trial:  a record of the trial of the Industr-
       ial Party, held in Moscow, November-December, 1930.  L., Modern Bks.,
       1931.    214p.

3325   The trial of Bukharin, Rykov, Borodin,&c. (March 1938):  report of court
       proceedings in the case of the anti-Soviet 'Bloc of Rights and Trotsky-
       ists' heard before the Military Collegium of the Supreme Court of the U.
       S.S.R., Moscow, March 2-13, 1938.  Moscow, People's Commissariat of Jus-
       tice, 1938.    800p.

3326   The trial of Piatakov, Radek, Sokolnikov, &c. (Jan. 1937):  report of c-
       ourt proceedings in the case of the anti-Soviet Trotskyite Centre;  hea-
       rd before the Military Collegium of the Supreme Court of the U.S.S.R.,
       Moscow, January 23-30, 1937.  Moscow, People's Commissariat of Justice,
       1937.    580p.

3327   The trial of Zinoviev, Kamenev, Smirnov, &c.  (Aug. 1936):  report of c-
       ourt proceedings;  the case of the Trotskyite-Zinovievite terrorist cen-
       tre, heard before the Military Collegium of the Supreme Court of the U.-
       S.S.R., Moscow, August 19-24, 1936.  Moscow, People's Commissariat of J-
       ustice, 1936.    180p.

3328   Tucker, R.C., Cohen, S.F.  The great purge trial.  N.Y., Grosset, 1965.
       725p.

3329   Weissberg, A.C.  Conspiracy of silence.  L., Hamilton, 1952.    509p.

3330   Wrecking activities at power stations in the Soviet Union.  L., Allen &
       Unwin, 1933.    798p.

3331   Yakir, P.  A childhood in prison.  N.Y., Coward;  L., Macmillan, 1972.
       155p.


E      The Second World War

(i)    General

3332   Hindus, M.  Hitler cannot conquer Russia.  Garden City, N.Y., Doubleday,
       1941.    299p.

3333   Hindus, M.  Mother Russia.  Garden City, N.Y., Doubleday, 1943.    395p.

3334   Jordan, P.  Russian glory.  L., Cresset P., 1942.    181p.

3335   Lesueur, L.  Twelve months that changed the world.  N.Y., Knopf, 1943.
       345p.

3336 Seely, C.S.   Russia and the battle of liberation.   Philadelphia, Dorr –
ance, 1942.   114p.

3337 Tolstoy, A.   My country:   articles and stories of the Great Patriotic W-
ar of the Soviet Union.   L., Hutchinson, 1944.   117p.

3338 Topolski, F.   Russia in war.   L., Methuen, 1942.   128p.

3339 Ward, H.F.   The Soviet spirit.   N.Y., International Publishers,   1944.
160p.

3340 Werth, A.   Russia at war, 1941–1945.   N.Y., Dutton;   L., Barrie & Rockliff, 1964.   1100p.

3341 Werth, A.   The year of Stalingrad:   an historical record and a study of
Russian mentality, methods and policies.   N.Y., Knopf, 1947.;   L., Hamilton, 1946.   478p.

3342 Winterton, P.   Report on Russia.   L., Cresset P., 1946.   138p.

3343 Zacharoff, L.   The voice of fighting Russia.   N.Y., Alliance Bk. Corp.,
1942.   336p.

(ii) <u>Political Aspects</u>

3344 Carroll, W.   We're in this with Russia.   Boston, Mass., Houghton, 1942.
264p.

3345 The crime of Katyn:   facts and documents;   with a foreword by General W.
Anders.   L., Polish Cultural Foundation, 1965.   303p.

3346 Dallin, A.   German rule in Russia, 1941–1945:   a study of occupation policies.   N.Y., St Martin's P.;   L., Macmillan, 1957.   695p.

3347 Dallin, A.   Odessa, 1941–1944:   a case study of Soviet territory under
foreign rule.   Santa Monica, Rand Corp., 1957.   488p.

3348 Fadeyev, A.A.   Leningrad in the days of the blockade.   L., Hutchinson,
1946.   104p.

3349 Fehling, H.M.   One great prison:   the story behind Russia's unreleased
POW's.   Boston, Mass., Beacon P., 1951.   175p.

3350 Fischer, G.   Soviet opposition to Stalin:   a case study in World War 2.
Cambridge, Mass., Harvard U.P., 1952.   230p.

3351 Fitzgibbon, L.   Katyn.   N.Y., Scribners, 1971.;   L., Stacey, 1972. 285p.

3352 Halpern, A.   Conducted tour.   N.Y., Sheed & Ward, 1945.   145p.;   Liberation – Russian style.   L., Max Love, 1945.   106p.

3353 Kalinin, M.I.   The Soviet President speaks:   speeches, broadcasts, and
articles on the Great Patriotic War of the Soviet Union.   L., Hutchinson,
1945.   79p.

3354  Kospoth, B.J.  Red wins.  L., Macdonald, 1946.  220p.

3355  Kuby, E.  The Russians and Berlin, 1945.  N.Y., Ballantine, 1969.;  L.,
      Heinemann, 1968.  372p.

3356  Mackiewicz, J.  The Katyn Wood murders.  N.Y.;  L., Hollis & Carter, 19-
      51.  252p.

3357  Moiseiwitch, M.  Heroes of the Soviet Union.  L., Skinner, 1943.  71p.

3358  New Soviet documents on Nazi atrocities.  L., Hutchinson, 1943.  128p.

3359  Nikitin, M.N., Vagin, P.I.  Crimes of the German fascists in the Lening-
      rad region.  L., Hutchinson, 1946.  128p.

3360  The people's verdict:  a full report of proceedings at the Krasnodar and
      Kharkhov German atrocity trials.  L., Hutchinson, 1945.  124p.

3361  Reitlinger, G.  The house built on sand:  the conflicts of German policy
      in Russia, 1939-1945.  N.Y., Viking;  L., Weidenfeld & Nicolson,  1960.
      459p.

3362  Russians tell the story:  sketches of the war on the Soviet-German front
      from 'Soviet War News'.  L., Hutchinson, 1944.  146p.

3363  Samarin, V.D.  Civilian life under the German occupation, 1942-1944. N.-
      Y., Research Program on the U.S.S.R., 1954.  90p.

3364  Soviet documents on Nazi atrocities.  L., Hutchinson, 1942.  192p.

3365  Soviet foreign policy during the Patriotic War:  documents and materials
      trans. by A. Rothstein.  N.Y.;  L., Hutchinson, 1946.  2 vols.

3366  Soviet government statements on Nazi atrocities.  L., Hutchinson, 1946.
      320p.

3367  Stalin's correspondence with Churchill, Attlee, Roosevelt, 1941-45. N.Y.,
      Dutton, 1958.  302p.;  Correspondence between the Chairman of the Counc-
      il of Ministers of the U.S.S.R. and the Presidents of the U.S.A. and the
      Prime Ministers of Great Britain during the Great Patriotic War of 1941-
      1945.  L., Lawrence & Wishart, 1958.;  Moscow, FLPH, 1957.  2 vols.

3368  Stalin, I.V.  The great patriotic war of the Soviet Union.  N.Y., Inter-
      national Publishers, 1945.  167p.

3369  Stalin, I.V.  War speeches, orders of the day, and answers to foreign p-
      ress correspondents during the Great Patriotic War.  N.Y.;  L., Hutchin-
      son, 1946.  140p.

3370  Steenberg, S.  Vlasov.  N.Y., Knopf, 1970.  230p.

3371  Strik-Strikfeldt, W.  Against Stalin and Hitler:  memoirs of the Russian
      Liberation Movement, 1941-1945.  N.Y., Day, 1973.;  L., Macmillan, 1970.
      270p.

3372  Trial of the organizers, leaders and members of the Polish diversionist
      organizations in the rear of the Red Army on the territory of Poland, L-
      ithuania and the Western region of  Byelorussia and the Ukraine:  verba-
      tim report.  L., Hutchinson, 1945.    240p.

3373  True to type:  a selection from letters and diaries of German soldiers
      and civilians collected on the Soviet-German front.  N.Y.;  L., Hutchin-
      son, 1945.    160p.

3374  Voznesensky, N.A.  War economy of the U.S.S.R. in the period of the Pat-
      riotic War.  Moscow, FLPH, 1948.    150p.

3375  Zawodny, J.K.  Death in the forest:  the story of the Katyn Forest mass-
      acre.  Notre Dame, U. of Notre Dame P., 1962.    252p.

(iii) Military Aspects

3376  Allen, W.E.D., Muratoff, P.  The Russian campaigns of 1941-43.  Harmond-
      sworth, Penguin Bks., 1944.    192p.

3377  Allen, W.E.D., Muratoff, P.  The Russian campaigns of 1944-1945.  Harmo-
      ndsworth, Penguin Bks., 1946.    332p.

3378  Armstrong, J.A.  Soviet partisans in World War II.  Madison, U. of Wisc-
      onsin P., 1964.    792p.

3379  Beck, A. and others.  Road to victory:  twelve tales of the Red Army. L.,
      Hutchinson, 1945.    174p.

3380  Bialer, S.  Stalin and his generals:  Soviet military memoirs of World
      War II.  N.Y., Pegasus, 1969.;  L., Souvenir, 1970.    644p.

3381  Bourke-White, M.  Shooting the Russian war.  N.Y., Simon & Schuster, 19-
      42.    287p.

3382  Brown, J.E.  Russia fights.  N.Y., Scribners, 1943.    276p.

3383  Caldwell, E.  All out on the road to Smolensk.  N.Y., Duell, 1942. 230p.

3384  Carell, P.  Hitler moves east:  1941-1943.  Boston, Mass., Little, 1965.
      Hitler's war on Russia:  the story of the German defeat in the East. L.,
      Harrap, 1964.    640p.

3385  Carell, P.  Scorched earth:  the Russian-German war, 1943-1944.  Boston,
      Mass., Little, 1970.;  Hitler's war on Russia.  Vol.2,  Scorched earth.
      L., Harrap, 1970.    556p.

3386  Carse, R.  A cold corner of hell:  the story of the Murmansk convoys,
      1941-45. Garden City, N.Y., Doubleday, 1969.    268p.

3387  Carter, D.  Russia's secret weapon.  L., Muller, 1944.    103p.

3388  Chuikov, V.I.  The beginning of the road.  N.Y., Holt, 1964.  364p.; L.,
      MacGibbon & Kee, 1963.    388p.

3389  Clark, A.  Barbarossa:  the Russian—German conflict, 1941—1945.  N.Y.,
      Morrow, 1965.  577p.;  L., Hutchinson, 1965.  444p.

3390  Cox, G.  The Red Army moves.  L., Gollancz, 1941.  278p.

3391  Craig, W.  Enemy at the gates:  the battle for Stalingrad.  N.Y., Reader-
      's Digest P., 1973.  457p.

3392  Dixon, C.A., Heilbrunn, O.  Communist guerilla warfare.  L., Allen & Un-
      win, 1954.  229p.

3393  Edelstadt, V.  Young fighters of the Soviet.  N.Y., Knopf, 1944.  104p.

3394  The epic story of Stalingrad.  L., Hutchinson, 1943.  118p.

3395  Eremenko, A.I.  The arduous beginning.  Moscow, Progress, 1966.  329p.

3396  Falls, C.  Ordeal by battle.  L., Methuen, 1943.  168p.

3397  Fineberg, J.  Heroic Leningrad — documents, sketches and stories.  Mos-
      cow, FLPH, 1945.  151p.

3398  Gafencu, G.  Prelude to the Russian campaign.  L., Muller, 1946. 348p.

3399  Golovko, A.G.  With the Red Fleet:  the war memoirs of the late Admiral
      Arseni  G. Golovko.  L., Putnam, 1965.  248p.

3400  Gorbatov, A.G.  Years of my life:  the memoirs of a General of the Sovi-
      et Army.  N.Y., Norton, 1965.;  L., Constable, 1964.  222p.

3401  Gorlitz, W.  Paulus and Stalingrad:  a life of Field—Marshall Friedrich
      Paulus.  N.Y., Citadel;  L., Methuen, 1963.  301p.

3402  Goure, L.  The siege of Leningrad.  Stanford, Stanford U.P., 1962. 363p.

3403  Hassel, S.  The legion of the damned.  L., Allen & Unwin, 1957.  298p.

3404  Higgins, T.  Hitler and Russia:  the Third Reich in a two—front war, 19—
      37—1943.  N.Y., Macmillan;  L., Collier—Macmillan, 1966.  310p.

3405  Hooper, A.D.  Through Soviet Russia and Soviet Finnish campaign,  1940.
      L., Muller, 1945.  140p.

3406  Howell, E.M.  The Soviet partisan movement, 1941—44.  Washington, USGPO,
      1956.  217p.

3407  Ignatov, P.K.  Partisans of the Kuban.  L., Hutchinson, 1945.  212p.

3408  Isakov, I.S.  The Red Fleet in the Second World War.  L., Hutchinson,
      1947.  124p.

3409  Jackson, W.G.F.  Seven roads to Moscow.  N.Y., Philosophical Library,
      1958.;  L., Eyre & Spottiswoode, 1957.  334p.

3410  Jukes, G.  The defence of Moscow.  N.Y., Ballantine;  L., Macdonald, 19—
      70.    158p.

3411  Jukes, G.  Kursk:  the clash of armour.  N.Y., Ballantine;  L., Macdonald,
      1969.    160p.

3412  Jukes, G.  Stalingrad:  the turning point.  N.Y., Ballantine;  L., Macd-
      onald, 1968.    160p.

3413  Keegan, J.  Barbarossa:  invasion of Russia, 1941.  L., Macdonald, 1971.
      160p.

3414  Kerr, W.B.  The Russian army:  its men, its leaders and its battles.  N.Y.,
      Knopf, 1944.    250p.

3415  Leach, B.A.  German strategy against Russia, 1939—1941.  Oxford, Claren-
      don P., 1973.    308p.

3416  Lukas, R.C.  Eagles east:  the Army Air Forces and the Soviet Union, 19—
      41—1945.  Tallahasee, Florida State U.P., 1970.    256p.

3417  Orgill, D.  T—34:  Russian armor.  N.Y., Ballantine, 1971.    159p.

3418  Paneth, P.  The epic of the Soviet cities.  L., Alliance P., 1944. 128p.

3419  Pavlenko, P.  The forest guerrillas:  a study of the partisans of Lake
      Ilmen.  L., Routledge, 1944.    114p.

3420  Pavlov, D.V.  Leningrad 1941:  the blockade.  Chicago, U. of Chicago P.,
      1965.    186p.

3421  Plivier, T.  Stalingrad.  N.Y., Appleton, 1948.  357p.;  Stalingrad: the
      death of an army.  L., Atheneum, 1948.    411p.

3422  Polevoi, B.  From Belgorod to the Carpathians.  L., Hutchinson, 1945.
      164p.

3423  Poliakov, A.  White mammoths:  the dramatic story of Russian tanks in a-
      ction.  N.Y., Dutton, 1943.  189p.  Westbound Tanks:  adventures of five
      Soviet heavy tanks from factory to action.  L., Hutchinson, 1943.  100p.

3424  Ponomarenko, P.K. and others.  Behind the front lines:  being an account
      of the military activities, exploits, adventures and day to day life of
      the Soviet guerrillas operating behind the German lines.  L., Hutchin —
      son, 1945.    160p.

3425  Rokossovski, K.K.  A soldier's duty.  Moscow, Progress, 1970.    340p.

3426  Salisbury, H.E.  The 900 days:  the siege of Leningrad.  N.Y., Harper,
      1969.;  The siege of Leningrad.  L., Secker & Warburg, 1969.    635p.

3427  Sammis, E.R.  Last stand at Stalingrad:  the battle that saved the world.
      N.Y., Macmillan;  L., Collier—Macmillan, 1966.    96p.

3428   Schofield, B.B.   The Russian convoys.   Chester Springs, Dufour;   L., Batsford, 1964.   224p.

3429   Schroter, H.   Stalingrad.   N.Y., Dutton;   L., Joseph, 1958.   263p.

3430   Seaton, A.   The Russo-German war, 1941-1945.   N.Y., Praeger;   L., Barker,
1971.   628p.

3431   Seaton, A.   The battle for Moscow, 1941-42.   L., Hart-Davies, 1971. 320p

3432   Seth, R.   Operation Barbarossa:   the battle for Moscow.   L., Blond, 1964.
191p.

3433   Seth, R.   Stalingrad:   point of return;   the story of the battle, August
1942-February 1943.   N.Y., Coward;   L., Gollancz, 1959.   254p.

3434   Sevruk, V.   Stalingrad, 1941-1942:   recollections, stories, reports.   M-
oscow, Progress, 1970.   278p.

3435   Shtemenko, S.M.   The Soviet General Staff at war (1941-1945).   Moscow,
Progress, 1970.   399p.

3436   Skomorovsky, B., Morris, E.G.   The siege of Leningrad:   the saga of the
greatest siege of all time as  told by the letters, documents and stories of the brave people who withstood it.   N.Y., Dutton, 1944.   196p.

3437   Sloan, P.   Russia resists.   L., Muller, 1941.   117p.

3438   Snow, E.   Glory and bondage.   L., Gollancz, 1945.   263p.

3439   Strategy and tactics of the Soviet-German war;   by officers of the Red
Army and the Soviet War correspondents.   L., Hutchinson, 1942.   148p.

3440   Taylor, J.E.   Northern escort.   L., Allen & Unwin, 1945.   127p.

3441   Thorwald, J.   Flight in the winter:   Russia conquers, January to May 19-
45.   N.Y., Pantheon, 1951. 318p.;   L., Hutchinson, 1953.   255p.

3442   Tikhonov, N.   The defence of Leningrad.   L., Hutchinson, 1943.   136p.

3443   Turney, A.W.   Disaster at Moscow:   von Bock's campaigns, 1941-1942.   Al-
buquerque, U. of New Mexico P., 1970.;   L., Cassell, 1971.   228p.

3444   Uebe, K.   Russian reactions to German air power in World War II.   Maxwell Air Force Base, Ala., USAF Historical Division, Air U., 1964.   146p.

3445   Voyetekhov, B.   The last days of Sevastopol.   N.Y., Knopf, 1943. 225p.
L., Cassell, 1943.   150p.

3446   Wagner, R.   The Soviet Air Force in World War II:   the official history;
originally published by the Ministry of Defense of the U.S.S.R.   Garden
City, N.Y., Doubleday, 1973.   440p.

3447   Werth, A.   Leningrad.   N.Y., Knopf;   L., Hamilton, 1944.   190p.

3448 Werth, A. Moscow war diary. N.Y., Knopf, 1942. 297p.; Moscow '41. L., Hamilton, 1942. 268p.

3449 Wykes, A. The siege of Leningrad: epic of survival. N.Y., Ballantine; L., Macdonald, 1969. 160p.

3450 Zacharoff, L. "We made a mistake" - Hitler: Russia's surprising defence against Germany. N.Y., Appleton, 1941. 213p.; "We made a mistake" - Hitler: Russia's amazing defence. L., Lane, 1942. 156p.

3451 Zhukov, G.K. Marshal Zhukov's greatest battles; ed. by H.E. Salisbury. N.Y., Harper; L., Macdonald, 1969. 304p.

3452 Zieser, B. The road to Stalingrad. N.Y., Ballantine, 1956. 152p.; L., Elek, 1956. 208p.

(iv) Personal Accounts

3453 Armonas, B., Nasvytis, A.L. Leave your tears in Moscow. Philadelphia, Lippincott, 1961. 222p.

3454 Bauer, J. As far as my feet will carry me. L., Deutsch, 1957. 254p.

3455 Beattie, E.W. Passport to war. L., Peter Davies, 1943. 331p.

3456 Becker, H. Devil on my shoulder. L., Jarrolds, 1955. 216p.

3457 Begin, M. White nights: the story of a prisoner in Russia. L., Macdonald, 1957. 240p.

3458 Cassidy, H.C. Moscow dateline. L., Cape, 1943. 256p.

3459 Czapski, J. This inhuman land. L., Chatto & Windus, 1951. 301p.

3460 Demianova, G. Comrade Genia: the story of a victim of German bestiality in Russia, told by herself. L., Nicholson & Watson, 1941. 141p.

3461 Devilliers, C. Lieutenant Katia. L., Constable, 1964. 256p.

3462 Dibold, H. Doctor at Stalingrad: the passion of a captivity. L., Hutchinson, 1958. 191p.

3463 Einsiedel, H. von. I joined the Russians: a captured German flier's diary of the Communist temptation. New Haven, Yale U.P., 1953. 306p.; The shadow of Stalingrad: being the diary of a temptation. L., Wingate, 1953. 254p.

3464 Emmens, R.G. Guests of the Kremlin. N.Y., Macmillan, 1949. 291p.

3465 Gerlach, H. Nightmare in red. Carol Stream, Creation House, 1970. 239p

3466 Gilboa, Y.A. Confess! confess!: eight years in Soviet prisons. Boston, Mass., Little, 1968. 304p.

3467  Gollwitzer, H.  Unwilling journey:  a diary from Russia.  Philadelphia, Muhlenberg P., 1954.;  L., SCMP, 1953.    316p.

3468  Haape, H.  Moscow train stop:  a doctor's experiences with the German s-pearhead in Russia.  L., Collins, 1957.    384p.

3469  Haldane, C.F.  Russian newsreel:  an eyewitness account of the Soviet U-nion at war.  L., Secker & Warburg, 1942.    207p.

3470  Herling, G.  A world apart.  N.Y., New American Library, 1952.    243p.

3471  Inber, V.  Leningrad diary.  N.Y., St Martin's P.; L., Hutchinson, 1971. 207p.

3472  Kosterina, N.  The diary of Nina Kosterina.  N.Y., Crown, 1968.; L., V-allentine, Mitchell, 1972.    192p.

3473  Krieger, E.  From Moscow to the Prussian frontier.  L., Hutchinson, 1945 136p.

3474  Last letters from Stalingrad.  McLean, Coronet P., 1955.  60p.; L., M-ethuen, 1956.    70p.

3475  Lipper, E.  Eleven years in Soviet prison camps.  Chicago, Regnery; L., Hollis & Carter, 1951.    310p.

3476  Magidoff, N.I.  Nila, her story as told to Willie Snow Ethridge.  N.Y., Simon & Schuster, 1956.    241p.

3477  Maks, L.  Russia by the back door.  L., Sheed & Ward, 1954.    264p.

3478  Malaparte, C.  The Volga rises in Europe.  L., Redman, 1957.    281p.

3479  Moats, A.-L.  Blind date with Mars.  Garden City, N.Y., Doubleday, 1943. 486p.

3480  Nork, K.  Hell in Siberia.  L., Hale, 1957.    222p.

3481  Pabst, H.  The outermost frontier:  a German soldier in the Russian cam-paign.  L., Kimber, 1957.    204p.

3482  Rawicz, L., Downing, R.  The long walk:  a gamble for life.  N.Y., Harp-er; L., Constable, 1956.    246p.

3483  Skrjabina, E.  Siege and survival:  the odyssey of a Leningrader.  Car-bondale, Southern Illinois U.P., 1971.    174p.

3484  Stypulkovski, Z.  Invitation to Moscow.  N.Y., Walker, 1962.    359p.

3485  Vogeler, R.A.  I was Stalin's prisoner.  N.Y., Harcourt, 1952.    314p.

3486  Wigmans, J.H.  Ten years in Russia and Siberia.  L., Darton, 1964.234p.

3487  Wittlin, T.  A reluctant traveller in Russia.  N.Y., Rinehart, 1952.

280p.; L., Hodge, 1952.    237p.

3488    Zieser, B.  In their shallow graves.  L., Elek, 1956.    208p.


F    The Khrushchev period

3489    Boffa, G.  Inside the Khrushchev era.  N.Y., Marzani, 1959.;  L., Allen
        & Unwin, 1960.    226p.

3490    Brumberg, A.  Russia under Khrushchev:  an anthology from 'Problems of
        Communism'.  N.Y., Praeger;  L., Methuen, 1962.    660p.

3491    Crankshaw, E.  Krushchev's Russia.  Harmondsworth, Penguin, 1959. 175p.

3492    Crankshaw, E.  Russia without Stalin:  the emerging pattern.  N.Y., Vik-
        ing;  L., Joseph, 1956.    287p.

3493    Current Digest of the Soviet Press.  Current Soviet policies:  the doc-
        umentary record of the nineteenth Communist Party Congress and the reor-
        ganization after Stalin's death.  N.Y., Praeger, 1953.    268p.

3494    Current Digest of the Soviet Press.  Current Soviet policies,2:  a docu-
        mentary record, 1953-1956, from the death of Beria through the Twentieth
        Communist Party Congress and the reevaluation of Stalin.  N.Y., Praeger,
        1956.    256p.

3495    Current Digest of the Soviet Press.  Current Soviet policies, 3:  the d-
        ocumentary record of the extraordinary 21st Congress of the Communist P-
        arty of the Soviet Union;  with a Who's Who of the Central Committee, co-
        mp. by M. Neuweld.  N.Y., Columbia U.P., 1960.    230p.

3496    Current Digest of the Soviet Press.  Current Soviet policies, 4:  the d-
        ocumentary record of the 22nd Congress of the Communist Party of the So-
        viet Union;  with a Who's Who of the Central Committee,  comp. by M. Ne-
        uweld.  N.Y., Columbia U.P., 1962.    248p.

3497    Dallin, D.J.  The changing world of Soviet Russia.  New Haven, Yale U.P.,
        1956.    422p.

3498    Deutscher, I.  Russia after Stalin;  with a new introduction by M. Lieb-
        man.  Indianapolis, Bobbs;  L., Cape, 1969.    174p.

3499    Dirscherl, D.  The new Russia:  communism in evolution.  Dayton, Pflaum,
        1968.    203p.

3500    Embree, G.D.  The Soviet Union between the 19th and 20th Party Congress-
        es, 1952-1956.  The Hague, Nijhoff, 1959.    365p.

3501    Hearst, W.R. and others.  Khrushchev and the Russian challenge.  N.Y.,
        Avon, 1961.    255p.

3502    Hindus, M.G.  Crisis in the Kremlin.  N.Y., Doubleday, 1953.    319p.

3503 Hyland, W., Shryock, R.W. The fall of Khrushchev. N.Y., Funk & Wagnall; L., Pitman, 1970. 209p.

3504 Institute for the Study of the U.S.S.R. Report on the Soviet Union in 1956: a symposium. Munich, 1956. 218p.

3505 Jacobs, D.N. The new communist manifesto and related documents. 2nd ed. Evanston, Row, Peterson, 1962. 250p.

3506 Laqueur, W.Z., Labedz, L. The future of Communist society. N.Y., Praeger, 1962. 196p.

3507 Lazareff, H., Lazareff, P. The Soviet Union after Stalin. L., Odhams, 1955. 254p.

3508 Leonhard, W. The Kremlin since Stalin. N.Y., Praeger; L., Oxford U.P., 1962. 403p.

3509 Malenkov, G.M. Report to the nineteenth party congress on the work of the Central Committee of the C.P.S.U.(B). Moscow, FLPH, 1952. 147p.

3510 Page, M. The day Khrushchev fell. N.Y., Hawthorn, 1965. 224p.

3511 Page, M. Burg, D. Unpersoned: the fall of Nikita Sergeyevitch Khrushchev. L., Chapman & Hall, 1966. 174p.

3512 Pethybridge, R. A key to Soviet politics: the crisis of the anti-party group. N.Y., Praeger, 1962. 207p.

3513 Program of the Communist Party of the Soviet Union; special preface to the American edition by N.S. Khrushchev. N.Y., International Publications, 1963. 143p.

3514 Ronchey, A. Russia in the thaw. N.Y., Norton, 1964. 249p.

3515 Rush, M. The rise of Khrushchev. Washington, Public Affairs P., 1958. 116p.

3516 Salisbury, H.E. Moscow journal: the end of Stalin. Chicago, U. of Chicago P., 1961. 441p.

3517 Salisbury, H.E. Stalin's Russia and after. L., Macmillan, 1955. 329p.

3518 Schapiro, L. The U.S.S.R. and the future: an analysis of the new program of the C.P.S.U. N.Y.; L., Praeger, 1962. 324p.

3519 Stipp, J.L. Soviet Russia today: patterns and prospects. N.Y., Harper, 1956. 270p.

3520 Swearer, H.R., Rush, M. The politics of succession in the U.S.S.R.: materials on Khrushchev's rise to leadership. Boston, Mass., Little, 1964. 324p.

3521 Ulam, A.B. The new face of Soviet totalitarianism. Cambridge, Mass., Harvard U.P., 1963. 236p.

3522   Werth, A.   Russia under Khrushchev.   N.Y., Hill & Wang, 1962.   352p.; T-
he Khrushchev phase:  the Soviet Union enters the 'decisive' sixties. L.,
Hale, 1961.   284p.

3523   Young, G.  Stalin's heirs.  L., Verschoyle, 1953.   156p.


G      The Brezhnev — Kosygin period

3524   Conquest, R.   Russia after Khrushchev.   N.Y., Praeger;  L., Pall Mall,
1965.   267p.

3525   Diamond, S.   The Soviet Union since Khrushchev:  new trends and old problems.   N.Y., Academy of Political Science, 1965.   116p.

3526   Kassof, A.   Prospects for Soviet society.   N.Y., Praeger;  L., Pall Mall
P., 1968.   582p.

3527   Kudryavtsev, V.   The 24th C.P.S.U. Congress and the struggle for peace.
Moscow, Novosti, 1972.   112p.

3528   Shub, A.   An empire loses hope:  the return of Stalin's ghost.  L., Cape,
1971.   474p.

3529   Soviet Affairs Symposium, 1st, Garmisch-Partenkirchen, 1967.   Papers pr-
esented at the first Soviet Affairs Symposium.   Garmisch, U.S. Army Institute for Advanced Russian and East European Studies, 1967.   140p.

3530   Soviet Affairs Symposium, 2nd, Garmisch-Partenkirchen, 1968.   The 51st
year:  the jubilee ends, the problems multiply.   Garmisch, U.S. Army Institute for Advanced Russian and East European Studies, 1968.   99p.

3531   Soviet Affairs Symposium, 3d, Garmisch-Partenkirchen, 1969.   Soviet Strategy for the 70's.   Garmisch,  U.S. Army Institute for Advanced Russian
and East European Studies, 1969.   143p.

3532   Strong, J.W.   The Soviet Union under Brezhnev and Kosygin:  the transition years.   N.Y., Van Nostrand, 1971.   277p.

3533   Tatu, M.   Power in the Kremlin from Krushchev to Kosygin.   N.Y., Viking;
L., Collins, 1969.   570p.

3534   Voices of tomorrow:  the 24th Congress of the Communist Party of the Soviet Union.   N.Y., NWR Publications, 1971.   192p.


H      Foreign Relations

(i)    General

3535   Adams, A.E.   Readings in Soviet foreign policy:  theory and practice. B-
oston, Mass., Heath, 1961.   420p.

3536   Anisimov, O.   The ultimate weapon.  Chicago, Regnery, 1953.   163p.

3537   Arnot, R.P.   Soviet Russia and her neighbors.   N.Y., Vanguard, 1927.
168p.

3538   Aspaturian, V.V.   Process and power in Soviet foreign policy.   Boston,
Mass., Little, 1971.   939p.

3539   Atkinson, J.D.   The edge of war.   Chicago, Regnery, 1960.   318p.

3540   Barghoorn, F.C.   Soviet foreign propaganda.   Princeton, Princeton U.P.,
1964.   329p.

3541   Barghoorn, F.C.   The Soviet cultural offensive:   the role of cultural d-
iplomacy in Soviet foreign policy.   Princeton, Princeton U.P.,   1960.
353p.

3542   Beloff, M.   The foreign policy of Soviet Russia, 1929–1941.   L., Oxford
U.P., 1947–49.   2 vols.

3543   Berzins, A.   The two faces of coexistence.   N.Y., Speller, 1967.   335p.

3544   Bessedovsky, G.   Revelations of a Soviet diplomat.   L., Williams & Norgate, 1931.   276p.

3545   Bishop, D.G.   Soviet foreign policy:   documents and readings.   Syracuse,
Syracuse U.P., 1952.   223p.

3546   Bouscaren, A.T.   Soviet expansion and the west.   San Francisco, Pacific
States, 1949.   199p.

3547   Bouscaren, A.T.   Soviet foreign policy:   a pattern of persistence. N.Y.,
Fordham U.P., 1962.   187p.

3548   Brzezinski, Z.K.   The Soviet bloc:   unity and conflict.   Rev. ed.   N.Y.,
Praeger, 1961.   543p.

3549   Campbell, J.R.   Soviet policy and its critics.   L., Gollancz, 1939.
381p.

3550   Carman, E.D.   Soviet imperialism:   Russia's drive towards world domination.   Washington, Public Affairs, 1950.   175p.

3551   Carr, E.H.   The Soviet impact on the western world.   N.Y.; L., Macmillan, 1946.   116p.

3552   Carroll, E.M.   Soviet communism and western opinion, 1919–1921.   Chapel
Hill, U. of North Carolina P., 1965.   302p.

3553   Chamberlin, W.H.   Beyond containment.   Chicago, Regnery, 1953.   406p.

3554   Clemens, D.S.   Yalta.   L., Oxford U.P., 1972.   356p.

3555   Coates, W.P.   World affairs and the U.S.S.R.   L., Lawrence & Wishart,
1939.   251p.

3556  Columbia University. _Russian Institute_. The anti-Stalin campaign and international communism: a selection of documents. N.Y., Columbia U.P., 1956.   338p.

3557  Conference on a century of Russian foreign policy, Yale University, 1961. Russian foreign policy: essays in historical perspective;  ed by I.J. Lederer. New Haven, Yale U.P., 1962.   620p.

3558  Corry, J.A.  Soviet Russia and the western alliance.  Toronto, Canadian Institute of International Affairs, 1958.   102p.

3559  Cousins, N.  The improbable triumvirate:  John F. Kennedy, Pope John, Nikita Khrushchev. N.Y., Norton, 1972.   171p.

3560  Crozier, B.  The peacetime strategy of the Soviet Union:  report of a study group of the Institute for the Study of Conflict, London, Sept. 1972 -Jan. 1973.  L., Institute for the Study of Conflict, 1973.   83p.

3561  Dallin, A.  Soviet conduct in world affairs:  a selection of readings. N.Y., Columbia U.P., 1960.   318p.

3562  Dallin, D.J.  The big three:  the United States, Britain and Russia.  New Haven, Yale U.P., 1945.;  L., Allen & Unwin, 1946.   232p.

3563  Dallin, D.J.  Soviet foreign policy after Stalin.  Philadelphia, Lippincott, 1961.;  L., Methuen, 1962.   543p.

3564  Dallin, D.J.  Soviet Russia's foreign policy, 1939-1942.  New Haven, Yale U.P., 1942.   452p.

3565  Dark, E.P.  The world against Russia?  Sydney, Pinchgut P., 1948.   352p.

3566  Davis, J.  Behind Soviet power:  Stalin and the Russians.  N.Y., Reader's P., 1946.   120p.

3567  Dean, V.M.  Russia — menace or promise?  2nd ed.  N.Y., Holt,   1947. 158p.

3568  Degras, J.T.  Calendar of Soviet documents on foreign policy, 1917-1941. L., R.I.I.A., 1948.   348p.

3569  Degras, J.T.  Soviet documents on foreign policy.  L., Oxford U.P., 1951-53.   3 vols.

3570  Dennis, A.L.P.  The foreign policies of Soviet Russia.  N.Y., Dutton; L., Dent, 1924.   500p.

3571  Deutscher, I.  The great contest:  Russia and the West.  N.Y.;  L., Oxford U.P., 1960.   86p.

3572  Deutscher, I.  Russia, China, and the West:  a contemporary chronicle, 1953-1966.  N.Y.;  L., Oxford U.P., 1970.   360p.

3573  Dinerstein, H.S.  Fifty years of Soviet foreign policy.  Baltimore, Johns Hopkins P., 1968.    73p.

3574  Donnelly, D.  Struggle for the world:  the Cold War, 1917—1965.  N.Y.,
      St Martin's P.;  L., Collins, 1965.    512p.

3375  Drane, J.F.  Pilgrimage to Utopia.  Milwaukee, Bruce, 1965.    155p.

3576  Dulles, E.L., Crane, R.D.  Detente:  cold war strategies in transition.
      N.Y., Praeger, 1965.    307p.

3577  Duncan, W.R.  Soviet policy in developing countries.  Waltham, Ginn, 19—
      70.    350p.

3578  Ermarth, F.W.  Internationalism, security and legitimacy:  the challenge
      to Soviet interests in East Europe, 1964—1968.  Santa Monica, Rand Corp.,
      1969.    162p.

3579  Eudin, X.J., Fisher, H.H.  Soviet Russia and the West, 1920—1927:  a do-
      cumentary survey.  Stanford, Stanford U.P., 1957.    450p.

3580  Eudin, X.J., Slusser, R.M.  Soviet foreign policy, 1928—1934:  documents
      and materials.  University Park, Pennsylvania U.P., 1967.    2 vols.

3581  Feis, H.  Between war and peace:  the Potsdam Conference.  Princeton, P-
      rinceton  U.P., 1960.    367p.

3582  Feis, H.  Churchill, Roosevelt, and Stalin:  the war they waged and the
      peace they sought.  Princeton, Princeton U.P., 1957.    692p.

3583  Fischer, L.  The great challenge.  N.Y., Duell, 1946.;  L., Cape, 1947.
      358p.

3584  Fischer, L.  Oil imperialism:  the international struggle for petroleum.
      N.Y., International Publishers, 1926.    256p.

3585  Fischer, L.  The road to Yalta:  Soviet foreign relations 1941—1945. N.Y.,
      Harper, 1972.    238p.

3586  Fischer, L.  Russia's road from peace to war:  Soviet foreign relations.
      N.Y., Harper, 1969.    499p.

3587  Fischer, L.  The Soviets in world affairs:  a history of the relations
      between the Soviet Union and the rest of the world, 1917—1929. 2nd ed.
      Princeton, Princeton U.P., 1951.    2 vols.

3588  Fisher, H.H.  America and Russia in the world community.  Claremont, Cl-
      aremont College, 1946.    175p.

3589  Flegon, A.  Soviet foreign trade technique:  an inside guide to Soviet
      foreign trade.  L., Flegon P., 1965.    148p.

3590  Fleming, D.F.  The cold war and its origins, 1917—1960.  Garden City, N.
      Y., Doubleday, 1961.    2 vols.

3591  Fletcher, W.C.  Religion and Soviet foreign policy, 1945-1970.  L., Oxford U.P., 1973.  179p.

3592  Fontaine, A.  History of the cold war from the October Revolution to the Korean War, 1917-1950.  L., Secker & Warburg, 1968.  432p.

3593  Foote, J.  Russian and Soviet imperialism.  Richmond, Foreign Affairs Publishing, 1972.  272p.

3594  Foust, C.M., Lerner,,W.  The Soviet world in flux:  six essays.  Atlanta Southern Regional Education Board, 1967.  173p.

3595  Gehlen, M.P.  The politics of coexistence:  Soviet methods and motives.  Bloomington, Indiana U.P., 1967.  334p.

3596  Gibney, F.  The Khrushchev pattern.  N.Y., Duell, 1961.  280p.

3597  Gilbert, R.  Competitive co-existence:  the new Soviet challenge.  N.Y., Bookmailer, 1956.  182p.

3598  Goldman, M.I.  Soviet foreign aid.  N.Y.; L., Praeger, 1967.  265p.

3599  Goldwin, R.A. and others.  Readings in Russian foreign policy.  N.Y., Oxford U.P., 1959.  775p.

3600  Goode, W.T.  Is intervention in Russia a myth?:  an excursion into recent political history.  L., Williams & Norgate, 1931.  126p.

3601  Goodman, E.R.  The Soviet design for a world state.  N.Y., Columbia U.P., 1960.  512p.

3602  Graebner, N.A.  The cold war:  ideological conflict or power struggle.  Boston, Mass., Heath, 1964.  105p.

3603  Graham, M.W.  The Soviet security system.  N.Y.; Worcester, Mass., Carnegie Endowment for International Peace, 1929.  89p.

3604  Great Britain.  Central office of Information.  Russia, China and the West.  L., H.M.S.O., 1968.  114p.

3605  Griffith, W.E.  Cold war and coexistence:  Russia, China, and the United States.  Englewood Cliffs, Prentice-Hall, 1971.  115p.

3606  Gurian, W. and others.  Soviet imperialism;  its origins and tactics.  Notre Dame, Notre Dame U.P., 1953.  166p.

3607  Haines, C.G.  The threat of Soviet imperialism.  Baltimore, Johns Hopkins P., 1954.  402p.

3608  Hamrell, S. Widstrand, C.G.  The Soviet bloc, China and Africa.  L., Pall Mall P., 1965.;  Uppsala, Scandinavian Institute of African Studies, 1964.  173p.

3609  Hanak, H.  Soviet foreign policy since the death of Stalin.  L., Routledge, 1972.    340p.

3610  Harper, S.N.  The Soviet Union and world problems.  Chicago, U. of Chic-
      ago P., 1935.    253p.

3611  Harriman, A.  Peace with Russia?  L., Gollancz, 1960.    174p.

3612  Hayter, W.  Russia and the world:  a study in Soviet foreign policy. N.Y.,
      Taplinger;  L., Secker & Warburg, 1970.    133p.

3613  Heater, D.  The cold war.  L., Oxford U.P., 1965.    80p.

3614  Herz, M.F.  Beginning of the cold war.  Bloomington, Indiana U.P., 1966.
      214p.

3615  Hoffman, E.P., Fleron, F.J.  The conduct of Soviet foreign policy.  Chi-
      cago, Aldine;  L., Butterworths, 1971.    478p.

3616  Huszar, G.B. de.  Soviet power and policy.  N.Y., Crowell, 1955.  598p.

3617  The impact of the Russian Revolution 1917-1967:  the influence of Bolsh-
      evism on the world outside Russia.  L., Oxford U.P., 1967.    357p.

3618  Ingram, K.  History of the cold war, 1945-1953.  N.Y., Philosophical Li-
      brary;  L., Finlayson, 1955.    239p.

3619  Ingrim, R.  After Hitler, Stalin?  Milwaukee, Bruce, 1946.    255p.

3620  Israelyan, V.  Soviet foreign policy:  a brief review 1955-1965.  Moscow,
      Progress, 1967.    284p.

3621  Joesten, J.  What Russia wants.  N.Y., Duell, 1944.    214p.

3622  Jones, G.J.  From Stalin to Krushchev.  L., Linden P., 1960.    206p.

3623  Joshua, W.  Arms for the third world:  Soviet military aid diplomacy. B-
      altimore, Johns Hopkins P., 1969.    169p.

3624  Karski, J.  Story of a secret state.  L., Hodder & Stoughton, 1945. 318p.

3625  Keeton, G.W., Schlesinger, R.  Russia and her western neighbours.  L.,
      Cape, 1942.    155p.

3626  Kelly, D.V.  Beyond the iron curtain.  L., Hollis & Carter, 1954.  83p.

3627  Kennan, G.F.  Russia, the atom and the West.  N.Y., Harper, 1958.;  L.,
      Oxford U.P., 1957.    120p.

3628  Kennan, G.F.  Russia and the West under Lenin and Stalin.  Boston, Mass.,
      Little;  L., Hutchinson, 1961.    411p.

3629  Kennan, G.F.  Soviet foreign policy, 1917-1941.  Princeton, Van Nostrand,
      1960.    192p.

3630   Khrushchev, N.S.  For victory in peaceful competition with capitalism; with a special preface written for the English edition.  L., Hutchinson, 1960.    784p.

3631   Kohler, F.D. and others.  Soviet strategy for the seventies:  from cold war to peaceful cosxistence.  Coral Gables, U. of Miami, Center for Advanced International Studies, 1973.    241p.

3632   Kohler, F.D.  Understanding the Russians:  a citizen's primer.  N.Y., Harper, 1970.    441p.

3633   Korostovetz, W.K.  Europe in the melting pot.  L., Hutchinson,1938. 320p

3634   Kulski, W.W.  Peaceful co-existence:  an analysis of Soviet foreign policy.  Chicago, Regnery, 1959.    662p.

3635   Kulski, W.W.  The Soviet Union in world affairs:  a documented analysis, 1964-1972.  Syracuse, Syracuse U.P., 1973.    526p.

3636   Lafeber, W.  The origins of the cold war, 1941-1947:  a historical problem with interpretations and documents.  N.Y., Wiley, 1971.    172p.

3637   Laserson, M.M.  Russia and the western world: the place of the Soviet Union in the comity of nations.  N.Y.; L., Macmillan, 1945.    275p.

3638   Lasky, V.  The ugly Russian.  N.Y., Simon & Schuster, 1965.    313p.

3639   Lerche, C.O.  The cold war — and after.  Englewood Cliffs, Prentice, 1965.    150p.

3640   Librach, J.  The rise of the Soviet empire:  a study of Soviet foreign policy.  N.Y., Praeger; L., Pall Mall P., 1964.    382p.

3641   Litvinov, M.  Against aggression:  speeches by Maxim Litvinov, together with texts of treaties and of the Covenant of the League of Nations.  L., Lawrence & Wishart, 1939.    208p.

3642   London, K.  The making of foreign policy.  Philadelphia, Lippincott, 1965.    358p.

3643   Lukacs, J.  A new history of the cold war.  Garden City, N.Y., Anchor Bks.,1966.    426p.

3644   Mackintosh, J.M.  Strategy and tactics of Soviet foreign policy.  Rev. ed.  N.Y.; L., Oxford U.P., 1963.    353p.

3645   Mager, N.H., Katel, J.  Conquest without war:  an analytical anthology of the speeches, interviews and remarks of Nikita Sergeyevich Khrushchev's statements.  N.Y., Simon & Schuster, 1961.    545p.

3646   Mair, G.B.  The day Khrushchev panicked.  L., Cassell, 1961.    172p.

3647   Mamatey, V.S.  Soviet Russian imperialism.  Princeton, Van Nostrand, 1964.    191p.

3648   Margulies, S.R.  The pilgrimage to Russia:  the Soviet Union and the tr-
eatment of foreigners, 1924-1937.  Madison, U. of Wisconsin  P., 1968.
290p.

3649   Marks, S.J.  The bear that walks like a man:  a diplomatic and military
analysis of Soviet Russia.  Philadelphia, Dorrance, 1943.   340p.

3650   Miller, R.H.  The evolution of the cold war from confrontation to containment.  N.Y., Holt, 1972.   141p.

3651   Molotov, V.M.  Problems of foreign policy:  speeches and statements, April 1945-November 1948.  Moscow, FLPH, 1949.   610p.

3652   Montgomery, B.L.  An approach to sanity:  a study of East-West relations.
Cleveland, World, 1960.;  L., Collins, 1959.   94p.

3653   Morray, J.P.  From Yalta to disarmament:  cold war debate.  N.Y., Monthly Review P., 1961.;  L., Merlin P., 1962.   368p.

3654   Mosely, P.E.  The Kremlin and world politics:  studies in Soviet policy
and action.  N.Y., Vintage Bks., 1960.   557p.

3655   Mosely, P.E.  The Soviet Union, 1922-1962:  a 'Foreign Affairs' reader.
N.Y, Praeger, 1963.   497p.

3656   Murphy, J.T.  Russia on the march:  a study of Soviet foreign policy. L.,
Lane, 1941.   128p.

3657   National Peace Council.  Commission on East-West relations.  Two worlds
in focus:  studies of the cold war.  L., National Peace Council, 1950.
133p.

3658   Nearing, S.  The Soviet Union as a world power.  N.Y., Island Workshop
P., 1945.   105p.

3659   Neumann, W.L.  After victory:  Churchill, Roosevelt, Stalin and the making of the peace.  N.Y., Harper, 1967.   212p.

3660   Norborg, C.S.  Operation Moscow.  N.Y., Dutton, 1947.   319p.

3661   Overstreet, H., Overstreet, B.  The war called peace:  Khrushchev's communism.  N.Y., Norton, 1961.   368p.

3662   Oliva, L.J.  Russia and the West from Peter to Khrushchev.  Boston, Mass.,
Heath, 1966.   289p.

3663   Paloczi-Horvath, G.  The facts rebel:  the future of Russia and the West.
L., Secker & Warburg, 1964.   256p.

3664   Pares, B.  Russia and the peace.  N.Y., Macmillan;  Harmondsworth, Penguin, 1944.   293p.

3665   Pentony, D.E.  Red world in tumult:  communist foreign policies.  San F-
rancisco, Chandler, 1962.   299p.

3666  Pentony, D.E.  Soviet behavior in world affairs:  communist foreign pol-
      icies.  San Francisco, Chandler, 1962.    308p.

3667  Pittman, J., Pittman, M.  Peaceful coexistence: its theory and practice
      in the Soviet Union.  N.Y., International Publishers, 1964.    156p.

3668  Pritt, D.N.  Must the war spread?  Harmondsworth, Penguin, 1940.  256p.

3669  Pritt, D.N.  Russia is for peace.  L., Lawrence & Wishart, 1951.  106p.

3670  Problems of Soviet foreign policy.  Munich, Institute for the Study of
      the U.S.S.R., 1959.    141p.

3671  Ra'anan, U.  The U.S.S.R. arms the third world:  case studies in Soviet
      foreign policy.  Cambridge, Mass., MITP., 1969.    256p.

3672  Rees, D.  The age of containment:  the Cold War, 1945-1965.  N.Y., St M-
      artin's P., L., Macmillan, 1967.    156p.

3673  Rosser, R.F.  An introduction to Soviet foreign policy.  Englewood Clif-
      fs, Prentice, 1969.    391p.

3674  Rothstein, A.  Peaceful coexistence.  Harmondsworth, Penguin,1955. 192p.

3675  Rubinstein, A.Z.  The foreign policy of the Soviet Union.  3rd ed. N.Y.,
      Random, 1972.    474p.

3676  Rush, M.  The international situation and Soviet foreign policy:  key r-
      eports by Soviet leaders from the Revolution to the present.  Columbus,
      Merrill, 1969.    358p.

3677  Sayers, M., Kahn, A.E.  The great conspiracy:  the secret war against S-
      oviet Russia.  Boston, Little, 1946.    433p.

3678  Schubart, W.  Russia and western man.  N.Y., Ungar, 1950.    300p.

3679  Seton-Watson, H.  From Lenin to Malenkov:  the history of world communi-
      sm.  N.Y., Praeger, 1953.    377p.

3680  Seton-Watson, H.  Neither war nor peace:  the struggle for power in the
      postwar world.  N.Y., Praeger; L., Methuen, 1960.    504p.

3681  Seton-Watson, H.  The new imperialism.  Rev. ed.  Totowa, Rowman & Litt-
      lefield;  L., Bodley Head, 1971.    144p.

3682  Shub, D.  The choice.  N.Y., Duell, 1950.    205p.

3683  Shulman, M.D.  Beyond the cold war.  New Haven, Yale U.P., 1966.    111p.

3684  Shulman, M.D.  Stalin's foreign policy reappraised.  Cambridge, Mass.,
      Harvard U.P., 1963.    320p.

3685  Snow, E.  Stalin must have peace.  N.Y., Random, 1947.    184p.

3686  The Soviet Union and peace; preface by H. Barbusse. L., Lawrence, 1929. 292p.

3687  The Soviet Union in Europe and the Near East: her capabilities and intentions. L., Royal United Services Institute, 1970.  108p.

3688  Sternberg, F. How to stop the Russians without war. N.Y., Day, 1948. 146p.

3689  Thompson, J.M. Russia, Bolshevism and the Versailles Peace. Princeton, Princeton, U.P., 1966.  430p.

3690  Thornton, T.P. The third world in Soviet perspective: studies by Soviet writers on the developing areas. Princeton, Princeton U.P.,  1964. 335p.

3691  Tokaev, G.A. Stalin means war. L., Weidenfeld & Nicolson, 1951. 214p.

3692  Tran-Tam. The storm within communism: a documentary study. Saigon, Free Pacific Editions, 1959.  150p.

3693  Trefousse, H.L. The cold war: a book of documents. N.Y., Putnam,1965. 296p.

3694  Triska, J.F., Finley, D.D. Soviet foreign policy. N.Y., Macmillan, 1968.  518p.

3695  Trush, M. Soviet foreign policy: early years. Moscow, Novosti P. Agency, 1970.  286p.

3696  Ulam, A.B. Expansion and co-existence: the history of Soviet foreign policy, 1917-1967. N.Y., Praeger; L., Secker & Warburg, 1968. 775p.

3697  Wade, R.A. The Russian search for peace, February – October 1917. Stanford, Stanford U.P., 1969.  196p.

3698  Warth, R.D. Soviet Russia in world politics. N.Y., Twayne; L., Vision P., 1963.  544p.

3699  Weeks, A.L. The other side of coexistence: an analysis of Russian foreign policy. N.Y., Pitman, 1970.  304p.

3700  Wesson, R.G. Soviet foreign policy in perspective. Homewood, Dorsey, 1969.  472p.

3701  Whelan, J.G. and others. Soviet empire: study in discrimination and abuse of power. Washington, USGPO, 1965.  197p.

3702  Winks, R.W. The cold war from Yalta to Cuba. N.Y., Macmillan; L., Collier-Macmillan, 1964.  106p.

3703  Wolfe, H.C. The imperial Soviets. N.Y., Doubleday, 1940.  294p.

3704 Yakhontoff, V.A. U.S.S.R.: foreign policy. N.Y., Coward, 1945. 311p.

(ii) <u>Africa</u>

3705 Brzezinski, Z.K. Africa and the communist world. Stanford, Stanford U. P., 1963. 272p.

3706 Cohn, H.D. Soviet policy towards Black Africa: the focus on national integration. N.Y.; L., Praeger, 1972. 316p.

3707 Klinghoffer, A.J. Soviet perspectives on African socialism. Rutherford, Farleigh Dickinson U.P., 1969. 276p.

3708 Legvold, R. Soviet policy in West Africa. Cambridge, Mass., Harvard U. P., 1970. 372p.

3709 Lessing, P. Africa's red harvest. N.Y., Day; L., Joseph, 1962. 207p.

3710 Morison, D.L. The U.S.S.R. and Africa. N.Y.; L., Oxford U.P., 1964. 124p.

(iii) <u>America</u>

(a) <u>Canada</u>

3711 Balawyder, A. Canadian—Soviet relations between the world wars. Toronto, U. of Toronto P., 1972. 248p.

(b) <u>United States</u>

3712 Alperovitz, G. Atomic diplomacy: Hiroshima and Potsdam; the use of the atomic bomb and the American confrontation with Soviet power. N.Y., Simon & Schuster, 1965.; L., Secker & Warburg, 1966. 317p.

3713 America's message to the Russian people. Boston, Mass., Marshall Jones, 1918. 154p.

3714 Barghoorn, F.C. The Soviet image of the United States: a study in distortion. N.Y., Harcourt, 1950. 297p.

3715 Beggs, R. The Cuban missile crisis. Harlow, Longman, 1971. 101p.

3716 Beitzell, R. The uneasy alliance: America, Britain and Russia, 1941–1943. N.Y., Knopf, 1972. 404p.

3717 Bell, C. Negotiation from strength: a study in the politics of power. N.Y., Knopf, 1963. 248p.; L., Chatto & Windus, 1962. 223p.

3718 Bennett, E.M. Recognition of Russia: an American foreign policy dilemma. Waltham, Mass., Blaisdell, 1970. 226p.

3719 Bishop, D.G. The Roosevelt—Litvinov agreements: the American view. Syracuse, Syracuse U.P., 1965. 297p.

3720  Bohlen, C.E.  Witness to history, 1929–1969.  L., Weidenfeld & Nicolson, 1973.    562p.

3721  Bose, T.C.  American Soviet relations 1921–1933.  Calcutta, Mukhopadhyay, ay, 1967.    228p.

3722  Browder, E.  War or peace with Russia?  N.Y., Wyn, 1947.    190p.

3723  Browder, R.P.  The origins of Soviet–American diplomacy.  Princeton, Princeton U.P., 1953.    256p.

3724  Brown, D.B.  Soviet attitudes towards American writing.  Princeton, Princeton U.P., 1962.    338p.

3725  Bullitt, W.C.  The Bullitt mission to Russia:  testimony before the Committee on Foreign Relations, U.S. Senate, of William C. Bullitt.  N.Y., Huebsch, 1919.    151p.

3726  Campaigne, J.G.  American might and Soviet myth.  Chicago, Regnery, 1962.  218p.

3727  Carr, A.H.Z.  Truman, Stalin and peace.  Garden City, N.Y., Doubleday, 1950.    256p.

3728  Clubb, O.E.  The United States and the Sino–Soviet bloc in the Southeast Asia.  Washington, Brookings Institution, 1962.    173p.

3729  Condoide, M.V.  Russian–American trade.  Columbus, Ohio State U., Bureau of Business Research, 1946.    160p.

3730  Crocker, G.N.  Roosevelt's road to Russia.  Chicago, Regnery, 1959. 312p

3731  Cumming, C.K., Pettit, W.W.  Russian–American relations, March 1917–March 1920:  documents and papers.  N.Y., Harcourt, 1920.    375p.

3732  Davies, J.E.  Mission to Moscow.  N.Y., Simon & Schuster, 1941.;  L., Gollancz, 1942.    683p.

3733  Dawson, R.H.  The decision to aid Russia, 1941; foreign policy and domestic politics.  Chapel Hill, U. of North Carolina P., 1959.    315p.

3734  Dean, V.M.  The United States and Russia.  Cambridge, Mass., Harvard U.P., 1947.    321p.

3735  Deane, J.R.  The strange alliance:  the story of our efforts at war-time co-operation with Russia.  N.Y., Viking, 1947.    333p.

3736  Dennett, R., Johnson, J.E.  Negotiating with the Russians.  Boston, Mass., World Peace Foundation, 1951.    310p.

3737  Divine, R.A.  The Cuban missile crisis.  Chicago, Quadrangle, 1971. 248p

3738  Dobriansky, L.E.  U.S.A. and the Soviet myth.  Old Greenwich, Devin-Adair, 1971.    274p.

3739    Draper, T.   American communism and Soviet Russia:   the formative period.
        N.Y., Viking P.;   L., Macmillan, 1960.     558p.

3740    Druks, H.   Harry S. Truman and the Russians, 1945-1953.   N.Y., Speller,
        1967.     291p.

3741    Dunham, D.C.   Kremlin target:   U.S.A.;   conquest by propaganda.   N.Y.,
        Washburn, 1961.     274p.

3742    Farnsworth, B.   William C. Bullitt and the Soviet Union.   Bloomington,
        Indiana U.P., 1967.     244p.

3743    Filene, P.G.   Americans and the Soviet experiment, 1917-1933.   Cambridge,
        Mass., Harvard U.P., 1967.     389p.

3744    Filene, P.G.   American views of Soviet Russia, 1917-1965.   Homewood, Do-
        rsey, 1968.     404p.

3745    Fischer, L.   Russia, America, and the world.   N.Y., Harper, 1961. 245p.

3746    Fischer, L.   Why recognise Russia?:   the arguments for and against the
        recognition of the Soviet Government by the United States.   N.Y., Ballou,
        1931.     298p.

3747    Foner, P.S.   The Bolshevik revolution, its impact on American radicals,
        liberals and labor.   N.Y., International Publications, 1967.     304p.

3748    Francis, D.R.   Russia from the American Embassy, April 1916-November 19-
        18.   N.Y., Scribner's, 1921.     361p.

3749    Griffith, W.E.   Cold war and coexistence:   Russia, China and the United
        States.   Englewood Cliffs, Prentice, 1971.     115p.

3750    Harriman, W.A.   America and Russia in a changing world:   a half century
        of observation.   Garden City, N.Y., Doubleday;   L., Allen & Unwin, 1971.
        218p.

3751    Harriman, W.A.   Peace with Russia?   N.Y., Simon & Schuster, 1959.   174p.

3752    Herring, G.C.   Aid to Russia, 1941-1946:   strategy, diplomacy, the orig-
        ins of the cold war.   N.Y., Columbia U.P., 1973.     365p.

3753    Hess, G.R.   America and Russia:   from cold war confrontation to coexist-
        ence.   N.Y., Crowell, 1973.     148p.

3754    Jones, R.H.   The roads to Russia:   United States lend-lease to the Soviet
        Union.   Norman, U. of Oklahoma P., 1969.     326p.

3755    Kennan, G.F.   Soviet-American relations, 1917-1920.   Princeton, Princet-
        on U.P.;   L., Faber, 1956.     2 vols.

3756    Khrushchev, N.S.   Khrushchev in America:   full texts of the speeches ma-
        de by N.S. Khrushchev on his tour of the United States, September 15-27,
        1959.   N.Y., Crosscurrents, 1960.     231p.

3757  Kim, Y.H.  Patterns of competitive coexistence:  U.S.A. v U.S.S.R.
      N.Y., Putnam, 1966.    484p.

3758  Labin, S., Lyons, D.  Fifty years:  the U.S.S.R. versus the U.S.A.  N.Y.,
      Twin Circle, 1968.    236p.

3759  Lafeber, W.  America, Russia and the cold war, 1945-1971.  2nd ed. N.Y.,
      Wiley, 1972.    339p.

3760  Lape, E.E., Read, E.F.  The United States and the Soviet Union:  a repo-
      rt on the controlling factors in the relations between the United States
      and the Soviet Union.  N.Y., American Foundation, Committee on Russian-
      American relations, 1931.    279p.

3761  Lasch, C.  The American liberals and the Russian Revolution.  N.Y., Col-
      umbia U.P., 1962.    290p.

3762  Liston, R.A.  The United States and the Soviet Union:  a background book
      on the struggle for power.  N.Y., Parents' Magazine P., 1973.    284p.

3763  Lovenstein, M.  American opinion of Soviet Russia.  Washington, American
      Council on Public Affairs, 1941.    210p.

3764  McSherry, J.E.  Khrushchev and Kennedy in retrospect.  Palo Alto, Open-
      Door P., 1971.    233p.

3765  Marzani, C.  We can be friends.  N.Y., Topical Bks. Publishers,  1952.
      380p.

3766  Mayer, A.J.  Wilson vs Lenin:  political origins of the new diplomacy,
      1917-1918.  Cleveland, World, 1964.    435p.

3767  Meiburger, A.  The efforts of Raymond Robins toward the recognition of
      Soviet Russia.  Washington, Catholic U. of America P., 1958.    222p.

3768  Neal, F.W.  U.S. foreign policy and the Soviet Union.  Santa Barbara, C-
      enter for Study of Democratic Institutions, 1961.    60p.

3769  Nenoff, S.  Two worlds, U.S.A. - U.S.S.R.  Chicago, Midland, 1946. 320p.

3770  Parker, W.H.  The superpowers:  the United States and the Soviet Union.
      N.Y., Wiley; L., Macmillan, 1972.    347p.

3771  Paterson, T.G.  Soviet-American confrontation:  postwar reconstruction
      and the origins of the cold war.  Baltimore, Johns Hopkins P.,  1973.
      287p.

3772  Rapoport, A.  The big two:  Soviet-American perceptions of foreign poli-
      cy.  N.Y., Pegasus, 1971.    249p.

3773  Roberts, C.M.  Can we meet the Russians halfway?  Garden City, N.Y., Do-
      ubleday, 1958.    96p.

3774  Roberts, H.L.  Russia and America:  dangers and prospects.  N.Y., Harper,

1956.    251p.

3775    Robins, R., Hard, W.    Raymond Robins' own story.    N.Y., Harper,    1920.
248p.

3776    Rock, U.P.    A strategy of interdependence:    a program for the control of
conflict between the United States and the Soviet Union.    N.Y., Scribners, 1964.    399p.

3777    Root, E.    The United States and the war:    the mission to Russia, political addresses.    Cambridge, Mass., Harvard U.P., 1918.    362p.

3778    Schuman, F.L.    American policy towards Russia since 1917:    a study of d-
iplomatic history, international law and public opinion.    L., Lawrence,
1929.    399p.

3779    Schuman, F.L.    The cold war:    retrospect and prospect.    Baton Rouge, Lo-
uisiana State U.P., 1962.    104p.

3780    Schwartz, A.J.    America and the Russo-Finnish war.    Washington, Public
Affairs P., 1960.    103p.

3781    Slusser, R.M.    The Berlin crisis of 1961:    Soviet-American relations and
the struggle for power in the Kremlin, June-November 1961.    Baltimore,
Johns Hopkins P., 1973.    510p.

3782    Smith, W.B.    My three years in Moscow.    Philadelphia, Lippincott, 1950.
346p.; Moscow mission, 1946-1949.    L., Heinemann, 1950.    337p.

3783    Sobel, R.    The origins of interventionism:    the United States and the R-
usso-Finnish war.    N.Y., Bookman Associates, 1960.    204p.

3784    Sorokin, P.A.    Russia and the United States.    2nd ed.    L., Stevens, 1950
213p.

3785    Standley, W.H., Ageton, A.A.    Admiral ambassador to Russia.    Chicago, R-
egnery, 1955.    524p.

3786    Stettinus, E.R., Johnson, W.    Roosevelt and the Russians:    the Yalta Conference.    Garden City, N.Y., Doubleday, 1949.    367p.; L., Cape, 1950.
320p.

3787    Stoessinger, J.G.    Nations in darkness:    China, Russia, and America. N.Y
Random, 1971.    197p.

3788    Strakhovsky, L.I.    American opinion about Russia, 1917-1920.    Toronto,
U. of Toronto P., 1961.    135p.

3789    Sutton, A.C.    National suicide:    military aid to the Soviet Union.    New
Rochelle, Arlington House, 1973.    283p.

3790    Thayer, C.W.    Bears in the caviar.    Philadelphia, Lippincott, 1950. 303p

3791    Ulam, A.B.    The rivals:    America and Russia since World War II.    N.Y.,

Viking. 1971.; L., Allen Lane, 1973.    405p.

3792  U.S.A.  Department of State.  Papers relating to the foreign relations
      of the United States, 1918–1919:  Russia.  Washington, USGPO, 1931–37.
      4 vols.

3793  U.S.A.  Department of State.  Foreign relations of the United States: d-
      iplomatic papers;  the Soviet Union, 1933–1939.  Washington, USGPO, 1952.
      1034p.

      (c)  Latin America

3794  Russia in the Caribbean.  Washington, Georgetown U., Center for Strateg-
      ic and International Studies, 1973.    2 vols.

3795  Bethel, P.D.  The losers:  the definitive report, by an eye–witness, of
      the communist conquest of Cuba and the Soviet penetration in Latin Amer-
      ica.  New Rochelle, Arlington House, 1969.    615p.

3796  Clissold, S.  Soviet relations with Latin America, 1918–1968:  a docume-
      ntary survey.  N.Y.;  L., Oxford U.P., 1970.    313p.

3797  Jackson, D.B.  Castro, the Kremlin and communism in Latin America.  Bal-
      timore, Johns Hopkins P., 1969.    163p.

3798  Oswald, J.G., Carlton, R.G.  Soviet image of contemporary Latin America;
      a documentary history, 1960–1968.  Austin, U. of Texas P., 1970.  365p.

3799  Oswald, J.G., Strover, A.J.  The Soviet Union and Latin America.  N.Y.;
      L., Praeger, 1970.    190p.

3800  Weyl, N.  Red star over Cuba:  the Russian assault on the Western hemis-
      phere.  N.Y., Devin–Adair, 1960.    222p.

(iv)  Asia

      (a)  General

3801  Abhayavardhan, H.  Russo–American rivalry in Asia.  Bombay, Vora, 1954.
      182p.

3802  Beloff, M.  Soviet policy in the Far East, 1944–1951.  N.Y., Oxford U.P.,
      1953.    278p.

3803  Creel, G.  Russia's race for Asia.  N.Y., Bobbs, 1949.    264p.

3804  Dallin, D.J.  The rise of Russia in Asia.  New Haven, Yale U.P., 1949.;
      L., Hollis & Carter, 1950.    293p.

3805  Dallin, D.J.  Soviet Russia and the Far East.  New Haven, Yale U.P., 19–
      48.;  L., Hollis & Carter, 1949.    398p.

3806  Dodge, N.T.  The Soviets in Asia.  Mechanicsville, Cremona Foundation,
      1972.    108p.

3807   Eudin, X.J., North, R.C.   Soviet Russia and the East, 1920-1927:   a doc-
       umentary survey.   Stanford, Stanford U.P., 1957.   478p.

3808   Fuse, K.   Soviet policy in the Orient.   Peking, Enjinsha, 1927.   409p.

3809   Jukes, G.   The Soviet Union in Asia.   Sydney, Angus & Robertson,   1973.
       304p.

3810   Kapur, H.   The embattled triangle:   Moscow-Peking-India.   New Delhi, Ab-
       hinav, 1973.   175p.

3811   McLane, C.B.   Soviet strategies in Southeast Asia:   an exploration of e-
       astern policy under Lenin and Stalin.   Princeton, Princeton U.P., 1966.
       581p.

3812   Mandel, W.   Soviet source materials on U.S.S.R. relations with East Asia
       1945-1950;   with an introductory survey of Soviet Far Eastern policy sin-
       ce Yalta by M. Beloff.   N.Y., Institute of Pacific Relations, Internati-
       onal Secretariat, 1950.   289p.

3813   Moore, H.   Soviet Far Eastern policy, 1931-1945.   Princeton, Princeton
       U.P., 1945.   284p.

3814   Saunders, J.R.   The challenge of world communism in Asia.   Grand Rapids,
       Eerdmans, 1964.   725p.

3815   Tompkins, P.   American-Russian relations in the Far East.   N.Y., Macmil-
       lan, 1949.   426p.

   (b) Middle East

3816   Becker, A.S., Horelick, A.L.   Soviet policy in the Middle East.   Santa
       Monica, Rand Corp., 1970.   128p.

3817   Confino, M., Shamir, S.   The U.S.S.R. and the Middle East.   N.Y., Wiley;
       Jerusalem, Israel Universities P., 1973.   441p.

3818   Dagan, A.   Moscow and Jerusalem:   twenty years of relations between Isr-
       ael and the Soviet Union.   N.Y.; L., Abelard, 1970.   255p.

3819   Donovan, J.   U.S. and Soviet policy in the Middle East, 1945-56.   N.Y.,
       Facts on File, 1972.   282p.

3820   Fatemi, N.S.   The diplomatic history of Persia, 1917-1923:   Anglo-Russi-
       an power politics in Iran.   N.Y., Russell F. Moore, 1952.   331p.

3821   Hirschmann, I.A.   Red star over Bethlehem:   Russia drives to capture the
       Middle East.   N.Y., Simon & Schuster; L., Baker, 1971.   192p.

3822   Hurewitz, J.C.   Soviet-American rivalry in the Middle East.   N.Y., Prae-
       ger, 1969.   250p.

3823   Kapur, H.   Soviet Russia and Asia, 1917-1927:   a study of Soviet policy
       towards Turkey, Iran and Afghanistan.   N.Y., Humanities, 1967.;·

L., Joseph, 1966.    265p.

3824  Klieman, A.S.  Soviet Russia and the Middle East.  Baltimore, Johns Hopkins P., 1970.    107p.

3825  Landis, L.  Politics and oil:  Moscow in the Middle East.  N.Y., Dunellen, 1973.    201p.

3826  Laqueur, W.Z.  The Soviet Union and the Middle East.  N.Y., Praeger; L., Routledge, 1959.    366p.

3827  Laqueur, W.Z.  The struggle for the Middle East:  the Soviet Union and the Middle East, 1958-70.  Rev. ed.  Baltimore; Harmondsworth, Penguin, 1972.    267p.

3828  Lenczowski, G.  Russia and the west in Iran, 1918-1948:  a study in big-power rivalry.  Ithaca, Cornell U.P., 1949.    383p.

3829  McLane, C.B.  Soviet-Middle East relations.  London, Central Asian Research Centre, 1973.    126p.

3830  Nollau,G., Wiehe, J.  Russia's south flank:  Soviet operations in Iran, Turkey and Afghanistan.  N.Y., Praeger; L., Pall Mall P., 1963.    171p.

3831  Page, S.  The U.S.S.R. and Arabia:  the development of Soviet policies and attitudes towards the countries of the Arabian peninsula, 1955-70.  Central Asian Research Centre, 1971.    149p.

3832  Pennar, J.  The U.S.S.R. and the Arabs:  the ideological dimension. N.Y., Crane; L., Hurst, 1973.    180p.

3833  Smolansky, O.M.  The Soviet Union and the Arab East under Khrushchev. Lewisburg, Bucknell U.P., 1973.    326p.

3834  The U.S.S.R. and the Middle East:  problems of peace and security.  Moscow, Novosti P. Agency, 1972.    294p.

3835  Yodfat, M.  Arab politics in the Soviet mirror.  N.Y., Wiley;  Jerusalem Israel Universities P., 1973.    332p.

(c)  China

3836  Aitchen, K.W.  China and the Soviet Union:  a study of Sino-Soviet relations.  L., Methuen, 1950.    434p.

3837  Clubb, O.E.  China & Russia:  the 'great game'.  N.Y., Columbia U.P., 1971.    578p.

3838  Pavlovsky, M.N.  Chinese-Russian relations.  N.Y., Philosophical Library, 1949.    194p.

3839  Akimova, V.V. Vishnyakova-.  Two years in revolutionary China, 1925-1927. Cambridge, Mass., Harvard U., East Asian Research Centre, 1971.    352p.

3840  Brandt, C.  Stalin's failure in China, 1924-1927.  Cambridge, Mass., Harvard U.P., 1958.  226p.

3841  Chiang Kai-Shek.  Soviet Russia in China:  a summing-up at seventy.  N.Y., Farrar; L., Harrap, 1957.  392p.

3842  Hidaka, N.  Manchouko-Soviet border issues.  Dairen, Manchuria Daily News, 1938.  261p.

3843  McLane, C.B.  Soviet policy and the Chinese communists, 1931-1946.  N.Y., Columbia U.P., 1958.  310p.

3844  North, R.C.  Moscow and Chinese communists.  Stanford, Stanford U.P., 1954.  306p.

3845  Soviet plot in China.  Peking, Metropolitan Police Headquarters, 1928.  162p.

3846  Tang, P.S.H.  Russian and Soviet policy in Manchuria and Outer Mongolia, 1911-1931.  Durham, N.C., Duke U.P., 1959.  494p.

3847  Trotsky, L.  Problems of the Chinese Revolution; with appendices by Zinoviev, and others.  N.Y., Pioneer, 1932.  432p.

3848  Weigh, Ken-Shen.  Russo-Chinese diplomacy.  Shanghai, Commercial, 1928.  382p.

3849  Whiting, A.S.  Soviet policies in China, 1917-1924.  N.Y., Columbia U.P., 1954.  350p.

3850  Wilbur, C.M., Hsia, L.-Y.  Documents on communism, nationalism, and Soviet advisers in China, 1918-1927:  papers seized in the 1927 Peking raid.  N.Y., Columbia U.P., 1956.  617p.

3851  Wu, A.K.  China and the Soviet Union:  a study of Sino-Soviet relations.  N.Y., Day; L., Methuen, 1950.  434p.

3852  Ambroz, A.  Realignment of world power:  the Russo-Chinese schism under the impact of Mao Tse-Tung's last revolution.  N.Y., Speller, 1972.  2 vols.

3853  An, T-S.  The Sino-Soviet territorial dispute.  Philadelphia, Westminster P., 1973.  254p.

3854  Boorman, H.L.  Moscow-Peking axis:  strengths and strains.  N.Y., Harper, 1956.  227p.

3855  Chin Szu-K'ai.  Communist China's relations with the Soviet Union, 1949-1957.  Kowloon, Union Research Institute, 1961.  143p.

3856  Chin, C.S.  A study of Chinese dependence upon the Soviet Union for economic development as a factor in Communist China's foreign policy.  Kowloon, Union Research Institute, 1959.  196p.

3857   Clark, M.G.  Development of China's steel industry and Soviet technical
       aid.  Ithaca, Cornell U., N.Y. State School of Industrial & Labor Relat-
       ions, 1973.    160p.

3858   Crankshaw, E.  The new cold war: Moscow v. Pekin.  Baltimore; Harmond-
       sworth, Penguin, 1963.    167p.

3859   Doolin, D.J.  Territorial claims in the Sino-Soviet conflict:  documents
       and analysis.  Stanford, Hoover Institution P., 1965.    77p.

3860   Floyd, D.  Mao against Khrushchev:  a short history of the Sino-Soviet
       conflict.  N.Y., Praeger;  L., Pall Mall P., 1964.    456p.

3861   Fokkema, D.W.  Literary doctrine in China and Soviet influence, 1956-
       1960. The Hague, Mouton, 1965.    296p.

3862   Garthoff, R.L.  Sino-Soviet relations.  N.Y.; L., Praeger, 1966.  285p.

3863   Gittings, J.  The Sino-Soviet dispute, 1956-63:  extracts from recent
       documents. N.Y.; L., Oxford U.P., 1964.    77p.

3864   Gittings, J.  Survey of the Sino-Soviet dispute:  a commentary and extr-
       acts from the recent polemics, 1963-1967.  N.Y.; L., Oxford U.P., 1968.
       410p.

3865   Griffith, W.E.  Sino-Soviet relations, 1964-1965.  Cambridge, Mass.,MITP.,
       1967.    504p.

3866   Griffith, W.E.  The Sino-Soviet rift; analysed and documented.  Cambrid-
       ge, Mass., MITP.; L., Allen & Unwin, 1964.    508p.

3867   Hudson, G.F. and others. The Sino-Soviet dispute; documented and analy-
       sed.  N.Y., Praeger, 1961.    227p.

3868   International Conference on Sino-Soviet Bloc Affairs, 3rd, Lake Kawaguc-
       hi, 1960.  Unity and contradiction:  major aspects of Sino-Soviet relat-
       ions;  ed. by K. London.  N.Y., Praeger, 1962.    464p.

3869   Isenberg, I.  The Russian-Chinese rift:  its impact on world affairs. N.
       Y., Wilson, 1966.    221p.

3870   Jackson, W.A.D.  The Russo-Chinese borderlands:  zone of peaceful conta-
       ct or potential conflict.  2nd ed.  Princeton, Van Nostrand, 1968. 156p.

3871   Kalb, M.L.  Dragon in the Kremlin:  a report on the Russian-Chinese all-
       iance.  N.Y., Dutton; L., Gollancz, 1961.    258p.

3872   Klochko, M.A.  Soviet scientist in Red China.  N.Y., Praeger, 1964. 213p.

3873   Kruchinin, A., Olgin, V.  Territorial claims of Mao Tse-Tung:  history
       and modern times.  Moscow, Novosti P. Agency, 1971.    111p.

3874   Labedz, L., Urban, G.R.  The Sino-Soviet conflict:  eleven radio discus-
       sions.  Chester Springs, Dufour; L., Bodley Head, 1965.    192p.

3875  Langer, P.F.  The Soviet Union, China and the Pathet Lao:  analysis and chronology.  Santa Monica, Rand Corp., 1972.  121p.

3876  Levine, D.C.  The rift:  the Sino-Soviet conflict.  Jacksonville, Harris -Wolfe, 1968.  217p.

3877  Mayer, P.  Sino-Soviet relations since the death of Stalin.  Kowloon, Union Research Institute, 1962.  172p.

3878  Mehnert, K.  Peking and Moscow.  N.Y., Putnam;  L., Weidenfeld & Nicolson, 1963.  522p.

3879  Metaxas, A.  Moscow or Peking?  Chester Springs, Dufour, 1965.;  L., Chatto & Windus, 1961.  110p.

3880  Moseley, G.  A Sino-Soviet cultural frontier:  the Ili-Kazakh Autonomous Chou.  Cambridge, Harvard U., East Asian Research Center, 1966.  171p.

3881  Ronchey, A.  The two red giants:  an analysis of Sino-Soviet relations.  N.Y., Norton, 1965.  117p.

3882  Rupen, R.A., Farrell, R.  Vietnam and the Sino-Soviet dispute.  N.Y.; L., Praeger, 1967.  120p.

3883  Salisbury, H.E.  War between Russia and China.  N.Y., Norton, 1969. 224p; The coming war between Russia and China.  L., Secker & Warburg,  1969. 200p.

3884  Sheng, Y.  Sun Yat-Sen University in Moscow and the Chinese revolution; a personal account.  Lawrence, U. of Kansas, Center for East Asian Studies, 1971.  270p.

3885  The Sino-Soviet dispute.  N.Y., Scribner's;  Bristol, Keesing's  1969. 120p.

3886  Swearingen, R.  Soviet and Chinese communist power in the world today.  N.Y., Basic, 1966.  138p.

3887  Tang, P.S.H.  The Twenty-second Congress of the Communist Party of the Soviet Union and Moscow-Tirana-Peking relations.  Washington, Research Institute on the Sino-Soviet Bloc, 1962.  141p.

3888  Treadgold, D.W.  Soviet and Chinese communism:  similarities and differences.  Seattle, U. of Washington P., 1967.  452p.

3889  US.A.  Congress.  House of Representatives.  Foreign Affairs Committee.  Sino-Soviet conflict:  report on Sino-Soviet conflict and its implications, together with hearings.  Washington, USGPO, 1965.  412p.

3890  Wei, H.  China and Soviet Russia.  Princeton, Van Nostrand, 1956.  379p.

3891  Whiting, A.S., Sheng Shih-Tsai.  Sinkiang:  pawn or pivot?  East Lansing, Michigan State U.P., 1958.  314p.

3892 Yin, J. Sino-Soviet dialogue on the problem of war. The Hague, Nijhoff, 1971. 247p.

3893 Zablocki, C.J. Sino-Soviet rivalry, implications for U.S. policy. N.Y., Praeger, 1966. 240p.

3894 Zagoria, D.S. The Sino-Soviet conflict, 1956-1961. Princeton, Princeton U.P., 1962. 484p.

(d) The Indian sub-continent.

3895 Budhraj, V.S. Soviet Russia- and the Hindustan subcontinent. New Delhi, Somaiya, 1973. 296p.

3896 Kidran, M. Pakistan's trade with Eastern bloc countries. N.Y.; L., Praeger, 1972. 131p.

3897 Chopra, P. Before and after the Indo-Soviet treaty. New Delhi, S. Chand , 1971. 175p.

3898 Datar, A.L. India's economic relations with the U.S.S.R. and Eastern Europe, 1953-1969. Cambridge, Cambridge U.P., 1972. 278p.

3899 Druhe, D.N. Soviet Russia and Indian Communism, 1917-1947; with an epilogue covering the situation today. N.Y., Bookman, 1960. 429p.

3900 Imam, Z. Colonialism in East-West relations: a study of Soviet policy towards India and Anglo-Soviet relations, 1917-1947. New Delhi, Eastman, 1969. 531p.

3901 Kapur, H. The Soviet Union and the emerging nations: a case study of Soviet policy towards India. L., Joseph, 1972. 124p.

3902 Kaushik, D. Soviet relations with India and Pakistan. Delhi, Vikas, 1971. 119p.

3903 Kautsky, J.H. Moscow and the Communist Party of India: a study in the post-war evolution of international communist strategy. N.Y., Wiley; L., Chapman & Hall, 1956. 220p.

3904 Kulkarni, M. Indo-Soviet political relations since the Bandung Conference of 1955. Bombay, Vora, 1968. 216p.

3905 Menon, K.P.S. The Indo-Soviet treaty: setting and sequel. 2nd ed. Delhi, Vikas, 1972. 156p.

3906 Naik, J.A. Soviet policy towards India from Stalin to Brezhnev. Delhi, Vikas, 1970. 201p.

3907 Neelkant, K. Partners in peace: a study in Indo-Soviet relations. Delhi, Vikas, 1972. 201p.

3908 Prasad, B. Indo-Soviet relations, 1947-1972: a documentary study. Bombay, Allied Publications, 1973. 494p.

3909 Samra, C.S.S. India and Anglo—Soviet relations, 1917—1947. Bombay, As—
ia Publishing House, 1959.    186p.

3910 Stein, A.  India and the Soviet Union:  the Nehru era.  Chicago, U. of
Chicago P., 1969.    320p.

3911 Suri, S.L.  Red star over India?  Delhi, M. Gulab Singh, 1965.    89p.

(e)  Indonesia

3912 Dake, A.C.A.  In the spirit of the Red Banteng:  Indonesian communists
between Moscow and Peking 1959—1965.  The Hague, Mouton, 1973.    479p.

3913 McVey, R.T.  The Soviet view of the Indonesian revolution:  a study in
the Russian attitude towards Asian nationalism.  Ithaca, Cornell U., De—
pt. of Far Eastern Studies, Southeast Asia Program, Modern Indonesian P—
roject, 1958.    86p.

(f)  Japan

3914 Feis, H.  Contest over Japan.  N.Y., Norton, 1967.    187p.

3915 Hata, I.  Reality and illusion:  the hidden crisis between Japan and the
U.S.S.R., 1932—1934.  N.Y., Columbia U., East Asian Institute, 1967. 60p

3916 Hindus, M.  Russia and Japan.  Garden City, N.Y., Doubleday, 1942. 254p.

3917 Lensen, G.A.  Japanese diplomatic and consular officials in Russia:  a
handbook of Japanese representatives in Russia from 1874 to 1968.  Tall—
ahassee, Diplomatic P., 1968.    230p.

3918 Lensen, G.A.  Japanese recognition of the U.S.S.R.:  Soviet—Japanese re—
lations 1921—1930.  Tokyo, Sophia U. in cooperation with the Diplomatic
P., Tallahassee, 1970.    419p.

3919 Lensen, G.A.  The strange neutrality:  Soviet—Japanese relations during
the Second World War, 1941—1945.  Tallahassee, Diplomatic P., 1972. 332p.

3920 Vishwanathan, S.  Normalization of Japanese—Soviet relations, 1945—1970.
Tallahassee, Diplomatic P., 1973.    190p.

(v)  Europe

(a)  General

3921 Bennett, T.H.  The Soviets and Europe, 1938—41.  Geneva, U. of Geneva,
Institute of International Studies, 1952.    112p.

3922 Bishop, R., Crayfield, E.S.  Russia astride the Balkans.  N.Y., McBride,
1948.  253p.; L., Evans, 1949.    287p.

3923 Borsody, S.  The triumph of tyranny:  the Nazi and Soviet conquest of C—
entral Europe.  N.Y., Macmillan; L., Cape, 1960.    285p.

3924    Dallin, D.J.  Russia and postwar Europe.  New Haven, Yale U.P.,  1943.
        230p.

3925    Wagner, W.  The partitioning of Europe:  a history of the Soviet expans-
        ion up to the cleavage of Germany 1918-1945.  Stuttgart, 1959.    240p.

        (b)  Eastern Europe

3926    Bromke, A.  The communist states at the crossroads;  between Moscow and
        Peking.  N.Y., Praeger, 1965.    270p.

3927    Bromke, A., Rakowska-Harmstone, T.  The communist states in disarray,19-
        65-1971.  Minneapolis, U. of Minnesota P., 1972.    363p.

3928    Brzezinski, Z.K.  The Soviet bloc:  unity and conflict.  Rev. ed.  Camb-
        ridge, Mass., Harvard U.P., 1967.    599p.

3929    Czerwinski, E.J.,Piekalkiewicz, J.  The Soviet invasion of Czechoslovak-
        ia:  its effects on Eastern Europe.  N.Y.;  L., Praeger, 1972.    214p.

3930    Dallin, D.J.  Russia and postwar Europe.  New Haven, Yale U.P., 1943.
        230p.

3931    Gluckstein, Y.  Stalin's satellites in Europe.  L., Allen & Unwin, 1952.
        334p.

3932    How did the satellites happen?:  a study of the Soviet seizure of Easte-
        rn Europe, by a student of affairs.  L., Batchworth, 1952.    304p.

3933    Ionescu, G.  The breakup of the Soviet Empire in Eastern Europe.  Balti-
        more;  Harmondsworth, Penguin, 1965.    168p.

3934    Lehrmann, H.  Russia's Europe.  N.Y., Appleton, 1947.    341p.

3935    Nagy, F.  The struggle behind the Iron Curtain.  L., Macmillan, 1949.
        472p.

3936    Pethybridge, R.  The development of the communist bloc.  Boston, Mass.,
        Heath, 1966.    244p.

3937    Rothschild, J.  Communist Eastern Europe.  N.Y., Walker, 1964.    168p.

3938    Schwartz, H.  Eastern Europe in the Soviet shadow.  Aylesbury, Abelard,
        1973.    117p.

        (c)  Albania

3939    Griffith, W.E.  Albania and the Sino-Soviet rift.  Cambridge, Mass.,MITP.,
        1963.    423p.

        (d)  Austria

3940    Allard, S.  Russia and the Austrian State Treaty:  a case study of Sovi-
        et policy in Europe.  University Park, Pennsylvania State U.P.,  1970.

248p.

3941 Stearman, W.L.  The Soviet Union and the occupation of Austria:  an analysis of Soviet policy in Austria, 1945–1955.  Bonn, Siegler, 1962. 192p

(e)  Czechoslovakia

3942 Nemec, F. Moudry, V.  The Soviet seizure of Subcarpathian Ruthenia.  Toronto, Anderson, 1955.    375p.

3943 Stransky, J.  East wind over Prague.  L., Hollis & Carter, 1950.  244p.

(f)  Finland

3944 Citrine, W.  My Finnish diary.  L., Penguin, 1940.    192p.

3945 Clark, D.  Three days to catastrophe.  L., Hamilton, 1966.    228p.

3946 Coates, W.P., Coates, Z.K.  Russia, Finland and the Baltic.  L., Lawrence & Wishart, 1940.    144p.

3947 Coates, W.P., Coates, Z.K.  Soviet–Finnish campaign, military and political, 1939–1940.  L., Eldon, 1942.    172p.

3948 Condon, R.W.  The winter war:  Russia against Finland.  N.Y., Ballantine L., Pan, 1972.    160p.

3949 Cox, G.  The Red Army moves.  L., Gollancz;  Toronto, Ryerson,1941. 278p

3950 Elliston, H.B.  Finland fights.  Boston, Mass., Little, 1940.  443p.; L., Harrap, 1940.    394p.

3951 Engle, E., Paananen, L.  The winter war:  the Russo–Finnish conflict, 1939–40. N.Y., Scribner's 1972.;  L., Sidgwick & Jackson, 1973.    176p.

3952 Finland.  Ministry for Foreign Affairs.  The Finnish blue book:  the development of Finnish–Soviet relations during the autumn of 1939, including the official documents and the peace treaty of March 12, 1940.  Philadelphia, Lippincott, 1940.;  The development of Finnish–Soviet relations during the autumn of 1939, including the official documents.  L., Harrap; Helsinki, Oy. Suomen kirja, 1940.    113p.

3953 Finland.  Ministry for Foreign Affairs.  Finland reveals her secret documents on Soviet policy:  March 1940–June 1941.  N.Y., Funk, 1941. 109p.

3954 Halter, H.  Finland breaks the Russian chains.  L., Hamilton,1940. 232p.

3955 Jakobson, M.  The diplomacy of the Winter War:  an account of the Russo–Finnish war, 1939–1940.  Cambridge, Mass., Harvard U.P., 1961.    281p.

3956 Krosby, H.P.  Finland, Germany, and the Soviet Union, 1940–1941.:  the Petsamo dispute.  Madison, U. of Wisconsin P., 1968.    276p.

3957 Langdon–Davies, J.  Invasion in the snow:  a study of mechanized war.

Boston, Mass., Houghton, 1941.; Finland: the first total war. L., Routledge, 1941.   202p.

3958   Smith, C.J.   Finland and the Russian Revolution, 1917-1922.   Athens, U. of Georgia P., 1958.   251p.

3959   Soderhjelm, H.   The red insurrection in Finland in 1918:   a study based on documentary evidence.   L., Harrison, 1920.   159p.

3960   Tanner, V.A.   The winter war:   Finland against Russia, 1939-1940.   Stanford, Stanford U.P., 1957.   274p.

3961   Upton, A.F.   Finland in crisis, 1940-41:   a study in small-power politics.   Ithaca, Cornell U.P., 1965.   318p.

3962   Ward, E.   Despatches from Finland, January-April 1940.   L., Lane, 1940.   160p.

(g)   France

3963   Grosser, A.   Franco-Soviet relations today.   Santa Monica, Rand Corp., 1967.   103p.

3964   Rieber, A.J.   Stalin and the French Communist Party, 1941-1947.   N.Y., Columbia U.P., 1962.   395p.

3965   Scott, W.E.   Alliance against Hitler:   the origins of the Franco-Soviet pact.   Durham, N.C., Duke U.P., 1962.   296p.

(h)   Germany

3966   Carr, E.H.   German-Soviet relations between the two world wars, 1919-1939.   Baltimore, Johns Hopkins P., 1951.   146p.

3967   Dyck, L.   Weimar Germany and Soviet Russia, 1926-1933:   a study in diplomatic instability.   L., Chatto & Windus, 1966.   279p.

3968   Embree, G.D.   The Soviet Union and the German question, September 1958-June 1961.   The Hague, Nijhoff, 1963.   330p.

3969   Fischer, L.   Stalin and Hitler:   the reasons for and the results of the Nazi-Bolshevik past.   L., Penguin, 1941.   95p.

3970   Fischer, R.   Stalin and German communism:   a study in the origins of the State Party.   Cambridge, Mass., Harvard U.P., 1949.   687p.

3971   Freund, G.   Unholy alliance:   Russian-German relations from the Treaty of Brest-Litovsk to the Treaty of Berlin.   N.Y., Harcourt;   L., Chatto & Windus, 1957.   283p.

3972   Hilger, G., Meyer, A.G.   The incompatible allies:   a memoir-history of German-Soviet relations, 1918-1941.   N.Y., Macmillan, 1953.   350p.

3973   Klimov, G.   The terror machine:   the inside story of the Soviet administration in Germany. N.Y., Praeger; L., Faber, 1953.    400p.

3974  Kochan, L.  Russia and the Weimar Republic.  Cambridge, Bowes,    1954.
      190p.

3975  Kuklick, B.  American policy and the division of Germany:  the clash with
      Russia over reparations.  Ithaca, Cornell U.P., 1972.    286p.

3976  Laqueur, W.Z.  Russia and Germany:  a century of conflict.  Boston, Mass.,
      Little;  L., Weidenfeld & Nicolson, 1965.    367p.

3977  McSherry, J.E.  Stalin, Hitler and Europe.  Cleveland, World,  1968-73.
      2 vols.

3978  Magnes, J.L.  Russia and Germany at Brest-Litovsk:  a documentary histo-
      ry of the public negotiations.  N.Y., Rand School of Social Science,1919.
      192p.

3979  Melville, C.F.  The Russian face of Germany:  an account of the secret
      military relations between the German and Soviet-Russian governments. L.,
      Wishart, 1932.    230p.

3980  Nettl, J.P.  The Eastern Zone and Soviet policy in Germany, 1945-50. L.,
      Oxford U.P., 1951.    324p.

3981  Newman, B.  The captured archives:  the story of the Nazi-Soviet docume-
      nts.  L., Latimer House, 1948.    222p.

3982  Rosenbaum, K.  Community of fate:  German-Soviet diplomatic relations
      1922-1928. Syracuse, Syracuse U.P., 1965.    325p.

3983  Rossi, A.  The Russo-German alliance, August 1939-June 1941.  L., Chapman
      & Hall, 1950.    218p.

3984  Schaffer, G.  Russian Zone.  L., Allen & Unwin, 1947.    192p.

3985  Scott, J.  Duel for Europe:  Stalin versus Hitler.  Boston, Mass., Hough-
      ton, 1942.    381p.

3986  Sontag, R.J., Beddie, J.S.  Nazi-Soviet documents 1939-1941:  documents
      from the archives of the German Foreign Office as released by the Depar-
      tment of State.  N.Y., Didier, 1948.    362p.

3987  Speier, H.  Divided Berlin:  the anatomy of Soviet political blackmail.
      N.Y., Praeger;  L., Thames & Hudson, 1961.    201p.

3988  Tetens, T.H.  Germany plots with the Kremlin.  N.Y., Schuman, 1953. 294p.

3989  U.S.A.  Dept. of State.  Proceedings of the Brest-Litovsk Peace Confere-
      nce:  the peace negotiations between Russia and the Central Powers, 21
      Nov. 1917-3 March 1918.  Washington, USGPO, 1918.    187p.

3990  Weinberg, G.L.  Germany and the Soviet Union, 1939-1941.  Reprint with
      revisions.  Leyden, Brill, 1972.    218p.

3991  Wheeler-Bennett, J.W.  Brest-Litovsk:  the forgotten peace.  L., Macmillan, 1938.    478p.

3992  Zeman, Z.A.B.  Germany and the revolution in Russia, 1915-1918:  documents from the archives of the German Foreign Ministry.  N.Y.;  L., Oxford U.P., 1958.    157p.

(j)  Great Britain

3993  Arnot, R.P.  The impact of the Russian revolution in Britain.  L., Lawrence & Wishart, 1967.    191p.

3994  Bilainkin, G.  Maisky:  ten years' ambassador.  L., Allen & Unwin, 1944.  400p.

3995  Bilainkin, G.  Diary of a diplomatic correspondent.  L., Allen & Unwin, 1942.    272p.

3996  Bilainkin, G.  Second diary of a diplomatic correspondent.  L., Low, 19-47.    423p.

3997  Coates, W.P., Coates, Z.K.  A history of Anglo-Soviet relations.  L., Lawrence & Wishart, 1943-58.    2 vols.

3998  Crankshaw, E.  Russia and Britain.  N.Y., Hastings;  L., Collins, 1944.  128p.

3999  Dewhurst, C.H.  Close contact.  L., Allen & Unwin, 1954.    174p.

4000  Elvin, H.  A cockney in Moscow.  L., Cressett, 1958.    222p.

4001  Graubard, S.R.  British labour and the Russian revolution, 1917-1924.  Cambridge, Mass., Harvard U.P., 1957.    305p.

4002  Gollancz, V.  Russia and ourselves.  L., Gollancz;  Toronto, Ryerson P., 1941.    131p.

4003  Hayter, W.  The Kremlin and the Embassy.  N.Y., Macmillan;  L., Hodder & Stoughton, 1966.    160p.

4004  Hilton, Rl  Military attache in Moscow.  Boston, Mass., Beacon P., 1951.;  L., Hollis & Carter, 1950.    232p.

4005  Maisky, I.M.  Before the storm.  L., Hutchinson, 1944.    176p.

4006  Maisky, I.M.  Journey into the past.  L., Hutchinson, 1962.    288p.

4007  Maisky, I.M.  Memoirs of a Soviet ambassador:  the War, 1939-43.  N.Y., Scribner's, 1968.    408p.

4008  Maisky, I.M.  Who helped Hitler?  L., Hutchinson, 1964.    216p.

4009  Nabokoff, C.  The ordeal of a diplomat.  L., Duckworth, 1921.    320p.

4010 Trevelyan, H. Worlds apart: China 1953-5, Soviet Union 1962-5. L., Macmillan, 1971. 320p.

4011 Ullman, R.H. Anglo-Soviet relations, 1917-1921. Princeton, Princeton U.P., 1961-72. 3 vols.

4012 Umiastowski, R. Poland, Russia and Great Britain, 1941-1945. L., Hollis & Carter, 1947. 544p.

(k) Hungary

4013 Nyarady, M. My ringside seat in Moscow. N.Y., Crowell, 1952. 297p.

(l) Netherlands.

4014 Oudendijk, W.J. Ways and by-ways in diplomacy. L., Peter Davies, 1939. 386p.

(m) Norway

4015 Gilberg, T. The Soviet Communist Party and Scandinavian communism: the Norwegian case. Oslo, Universitetsforlaget, 1973. 271p.

4016 Orvik, N. Europe's Northern Cap and the Soviet Union. Cambridge, Mass., Harvard U.P., 1963. 64p.

(n) Poland

4017 Budurowycz, B.B. Polish-Soviet relations, 1932-1939. N.Y., Columbia U. P., 1963. 229p.

4018 Cardwell, A.S. Poland and Russia: the last quarter century. N.Y., Sheed & Ward, 1943. 251p.

4019 Davies, N. White eagle, red star: the Polish-Soviet war, 1919-20. N.Y., St Martin's P.; L., Macdonald, 1972. 318p.

4020 General Sikorski Historical Institute. Documents on Polish-Soviet relations 1939-1945. L., Heinemann, 1961-67. 2 vols.

4021 Korbel, J. Poland between East and West: Soviet and German diplomacy toward Poland, 1919-1933. Princeton, Princeton U.P., 1963. 321p.

4022 Korostovetz, W.K. The rebirth of Poland. L., Bles, 1928. 317p.

4023 Kot, S. Conversations with the Kremlin and dispatches from Russia. N.-Y.; L., Oxford U.P., 1963. 285p.

4024 Kusnierz, B. Stalin and the Poles: an indictment of the Soviet leaders. L., Hollis & Carter, 1949. 317p.

4025 Mikolajczyk, S. The rape of Poland: pattern of Soviet aggression. N.-Y., McGraw-Hill, 1948. 309p.; The pattern of Soviet domination. L., Low, 1948. 353p.

4026  Orme, A.  From Christmas to Easter:  a guide to a Russian occupation. L.,
      Hodge, 1949.    343p.

4027  Poland. Ministry of Foreign Affairs.  The Polish white book:  official
      documents concerning Polish-German and Polish-Soviet relations, 1933-19-
      39.  L., Hutchinson, 1940.    222p.

4028  Shotwell, J.T., Laserson, M.M.  Poland and Russia, 1919-1945.  N.Y., Co-
      lumbia U.P., 1945.    114p.

4029  Stypulkowski, Z.  Invitation to Moscow.  L., Thames & Hudson,    1951.
      360p.

4030  Wandycz, P.S.  Soviet-Polish relations, 1917-1921.  Cambridge, Mass., H-
      arvard U.P., 1969.    403p.

      (o)  Spain

4031  Bolloten, B.  The grand camouflage:  the communist conspiracy in the Sp-
      anish Civil War.  N.Y., Praeger; L., Hollis & Carter, 1961.    350p.

4032  Cattell, D.T.  Communism and the Spanish Civil War.  N.Y., Russell & Ru-
      ssell, 1965.    290p.

4033  Cattell, D.T,  Soviet diplomacy and the Spanish Civil War.  Berkeley, C-
      alifornia U.P., 1957.    204p.

4033a Maisky, I.M.  Spanish notebooks.  L., Hutchinson, 1966.    208p.

      (p)  Yugoslavia

4034  Armstrong, H.F.  Tito and Goliath.  N.Y., Macmillan; L., Gollancz, 1951.
      318p.

4035  Bass, R.H., Marbury, E.  The Soviet-Yugoslav controversy, 1948-1958:  a
      documentary record.  N.Y., Prospect Bks., 1959.    225p.

4036  Benes, V. and others.  The second Soviet-Yugoslav dispute:  full text of
      main documents, April-June 1958, with an introductory analysis.  Bloomi-
      ngton, Indiana U., 1959.    272p.

4037  Dedijer, V.  The battle Stalin lost:  memoirs of Yugoslavia, 1948-1953.
      N.Y., Grosset, 1972.    341p.

4038  Dedijer, V.  Tito speaks:  his self portrait and struggle with Stalin.
      L., Weidenfeld & Nicolson, 1953.    456p.

4039  Djilas, M.  Conversations with Stalin.  N.Y., Harcourt; L., Hart-Davies,
      1962.    192p.

4040  Farrell, B.  Jugoslavia and the Soviet Union, 1948-1956:  an analysis wi-
      th documents.  Hamden, Shoe String P., 1956.    220p.

4041  Hodgkinson, H.  Challenge to the Kremlin.  N.Y., Praeger, 1952.; West and east of Tito.  L., Gollancz, 1952.    190p.

4042  Tomasic, D.A., Strmecki, J.  National communism and Soviet strategy.  W-
ashington, Public Affairs P., 1957.    222p.

4043  Ulam, A.B.  Titoism and the Cominform.  Cambridge, Mass., Harvard U.P.,
1952.    243p.

4044  White, L.  Balkan Caesar:  Tito versus Stalin.  N.Y., Scribner's, 1951.
245p.

4045  Yindrich, J.  Tito v. Stalin:  the battle of the marshals.  L., Benn,
1950.    215p.


J    Biographies

4046  Lunacharsky, A.  Revolutionary silhouettes.  N.Y., Hill & Wang,  1968.
155p.

4047  Wolfe, B.D.  Strange communists I have known.  N.Y., Stein & Day, 1965.
222p.

4048  Allilueva, A.  The Alliluyev memoirs:  recollections of Svetlana Stalin's
maternal aunt Anna Alliluyeva and her grandfather Sergei Alliluyev.L.,
Joseph, 1968.    238p.

4049  Allilueva, S.  Only one year.  N.Y., Harper;  L., Hutchinson, 1969. 415p.

4050  Allilueva, S.  Twenty letters to a friend.  N.Y., Harper;  L., Hutchinson
1967.    246p.

4051  Biagi, E.  Svetlana:  an intimate portrait.  N.Y., Funk & Wagnalls;  Svetlana:  the inside story.  L., Hodder & Stoughton, 1967.    158p.

4052  Ebon, M.  Svetlana:  the story of Stalin's daughter.  N.Y., New American
Library, 1967.    192p.

4053  Hudson, J.A.  Svetlana Alliluyeva:  flight to freedom.  N.Y., Tower, 19-
67.    174p.

4054  Wittlin, T.  Commissar:  the life and death of Lavrenty Pavlovich Beria.
N.Y., Macmillan, 1972.;  L., Angus & Robertson, 1973.    566p.

4055  Cohen, S.F.  Bukharin and the Bolshevik revolution:  a political biograp
hy, 1888-1938.  N.Y., Knopf, 1973.    495p.

4056  Bromage, B.  Man of terror:  Dzherzhynski,  L., Owen, 1956.    223p.

4057  Dzherzhynski, F.E.  Prison diary and letters.  Moscow, FLPH, 1959. 306p.

4058  Jaxa-Ronikier, B.  The red executioner Djierjinski (The good heart).  L.,
Archer, 1935.    316p.

4059   Ivanov-Razumnik, R.V.   The memoirs of Ivanov-Razumnik.   N.Y.;   L., Oxford U.P., 1965.   374p.

4060   Alexandrov, V.   Khrushchev of the Ukraine:   a biography.   N.Y., Philosophical Library, 1957.   216p.;   L., Gollancz, 1957.   176p.

4061   Crankshaw, E.   Khrushchev:   a career.   N.Y., Viking;   L., Collins, 1966.   320p.

4062   Frankland, M.   Khrushchev.   N.Y., Stein & Day;   Harmondsworth, Penguin, 1966.   213p.

4063   Kellen, K.   Khrushchev:   a political portrait.   N.Y., Praeger;   L., Thames & Hudson, 1961.   271p.

4064   Khrushchev, N.S.   Khrushchev remembers.   Boston, Mass., Little, 1970.;   L., Deutsch, 1971.   639p.

4065   Khrushchev, N.S.   Khrushchev speaks:   selected speeches, articles, and press conferences, 1949-1961;   ed. by T.P. Whitney.   Ann Arbor, U. of Michigan P., 1963.   466p.

4066   Linden, C.A.   Khrushchev and the Soviet leadership.   Baltimore, Johns Hopkins P., 1966.   270p.

4067   MacGregor-Hastie, R.   The life and times of N. Krushchev.   L., Hamilton, 1959.   158p.

4068   Paloczi-Horvath, G.   Khrushchev:   the making of a dictator.   Boston, Mass., Little, 1960.   314p.;   Khrushchev:   the road to power.   L., Secker & Warburg, 1960.   304p.

4069   Pistrak, L.   The grand tactician:   Khrushchev's rise to power.   N.Y., Praeger;   L., Thames & Hudson, 1961.   296p.

4070   Salisbury, H.E.   Khrushchev's 'Mein Kampf'.   N.Y., Belmont, 1961.   208p.

4071   Kollontai, A.   The autobiography of a sexually emancipated Communist woman.   N.Y., Herder & Herder, 1971.;   L., Orbach & Chambers, 1972.   137p.

4072   Palencia, I. de.   Aleksandra Kollontay.   N.Y., Longmans, 1947.   309p.

4073   Krassin, L.   Leonid Krassin:   his life and work.   L., Skeffington, 1929.   284p.

4074   McNeal, R.H.   Bride of the revolution:   Krupskaya and Lenin.   Ann Arbor, U. of Michigan P., 1972.;   L., Gollancz, 1973.   326p.

4075   Balabanoff, A.   Impressions of Lenin.   Ann Arbor, U. of Michigan P., 1964.   152p.

4076   Charnock, J.   Red revolutionary:   a life of Lenin.   N.Y., Hawthorn, 1970.   138p.

4077　Conquest, R.　V.I. Lenin.　N.Y., Viking, 1972.　152p.

4078　Deutscher, T.　Not by politics alone:　the other Lenin.　L., Allen & Unwin, 1973.　256p.

4079　Fischer, E., Marek, F.　The essential Lenin.　N.Y., Herder & Herder, 1972.;　Lenin in his own words.　L., Allen Lane, 1972.　190p.

4080　Fischer, L.　The life of Lenin.　N.Y., Harper, 1964.　703p.

4081　Fox, R.　Lenin:　a biography.　L., Gollancz, 1933.　320p.

4082　Fulop-Miller, R.　Lenin and Gandhi.　L., Putnam, 1927.　343p.

4083　Gorky, M.　Lenin:　a biographical essay.　Edinburgh, University Texts, 1967.　62p.

4084　Gourfinkel, N.　Lenin.　N.Y., Grove P.; L., Evergreen, 1961.　193p.

4085　Hill, C.　Lenin and the Russian Revolution.　N.Y., Macmillan, 1950.; L., English Universities P., 1947.　245p.

4086　Hill, E., Mudie, D.　The letters of Lenin.　L., Chapman & Hall, 1937. 495p.

4087　Hollis, C.　Lenin:　portrait of a professional revolutionary.　L., Longmans, 1938.　285p.

4088　Kerzhentsev, P.　Life of Lenin.　Moscow, Co-operative Publishing Society of Foreign Workers, 1937.　336p.

4089　Krupskaya, N.K.　Reminiscences of Lenin.　L., Lawrence & Wishart;　Moscow FLPH, 1959.　553p.

4090　Lenin:　a biography;　tr. by V. Dutt.　L., Lawrence & Wishart, 1955. 272p.

4091　Levine, I.E.　Lenin:　the man who made a revolution.　N.Y., Messner, 1969.;　Folkestone, Bailey & Swinfen, 1970.　189p.

4092　Lewin, M.　Lenin's last struggle.　N.Y., Pantheon, 1968.　193p.

4093　Liversidge, D.　Lenin:　genius of revolution.　N.Y., Watts, 1969.　186p.

4094　Lukacs, G.　Lenin:　a study on the unity of his thought.　Cambridge, Mass., MITP., 1971; L., NLB, 1970.　104p.

4095　Mailloux, K.F. Mailloux, H.P.　Lenin:　the exile returns.　Princeton, Auerbach, 1972.　326p.

4096　Marcu, V.　Lenin.　L., Gollancz, 1928.　419p.

4097　Marx-Engels-Lenin Institute,　Lenin.　L., Hutchinson, 1943.　204p.

4098 Maxton, J. Lenin. L., Peter Davies, 1932. 183p.

4099 Mirsky, D.S. Lenin. L., Holme P., 1931. 226p.

4100 Morgan, M.C. Lenin. Athens, Ohio U.P.; L., Arnold, 1971. 236p.

4101 Page, S.W. Lenin and world revolution. N.Y., N.Y.U.P., 1959. 252p.

4102 Payne, R. The life and death of Lenin. N.Y., Simon & Schuster; L., W. H. Allen, 1964. 672p.

4103 Possony, S.T. Lenin: the compulsive revolutionary. Rev. British ed. L., Allen & Unwin, 1966. 493p.

4104 Possony, S.T. Lenin reader. Chicago, Henry Regnery, 1966. 561p.

4105 Schapiro, L., Reddaway, P. Lenin: the man, the theorist, the leader; a reappraisal. N.Y., Praeger; L., Pall Mall P., 1967. 317p.

4106 Shub, D. Lenin. Rev. ed. Harmondsworth, Penguin, 1966. 496p.

4107 Shukman, H. Lenin and the Russian revolution. N.Y., Putnam, 1967. 224p

4108 Silverman, S.N. Lenin. Englewood Cliffs, Prentice-Hall, 1972. 213p.

4109 Sweezy, P.M., Magdoff, H. Lenin today: eight essays; on the hundredth anniversary of Lenin's birth. N.Y., Monthly Review, 1970. 125p.

4110 Theen, R.H.W. Lenin: genesis and development of a revolutionary. Philadelphia, Lippincott, 1973. 194p.

4111 Trotsky, L. Lenin. L., Harrap, 1925. 247p.

4112 Trotsky, L. Lenin: notes for a biographer; introduction by B.D. Wolfe. N.Y., Putnam, 1971. 224p.; On Lenin: notes towards a biography. L., Harrap, 1971. 204p.

4113 Trotsky, L. The young Lenin. Garden City, N.Y., Doubleday; Newton Abbot, David & Charles, 1972. 224p.

4114 Veale, F.J.P. The man from the Volga: a life of Lenin. L., Constable, 1932. 288p.

4115 Vernadsky, G. Lenin: red dictator. New Haven, Yale U.P., 1931. 351p.

4116 Vladimir Lenin: a political biography. N.Y., International Publishers, 1944. 288p.

4117 Volsky, N.V. The early years of Lenin by N.V. Valentinov. Ann Arbor, U. of Michigan P., 1969. 302p.

4118 Volsky, N.V. Encounters with Lenin. N.Y.; L., Oxford U.P., 1968. 274p.

4119   Warth, R.D.   Lenin.   N.Y., Twayne, 1973.     198p.

4120   Zetkin, C.   Reminiscences of Lenin.   L., Modern Bks., 1929.     78p.

4121   Litvinov, M.M.   Notes for a journal;   introduction by E.H. Carr.   N.Y.,
       Morrow, 1955.   347p.;   L., Deutsch, 1955.   303p.   (Probably a forgery.)

4122   Pope, A.U.   Maxim Litvinoff.   N.Y., Fischer, 1943.;   L., Secker & Warbu-
       rg, 1944.   530p.

4123   Luria, A.R.   The man with a shattered world:   the history of a brain wo-
       und.   N.Y., Basic, 1972.     165p.

4124   Ebon, M   Malenkov:   a biographical study of Stalin's successor.   N.Y.,
       McGraw-Hill, 1953.   284p.;   L., Weidenfeld & Nicolson, 1953.     152p.

4125   Svanidze, B.   Georgiy Malenkov:   a portrait sketch from life by Stalin's
       nephew.   L., Wingate, 1954.     160p.

4126   Bromage, B.   Molotov:   the story of an era.   L., Owen, 1956.     256p.

4127   Serge, V.   Memoirs of a revolutionary, 1901-1941.   L., Oxford U.P., 1963.
       401p.

4128   Steinberg, I.   Spiridonova:   revolutionary terrorist.   L., Methuen, 1936.
       313p.

4129   Adams, A.E.   Stalin and his times.   N.Y., Holt, 1972.     243p.

4130   Amba, A.   I was Stalin's bodyguard.   L., Muller, 1952.     256p.

4131   Backer, G.   The deadly parallel:   Stalin and Ivan the Terrible.   N.Y.,
       Random, 1950.   240p.

4132   Baikaloff, A.V.   I knew Stalin.   L., Burns Oates, 1940.     142p.

4133   Barbusse, H.   Stalin.   L., Lane, 1935.     324p.

4134   Basseches, N.   Stalin.   N.Y., Dutton, 1952.   384p.;   L., Staples, 1952.
       404p.

4135   Bigland, E.   The riddle of the Kremlin.   L., Collins, 1940.     192p.

4136   Cole, D.M.   Josef Stalin:   man of steel.   L., Rich & Cowan, 1942. 136p.

4137   Delbars, Y.   The real Stalin.   L., Allen & Unwin, 1953.     439p.

4138   Deutscher, I.   Stalin:   a political biography.   2nd ed.   N.Y.; L., Oxf-
       ord U.P., 1967.     661p.

4139   Essad-Bey.   Stalin:   the career of a fanatic.   L., Lane, 1932.     391p.

4140   Feldman, A.B.   Stalin:   red lord of Russia, 1879-1953.   Philadelphia, M-
       ercury, 1962.     253p.

4141   Fischer, L.   The life and death of Stalin.   N.Y., Harper, 1952.   272p.;
       L., Cape, 1953.   255p.

4142   Fishman, J.,Hutton, J.B.   The private life of Josif Stalin.   L., W.H. A-
       llen, 1962.   214p.

4143   Graham, S.   Stalin:   an impartial study of the life and work of Joseph
       Stalin.   2nd ed.   L., Hutchinson, 1939.   159p.

4144   Hutton, J.B.   Stalin — the miraculous Georgian.   L., Spearman,   1961.
       375p.

4145   Hyde, H.M.   Stalin:   the history of a dictator.   N.Y., Farrar, 1972.; L.,
       Hart-Davies, 1971.   679p.

4146   King-Hall, S.   Three dictators:   Mussolini, Hitler, Stalin.   L., Faber,
       1964.   132p.

4147   Kolarz, W.   Stalin and eternal Russia.   L., Drummond, 1944.   144p.

4148   Levine, I.D.   Stalin:   a biography.   L., Cape, 1931.   336p.

4149   Levine, I.D.   Stalin's great secret.   N.Y., Coward, 1956.   126p.

4150   Liversidge, D.   Joseph Stalin.   N.Y., Watts, 1969.   188p.

4151   Ludwig, E.   Stalin.   N.Y., Putnam, 1942.   248p.

4152   Lyons, E.   Stalin:   a czar of all the Russias.   L., Harrap, 1940.   255p.

4153   Marx-Engels-Lenin Institute, Moscow.   Joseph Stalin:   a political biog-
       raphy.   N.Y., International Publishers, 1949.   128p.

4154   Monitor.   The death of Stalin:   an investigation by 'Monitor'.   L., Win-
       gate, 1958.   144p.

4155   Murphy, J.T.   Stalin, 1879-1944.   L., Lane, 1945.   251p.

4156   Orlov, A.   The secret history of Stalin's crimes.   N.Y., Random,   1953.
       366p.

4157   Payne, R.   The rise and fall of Stalin.   N.Y., Simon & Schuster,   1965.;
       L., W.H. Allen, 1966.   767p.

4158   Ray, O.   Stalin:   the red czar.   L., Pilot P., 1939.   128p.

4159   Rigby, T.H.   Stalin.   Englewood Cliffs, Prentice, 1966.   189p.

4160   Roberts, E.M.   Stalin:   man of steel.   N.Y., Roy;   L., Methuen,   1968.
       95p.

4161   Sethi, S.S.   Stalin lives on:   a narrative of his life and struggle.   N-
       ew Delhi, Cosmopolitan Publications, 1953.   247p.

4162  Smith, E.E.  The young Stalin:  the early years of an elusive revolutio-
      nary.  N.Y., Farrar, 1967.;  L., Cassell, 1968.    470p.

4163  Souvarine, B.  Stalin:  a critical survey of Bolshevism.  L., Secker &
      Warburg, 1939.    690p.

4164  Stalin, J.V.  The essential Stalin: major theoretical writings, 1905-52.
      Garden City, N.Y., Anchor Bks., 1972.;  L., Croom Helm, 1973.    511p.

4165  Svanidze, B.  My uncle Joe.  L., Heinemann, 1952.    190p.

4166  Trotsky, L.  Stalin:  an appraisal of the man and his influence.  N.Y.;
      L., Harper, 1941.    516p.

4167  Tucker, R.C.  Stalin as revolutionary, 1879-1929:  a study in history and
      personality.  N.Y., Norton, 1973.    519p.

4168  Ulam, A.B.  Stalin:  the man and his era.  N.Y., Viking P., 1973.  760p.

4169  Warth, R.D.  Joseph Stalin.  N.Y., Twayne, 1969.    176p.

4170  Yaroslavsky, E.  Landmarks in the life of Stalin.  L., Lawrence & Wisha-
      rt, 1942.    191p.

4171  Mehring, W.  Timoshenko:  marshal of the Red Army.  N.Y., Unger,  1942.
      191p.

4172  Deutscher, I.  The prophet armed:  Trotsky, 1879-1921.  N.Y.;  L., Oxfo-
      rd U.P., 1954.    540p.

4173  Deutscher, I.  The prophet unarmed:  Trotsky, 1921-1929.  N.Y.,  L., Ox-
      ford U.P., 1959.    490p.

4174  Deutscher, I.  The prophet outcast:  Trotsky, 1929-1940.  N.Y.;  L., Ox-
      ford U.P., 1963.    543p.

4175  Howe, I.  The basic writings of Trotsky.  N.Y., Vintage, 1965;  L., Sec-
      ker & Warburg, 1964.    427p.

4176  Leon Trotsky:  the man and his work;  reminiscences and appraisals by J.
      Hansen and others.  N.Y., Merit, 1969.    128p.

4177  Meijer, J.M.  The Trotsky papers, 1917-1922.  The Hague, Mouton, 1964-71.
      2 vols.

4178  Mosley, N.  The assassination of Trotsky.  L., Joseph, 1972.    185p.

4179  Salazar, L.A.S., Gorkin, J.  Murder in Mexico:  the assassination of Le-
      on Trotsky.  L., Secker & Warburg, 1950.    235p.

4180  Smith, I.H.  Trotsky.  Englewood Cliffs, Prentice, 1973.    181p.

4181  Trotsky, L.  The age of permanent revolution:  a Trotsky anthology. N.Y.,
      Dell, 1964.    384p.

4182 Trotsky, L. Diary in exile, 1935. Cambridge, Mass., Harvard U.P.,1958. 218p.; L., Faber, 1959. 176p.

4183 Trotsky, L. The essential Trotsky. N.Y., Barnes & Noble; L., Allen & Unwin, 1964. 251p.

4184 Trotsky, L. Military writings. N.Y., Merit, 1969. 158p.

4185 Trotsky, L. My life. N.Y., Scribner, 1930. 613p.

4186 Trotsky, L. The writings of Leon Trotsky. N.Y., Merit, 1969- . Vol1-

4187 Weiss, P. Trotsky in exile. L., Methuen, 1972. 126p.

4188 Wyndham, F., King, D. Trotsky: a documentary. N.Y., Praeger; L., Allen Lane, 1972. 204p.

4189 Wheatley, D. Red eagle: the story of the Russian Revolution and of Klementy Efremovitch Voroshilov, Marshal and Commissar for Defence of the U.S.S.R. L., Hutchinson, 1937. 390p.

4190 Chaney, O.P. Zhukov. Norman, U. of Oklahoma P., 1971.; Newton Abbot, David & Charles, 1972. 512p.

4191 Zhukov, G.K. The memoirs of Marshal Zhukov. N.Y., Delacorte; L., Cape, 1971. 703p.

- 237 -

VIII  THE NATIONALITIES

A     General

4192  Barghoorn, F.C.   Soviet Russian nationalism.   N.Y., Oxford U.P., 1956.
      330p.

4193  Boersner, D.   The Bolsheviks and the national and colonial question, 19-
      17-1928.   N.Y., Lounz;  Geneva, Droz, 1957.     285p.

4194  Conquest, R.   The last empire.   L., Ampersand, 1962.     132p.

4195  Conquest, R.   The nation killers:  the Soviet deportation of nationalit-
      ies.   N.Y., St Martin's P.;  L., Macmillan, 1970.     222p.

4196  Conquest, R.   Soviet nationalities policy in practice.   N.Y., Praeger;
      L., Bodley Head, 1967.     160p.

4197  Deker, N.K., Lebed, A.   Genocide in the U.S.S.R.:  studies in group des-
      truction.   N.Y., Scarecrow P., 1958.     280p.

4198  Dzyuba, I.   Internationalism or Russification:  a study in the Soviet n-
      ationalities problem.   L., Weidenfeld & Nicolson, 1968.     240p.

4199  Gecys, C.C.   Two worlds.   N.Y., Fordham U., Institute of Contemporary R-
      ussian Studies, 1965.     398p.

4200  Goldhagen, E.   Ethnic minorities in the Soviet Union.   N.Y.; L., Praeger,
      1968.     351p.

4201  Kohn, H.   Nationalism in the Soviet Union.   N.Y., Columbia U.P.;  L., R-
      outledge, 1933.     164p.

4202  Kolarz, W.   Russia and her colonies.   N.Y., Praeger, 1953.;  L., Philip,
      1952.     334p.

4203  Lewis, E.G.   Multilingualism in the Soviet Union:  aspects of language
      policy and its implementation.   The Hague, Mouton, 1972.     332p.

4204  Low, A.D.   Lenin on the question of nationality.   N.Y., Bookman Associa-
      tes, 1958.     193p.

4205  Mikhailov, N.N.   The sixteen republics of the Soviet Union.   Rev. ed. L.,
      Soviet News, 1955.     100p.

4206  Padmore, G., Pizer, D.   How Russia transformed her colonial empire:  a
      challenge to the imperialist powers.   L., Dobson, 1946.     178p.

4207  Schlesinger, R.   The nationalities problem and Soviet administration; c-
      hanging attitudes in Soviet Russia:  selected readings on the development
      of Soviet nationalism.   N.Y., Humanities;  L., Routledge, 1956.     299p.

4208  Scottish League for European Freedom.   The struggle and weakness of Red

Russia: congress of delegates of independence movements within the U.S.-S.R. held in Edinburgh, 12th, 13th and 14th June 1950. Edinburgh, Scottish League for European Freedom, 1950.    143p.

4209  Smal-Stocki, R.  The captive nations:  nationalism of the non-Russian n-ations in the Soviet Union.  N.Y., Bookman, 1960.    118p.

4210  Smal-Stocki, R.  The nationality problem of the Soviet Union and Russian Communist imperialism.  Milwaukee, Bruce, 1952.    474p.

4211  Society for the Defence of Freedom in Asia.  The Soviet prisonhouse of nationalities:  a study of the Russian experiment in solving the national question.  Calcutta. 1955.    226p.

4212  Sprudzs, A., Rusis, A.  Res Baltica:  a collection of essays in honor of the memory of Dr. A. Bilmanis (1887-1948.).  Leyden, Sijthoff, 1968.303p.

4213  Stahl, K.M.  British and Soviet colonial systems.  N.Y., Praeger;  L., Faber, 1951.    114p.

4214  Stalin, I.V.  Marxism and the national and colonial question. N.Y., International Publishers, 1936.    304p.

4215  Symonolewicz, K.  Symmons— Non-slavic peoples of the Soviet Union:  a brief ethnographical survey.  Meadville, Maplewood P., 1972.    168p.

4216  Tsamerian, I.P., Ronin, S.L.  Equality of rights between races and nationalities in the U.S.S.R.  Paris, Unesco, 1962.    106p.

4217  Yarmolinsky, A.  The Jews and other minor nationalities under the Soviets.  N.Y., Vanguard P., 1929.    182p.


B    The Baltic nations

4218  Berzins, A.  The unpunished crime.  N.Y., Speller, 1963.    314p.

4219  Dunn, S.P.  Cultural processes in the Baltic area under Soviet rule.  Berkeley, U. of California P., 1966.    92p.

4220  Kalme, A.  Total terror:  an expose of genocide in the Baltic.  N.Y., Appleton, 1951.    310p.

4221  Manning, C.A.  The forgotten republics.  N.Y., Philosophical Library, 1952.    264p.

4222  Meiksins, G.  The Baltic riddle:  Finland, Estonia, Latvia, Lithuania — keypoints of European peace.  N.Y., Fisher, 1943.    271p.

4223  Newman, B.  Baltic background.  L., Hale, 1948.    280p.

4224  Oras, A.  Baltic eclipse.  L., Gollancz, 1948.    307p.

4225  Page, S.W.  The formation of the Baltic states:  a study of the effects of great power politics upon the emergence of Lithuania, Latvia, and Estonia. Cambridge, Mass., Harvard U.P., 1959.    193p.

4226    Pick, F.W.    The Baltic nations: Estonia, Latvia and Lithuania.    L., Boreas, 1945.    172p.

4227    Ruhl, A.    New masters of the Baltic.    N.Y., Dutton, 1922.    239p.

4228    Scott, A.M.    Beyond the Baltic.    L., Butterworth, 1925.    316p.

4229    Silde, A.    The profits of slavery: Baltic forced laborers and deportees under Stalin and Khrushchev.    Stockholm, 1958.    302p.

4230    Sweetenham, J.A.    The tragedy of the Baltic states:  a report compiled from official documents and eyewitnesses stories.    L., Hollis & Carter, 1952.    216p.

4231    Tarulis, A.N.    American-Baltic relations, 1918-1922:  the struggle over recognition.    Washington, Catholic U.P., 1965.    386p.

4232    Tarulis, A.N.    Soviet policy toward the Baltic States, 1918-1940.    Notre Dame, U. of Notre Dame P., 1959.    276p.

4233    Ziedonis, A. and others.    Problems of mininations:  Baltic perspectives. San Jose, California State U., Association for the Advancement of Baltic Studies, 1973.    214p.

4234    Rubulis, A.    Baltic literature:  a survey of Finnish, Estonian, Latvian and Lithuanian literatures.    Notre Dame, U. of Notre Dame P., 1970. 215p.

4235    Bourgeois, C.    A priest in Russia and the Baltic.    L., Burns, Oates; Dublin, Clunmore & Reynolds, 1953.    146p.

4236    Jackson, J.H.    Estonia.    2nd ed.    N.Y., Macmillan, 1949.;    L., Allen & Unwin, 1948.    272p.

4237    Kabin, J.    Estonia yesterday and today.    Moscow, Progress, 1971.    166p.

4238    Kareda, E.    Estonia in the Soviet grip:  life and conditions under Soviet occupation, 1947-1949.    West Byfleet, Boreas, 1949.    100p.

4239    Kareda, E.    Technique of economic Sovietization:  a Baltic experience. West Byfleet, Boreas, 1947.    127p.

4240    Korp, A.    Welcome to Estonia.    Tallinn, Eesti Raamat, 1970.    117p.

4241    Nodel, E.    Estonia:  nation on the anvil.    N.Y., Bookman, 1964.    207p.

4242    Raud, V.    Estonia:  a reference book.    N.Y., Nordic P., 1953.    158p.

4243    Tomingas, W.    The Soviet colonization of Estonia.    N.Y., Kultur Publishing House, 1973.    312p.

4244    Tumulus, G.    I am an Estonian:  the Baltics and the metamorphoses of the

Russian Empire. N.Y., Exposition P., 1959.   186p.

4245   Uustalu, E.   The history of the Estonian people.   L., Boreas, 1952. 266p.

4246   Viirsaule, E.   Women and youth in occupied Estonia.   L., Boreas, 1955. 69p.

4247   Koressaar, V., Rannit, A.   Estonian poetry and language:   studies in ho-
       nor of Ants Oras.   Stockholm, Estonian Learned Society in America, 1965.
       301p.

4248   Uustalu, E.   Aspects of Estonian culture.   L., 1961.   332p.

4249   Berg, A.   Latvia and Russia:   one problem of the world-peace considered.
       L., Dent, 1920.   93p.

4250   Bilmanis, A.   Latvia as an independent state.   Washington, Latvian Lega-
       tion, 1947.   405p.

4251   Bilmanis, A.   Latvia and her Baltic neighbourhood.   Washington, Latvian
       Legation, 1942.   143p.

4252   Blodnieks, A.   The undefeated nation.   N.Y., Speller, 1960.   312p.

4253   Feld, M.J., Peterman, I.H.   The hug of the bear.   N.Y., Holt, 1961. 305p

4254   Kalnberzins, J. Ten years of Soviet Latvia.   Moscow, FLPH, 1951.   271p.

4255   King, G.J.   Economic politics in occupied Latvia:   a manpower management
       study.   Tacoma, Pacific Lutheran U.P., 1965.   304p.

4256   Latvia in 1939-1942:   background, Bolshevik and Nazi occupation, hopes
       for future.   Washington, Latvian Legation, 1942.   137p.

4257   Ludovici, L.J.   Tomorrow sometimes comes:   ten years against tyranny. L.,
       Odhams, 1958.   224p.

4258   Popoff, G.   The city of the red plague:   Soviet rule in a Baltic town.
       L., Allen & Unwin, 1932.   343p.

4259   Spekke, A.   Latvia and the Baltic problem:   sketch of recent history. L.,
       1956.   96p.

4260   Tallents, S.   Man and boy.   L., Faber, 1943.   431p.

4261   Voss, A.   Lenin's behests and the making of Soviet Latvia.   Moscow, Pro-
       gress, 1970.   104p.

4262   Watson, H.A.G.   An account of a mission to the Baltic States in the year
       1919; with a record of subsequent events.   L., Waverley P., 1957.   68p.

4263   Watson, H.A.G.   The Latvian republic:   the struggle for freedom.   N.Y.,
       Hillary House, L., Allen & Unwin, 1965.   102p.

4264   Matthews, W.K.   A century of Latvian poetry:   an anthology.   L., Calder, 1958.   140p.

4265   Lesins, K.   The wine of eternity:   short stories from the Latvian tr. by R. Speirs, H. Kundzins.   Minneapolis, U. of Minnesota P., 1957.   179p.

4266   Upits, A.   Outside paradise, and other stories;   tr. from the Lettish by T. Zalite.   Moscow, FLPH, 1960.   367p.

4267   Baronas, A.   Footbridges and abysses.   N.Y., Manyland Bks., 1965.   229p.

4268   Chase, T.J.   The story of Lithuania.   N.Y., Stratford House, 1946. 392p.

4269   Harrison, E.J.   Lithuania's fight for freedom.   N.Y., Lithuanian American Information Center, 1952.   95p.

4270   Harrison, E.J.   Lithuania past and present.   N.Y., McBride, 1922.   230p. L., Fisher Unwin, 1922.   224p.

4271   Kaslas, B.J.   The U.S.S.R.- German aggression against Lithuania.   N.Y., Speller, 1973.   543p.

4272   Maciuika, B.V.   Lithuania in the last 30 years.   New Haven, Human Relations Area Files, 1955.   411p.

4273   Rozanskas, E.   Documents accuse;   compiled and commented by B. Baranauskas and K. Ruksenas.   Vilnius, Gintaras, 1970.   310p.

4274   Sabaliunas, L.   Lithuania in crisis:   nationalism to communism, 1939-1940.   Bloomington, Indiana U.P., 1972.   293p.

4275   Savasis, J.   The war against God in Lithuania.   N.Y., Manyland Bks.,1966. 134p.

4276   Senn, A.E.   The emergence of modern Lithuania.   N.Y., Columbia U.P.,1959. 272p.

4277   Senn, A.E.   The great powers, Lithuania and the Vilna question, 1920-1928.   Leyden Brill, 1966.   242p.

4278   Simutis, A.   The economic reconstruction of Lithuania after 1918.   N.Y., Columbia U.P., 1942.   148p.

4279   Stukas, J.J.   Awakening Lithuania:   a study on the rise of modern Lithuanian nationalism.   Madison, Florham Park P., 1966.   187p.

4280   Tauras, K.V.   Guerrilla warfare on the amber coast.   N.Y., Voyages P., 1963.   293p.

4281   Vardys, V.S.   Lithuania under the Soviets:   portraits of a nation. 1940-65.   N.Y.; L., Praeger, 1965.   299p.

C     Belorussia

4282    Borodina, V.P. and others. Soviet Byelorussia. Moscow, Progress, 1972. 169p.

4283    Lubachko, I.S. Belorussia under Soviet rule, 1917–1957. Lexington, U.P. of Kentucky, 1972.    219p.

4284    Vakar, N.P. Belorussia: the making of a nation; a case study. Cambridge, Mass., Harvard U.P., 1956.    297p.

4285    Adamovich, A. Opposition to Sovietization in Belorussian literature (1917–1957). N.Y., Scarecrow P., 1958.    204p.

4286    Bryl, Y. Short stories; tr. by D. Skvirsky. Moscow, FLPH, 1954. 60p.

4287    Like water, like fire: an anthology of Byelorussian poetry from 1828 to the present day; tr. by V. Rich. L., Allen & Unwin, 1971.    347p.

4288    Seduro, V. The Byelorussian theater and drama. N.Y., Research Program on the U.S.S.R., 1955.    517p.


D     Ukraine

4289    Adams, A.E. Bolsheviks in the Ukraine: the second campaign, 1918–1919. New Haven, Yale U.P., 1963.    440p.

4290    Armstrong, J.A. Ukrainian nationalism. 2nd ed. N.Y., Columbia U.P., 1963.    361p.

4291    Benyukh, O., Singh, D. Burglars of hearts: travelogue. Bombay, Jaico Publishing House, 1969.    232p.

4292    Bilinski, Y. The second Soviet republic: the Ukraine after World War II. New Brunswick, Rutgers U.P., 1964.    539p.

4293    Borys, J. The Russian Communist Party and the Sovietization of Ukraine; a study in self-determination of nations. Stockholm, Norstedt, 1960. 374p.

4294    Bregy, P., Obolensky, S. The Ukraine: Russian land. L., Selwyn & Blount, 1940.    260p.

4295    Browne, M. Ferment in the Ukraine: documents by V. Chornovil and others. N.Y., Praeger; L., Macmillan, 1971.    267p.

4296    Chamberlin, W.H. The Ukraine: a submerged nation. N.Y., Macmillan, 1944.    91p.

4297    Chornovil, V. The Chornovil papers. N.Y., McGraw-Hill, 1968.    246p.

4298    Comite des delegations juives, Paris. The programs in the Ukraine under the Ukrainian governments (1917–1921). L., Bale, 1927.    286p.

4299    Dmytryshyn, B. Moscow and the Ukraine, 1918–1953: a study of Russian

Bolshevik nationality policy. N.Y., Bookman, 1956.    310p.

4300  Dushnyck, W.  In quest of freedom, 1918-1958:  in commemoration of the fortieth anniversary of Ukrainian independence.  N.Y., Ukrainian Congress Committee of America, 1958.    87p.

4301  Fedenko, P.  Ukraine:  her struggle for freedom.  Augusburg, 1951.  80p.

4302  Fedyshyn, O.S.  Germany's drive to the East and the Ukrainian revolution 1917-1918.  New Brunswick, Rutgers U.P., 1971.    401p.

4303  Gora, D.  Russian dance of death.  Claremont, Key Books, 1930.    186p.

4304  Holubnychy, V.  The industrial output of the Ukraine 1913-1956.  Munich, 1957.    63p.

4305  Hryhorijiv, N.Y.  The war and Ukrainian democracy:  a compilation of documents from past and present.  Toronto, 1945.    206p.

4306  Hryshko, V.I.  Experience with Russia.  N.Y., Ukrainian Congress Committee of America, 1956.    179p.

4307  Kamenetsky, I.  Hitler's occupation of the Ukraine, 1941-1944.  Milwaukee, Marquette U.P., 1956.    112p.

4308  Korostovetz, V.  Seed and harvest.  L., Faber, 1931.    387p.

4309  Kostiuk, H.  Stalinist rule in the Ukraine:  a study of the decade of mass terror, 1929-39.  N.Y., Praeger, 1961.    162p.

4310  Luznycky, G.  Persecution and destruction of the Ukrainian Church by the Russian Bolsheviks.  N.Y., Ukrainian Congress Committee of America, 1960. 64p.

4311  Majstrenko, I.  Borotbism:  a chapter in the history of Ukrainian communism.  N.Y., Research Program on the U.S.S.R., 1954.    325p.

4312  Manning, C.A.  Twentieth-century Ukraine.  N.Y., Bookman Associates, 19-51.    243p.

4313  Manning, C.A.  Ukraine under the Soviets.  N.Y., Bookman Associates, 19-53.    223p.

4314  Margolin, A.D.  From a political diary:  Russia, the Ukraine and America 1905-1945.  N.Y., Columbia U.P., 1946.    250p.

4315  Martovych, O.R.  Ukrainian liberation movement in modern times.  Edinburgh, Scottish League for European Freedom, 1953.    777p.

4316  Mazlach, S., Shakhrai, V.  On the current situation in the Ukraine.  Ann Arbor, U. of Michigan P., 1970.    220p.

4317  Mirchuk, I.  Ukraine and its people:  a handbook with maps, statistical tables and diagrams.  Munich, Ukrainian Free U.P., 1949.    280p.

4318    Moroz, V.  Among the snows:  protest writings from Ukraine.  L., Ukrain-
        ian Information Service, 1971.    65p.

4319    Muldavin, A.  The red fog lifts.  N.Y., Appleton, 1931.    311p.

4320    Nahayewsky, I.  History of the modern Ukrainian state 1917-1923.  Munich,
        Ukrainian Free U. and Academy of Arts and Sciences, 1966.    317p.

4321    Nikitin, P.  Organization and utilization of forests in the Ukrainian S.
        S.R.  N.Y., Research Program on the U.S.S.R., 1955.    85p.

4322    Oshmachka, T.  Red assassins:  a factual story of how the Ukraine lost
        its freedom.  Minneapolis, Dennison, 1959.    375p.

4323    Peters, V.  Nestor Makhno:  the life of an anarchist.  Winnipeg, Echo B-
        ks., 1970.    133p.

4324    Pidhainy, O.S.  The Ukrainian republic in the Great East-European Revol-
        ution.  Toronto, New Review Bks., 1966-        Vol.1-

4325    Pidhainy, S.O.  The black deeds of the Kremlin:  a white book.  Toronto,
        Ukrainian Association of Victims of Russian Communist Terror, 1953-58.
        2 vols.

4326    Pigido, F.  Materials concerning Ukrainian-Jewish relations during the
        years of the Revolution (1917-1921):  collection of documents and testi-
        monies by prominent Jewish political workers.  Munich, 1956.

4327    Reshetar, J.S.  The Ukrainian revolution, 1917-1920:  a study in nation-
        alism.  Princeton, Princeton U.P., 1952.    363p.

4328    Rosenberg, J.N.  On the steppes:  a Russian diary.  N.Y., Knopf,  1927.
        215p.

4329    Shandruk, P.  Arms of valor.  N.Y., Speller;  L., Paterson, 1959.  320p.

4330    Sheridan, C.  Across Europe with Satanella.  L., Duckworth, 1925.  216p.

4331    Soviet Ukraine;  chief editorial board:  M.P. Bazhan and others.  Kiev,
        Academy of Sciences of the Ukrainian S.S.R., Editorial office of the Uk-
        rainian Soviet Encyclopedia, 1969.    572p.

4332    Stock, M.  Parents unknown:  a Ukrainian childhood.  L., Deutsch, 1971.
        269p.

4333    Sullivants, R.S.  Soviet politics and the Ukraine, 1917-1957.  N.Y., Co-
        lumbia U.P., 1962.    438p.

4334    Ukrainian Congress Committee of America.  Ukrainian resistance:  the sto-
        ry of the Ukrainian National Liberation Movement in modern times.  N.Y.,
        1949.    142p.

4335    Ukrainian Information Service.  Russian oppression in Ukraine:  reports
        and documents.  L., Ukrainian Publishers, 1962.    576p.

4336    Wasilewska, W.  The rainbow.  N.Y., Simon & Schuster, 1944.    230p.

4337    Wolycky, W.  On to Lviv and Kiev:  war memories, 1918-1920.  Toronto, U-krainian Echo, 1963.    238p.

4338    Cresson, W.P.  The Cossacks:  their history and country.  N.Y., Brentano, 1919.    239p.

4339    Gardo, L.  Cossack fury:  the experiences of a woman soldier with the White Russians.  L., Hutchinson, 1938.    256p.

4340    Hindus, M.  The Cossacks.  N.Y., Doubleday, 1945.;  L., Collins, 1946. 319p.

4341    Huxley-Blythe, P.J.  The East came West.  Caldwell, Caxton, 1964.  225p.

4342    Longworth, P.  The Cossacks.  L., Constable, 1969.    409p.

4343    Luckyj, G.S.N.  Literary politics in the Soviet Ukraine, 1917-1934.  N.-Y., Columbia U.P., 1956.    269p.

4344    Babayevski, S.P.  Cavalier of the gold star;  tr. by R. Kisch.  L., Lawrence & Wishart, 1955.    628p.

4345    Bahriany, I.  The hunters and the hunted.  N.Y., St Martin's P.;  L., Macmillan, 1956.    245p.

4346    Honchar, O.  Short stories;  tr. by V. Shneerson.  Moscow, FLPH, 1954. 268p.

4347    Luckyj, G.S.N.  Modern Ukrainian short stories.  Littleton, Ukrainian Academic P., 1973.    228p.

4348    Slavutych, Y.  The muse in prison:  eleven sketches of Ukrainian poets killed by Communists and twenty-two translations of their poems.  Jersey City, Svoboda, 1956.    62p.

4349    Struk, D.S.  A study of Vasyl Stefanyk:  the pain at the heart of existence.  Littleton, Ukrainian Academic P., 1973.    200p.


## E    Moldavian Republic

4350    Zlatova, E., Kotelnikov, V.  Across Moldavia.  Moscow, FLPH, 1959.  230p


## F    Transcaucasia

4351    Baldwin, O.  Six prisons and two revolutions:  adventures in Trans-Caucasia and Anatolia, 1920-21.  Garden City, N.Y., Doubleday;  L., Hodder & Stoughton, 1925.    271p.

4352    Beria, L.  On the history of the Bolshevik organisation in Transcaucasia. L., Lawrence & Wishart, 1939.    206p.

4353   Buxton, H.J.   Transcaucasia.  L., Faith, 1926.    98p.

4354   Donohoe, M.H.   With the Persian expedition.  L., Arnold, 1919.    276p.

4355   Dunsterville, L.C.   The adventures of Dunsterforce.  L., Arnold,  1920.
       323p.

4356   Farson, N.   The lost world of the Caucasus.  Garden City, N.Y., Double-
       day, 1958.;  Caucasian journey.  L., Evans, 1951.    154p.

4357   Kazemzadeh, F.   The struggle for Transcaucasia (1917-1921).  N.Y., Phil-
       osophical Library;  Oxford, Ronald, 1951.    356p.

4358   Sava, G.   Valley of forgotten people.  L., Faber, 1941.    295p.

4359   Tutaeff, D.   The Soviet Caucasus.  L., Harrap, 1942.    208p.

4360   Aslanyan, A.A. and others.   Soviet Armenia.  Moscow, Progress, 1971.
       255p.

4361   Hovannisian, R.G.   Armenia on the road to independence, 1918.  Berkeley,
       U. of California P., 1967.    364p.

4362   Hovannisian, R.G.   The republic of Armenia:  the first year, 1918-1919.
       Berkeley, U. of California P., 1971.    547p.

4363   Matossian, M.K.   The impact of the Soviet policies in Armenia.   Leyden,
       Brill, 1962.    239p.

4364   Nansen, F.   Armenia and the Near East.  L., Allen & Unwin, 1928.   324p.

4365   Nansen, F.   Through the Caucasus to the Volga.  N.Y., Norton,;  L., All-
       en & Unwin, 1931.    255p.

4366   Sarian, N.S.   I shall not die:  a tribute to the faithfulness of God.  L.,
       Oliphants, 1967.    176p.

4367   Totovents, V.   Scenes from an Armenian childhood.  L., Oxford U.P., 1962.
       182p.

4368   Yeghenian, A.Y.   The red flag at Ararat.  N.Y., The Women's P.,   1932.
       170p.

4369   Suny, R.G.   The Baku commune, 1917-1918:  class and nationality in the
       Russian Revolution.  Princeton, Princeton U.P., 1972.    412p.

4370   Antadze, K.D. and others.   Soviet Georgia.  Moscow, Progress, 1972. 211p

4371   Armstrong, H.C.   Unending battle.  L., Longmans, 1934.    302p.

4372   Avashvili, Z.   The independence of Georgia in international politics,
       1918-1921.  L., Headley, 1940.    286p.

4373   Ghambashidze, D.   Mineral resources of Georgia and Caucasia:  manganese industry of Georgia. L., Allen & Unwin, 1919. 182p.

4374 Kandelaki, C. The Georgian question before the free world: acts, documents, evidence. Paris, 1953. 218p.

4375 Kautsky, K. Georgia: a social-democrat peasant republic; impressions
and observations. L., International Bkshops, 1922. 112p.

4376 Keun, O. In the land of the Golden Fleece: through independent Menshe-
vist Georgia. L., Lane, 1924. 270p.

4377 Lang, D.M. A modern history of Soviet Georgia. N.Y., Grove, 1962.; A
modern history of Georgia. L., Weidenfeld & Nicolson, 1962. 298p.

4378 Lehmann, J. Prometheus and the Bolsheviks. N.Y., Knopf, 1938.; L., C-
resset P., 1937. 256p.

4379 Shafir, I.M. Secrets of Menshevik Georgia: the plot against Soviet Russia unmasked. L., Communist Party of Great Britain, 1922. 100p.

4380 Trotsky, L. Between Red and White: a study of some fundamental questions of revolution with particular reference to Georgia. L., Communist .
Party of Great Britain, 1922. 104p.

4381 Woytinsky, W.S. Stormy passage: a personal history through the Russian
revolution to democracy and freedom, 1905-1960. N.Y., Vanguard P., 1961.
550p.

4382 Rothstein, A. A people reborn: the story of North Ossetia. L., Lawrence & Wishart, 1954. 64p.

G    Soviet Central Asia

4383 Akhmedova, M. Their road to socialism: transition of the Central Asian
republics to socialism; general laws and special features. Moscow, Novosti, 1972. 112p.

4384 Allworth, E. Central Asia: a century of Russian rule. N.Y., Columbia
U.P., 1967. 552p.

4385 Allworth, E. The nationality question in Soviet Central Asia. N.Y., L.,
Praeger, 1973. 221p.

4386 Allworth, E. Soviet nationality problems. N.Y., Columbia U.P., 1971.
296p.

4387 American Federation of Labor. Free Trade Union Committee. Soviet imperialism plunders Asia. N.Y., The Committee, 1951. 112p.

4388 Bacon, E.E. Central Asians under Russian rule: a study in cultural change. Ithaca, Cornell U.P., 1966. 273p.

4389 Bailey, F.M. Mission to Tashkent. L., Cape, 1946. 294p.

4390   Bates, E.S.   Soviet Asia:   progress and problems.   L., Cape, 1942. 191p.

4391   Becker, S.   Russia's protectorates in Central Asia:   Bukhara and Khiva,
       1865-1924.   Cambridge, Mass., Harvard U.P., 1968.      416p.

4392   Blacker, L.V.S.   On secret patrol in high Asia.   L., Murray, 1922. 294p.

4393   Brun, A.H.   Troublous times:   experiences in Bolshevik Russia and Turke-
       stan.   L., Constable, 1931.      243p.

4394   Caroe, O.   Soviet empire:   the Turks of Central Asia and Stalinism. 2nd
       ed.   N.Y., St Martin's P.;   L., Macmillan, 1967.      308p.

4395   Carruthers, D.   Beyond the Caspian:   a naturalist in Central Asia.   L.,
       Oliver & Boyd, 1949.      290p.

4396   Central Asian Research Centre, and others.   Cities of Central Asia:   town
       plans, photographs and short descriptions of some of the major cities of
       Soviet Central Asia.   L., Luzac, 1961.      20p & 8 plans.

4397   Coates, W.P., Coates, Z.K.   Soviets in Central Asia.   N.Y., Philosophic-
       al Library;   L., Lawrence & Wishart, 1951.      288p.

4398   Conolly, V.   Beyond the Urals:   economic development in Soviet Asia.   L.,
       Oxford U.P., 1967.      420p.

4399   Czaplicka, M.A.   The Turks of Central Asia in history and at the present
       day:   an ethnological inquiry into the Pan-Turanian problem, and biblio-
       graphical material relating to the early Turks and the present Turks of
       Central Asia.   Oxford, Clarendon P., 1918.      242p.

4400   Davies, R.A., Steiger, A.J.   Soviet Asia:   democracy's first line of de-
       fence.   N.Y., Dial, 1942. 384p.;   L., Gollancz, 1943.      208p.

4401   Edelman, H.   How Russia prepared:   U.S.S.R. beyond the Urals.   L., Peng-
       uin, 1942.      127p.

4402   Elvin, H.   The incredible mile:   Siberia, Mongolia, Uzbekistan.   L., He-
       inemann, 1970.      263p.

4403   Fleming, P.   A forgotten journey.   L., Hart-Davies, 1952.      190p.

4404   Fox, R.   People of the steppes.   L., Constable, 1925.      246p.

4405   Goldman, B.   Red road through Asia:   a journey by the Arctic Ocean to S-
       iberia, Central Asia and Armenia:   with an account of the peoples now l-
       iving in those countries under the hammer and sickle.   L., Methuen, 1934.
       270p.

4406   Hayit, B.   Some problems of modern Turkistan history:   an analysis of S-
       oviet attacks on the alleged falsifiers of the history of Turkistan.   D-
       usseldorf, 1963.      60p.

4407   Hayit, B.   Soviet Russian colonialism and imperialism in Turkestan.   Cologne, 1965.    123p.

4408  Hostler, C.R.  Turkism and the Soviets:  the Turks of the world and their
      political objectives.  N.Y., Praeger;  L., Allen & Unwin, 1957.    244p.

4409  Inoue, Y.  Journey beyond Samarkand.  Tokyo;  Palo Alto, Kodansha, 1971.
      130p.

4410  Krader, L.  The peoples of Central Asia.  2nd ed.  Bloomington, Indiana
      U.P., 1966.    322p.

4411  Krist, G.  Alone through the forbidden land:  journeys in disguise thro-
      ugh Soviet Central Asia.  L., Faber, 1938.    271p.

4412  Krist, G.  Prisoner in a forbidden land.  L., Faber, 1938.    354p.

4413  Kunitz, J.  Dawn over Samarkand:  the rebirth of Central Asia.  L., Law-
      rence & Wishart, 1936.    348p.

4414  MacLean, F.  Back to Bokhara.  L., Cape, 1959.    156p.

4415  MacLean F.  A person from England and other travellers.  N.Y., Harper,
      1959.;  L., Cape, 1958.    384p.

4416  Maillart, E.K.  Turkestan solo:  one woman's expedition from the Tien S-
      han to Kizil Kum.  N.Y.;  L., Putnam, 1935.    301p.

4417  Mandel, W.  The Soviet Far East and Central Asia.  N.Y., Dial P., L.,
      Allen & Unwin, 1944.    158p.

4418  Mazaroff, P.S.  Hunted through Central Asia.  L., Blackwood, 1932. 332p.

4419  Nove, A., Newth, J.A.  The Soviet Middle East:  a communist model for d-
      evelopment.  N.Y., Praeger, 1966;  L., Allen & Unwin, 1967.    160p.

4420  Park, A.G.  Bolshevism in Turkestan, 1917-1927.  N.Y., Columbia U.P.,
      1957.    428p.

4421  Price, M.P.  War and revolution in Asiatic Russia.  L., Allen & Unwin,
      1918.    296p.

4422  Rywkin, M.  Russia in Central Asia.  N.Y., Collier Bks.;  L., Collier-M-
      acmillan, 1963.    191p.

4423  Schulyer, E.  Turkestan:  notes of a journey in Russian Turkestan, Koka-
      nd, Bukhara and Kuldja.  N.Y., Praeger, 1966.    340p.

4424  Sinor, D.  Inner Asia:  history, civilization, languages;  a syllabus.
      Bloomington, Indiana U., 1969.    261p.

4425  Taaffe, R.N.  Rail transportation and the economic development of Soviet
      Central Asia.  Chicago, U. of Chicago, Dept. of Geography, 1960.  186p.

4426  Tuzmuhamedov, R.  How the national question was solved in Soviet Central

Asia: a reply to falsifiers. Moscow, Progress, 1973.    203p.

4427  Wallace, H.A., Steiger, A.J.   Soviet Asia mission.  N.Y., Reynal & Hitchcock, 1946.    248p.

4428  Wheeler, G.   The peoples of Soviet Central Asia:  a background book.  L.,
Bodley Head, 1966.    126p.

4429  Wheeler, G.   Racial problems in Soviet Muslim Asia.  2nd ed.  L., Oxford
U.P., 1962.    67p.

4430  Wilson, H.C., Mitchell, E.R.  Vagabonding at fifty:  from Siberia to Turkestan.  N.Y., Coward;  L., Hutchinson, 1929.    335p.

4431  Zenkovsky, S.A.   Pan-Turkism and Islam in Russia.  Cambridge, Mass., Harvard U.P., 1960.    345p.

4432  Halpern, A.  Conducted tour.  N.Y., Sheed & Ward, 1945.    145p.

4433  Viktovich, V.  Kirghizia today:  travel notes.  Moscow, FLPH,    1960.
270p.

4434  Wardell, J.W.  In the Kirghiz steppes.  L., Galley P., 1961.    182p.

4435  Winner, T.G.  The oral art and literature of the Kazakhs of Russian Central Asia.  Durham, N.C., Duke U.P., 1958.    269p.

4436  Luknitskii, P.N.  Soviet Tajikstan.  Moscow, FLPH, 1954.    254p.

4437  Rakowska-Harmstone, T.  Russia and nationalism in central Asia:  the case of Tadzhikistan.  Baltimore, Johns Hopkins P., 1970.    326p.

4438  Craig-McKerrow, M.R.  The iron road to Samarcand.  L., De la More P.,
1932.    143p.

4439  Falk, J.C.  Incident in Bokhara.  N.Y., Exposition, 1970.    93p.

4440  Mannin, E.  South to Samarkand.  L., Jarrolds, 1936.    355p.

4441  Medlin, W.K. and others.  Education and development in Central Asia:  a
case study on social change in Uzbekistan.  Leyden, Brill, 1971.    285p.

4442  Medlin, W.K. and others.  Education and social change:  a study of the
role of the school in a technically developing society in Central Asia.
Ann Arbor, U. of Michigan, School of Education, 1965.    457p.

4443  Strong, A.L.  Red star in Samarkand.  N.Y., Coward, 1929.;  L.. Williams
& Norgate, 1930.    329p.

4444  X.Y.  From Moscow to Samarkand.  L., Hogarth P., 1934.    134p.

H    Siberia and the Soviet North

4445  Armstrong, T.E.  Russian settlement in the North.  Cambridge, Cambridge
      U.P., 1965.    223p.

4446  Ashton, J.M.  Icebound:  a trader's adventures in the Siberian Arctic.
      N.Y., Putnam, 1928.    255p.

4447  Barber, N.  Trans-Siberian.  L., Harrap, 1942.    180p.

4448  Bergman, S.  Through Kamchatka by dog-sled and skis.  L., Seeley Service,
      1927.    284p.

4449  Borodin, G.  Soviet and Tsarist Siberia.  L., Rich & Cowan, 1945.    168p.

4450  Botting, D.  One chilly Siberian morning.  L., Hodder & Stoughton, 1965.
      192p.

4451  Burnham, J.B.  The rim of mystery:  a hunter's wanderings in unknown Sib-
      erian Asia.  N.Y., Putnam, 1929.    281p.

4452  Burr, M.  In Bolshevik Siberia:  the land of ice and exile.  L., Wither-
      by, 1931.    224p.

4453  Channing, C.G.F.  Siberia's untouched treasure:  its future role in the
      world.  N.Y.; L., Putnam, 1923.    475p.

4454  Dibb, P.  Siberia and the Pacific:  a study of economic development and
      trade prospects.  N.Y., Praeger, 1972.    288p.

4455  Digby, B.  Tigers, gold and witchdoctors.  L., Lane, 1928.    341p.

4456  Dominique, P.  Secrets of Siberia.  L., Hutchinson, 1934.    288p.

4457  Egart, M.  The ferry:  sketches of the struggle for socialism in the Al-
      tai Mts.  L., Lawrence, 1932.    151p.

4458  Hautzig, E.  The endless steppe:  growing up in Siberia.  N.Y., Crowell,
      1968.; L., Hamilton, 1969.    243p.

4459  Huppert, H.  Men of Siberia:  sketchbook from the Kuzbas.  L., Lawrence,
      1934.    326p.

4460  Jochelson, W.  Peoples of Asiatic Russia.  N.Y., American Museum of Nat-
      ural History, 1928.    277p.

4461  Kirby, E.S.  The Soviet Far East.  L., Macmillan, 1971.    268p.

4462  Kolarz, W.  The peoples of the Soviet Far East.  N.Y., Praeger; L.,
      Philip, 1954.    194p.

4463  Krypton, C.  The Northern Sea Route and the economy of the Soviet North.
      N.Y., Praeger, 1956.    219p.

4464  Lengyel, E.  Secret Siberia.  N.Y., Random, 1943.; L., Hale, 1947.
      277p.

4465  Levin, M.G., Potapov, L.P.  The peoples of Siberia.  Chicago, U. of Chicago P., 1964.    948p.

4466  Lied, J.  Prospector in Siberia:  an autobiography.  N.Y., Oxford U.P.,
1945.  307p.;  Return to happiness.  L., Macmillan, 1943.    317p.

4467  Matters, L.  Through the Kara Sea:  the narrative of a voyage in a tramp
steamer through Arctic waters to the Yenisei River.  L., Skeffington,
1932.    283p.

4468  Moore, F.F.  Siberia today.  N.Y., Appleton, 1919.    333p.

4469  Mowat, F.  The Siberians.  Boston, Mass., Little, 1970.  360p.;  L., Heinemann, 1972.    313p.

4470  Norton, H.F.  The Far Eastern Republic of Siberia.  N.Y., Holt;  L., Allen & Unwin, 1923.    311p.

4471  Novomeysky, M.A.  My Siberian life.  L., Parrish, 1956.    352p.

4472  Phillips, G.D.R.  Dawn in Siberia:  the Mongols of Lake Baikal.  L., Muller, 1943.    196p.

4473  Portisch, H.  I saw Siberia.  L., Harrap, 1972.    210p.

4474  Rondiere, P.  Siberia.  N.Y., Ungar, 1967.;  L., Constable, 1966.  205p.

4475  St George, G.  Siberia:  the new frontier.  N.Y., McKay, 1969.    374p.

4476  Semushkin, T.  Children of the Soviet Arctic.  L., Hutchinson, 1944.
256p.

4477  Servadio, G.  A Siberian encounter.  N.Y., Farrar, 1972;  L., Weidenfeld
& Nicolson, 1971.    241p.

4478  Shinkarev, L.  The land beyond the mountains:  Siberia and its people t-
oday.  N.Y., Macmillan, 1973.    250p.

4479  Smolka, H.P.  40,000 against the Arctic:  Russia's polar empire.  L., H-
utchinson, 1937.    275p.

4480  Special Delegation of the Far Eastern Republic to the Washington Conference, 1922.  The Far Eastern Republic:  its natural resources, trade and
industry.  Washington, 1922.    368p.

4481  Staf, K.  Yakutia as I saw it.  Moscow, FLPH, 1958.    114p.

4482  Stanford, D.  Siberian odyssey.  N.Y., Dutton, 1964.;  Sun and snow:  a
Siberian adventure.  L., Longmans, 1963.    158p.

4483  Stephan, J.  Sakhalin:  a history.  Oxford, Clarendon P., 1971.    240p.

4484  Swenson, O.  Northwest of the world:  forty years trading and hunting in
northern Siberia.  N.Y., Dodd, 1944.    270p.

4485   Tchernavin, T.   My childhood in Siberia.   L., Oxford U.P., 1972.   112p.

4486   Thiel, E.   The Soviet Far East:   a survey of its physical and economic
       geography.   N.Y., Praeger;   L., Methuen, 1957.      388p.

4487   Woods, J.B.   Incredible Siberia.   N.Y., Dial, 1928.      261p.

IX    LEARNING

4488    Graham, L.R.   The Soviet Academy of Sciences and the Communist Party,
        1927-1932.  Princeton, Princeton U.P., 1967.    255p.

4489    Institute for the Study of the History and Culture of the U.S.S.R.   Aca-
        demic freedom under the Soviet regime:  a symposium of refugee scholars
        and scientists who have escaped from the U.S.S.R. on the subject 'Academ-
        ic freedom in the Soviet Union as a threat to the theory and practice of
        Bolshevik doctrine.'  Munich, 1954.    120p.

4490    Korol, A.G.   Soviet research and development:  its organization, person-
        nel and funds.  Cambridge, Mass., MITP., 1965.    375p.

4491    Medvedev, Z.A.   The Medvedev papers:  fruitful meetings between scienti-
        sts of the world;  and, Secrecy of correspondence is guaranteed by law.
        L., Macmillan, 1971.    471p.

4492    Nimitz, A.E.   Soviet expenditures on scientific research.   Santa Monica,
        Rand Corp., 1963.    77p.

4493    Vucinich, A.   The Soviet Academy of Sciences.  Stanford, Stanford U.P.,
        1956.    157p.


A    Science

4494    American Association for the Advancement of Science.   Soviet science: a
        symposium.  Washington, 1952.    108p.

4495    Ashby, E.   Scientist in Russia.  Baltimore;  Harmondsworth, Penguin, 19-
        47.    252p.

4496    Barnier, L.   Secrets of Soviet science.  N.Y., International Publications
        Service;  L., Wingate, 1959.    165p.

4497    Biew, A.M.   Kapitsa:  the story of the British-trained scientist who in-
        vented the Russian hydrogen bomb.  L., Muller, 1956.    288p.

4498    Crowther, J.G.   Soviet science.  N.Y., Dutton;  L., Kegan Paul,  1936.
        342p.

4499    DiPaola, R.A.   A survey of Soviet work in the theory of computer progra-
        mming.  Santa Monica, Rand Corp., 1967.    144p.

4500    Dorozynski, A.   The man they wouldn't let die.  N.Y., Macmillan,  1965.
        207p.

4501    Fridland, L.S.   The achievement of Soviet medicine.  N.Y., Twayne, 1961.
        352p.

4502    Galkin, K.   The training of scientists in the Soviet Union.  Moscow, FL-
        PH, 1959.    204p.

4503 Gouschev, S. Vassiliev, M. Russian science in the 21st century. N.Y., McGraw-Hill, 1960. 222p.

4504 Harvey, M.L. and others. Science and technology as an instrument of Soviet policy. Coral Gables, U. of Miami, Center for Advanced International Studies, 1972. 219p.

4505 Huxley, J.S. Heredity east and west: Lysenko and world science. N.Y., Schuman, 1949. 246p.; Soviet genetics and world science: Rysenko and the meaning of heredity. L., Chatto & Windus, 1949. 254p.

4506 Ipatieff, V.N. Life of chemist: memoirs. Stanford, Stanford U.P., 1946. 658p.

4507 Joravsky, D. The Lysenko affair. Cambridge, Mass., Harvard U.P., 1970. 459p.

4508 Joravsky, D. Soviet Marxism and natural science, 1917-1923. N.Y., Columbia U.P.; L., Routledge, 1961. 433p.

4509 Koshtoiants, K.S. Essays on the history of physiology in Russia. Washington, American Institute of Biological Sciences, 1964. 321p.

4510 Langdon-Davies, J. Russia puts the clock back: a study of Soviet science and some British scientists. L., Gollancz, 1949. 160p.

4511 Lebedinskii, A. What Russian scientists say about fallout. N.Y., Collier, 1962. 124p.; Soviet scientists on the danger of nuclear tests. Moscow, FLPH, 1960. 129p.

4512 Lenin Academy of Agricultural Sciences of the U.S.S.R. Proceedings, July 31- August 7, 1948: the situation in biological sciences. N.Y., International Publishers, 1949. 636p.

4513 Leningrad. Direct Current Research Institute. U.S.S.R. direct current research. N.Y., Macmillan, 1964. 287p.

4514 Lysenko, T.D. Heredity and its variables. Moscow, FLPH, 1951. 136p.

4515 Medvedev, Z.A. The rise and fall of T.D. Lysenko. N.Y., Columbia U.P., 1969. 284p.

4516 Melinskaya, S.I. Soviet science, 1917-70. Metuchen, Scarecrow, 1971- Vol. 1-

4517 Morton, A.G. Soviet genetics. L., Lawrence & Wishart, 1951. 176p.

4518 Parry, A. The Russian scientist. N.Y., Macmillan, 1973. 196p.

4519 Rabinovich, I.M. Structural mechanics in the U.S.S.R., 1917-1957. N.Y; L., Pergamon, 1960. 429p.

4520 Recent advances in Soviet science; with a foreword by A.W. Haslett. L., Todd, 1961. 224p.

4521 Zaleski, E. and others. Science policy in the U.S.S.R. Paris, Organis-
     ation for Economic Co-operation and Development, 1969.    615p.

4522 Zirkle, C. Death of a science in Russia: the fate of genetics as desc-
     ribed in Pravda and elsewhere. Philadelphia, U. of Pennsylvania P., 19-
     49.    319p.


B    Social Sciences

4523 Academy of Sciences of the U.S.S.R. Institute of Economics. Political
     economy: a text book. L., Lawrence & Wishart, 1957.    858p.

4524 Dunn, S.P. Sociology in the U.S.S.R.: a collection of readings from S-
     oviet sources. N.Y., International Arts & Sciences P., 1969.    281p.

4525 Fischer, G. Science and ideology in Soviet society. N.Y., Atherton P.,
     1967.    176p.

4526 Fischer, G. Science and politics: the new sociology in the Soviet Uni-
     on. Ithaca, Cornell U.P., 1964.    66p.

4527 Hare, R. Pioneers of Russian social thought: studies of non-Marxian f-
     ormation in nineteenth-century Russia and of its partial revival in the
     Soviet Union. L., Oxford U.P., 1951.    307p.

4528 Jasny, N. Soviet economists of the twenties: names to be remembered.
     Cambridge, Cambridge U.P., 1972.    217p.

4529 Ostrovitjanov, K.V. and others. Social sciences in the U.S.S.R. The H-
     ague, Mouton, 1965.    297p.

4530 Robinson, T.W. Game theory and politics: recent Soviet views. Santa
     Monica, Rand Corp., 1970.    127p.

4531 Simirenko, A. Soviet sociology: historical antecedents and current app-
     raisals. Chicago, Quadrange, 1966.; L., Routledge, 1967.    384p.

4532 Simirenko, A. Social thought in the Soviet Union. Chicago, Quadrangle,
     1969.    439p.

4533 Stolt, R.G. The western economy and its future as seen by Soviet econo-
     mists. Montreal, International Film and Publications Co., 1958.  102p.

4534 Turner, C.B. An analysis of Soviet views on John Maynard Keynes. Dur-
     ham, N.C., Duke U.P., 1969.    183p.


C    Psychology

4535 Babkin, B.P. Pavlov: a biography. Chicago, U. of Chicago P., 1948.;
     L., Gollancz, 1951.    365p.

4536 Bauer, R.A. The new man in Soviet psychology. Cambridge, Mass., Harvard U.P., 1952.    229p.

4537  Bauer, R. A.  Some views on Soviet psychology.  Washington, American Ps-
      ychological Association, 1962.    285p.

4538  Cole, M., Maltzman, I.  A handbook of contemporary Soviet psychology.  N.
      Y., Basic, 1969.    887p.

4539  Cuny, H.  Ivan Pavlov:  the man and his theories.  N.Y., Hill & Wang,19-
      65.    174p.

4540  Gautt, W.H. and others.  Pavlovian approach to psychopathology:  history
      and perspectives.  N.Y.;  Oxford, Pergamon, 1970.    341p.

4541  Handbook of Soviet psychology.  White Plains, International Arts & Scie-
      nces P., 1966.    148p.

4542  O'Connor, N.  Present-day Russian psychology:  a symposium by seventeen
      authors.  N.Y.;  Oxford, Pergamon, 1966.    201p.

4543  O'Connor, N.  Recent Soviet psychology.  N.Y., Liveright, 1962.; Oxford,
      Pergamon, 1961.    334p.

4544  Payne, T.R.  S.L. Rubinstein and the philosophical foundations of Soviet
      psychology.  Dordrecht, Reidel, 1969.    186p.

4545  Rahmani, L.  Soviet psychology:  philosophical, theoretical, and experi-
      mental issues.  N.Y., International Universities P., 1973.    440p.

4546  Simon, B.  Psychology in the Soviet Union.  L., Routledge, 1957.  350p.

4547  Soviet psychology:  a symposium.  N.Y., Philosophical Library, 1961.; L.,
      Vision P., 1962.    109p.

4548  Winn, R.B.  Psychotherapy in the Soviet Union.  N.Y., Grove, 1962. 207p.

4549  Wortis, J.  Soviet psychiatry.  Baltimore, Williams & Wilkins,    1950.
      314p.


D    History

4550  Black, C.E.  Rewriting Russian history:  Soviet interpretations of Russi-
      a's past.  2nd ed.  N.Y., Random, 1963.    431p.

4551  Eremenko, A.I.  False witnesses:  an exposure of falsified Second World
      War histories.  Moscow, FLPH, 1960.    144p.

4552  Gallagher, M.P.  The Soviet history of World War 2:  myths, memories and
      realities.  N.Y.;  L., Praeger, 1963.    205p.

4553  Heer, N.W.  Politics and history in the Soviet Union.  Cambridge, Mass.,
      MITP, 1971.    319p.

4554    Keep, J. Brisby, L.   Contemporary history in the Soviet mirror.  L., Allen & Unwin, 1964.    332p.

4555    Mazour, A.G.   Modern Russian historiography.  2nd ed.  Princeton, Van Nostrand, 1958.    260p.

4556    Mazour, A.G.   The writing of history in the Soviet Union.  Stanford, Stanford U.P., 1971.    383p.

4557    Mehnert, K.   Stalin versus Marx:   the Stalinist historical doctrine.  L., Allen & Unwin, 1952.    128p.

4558    Miller, M.O.   Archaeology in the U.S.S.R.   N.Y., Praeger;  L., Atlantic P., 1956.    232p.

4559    Mongait, A.L.   Archaeology in the U.S.S.R.;  tr. by M.W. Thompson.  Baltimore;  Harmondsworth, Penguin, 1961.    320p.

4560    Mongait, A.L.   Archaeology in the U.S.S.R.;  tr. by D. Skvirsky.  Moscow, FLPH, 1959.    428p.

4561    Nekrich, A.M.   'June 22, 1941';  Soviet historians and the German invasion.  Columbus, U. of South Carolina P., 1968.    322p.

4562    Pundeff, M.   History in the U.S.S.R.:   selected readings.  San Francisco, Chandler, 1967.    313p.

4563    Shteppa, K.F.   Russian historians and the Soviet state.  New Brunswick, Rutgers U.P., 1962.    437p.

4564    Solovyev, O.   The socialist revolution: facts and fiction;  criticisms of bourgeois concepts.  Moscow, Novosti Agency, 1972.    140p.

4565    Tillett, L.   The great friendship:   Soviet historians on the non-Russian nationalities.  Chapel Hill, U. of North Carolina P., 1969.    468p.

(v)    Linguistics

4566    Current Digest of the Soviet Press Association.  The Soviet linguistic controversy.  N.Y., King's Crown P., 1951.    98p.

4567    Prucha, J.   Soviet psycholinguistics.  Mouton, The Hague, 1972.  117p.

4568    Thomas, L.J.   The linguistic theories of N.Ja. Marr.  Berkeley, U. of California P., 1957.    176p.

(vi)    Philosophy

4569    Birjukov, B.W.   Two Soviet studies on Frege;  ed. by I. Angelelli.  Dordrecht, Reidel, 1964.    101p.

4570    Blakeley, T.J.   Soviet scholasticism.  Dordrecht, Reidel, 1963.    176p.

4571    Blakeley, T.J.   Soviet theory of knowledge.  Dordrecht, Reidel, 1964.

200p.

4572 Bochenski, J.M.  The dogmatic principles of Soviet philosophy (as of 19-
58):  synopsis of the 'Osnovy Marksistskoj Filosofii'with complete index.
Dordrecht, Reidel, 1963.    78p.

4573 Bochenski, J.M.  Soviet Russian dialectical materialism (Diamat).  Dordrecht, Reidel, 1963.    185p.

4574 De George, R.T.  Patterns of Soviet thought:  the origins and development of dialectical and historical materialism.  Ann Arbor, U. of Michigan P., 1966.    294p.

4575 De George, R.T.  Soviet ethics and morality.  Ann Arbor, U. of Michigan
P., 1969.    184p.

4576 Edie, J.M. and others.  Russian philosophy.  Chicago, Quadrangle, 1965.
3 vols.

4577 Filipov, A.P.  Logic and dialectic in the Soviet Union.  N.Y., Research
Program on the U.S.S.R., 1952.    89p.

4578 Graham, L.R.  Science and philosophy in the Soviet Union.  N.Y., Knopf,
1972.; L., Allen Lane, 1973.    584p.

4579 Kline, G.L.  Spinoza in Soviet philosophy:  a series of essays.  L., Routledge, 1952.    190p.

4580 Lazlo, E.  Philosophy in the Soviet Union:  a survey of the mid-sixties.
Dordrecht, Reidel, 1968.    212p.

4581 Shein, L.J.  Readings in Russian philosophical thought.  The Hague, Mouton, 1968.    293p.

4582 Shein, L.J.  Readings in Russian philosophical thought:  logic and aesth-
etics.  The Hague, Mouton, 1973.    337p.

4583 Simmons, E.J.  Continuity and change in Russian and Soviet thought.  Cambridge, Mass., Harvard U.P., 1955.    563p.

4584 Somerville, J.  Soviet philosophy:  a study of theory and practice. N.Y. ,
Philosophical Library, 1946.    269p.

4585 Wetter, G.A.  Dialectical materialism:  a historical and systematic survey of philosophy in the Soviet Union.  N.Y., Praeger, 1959.; L., Routledge, 1958.    609p.

INDEX OF NAMES

Arakelian, A., 1307

Aramilev, I.A., 2073

Ararat, Mt., 458,4368

Arbuzov, A., 2074-76

Archangel, 3188,3209

Archer, P., 1772

Arctic, 2817,2823,2826,2832,
 2835-37,4446,4476,4479

Armenia, 3202,4360-64,4368,
 4405

Armes, K., 2572

Armonas, B., 732,3453

Armstrong, H.C., 4371

Armstrong, H.F., 4034

Armstrong, J.A. 35,924,1357,
 1443,3378,4290

Armstrong, T.E., 2816-17,4445

Arnold, A.Z., 1296

Arnot, R.P., 3537,3993

Arossev, A., 2709

Arsenyev, V.K., 2077

Arthur, A., 2187

Arts Council of Great Britain,
 2781

Arzhak, N., 1056,2135

Ashbee, F., 2095

Ashby, E., 576,4495

Ashleigh, C., 2187

Ashmead-Bartlett, E., 365

Ashton, J.M., 4446

Asia, 3801-3920

Asirvatham, A., 1110

Aslanyan, A.A., 4360

Aspaturian, V.V., 1581,1590,3538

Association of American Law Schools,
 1773-74

Astrov, E., 3021

Aten, M., 3160

Athay, R.E., 1242

Atkinson, J., 2631

Atkinson, J.D., 3539

Atkinson, O., 577

Attlee, C.R., 3367

Austria, 3940-41

Auden, W.H., 2114,2650

Avashvili, Z., 4372

Avdeyenko, A.Y., 2078

Avdeyev, V.F., 2079

Avinov, M., 3304

Avrich, P., 3076,3131

Avtorkhanov, A., 1444-45

Azhaev, V., 2080

Azrael, G., 2138

Azrael, J.R., 925,1480

Baade, H.W., 1558

Babayevsky, S.P., 2081,4344

Babel, I., 2082-90

Babel, N., 2085,2088

Babitsky, P., 2710-11

Babkin, B.P., 4535

Bach, M., 2864

Backer, G., 4131

Bacon, E.E., 4388

Baczkowski, W., 578

Badigin, K.S., 2091

Baerlein, H.P.B., 3161

Bahriany, I., 4345

Baikal, Lake, 4472

Baikaloff, A.V., 932,4132

Bailey, F.M., 4389

Bailey, G., 816,1624

Baker, G.R., 1198

Baklanov, G.I., 2092-93

Bakshy, A., 2043,2152,2198,
    2223,2233,2239

Bakst, J., 2739

Baku, 3202,4369

Balabanova, A., 2094,3221,4075

Balawyder, A., 3711

Baldwin, H.W., 1686

Baldwin, O., 4351

Baldwin, R.N., 1002,1481

Bales, J.D., 2887

Balinsky, A., 1308

Balkans, 3922

Balkoff-Downe, T., 2501

Balter, B., 2095

Baltic Sea, 389,1009,3946

Baltic States, 98,4218-81

Balukhatuy, S.D., 2675

Balys, J., 101

Balzak, S.S., 274

Bandera, V.L., 1111

Bann, S., 1934

Baranauskas, B., 4273

Baransky, N.N., 275

Barashev, P., 2859

Barber, N., 520,4447

Barbusse, H., 383,4133

Bardukov, G., 2818

Barghoorn, F.C., 1482,3540-41,3714,4192

Barker, A.J., 1687

Barker, G.R., 1309

Barmine, A., 1582

Barna, Y., 2712

Barnier, L., 4496

Barnes, J., 2467,2481,2540

Baron, S.W., 2933

Baronas, A., 4267

Barou, N., 1446

Barry, D.D., 1775

Bartley, D.E., 1831

Bashkiroff, Z., 3077

Bashkirov, S.I., 2798

Basily, N.de, 2959

Basnett, F., 789

Bass, R.H., 4035

Basseches, N., 1688,4134

Bates, E.S., 4390

Bateson, E., 1008

Batsell, W.R., 1358

Battelle Memorial Institute, 135, 2862

Bauer, J., 3454

Bauer, R.A., 879-80,890,4536-37

Bauermeister, A., 1625

Baykov, A.M., 1243,1310

Bazhan, M.P., 4331

Bazhov, P., 2096

Beard, R., 69

Bearne, C.G., 1983,2015,2533

Beattie, E.W., 3455

Beatty, B., 3022

Beauchamp, J., 1070,1217

Beaujour, E.K., 2422

Bechhofer, C.E., 3222

Beck, A., 3379

Beck, F., 1483,3305

Becker, A.S., 204-05,235,1689, 3816,4391

Becker, H., 1011,3456

Beckmann, P., 1038

Beddie, J.S., 3986

Beggs, R., 3715

Begin, M., 3457

Beitzell, R., 3716

Bek, A., 2097-2100

Belfrage, S., 690

Belgorod, 2485,3422

Belgrade, 1917

Bell, C., 3717

Bell, R., 697

Bell, V., 2374

Bellew, H., 2761

Belli, M.M., 763

Beloff, M., 3542,3802

Belorussia, 103,3372,4282-85,4287-88

Belov, F., 1071

Belyayev, A.R., 2101-02

Benes, V., 4035

Benet, S., 1072

Ben-Horin, E., 1690

Bennett, E.M., 3718

Bennett, G., 3163

Bennett, T.M., 3921

Benningsen, A., 2926

Benningsen, G., 2865

Benton, W., 1832-33

Benyukh, O., 4291

Beraud, H., 344

Berchin, M., 1690

Berdyaev, N., 3023

Bereday, G.Z.F., 1834-36

Berg, A., 4249

Berg, L.S., 272

Bergaust, E., 2841

Berger, J., 2648,2782,3306

Bergman, S., 2819,4448

Bergson, A., 202,222,225-26,231,
    1112-13,1289,1311-12

Berhman, J., 1273

Beria, L.P., 1026,3494,4054,
    4352

Berkman, A., 335

Berlin, 1650,3355,3781,3971,3987

Berliner, J.S., 926,1244

Berman, H.J., 646,881,1678,
    1691-92,1776-78

Bernard, P.J., 1313

Bernaut, E., 1447,3319

Bernaut, R., 229,231

Bertensson, S., 2348-49

Berton, P.A., 95

Bertone, C.M., 60

Beryozka State Dance Company,
    2769

Berzins, A., 3543,4218

Bess, D., 488

Bessedovsky, G., 3544

Best, H., 2960,3024

Bethel, P.D., 3795

Bethell, N., 2570,2576

Beury, C.E., 3025

Bezsonov, Y., 1484

Biagi, E., 4051

Bialer, S., 3380

Bialoguski, M., 1626

Bienstock, G., 927

Bigland, E., 497,521,592,4135

Bilainkin, G., 3994-96

Bilinski, Y., 4292

Bill-Belozerkovsky, V., 2103

Bilmanis, A., 4212,4250-51

Bimstone, J., 2403

Binder, P., 882,965

Binyon, T.J., 2026

Bird, C., 2393

Birjukov, B.W., 4569

Birkos, A.S., 20

Bishop, D.G., 3545,3719

Bishop, R., 1074,3922

Bissonnette, G., 675

Bjork, L., 1290

Bose, T.C., 3721

Bosley, K., 2027

Bostock, A., 2148,2303,2319

Botchkareva, M., 3087

Botting, D., 4450

Botvinnik, M., 1902-05, 1924

Bourdeaux, M., 2889-91,2906

Bourke-White, M., 384,3381

Bouscaren, A.T., 1414,3546-47

Bowen, J.E., 1837

Bowen, V., 2408

Bower, H.M., 770

Bowers, F., 2676

Bowlt, J.E., 1934

Boyars, A., 2132

Brabant, J.M.P.van, 1245

Bradley, J., 3165

Bradshaw, M., 2677

Bragin, M.G., 2113

Braham, R.L., 75,76,888,1359

Brailsford, H.N., 1360,1448, 3132

Brandt, C., 3840

Brasher, C., 2824

Braverman, H., 1115

Bregy, P., 4294

Brest-Litovsk, 3065,3971,3978, 3989,3991

Breyer, S., 1694

Brezhnev, L.I., 3532,3906

Brinkley, G.A., 3166

Brinton, C., 3026

Brinton, L.N., 1091

Brisby, L., 4554

British Labour Delegation to Russia, 3133

British Trade Delegation, 336, 343

British Workers' Delegation, 614

Britton, L., 2603,2654-55

Broad, M., 829

Broadway, 457

Broderson, A., 933

Brodsky, J., 2114

Bromage, B., 4056,4126

Bromke, A., 3926-27

Bron, S.G., 186

Bronfenbrenner, U., 970

Brontman, L.K., 2820

Brooks, J., 2213

Browder, E., 3722

Browder, R.P., 3723

Brower, D.R., 1116

Brown, A., 2005,2065,2067,2336,2356,2430 2449,2477,2638

Brown, C., 2368-69,2371

Brown, D.B., 51,3724

Brown, D.R., 985

Brown, E.C., 934

Brown, E.J., 1938-40,2381

Brown, E.T., 433

Brown, G.W., 51

Brown, J., 471,698

Brown, J.E., 3382

Brown, K., 2602

Brown, W.A., 3224

Brown, W.J., 356,1628

Browne, M., 4295

Brumberg, A., 1053,3490

Brun, A.H., 385,4393

Brunovsky, V., 1487

Brutzkus, B., 1314

Bryant, L., 325,3088

Bryher, 2713

Bryl, Y., 4286

Brzezinski, Z.K., 1361-62,1371,
1485-86,1695,3548,3705,3928

Bubennov, M., 2115-16

Buber, M., 3307

Buchanan, G., 3090

Buchanan, M., 3089

Buchwald, N., 1074

Buck, P.S., 555

Budberg, M., 2202,2208,2220,
2397,2434,2439,2515

Budhraj, V.S., 3895

Budish, J.M., 1246

Budurowycz, B.B., 4017

Bukhara, 4391,4414,4423,4439

Bukharin, N.I., 83,1181-82,1415,
3316,3325,4055

Bulgakov, M., 2117-24

Bullitt, N., 472

Bullitt, W.C., 3725,3742

Bulloch, J., 1629

Bulygin, P., 3134

Bunyan, J., 1003,3027,3135

Burago, A., 2367

Burchett, W., 2842-43

Burg, D., 2132,2570,2576,2586,3511

Burma, 1586

Burnham, J.B., 4451

Burns, E., 1218,2615,2627,2645

Burr, M., 2077,2333-35,2337,2394,
2556,4452

Burrell, G.A., 410

Bury, H., 349

Business International S.A., Geneva,
1247

Butler, H., 2358

Butler, J., 1248

Butler, W.E., 1780-81

Buxhoevden, S., 3225

Buxton, C.R., 323

Buxton, D.F., 357

Buxton, H.J., 4353

Buzek, A., 1051

Byford-Jones, W., 733

Bykov, P.M., 3028

Bykov, V.U., 2125

Byron, R., 411


Cafferty, B., 1906

Caidin, M., 2844-45,2858

Cain, C.W., 1696

Caldwell, E., 522,3383

Callcott, M.S., 3308

Campaigne, J.G., 3726

Campbell, J.R., 1488,3549

Campbell, R.W., 1117,1315

Campbell, T.D., 412,1219

Campbell, W.H., 1249

Canada, 1660,3212,3711

Cang, J., 2934

Cantacuzene, Princess, 3091

Cantril, H., 1416,1449

Caplan, L., 1331

Capote, T., 677

Carden, P., 2089

Caribbean, 3794

Carlisle, O.A., 1941

Carlton, R.G., 27,92,3798

Carmichael, J., 3029

Carnegie, S., 804

Carpathians, 2485,3422

Carpozi, G., 1630,1645

Carr, A.H.Z., 3727

Carr, B., 473

Carr, E.H., 2961,2966,3030,3551,3966,
4121

Cardwell, A.S., 4018

Carell, P., 3384-85

Caroe, O., 4394

Carman, E.D., 3550

Carroll, E.M., 3552

Carroll, W., 3344

Carruthers, D., 4395

Carse, R., 3386

Carson, G.B., 1489

Carter, C., 625

Carter, D., 625,3387

Carter, G.M., 1363

Carter, H., 2678-79

Carter, J.R., 1250

Cartier-Bresson, H., 295

Casey, R.P., 2866

Cash, A., 3031

Cassidy, H.C., 533,3458

Castellane, B.V.de, 3226

Castle, J., 2151

Castro, F., 3798

Cattell, D.T., 1490,4032-33

Caucasus, 691,701,858,2824,3202,
4356,4359,4373

Cederholm, B., 1491

Central Asia, 4383-85,4388,4391,
4394-97,4399,4405,4410-11,
4417-18,4422,4425-26,4428,
4437,4441-42

Central Asian republics, 783

Central Asian Research Centre, 2927,
4396

Chamberlin, W.H., 373,534,1118,1342,
1364,2962,3032,3269,3553,4296

Chandler, G., 155

Chaney, O.P., 4190

Channing, C.G.F., 4453

Chapman, J.G., 232,236,1291

Chappelow, A., 664

Chapsal, M., 3060

Chapygin, A., 2126

Charnock, J., 717,4076

Charques, R., 2171-72

Chary, P.de, 2502

Chase, S., 358

Chase, T.J., 4268

Chavchavadze, P., 3304

Chayanov, A.V., 1220

Cheka, 1491,1540

Chekhov, A.P., 2144,2237

Chelyushkin, 2839

Chen, J., 2784

Cheng, C., 1251

Chernavin, T., 1492

Chernev, I., 1908

Chesterton, Mrs. C., 386,498,524

Chew, A.F., 251

Chiang Kai-Shek, 3841

Chin Szu-K'ai, 3855

Chin, C.S., 3856

China, 93-95,122,366,370,1066,1239,1251,
1259,1580,1883,3572,3604-05,3608,3728,
3749,3787,3795,3810,3836-94,3912,3926,
4010

Chinese Communist Party, 1619

Choat, H., 2209

Chopra, P., 3897

Chornovil, V., 4295,4297

Christopher, M., 474

'Chronicle of current events', 1061

Chronicler, 3169

Chudnovsky, M., 2764

Chuikov, V.I., 3388

Chukovskaia, L., 2127-28

Chukovskii, K.I., 971,2129

Chumandrin, M.F., 2130

Churchill, W.S., 3367,3582,3659

Churchward, L.G., 997,1365

Cianfarra, C.M., 2892

Ciliberti, C., 566

Ciliga, A., 511,1493

Ciszek, W.J., 1012-13,2893

Citrine, W., 499,524,3944

Clark, A., 3389

Clark, B., 2216

Clark, C., 199

Clark, D., 3945

Clark, F.L., 1091

Clark, J.S., 3227

Clark, M., 718

Clark, M.G., 1200,3857

Clarke, C., 1631

Clarke, J.S., 314

Clarke, P.H., 1909-10

Clarke, R.A., 197

Claudia, 500

Clayton, H., 2672

Clemens, D.S., 3554

Clemens, W.C., 86,1566

Clews, J.C., 1041

Cliff, T., 1417-18

Clifford, A., 593

Clissold, S., 3796

Clubb, O.E., 3728,3837

Coates, W.P., 475,1351,1592,2963,
   3167,3310-11,3555,3946-47,

3997,4397

Coates, Z.K., 475,1351,1592,2963,3167,
   3311,3946-47,3997,4397

Cohen, R., 2935

Cohen, S.F., 3328,4055

Cohn, H.D., 3706

Cohn, S.H., 1119

Cole, D.M., 1697,4136

Cole, J.P., 276

Cole, M., 535,4538

Cole, M.I., 434

Coleman, A.P., 145

Coleman, F.A., 3168

Coleman, L., 2374

Collard, D., 3312

College of Preceptors, 1838

Colquhon, J., 3228

Columbia University, Russian Institute,
   143,146,1593

Comecon, 1245,1267,1272

Cominform, 4043

Comite des delegations juives, 4298

Commissariat of Enlightenment, 1845

Committee for Economic Development, 1120

Communist International, 88,123,314,1595
   1598,1606,1610,1619-20,3227

Communist Party of the Soviet Union, 34-
   35,1316,1443-45,1453,1456-58,1460,14-
   63,1466-69,1471,1531,1552,1981,2939,
   3281-82,3513,3518,3527,3534,4293,4488

- 272 -

Communist Party Congress, 19th,
3493,3500,3509

Communist Party Congress, 20th,
3494,3500

Communist Party Congress, 21st,
3495

Communist Party Congress, 22nd,
3496,3887

Communist Party, Central Committee
3509

Comparative Education Society,
1836

Condoide, M.V., 1252,3729

Condon, R.W., 3948

Confino, M., 3817

Congress for Cultural Freedom,
1121

Conklin, D.W., 1221

Connor, W.D., 1000

Conolly, V., 480,1253-54,4398

Conover, H.S., 13

Conquest, R., 719,935,1075,1366,
1494-96,1784,2458,2868,3313,
3524,4077,4194-96

Constantini, O., 771

Conus, E., 986

Conway, W.M., 2785

Conyngham, W.J., 1316

Cooke, R.J., 2869

Cookridge, E.H., 1632-34

Cornell, R., 1367,1594

Corry, J.A., 3558

Corsini, R.P., 790

Cossacks, 774,3187,3244,3267,4338-40,
4342

Costello, B., 2340

Costello, D.P., 2340

Coulson, J.S., 1991

Counts, G.S., 375,387,1042,1839

Cournos, J., 1984,2140,2404

Cousins, N., 3559

Covan, J., 2558

Cowles, V., 516

Cox, G., 3390,3949

Craig, W., 3391

Craig-McKerrow, M.R., 413,4438

Crane, R.D., 1698,3576

Crankshaw, E., 594,3491-92,3858,3998,
4061

Crayfield, E.S., 3922

Creel, G., 3803

Cressey, G.B., 259

Cresson, W.P., 4338

Crichton, C.F.A.M.-M., 414

Crimea, 3202

Crocker, G.N., 3730

Crosfield, Joseph & Sons, 220,290,1255

Crosley, P.S., 3092

Crowe, B., 134

Crowley, E.L., 119,1229,1953

Crowther, J.G., 1840,4498

Crozier, B., 3560

Cuba, 3715,3737,3800

Cudahy, J., 3169

Cumming, C.K., 3731

Cummings, A.J., 3314

Cummings, E.E., 435

Curry, H., 4539

Curie, E., 536

'Current Digest of the Soviet Union'
    3493-96

Curtiss, J.S., 2894,3033

Cusack, E.D., 772

Czaplicka, M.A., 4399

Czapski, J., 1497,3459

Czarnomski, F.B., 635

Czechoslovakia, 1069,1775,3162,3176,
    3929,3942-43

Czerwinski, E.J., 3929

Czyrowski, N.L., 1122


D'Abernon, Viscount, 3170

Dagan, A., 3818

Daglish, R., 2102,2129,2252,2299,
    2315,2328,2529

Daiches, L., 720

Dake, A.C.A., 3912

Dallas, D., 636

Dallin, A., 72,82,1498,1567,1570,

3346-47

Dallin, D.J., 546,1004,1635,2964,3270,
    3497,3561-64,3804-05,3924,3930

Dalton, M., 2134

Dana, H.W.L., 50,2044

Dand, C.H., 3164

Daniel, Y., 1056,2131-35

Daniels, G., 2378

Daniels, R.V., 1499,2965,3034-35,3271

Dark, E.P., 3565

Darling, J., 415

Datar, A.L., 3898

Davidson-Houston, J.V., 699,871

Davie, D., 2445,2459

Davies, J.E., 3732

Davies, N., 4019

Davies, R.A., 4400

Davies, R.W., 1297,2961

Davis, J., 615,3272,3566

Davis, K.W., 1571

Davis-Poynter, R.G., 1942

Dawson, P.M., 501

Dawson, R.H., 3733

Day, R.B., 1183

Deacon, R.V., 1500

Deakin, F.W. 1636

Deal, R.L., 883

Dean, V.M., 3567,3734

Deane, J.R., 3735

De Beausobre, I., 1501

De Chessin, S., 374

Dedijer, V., 4037-38

De George, R.T., 1419,4574-75

Degras, J., 1317,1595,3568-69

Deineko, M.M., 1841

Deker, N.K., 4197

Delafield, E.M., 481

Delbars, Y., 4137

Dellenbrandt, J.A., 1184

Dellin, L.A.D., 1123

De Mauny, E., 840

Demianova, G., 3460

Denikin, A.I., 3171,3187,3202-03

Denisov, A., 1786

Dennen, L., 2936

Dennett, R., 3736

Dennis, A.L.P., 3570

Denno, T., 1420

Deriabin, P., 1450,1502,1637

Derrick, M., 2895

Derthick, L.G., 1842

Desai, P., 1256

De Silva, C.C., 805

Deutscher, I., 152,721,936,1596,
2966-67,3498,3571-72,4138,
4172-74,4078

Devilliers, C., 3461

Dewar, H., 1638

Dewar, M., 937,1257

Dewdney, J.C., 260

Dewey, J., 366,3309

Dewey, V., 2211,2236

Dewhirst, M., 1049

Dewhurst, C.H., 3999

De Witt, N., 928

Diamond, S., 3525

Dibb, P., 4454

Dibold, H., 3462

Dickey, J., 2167

Dickinson, T., 2714

Digby, B., 4455

Dikovski, S.V., 2136

Dillon, E.J., 367

Dinerstein, H.S., 1503,1699,3573

Dingle, R.J., 1597

DiPaola, R.A., 4499

Direct Current Research Institute, 4513

Dirscherl, D., 3499

Divine, R.A., 3737

Dixon, C.A., 3392

Dixon, R., 2314,2338,2389

Djilas, M., 4039

Dmytryshyn, B., 2968,4299

Dobb, M.H., 537,1124,1318

Dobbert, G., 1125

Dobriansky, L.E., 3738

Dobrovolsky, A., 1058

Dodge, N.T., 987,3806

Dohrs, M.E., 700

Dokuchayev, Y., 2859

Dolgopolov, Y., 1794

Dombrovskii, I., 2137

Dominique, P., 4456

Don River, 3219

Donnelly, D., 1277,3574

Donnelly, E., 2006,2190,2261,2263

Donohoe, M.H., 3172,4354

Donovan, J.B., 1639,3819

Doolin, D.J., 3859

Dornberg, J., 851

Dorosh, H., 1504

Dorosh, J.T., 5

Dorozynski, A., 4500

Dorr, R.L.C., 3036

Dosch-Fleurot, A., 3093

Dossick, J.J., 19

Doubassof, I., 1505

Douglas, W.O., 678

Douillet, J., 376

Dovzhenko, A., 2715,2732

Downing, R., 3482

Dowse, R.E., 914

Drachkovitch, M.M. 123,1421,1598-99,2970

Drane, J.F., 3575

Draper, T., 3739

Dreiser, T., 359

Drowne, T.B., 2658,2668

Druhe, D.N., 3899

Druks, H., 3740

Drum, K., 1700

Duddington, N., 2060,2362

Dudintsev, V., 2138-39

Dukes, P., 324,3173-34

Dulles, E.L., 3576

Duncan, Irma, 2765

Duncan, Isadora, 2765,2772

Duncan, W.R., 3577

Duner, P., 525

Dunham, D.C., 3741

Dunn, E., 1076

Dunn, R.W., 938

Dunn, S.P., 1076,4219,4524

Dunsheath, J., 701

Dunsterville, L.C., 3175,4355

Dupuy, R.E., 3176

Durant, W., 436

Duranty, W., 447,482,1451,1506,2969

- 276 -

Durasoff, S., 2896

Durov, V., 2140

Durstine, R.S., 448

Dushnyck, W., 4300

Dutt, V.L., 2016,2243,2516,4090

Dutton, G., 2059,2163

Duval, G.R., 1742

Dwinger, E.E., 3177-78

Dyboski, R., 3229

Dyck, L., 3967

Dykstra, G.O., 360

Dzherzhynski, F.E., 4056-58

Dziewanowski, M.K., 3037

Dzyuba, I., 4198

Eason, W., 246

East, W.G., 764,2971

East Asia, 3812

East European Fund, 138

Eastern Europe, 1066,1190-91,1239,
1248,1257,1266,1452,1796,3578,
3899,3926-38

Eastman, M., 1943,3094,3273-74

Eaton, R., 1507,3230

Ebon, M., 4052,4124

Eckhardt, H.von, 416

Economist Intelligence Unit, 252

Eddy, J.S., 388,449

Edelhertz, B., 377

Edelman, H., 4401

Edelman, M., 526,3315

Edelstadt, V., 3393

Edie, J.M., 4576

Edinburgh, 4208

Edmonds, R., 691

Edwards, C., 2680

Efremov, I.A., 2141-43

Efron, A., 1787

Egart, M., 4457

Eggington, J., 665

Ehrenburg, I., 2144-59

Eichenbaum, V.M., 3069,3155

Einsiedel, H.von, 647,3463

Eisenstein, S.M., 2712,2716-25,2727-30,
2735

Eissenstat, B.W., 1422

Ekart, A., 1015

El Campesino, 637

Elias, A., 248

Eliav, A.L., 2937

Eliot, G.F., 1701

Eliot, T.S., 1014

Eller, E.M., 1702

Ellis, C.H., 3179

Elliston, H.B., 3950

Ellman, M., 1319-20

Ellsworth, R., 1368

Fedyshyn, O.S., 4302

Fehling, H.M., 3349

Feifer, G., 856,1789,2586

Feiler, A., 379

Feinstein, E., 2635

Feis, H., 3581-82,3914

Feiwel, G., 1126

Felber, J.E., 873

Felker, J.L., 1321

Feld, M.J., 4253

Feldbrugge, F.J.M., 1790-91

Foldman, A.B., 4140

Felgenhauer, E., 2323,2621

Fen, E., 1985-86,2110,2673-74
3231

Fernbach, A.P., 1572

Feshbach, M., 245

Feuchtwanger, L., 483

Fialko, N.M., 2180

Fichelle, A., 296

Field, A., 988,1946

Field, M.G., 1092-93

Fiene, D.M., 2584

Filene, P.G., 3743-44

Filipov, A.P., 4577

Fineberg, A., 2262,3277

Fineberg, J., 2113,2155,2188,2279,
2470,2487,2539,3397

Finland, 3405,3780,3783,3944-62,4222,
4234

Finland, Ministry for Foreign Affairs,
3952-53

Finley, D.D., 3694

Fireside, H., 2900

Fischer, B., 747,1901,1912-13,1918

Fischer, E., 4079

Fischer, G., 144,885,1510,3350,4525-26

Fischer, J., 579-80

Fischer, L., 417,461,686,2972,3583-87,
3745-46,3969,4080,4141

Fischer, M., 547

Fischer, R., 3970

Fisher, H.H., 141,3027,3136,3215,3579,
3588

Fisher, J., 3038

Fisher, R.T., 978

Fisher, W.A., 922

Fishman, J., 4142

Fittkau, G.A., 1016

Fitzgibbon, L., 3351

Fitzpatrick, S., 1845

Fitzsimmons, T., 165,184

Flaherty, D.L., 1012-13,2893

Flambeau, V., 773

Flayderman, P.C., 2457

Flegon, A., 136-37,1258,3589

Fleming, D.F., 3590

Fleming, P., 3180,4403

Fleron, F.J., 3615

Fletcher, W.C., 74,2871,2873, 2901-02

Fleuchter, C.E., 703

Flor, G., 2157

Florinsky, M.T., 166,1370,1600

Flower, D., 2375

Floyd, D., 2051,2342,2575,3860

Fokkema, D.W., 3861

Folk Dance Company of the U.S.S.R., 2764

Folsom, F., 791

Fomichenko, I., 1707

Foner, P.S., 3747

Fontaine, A., 3592

Foot, M., 1942

Foote, A., 1640

Foote, J., 3593

Footman, D., 1601,3039,3181

Forman, A., 389

Forsh, O., 2181-82

Forsythe, G.E., 61

Foss, K., 380

Foster, L.A., 108

Foust, C.M., 3594

Fox, I.K., 294

Fox, R., 4081,4404

France, 931,1323,3963-65

France, P., 2105

France, T.D., 2520

Francis, D.R., 3095,3784

Francis, P.G., 509

Francis, S., 156

Franck, H.A., 462

Frank, R., 2571

Frank, W., 418

Frankland, M., 406

Frederickson, O.J., 2168

Freed, D., 2681

Freedman, R.O., 1259

Freeman, J., 939,1925

Freemantle, A., 2157

Frege, G., 4569

Fremantle, A., 2561,2563

French Communist Party, 3964

French, J., 2057

French, R.A., 792

Freund, G., 3971

Freund, H.A., 167

Friedburg, M., 1947,1988

Friedland, L.S., 1987

Friedman, E.M., 1127

Fridland, L., 1094,4501

Friedrich, C.J., 1371

Frolich, B., 765

Fromberg, D., 2013,2262,2331,
   2346,2610,2623

Frost, R., 768

Fry, A.R., 3137

Fry, D., 2500

Fry, J., 1095

Fuchs, K., 1658

Fullard, H., 253

Fulop-Miller, R., 1926,2682,4082

Furmanov, D., 2183

Fuse, K., 3808

Fusfeld, D.R., 1114


GPU, 1638,3315,3318

Gabovich, M., 2762

Gafencu, G., 3398

Gagarin, Y., 2840,2843,2846,
   2854

Galaktionov, V., 2056

Galanskov, Y., 1058

Galenson, W., 1202

Galkin, K., 4502

Gallagher, M.P., 1708,4552

Galler, M., 1511

Galli-Shohat, N., 2757

Galton, D., 2796

Gandhi, M., 4082

Gantt, W.H., 4540

Garbutt, P.E., 2807

Garder, M., 1709

Gardo, L., 4339

Garelik, J., 616

Garmisch-Partenkirchen, 3529-31

Garretson, R.C., 1128

Garry, S., 2271-72,2289,2431,2471-72,
   2526-28,2531,2615,2646

Garshin, V.M., 2184

Garthoff, R.L., 1710-13,3862

Gasiorowska, X., 2022

Gatland, W.K., 2847

Gaucher, R., 1512

Gazdanov, G., 2185-86

Gecys, C.C., 4199

Gehlen, M.P., 1453,3595

Geiger, H.K., 966

Geis, D., 872

Geller, Y.P., 1911

General Sikorski Historical Institute,
   4020

Georgia, 3202,4370,4372-77,4379-80

Gerasimov, I.P., 285

Gerlach, H., 3465

German Communist Party, 3970

German, F.C., 276

Germany, 744,3168,3361,3363,3373,3384-85
   3404,3415,3424,3430,3439,3444,3450,

3460,3468,3481,3925,3956,3966-
92,4021,4027,4271,4302,4561

Germany, Army, 3245

Germany, Foreign Office, 3986,3992

Gerschenkron, A., 214-15,217,219,
1213

Gerstenmaier, C., 1054

Ghambashidze, D., 4373

Ghana, 914

Gibberd, K., 567

Gibbons, P., 2497

Gibbs, H., 1602

Gibbs, P., 3232

Gibian, G., 49,1948,1989,2320

Gibney, F., 1454,1502,1637,3596

Gibson, M., 3278

Gibson, W.J., 463

Gibson-Cowan, 2287

Gide, A., 484,502

Giffen, J.H., 1260

Gilberg, T., 4015

Gilbert, R., 3597

Gilboa, Y.A., 2938,3466

Gilison, J., 1513

Gilmore, E., 657,774

Ginsburg, G., 1578

Ginsburg, M., 1990,2017,2662-63

Ginsburgs, G., 1792

Ginzburg, A., 1058

Gitelman, Z.Y., 2939

Gittings, J., 3863-64

Giudici, D., 2822

Gladkov, F., 2187

Gladstone, J.M., 48

Glaeser, E., 1129

Glagoleva, F., 2420

Glass, S., 2295

Glenny, M., 1949,2045,2120-22,2124,2137,
2569,2582,2598,2600

Gligoric, S., 1912

Gliksman, J.G., 940,1017,1514

Gluckstein, Y., 3931

Gobi Desert, 3186

Godden, G.M., 3138

Godin, W., 1483,3305

Godley, J., Lord Kilbracken, 704

Gohdes, C., 52

Goldberg, B.Z., 2940

Goldberg, D., 2941

Golder, F.A., 3139

Goldhagen, E., 4200

Goldina, M., 2209

Goldman, B., 4405

Goldman, E., 326,330

Goldman, G.G., 2942

Goldman, M.I., 292,1131,1261,3598

Goldstein, D.I., 106

Goldston, R.C., 2973,3040

Goldwin, R.A., 3599

Gollancz, V., 4002

Gollwitzer, H., 3467

Golombek, H., 1913

Golovko, A.G., 3395

Golubov, S., 2188

Goncharov, N.K., 1843

Gonzalez, V., 637

Goode, W.T., 306,3140,3600

Goodfriend, A., 617

Gooding, J., 793

Goodman, E.R., 1423,3601

Goodman, W.L., 1846,2498

Goold-Verschoyle, N., 2305

Gora, D., 4303

Gorbanevskaya, N., 1055,2191

Gorbatov, A.G., 1018,3400

Gorbatov, B., 2189-90

Gorchakov, N.M., 2683-85

Gorchakov, O., 2142,2173

Gordey, M., 638

Gordon, A.G., 3182

Gordon, M., 941,2670

Gorer, G., 962

Gorkin, J., 4179

Gorky St., 1684

Gorky, M., 1009,1950,1962,2010,2192-2251
3141,3295,4083

Gorlitz, W., 3401

Gorodetsky, N., 1991

Gorokhoff, B.I., 162

Gosstroi, 2806

Gould, K.M., 485,748

Goure, L., 979,1503,1714-15,3402

Gourfinkel, N., 2244,4084

Gouschev, S., 4503

Gouzenko, I., 595,2270

Gouzenko, S., 722

Graaff, F.de, 2161

Grady, E.G., 390

Graebner, N.A., 3602

Graebner, W., 527

Graham, G., 1716

Graham, L.R., 4488,4578

Graham, M.W., 3603

Graham, S. 628,4143

Granick, D., 929,1203,1322-23

Granin, D., 2252

Granovsky, A., 1641

Grant, A., 2287

Grant, D., 1847

Grant, N., 1848

Graubard, S.R., 4001

Graves, W.S., 3183

Gray, C., 2788

Gray, G.D.B., 581

Gray, W., 1793

Grazzini, G., 2587

Great Britain, 816,931,1095,1323,
3197,3367,3562,3716,3900,3909,
3993-4012,4213

Great Britain, Central office of
Information, 3604

Green, E., 2253

Green, M., 2476

Greenbaum, A.A., 2943

Greenwall, H.J., 368

Greer, T.V., 1262

Gregor, J., 2682

Gregory, J.S., 254,262,568

Grey, B., 2766

Grey, I., 2974

Gribachev, N., 2254

Grierson, J., 451

Grierson, P., 6

Griffin, F., 419

Griffith, H., 420,464,1927,2052

Griffith, W.E., 3605,3749,3865-66
3939

Griffiths, F., 1548

Grigoryan, L., 1794

Grimsted, P.K., 153

Grin, A., 2255

Grinko, G.F., 1345

Gripp, R.C., 1372

Groettrup, I., 705

Gross, H., 1123

Gross, R.E., 748

Grosser, A., 3963

Grossman, G., 221

Grossman, L., 2256

Grossman, V., 2257-63

Gruber, H., 1603

Gruber, R., 2823

Grunwald, C.de, 2872,2903

Grzybowski, K., 1560,1604,1795-96

Gsovski, V., 1796

Gubski, N., 2264-67

Guerney, B.G., 1950,1992,2068,2206,2616,
2664

Guest, L.H., 345

Guillaume, A., 1717

Guins, G.C., 2975

Guirey, C., 648

Gulia, G., 2268

Gumilevski, L., 2269

Gumilyov, N., 2042

Gunther, J., 687,749

Guralsky, J., 2341,2402

Gurevich, S., 1130

Gurian, W., 1373-74,1424,3606

Guterman, N., 2295,2354-55,2489

Guybon, M., 2573

Gyseghem, A.van, 2686


Haape, H., 3468

Haberman, G., 2245

Hadow, M., 1515

Haensel, P., 1132

Hahn, W.G., 1516

Haines, A.J., 1096

Haines, C.G., 3607

Hakim, K.A., 2928

Haldane, C.F., 3469

Hale, N.A., 110

Halle, F.W., 989-90

Hallett, R., 2090

Halliday, E.M., 3041,3184

Halperin, N.H., 1568

Halpern, A., 3352,4432

Halter, H., 3954

Hamilton, C.M., 452

Hammer, A., 1263

Hammond, T.T., 85,942

Hampel, E., 517

Hamrell, S., 3608

Hanak, H., 3609

Hanna, G., 2179,2512,2617

Hans, N., 1849

Hansen, J., 4176

Hanson, E.M., 2741

Hanson, L., 2741

Hanson, P., 1194

Hapgood, R., 2537

Harari, M., 2159,2318,2451-54,2546

Hard, W., 3096,3775

Hardbottle, R., 2806

Harding, S.M., 639,3233

Hardt, J.P., 196

Hardy, F.J., 640,1152

Hare, R., 1951,2246,4257

Harnwell, G.P., 723

Harper, F.M., 3097

Harper, K., 1993

Harper, S.N., 1375,1455,1517,1587,3610

Harriman, W.A., 3611,3750-51

Harris, G., 2425

Harris, R., 2904

Harris, T.L., 2905

Harrison, E.J., 4269-70

Harrison, M.E., 316,3234

Hartley, E., 2156,2618

Hartson, W.R., 1914

Harvard University, Library, 45,78,81,96

- 285 -

Harvard University, Russian Research Center, 147

Harvey, M.L., 4504

Haslett, A.W., 4520

Hassel, S., 3403

Hassman, H., 289

Hata, I., 3915

Hauer, M.M., 76

Hautzig, E., 4458

Hawker, L.R., 794

Hayit, B., 4406-07

Hayter, W., 3612,4003

Hayward, M., 1056,1936,1952-53, 2032,2062,2085,2300,2377,2451, 2545,2548,2575,2578,2873

Hazard, J.N., 38,1376,1797-99

Heald, E.T., 3098

Hearn, C.V., 1800

Hearst, W.R., 3501

Heater, D., 3613

Hechinger, F.M., 1850

Hecht, R.S., 658

Hecker, J.F., 2874-75

Heer, N.W., 4553

Heifetz, E., 2944

Heilbrunn, O., 1518,1642,3392

Heitman, S., 83

Helsinki University, Library, 1,26

Helstein, N., 2087,2425

Hemy, G.W., 2799

Hendel, S., 888,1377

Henderson, L.W., 750

Henry, P., 1994

Herling, A.K., 1005

Herling, G., 1019,3470

Herman, Y., 2271-74

Herrick, R.W., 1718

Herring, G.C., 3752

Herrington, L.M., 381

Herriot, E., 453

Herz, M.F., 3614

Hess, G.R., 3753

Hessen, S., 1849

Heymann, H., 1264

Hidaka, N., 3842

Hiebert, P.C., 3142

Higgins, M., 666

Higgins, T., 3404

Hiler, L., 2427

Hilger, G., 3972

Hill, C., 4085

Hill, E., 2284

Hill, G.A., 3185

Hill, P.S., 1844

Hilton, R., 607,4004

Hindus, M.G., 421,437,528,538,734,1077-78,2976-77,3078,3332-33,3502,3916,

4340

Hingley, R., 735,1519,2545,
2578,3042

Hippius, Z., 2275-78

Hird, J.W., 2978

Hiroshima, 3712

Hirsch, H., 1324

Hirsch, R., 1643

Hirschmann, I.A., 3821

Hitler, A., 3332,3371,3384-85,
3404,3450,3619,3965,3969,
3977,3985,4008,4146,4307

Hoare, S.J.G., 3099

Hodges, L.H., 706

Hodges, P., 3186

Hodgkins, J.A., 288,2801

Hodgkinson, H., 4041

Hodgman, D.R., 208,1204

Hodgson, J.E., 3187

Hodnett, G., 120

Hoffman, E.P., 3615

Hoffman, G.V., 889

Hogarth, C., 2201,2324,2522

Hogarth, L.J., 2241

Holdsworth, M., 90

Hollander, G.D., 1043

Hollander, P., 886-87

Hollis, C., 4087

Hollo, A., 2028,2653

Holmes, B., 865

Holst, J.J., 1719

Holt, R.T., 2979

Holthusen, J., 1954

Holubnychy, V., 213,4304

Holzman, F.D., 1298

Honchar, O., 4346

Hood, S., 2133

Hooper, A.D., 3405

Hooper, A.S., 486

Hooson, D.J., 263-64

Hoover Institution, 22

Hoover, C.B., 1133

Hoover, H., 3156

Hope, B., 766

Hopkins, E., 2221

Hopkins, M.W., 1050

Hopper, B., 391

Horak, S., 18

Horecky, P.L., 7,8,24,25,27,154

Horelick, A.L., 1720,3816

'Horizon', 3041

Horowitz, D., 152

Horrabin, J.F., 254

Horton, M.H., 1915

Hostler, B., 4408

Hough, J.F., 1459

Houghteling, J.L., 3100

Houghton, N., 2687-88

Houston, J.F., 679

Hovannisian, R.G., 4361-62

Howard-Johnston, X., 2904-05

Howe, I., 4175

Howell, E.M., 3406

Hoyland, J.S., 438

Hryhorijiv, N.Y., 4305

Hryshko, V.I., 4306

Hsia, L.-Y., 3850

Hubbard, L.E., 943,1222,1265,1299

Huberman, L., 2980

Hubman, H., 771

Hudgins, A., 2572

Hudson, G.F., 1378,2981,3867

Hudson, J.A., 4053

Hueck, C.de, 627

Huff, W.K., 427

Hughes, E., 707

Hughes, W.R., 618

Hulicka, I.M., 915

Hulicka, K., 915

Hullinger, E.W., 337

Humesky, A., 2061,2382

Huminik, J., 1644

Humphreys, T., 3285

Hunt, Sir J., 2824

Hunt, R.N.C., 9

Hungary, 1775,4013

Hunter, H., 1205

Hunter-Blair, K., 2213

Huntingdon, S.P., 1486

Huppert, H., 4459

Hurewitz, J.C., 3822

Hurlimann, M., 297

Huss, P.J., 1645

Huszar, G.B.de, 1379,3616

Hutchings, R., 1134,1206

Hutchinson, L., 3139

Hutton, J.B., 1646-48,3279,4142,4144

Huxley, J., 422,4505

Huxley-Blythe, P.J., 4341

Hyde, F., 2982

Hyde, H.M., 4145

Hyde, N.V., 2982

Hyland, W., 3503


Ielita-Wilczkovski, C., 2983

Ignatov, P.K., 2279,3407

Ikonnikov, A.A., 2383,2742

Ilf, I.A., 2280-85

Ili-Kazakh Autonomous Chou, 3880

Ilmen, Lake, 2469,3419

Ilyin-Genevsky, A.F., 3101

Imam, Z., 3900

Inber, V., 3471

Ingram, K., 3618

Ingrim, R., 3619

India, 767,1285,3810,3897-3911

Indonesia, 3912-13

Industrial Party, 3324

Inkeles, A., 890-91,916,1044

Inoue, Y., 4409

Institute for the Study of the
    History and Culture of the
    U.S.S.R., 892,4489

Institute for the Study of the
    U.S.S.R., 112-17,119,121,125,
    149,2929,3504

Institute of Economic Affairs, 1207

International Confederation of Free
    Labor Unions, 1006

International Labour Organization,
    944,947,960,1195,1572,1576

Intourist, 864

Ionescu, G., 1266,1520,3933

Ipatieff, V.N., 4506

Iran, 1253,3820,3823,3828,3830

Ironside, W.E., 3188

Isaacs, B., 2098,2184,2189,2330,
    2406,2551,2593,2661

Isakov, I.S., 3408

Isenberg, I., 3869

Ispahani, M.A.H., 751

Israel, 3818

Israelyan, V., 3620

Istrait, P., 392

Italy, 2109,2200,2395

'Italia', 2822

Ivanov, I., 1060

Ivanov, V., 2286-88

Ivanov-Razumnik, R.V., 4059

Izmerov, N.F., 293

'Izvestia', 2791

Jacka, E., 2163

Jackson, D.B., 3797

Jackson, J.H., 2907,4236

Jackson, R., 1721,3189

Jackson, W.A.D., 3870

Jackson, W.G.F., 3409

Jacquet, E., 736

Jacob, A., 569,822

Jacobs, D.N., 3505

Jacobsen, C.G., 1722

Jacobson, H.K., 1573,2019

Jacobson, J., 1425

Jacoby, S., 852

Jakobson, M., 3955

James, C.L.R., 1606

James, F.C., 708,1851

Jamgotch, N., 1584

Janse, R.S., 67

Japan, 122,3168,3198,3207,
  3914-20

Jarman, T.L., 439

Jasny, N., 191,1135,1208,1223-24,
  1300,1317,1325,4528

Jaworskyj, M., 1426

Jaxa-Ronikier, B., 4058

Jenkins, A.C., 582

Jochel, N., 2347

Jochelson, W., 4460

Joesten, J., 3621

John XXIII, Pope, 3559

Johnson, C., 1649

Johnson, D., 2018

Johnson, D.G., 1225

Johnson, E.L., 1801

Johnson, H., 512,539,583

Johnson, J., 393

Johnson, J.E., 3736

Johnson, P., 1928

Johnson, S., 823

Johnson, W., 3786

Johnson, W.H., 1852

Johnston, J., 2908

Johnstone, A., 680

Jonas, A.M., 1585

Jones, D.R., 763

Jones, G.J., 3622

Jones, G.V., 423

Jones, M., 752

Jones, R.H., 3754

Jones, S., 3102

Jones, T., 2642

Joravsky, D., 4507-08

Jordan, M., 2482

Jordan, P., 3334

Jorre, G., 265

Joshua, W., 3623

Jukes, G., 3410-12,3809

Jupp, G.A., 692

Juviler, P.H., 1380,1521


Kabin, J., 4237

Kagan, B., 2302

Kaganovich, L.M., 2804

Kahan, A., 1225

Kahn, A.E., 2767,3677

Kalashnik, M., 1723

Kalb, M.L., 693,809,3871

Kaledin, V.K., 1650

Kalinin, A., 2289

Kalinin, M.I., 1427,3353

Kalinikov, I.F., 2290-91

Kalme, A., 4220

Kalnberzins, J., 4254

Kamchatka, 2819,4448

Kamen, H., 2442

Kamenetsky, I., 4307

Kamenev, L.B., 3327

Kamm, H., 1355

Kandelaki, C., 4374

Kanet, R.E., 1381,2985

Kantner, J.F., 241

Kantorovich, L.V., 1185

Kapitsa, P.L., 4497

Kaplan, F.I., 945

Kaplan, N.M., 209-10,212,233,
   1136,1186,1292,1326

Kapp, Y., 1995,2150

Kapur, H., 3810,3823,3901

Kara Sea, 2826,4467

Karazin, N., 2292

Karcz, J.F., 1226-27

Kareda, E., 4238-39

Karlgren, A., 350

Karlinsky, S., 2636

Karpinsky, V.A., 893

Karski, J., 3624

Kaseninka, O., 608

Kaser, M.C., 1137,1267

Kaslas, B.J., 4271

Kassil, L.A., 2293-95

Kassoff, A., 894,980,3526

Katare, S.L., 1382

Katayev, V.P., 2296-2308

Katel, J., 3645

Katkoff, V., 1138

Katkov, G., 2986,3316

Katorga, 1030

Katterle, Z.B., 1853

Katyn Forest, 3345,3351,3356,3375

Katz, A., 1139

Katzenellenbaum, S.S., 1301

Kaufman, A., 2800

Kaun, A., 2038,2247

Kaushik, D., 3902

Kautsky, J.H., 3903

Kautsky, K., 2987,4375

Kaverin, V., 2309-13

Kay, N., 2743

Kayden, E.M., 2443,2446

Kaye, N., 2136

Kazakevich, E.G., 2314-16

Kazakhs, 4435

Kazakov, G., 284,1228

Kazakov, I.P., 2317-18

Kazakov, Y., 2010

Kazanina, H., 2175,2353

- 291 -

Kazemzadeh, F., 4357

Kaznacheev, A.I., 1586

Keegan, J., 3413

Keeling, E.H., 3235-36

Keeling, H.V., 3103

Keep, J., 4554

Keeton, G.W., 3317,3625

Kehler, H., 3104

Kellen, K., 4063

Keller, W., 737

Kelly, D.V., 3626

Kelly, M.N., 298,641

Kelsen, H., 1802

Kemball, R., 2106

Kenez, P., 3190

Kennedy, J.F., 3559,3764

Kennedy, M., 2596

Kennan, G.F., 3627-29,3755

Kerner, M., 1691-92

Kerner, R.J., 1140

Kerr, W., 1724,3414

Kerzhentsev, P., 4088

Ketlinskaya, V., 2319

Keun, O., 327,3237,4376

Keynes, J.M., 4534

Khachaturyan, A., 2758

Kharkov, 552,590,3360

Kharms, D., 2320

Khiva, 4391

Khmel, A., 1725

Khokhlov, N.E., 1651

Khrushchev, N.S., 667,1223,1237,1388,
    1454,1565,1609,1617,1928,2958,2964,
    3280-82,3291,3302,3489-91,3501,3503,
    3510-11,3513,3515,3520,3522,3524-25,
    3533,3559,3596,3622,3630,3645-46,
    3661-62,3756,3764,3833,4060-70,4229

Khvat, K.K.B., 2825

Khvat, L., 2825

Kidran, M., 3896

Kieser, G., 2988

Kiev, 691,877,4337

Kilbracken, John Godley, _Lord_, 704

Kilmarx, R.A., 1726

Kim, Y.H., 3757

Kindall, S.G., 3191

Kindermann, K., 1522

King, B., 570,1854-55

King, D., 4188

King, E.J., 1856

King, F., 584

King, G.J., 4255

King-Hall, S., 1607,4146

Kingsbury, J.A., 1098

Kingsbury, S.M., 991,1097

Kinkead, B., 2669

Kirghizia, 4433-34

Korostovetz, W.K., 3633,4022

Korp, A., 4240

Kosa, J., 895

Koshtoiants, K.S., 4509

Kosin, I., 2234

Koslow, J., 724

Kosmodemyanskaya, L.T., 2328

Kospoth, B.J., 3354

Kostering, N., 3472

Kostiuk, H., 4309

Kosygin, A.N., 3532-33

Kot, S., 4023

Koteliansky, S., 2276

Kotelnikov, V., 4350

Kotov, A., 1916

Koudrey, V., 3238

Kourdakov, S., 2909

Kournakoff, S.N., 1729

Koutaissoff, E., 846

Kovner, M., 1270

Kozera, E.S., 1390

Kozhenikov, V., 2329-31

Krader, L., 4410

Kramish, A., 2802

Krasnodar, 3360

Krasnov, N.N., 1020

'Krassin', 2829

Krassin, L., 4073

Kravchenko, V., 629,3283-85

Krebs, S.D., 2744

Kremlin, 724

Kreusler, A.A., 796,1859-60

Krieger, E., 3473

Krieger, F.J., 2848

Kriger, Y.G., 2332

Krist, G., 4411-12

Krivitsky, W.G., 1653

'Krokodil', 2786,2792,2794

Kronstadt, 3131,3149,3154,3155

Krosby, H.P., 3956

Kruchinin, A., 3873

Kruglak, T.E., 1052

Krupskaya, N.K., 160,4074,4089

Krylov, I.N., 1730

Krymov, V.P., 2333-39

Krypton, C., 4463

Kuban, 3407

Kubijovyc, V., 185

Kublin, H., 824

Kuby, E., 3355

Kucherov, S., 1805

Kudryavtsev, V., 3527

Kuhn, D., 841

Kuhn, F., 841

Kuklick, B., 3975

Kulchycka, L.W., 241

Kuldja, 4423

Kulkarni, M., 3904

Kulski, W.W., 1384,3634-35

Kundzins, H., 4265

Kunitz, J., 585,1955,1997,4413

Kunitz, S., 2062

Kuri, S., 99

Kursk, 3411

Kursky, A., 1328

Kushchevsky, I., 2340

Kushkina, R.I., 237

Kushner, M.D., 825

Kuznetsov, A., 2341-43

Kuznierz, B., 4024

Kuzbas, 4459

Kyaw Min, 649


Labedz, L., 140,1056,1609,1928,
    1952,2588,3506,3874

Labin, S., 3286,3758

La Fave, W.R., 1806

Lafeber, W., 3636,3759

Laird, B.A., 1230

Laird, R.D., 896,1079-81,1229-30

Lambton, A.K.S., 2927

Lamont, C., 440,571,650,2989

Lamont, M., 440

Landis, L., 3825

Lane, D., 1385

Lang, D.M., 4377

Langdon-Davies, J., 3957,4510

Langer, P.F., 3875

Langland, J., 2035

Langnas, T., 2450

Lann, Y.L., 2344-45

Lansbury, G., 307,3239

Lansbury, V., 513

Lansbury-Dutt, V., 2624

Lape, E.E., 3760

Lapenna, I., 1807-08

Laqueur, W., 140,151,1929,3506,3826-27,
    3976

Larsen, O., 1021

Larson, T.B., 1569

Lasch, C., 3761

Laserson, M.M., 3637,4028

Lashkova, V., 1058

Lasker, I.B., 1352

Lasky, V., 3638

Latham, P., 806

Lathe, H., 738

Latin America, 92,1241,3794-3800

Latour, C.F., 82

Latvia, 100,4222,4225-26,4234,4249-51,

MacColl, R., 659

MacConville, M., 1073

McCormick, A.O., 369

McCullagh, F., 2910,3193

MacDougall, A.R., 2765

McDuff, D., 2370

MacDuffie, M., 667

Mace, D.R., 967

Mace, V., 967

MacEoin, G., 2878

MacGregor-Hastie, R., 739,4067

Maciuika, B.V., 4272

McKane, R., 2063

McKelvey, R.G., 1580

MacKenzie, F.A., 2911

McKenzie, K.E., 1610

Mackiewicz, J., 3356

Mackiewicz, S., 424

Mackintosh, J.M., 3644

Mackintosh, M., 1735

McKnight, F.R., 753

McLane, C.B., 2829,3811,3843

MacLean, F., 620,4414-15

McLean, H., 1957,2670

McLeod, J., 2689-91

McNeal, R.H., 34,1388,2993, 4074

McSherry, J.E., 3764,3977

McVey, R.T., 3913

McWilliams, M.S., 353

McWilliams, R.F., 353

Maddison, A., 1147

Magadan, 1549

Magarshack, D., 2454,2456,2495,2657,2692

Magdoff, H., 4109

Mager, N., 3645

Magidoff, N.I., 3476

Magidoff, R., 609,653,2018-19

Magner, T.F., 53

Magnes, J.L., 3978

Magnus, B., 3194

Magnus, L., 2364

Maguire, R.A., 1958

Mahaney, W.L., 1574

Mahanta, K.C., 754

Mahmuduzzafar, S., 660

Maichel, K., 2,21-22

Maillart, E.K., 4416

Mailloux, H.P., 4095

Mailloux, K.F., 4095

Mair, G.B., 725,3646

Maisky, I.M., 3994,4005-08,4033a

Majstrenko, I., 4311

Makarenko, A., 1837,1846,1862-64

Makarenko, G.S., 1862

Makeev, N., 338

Makhno, N., 4323

Maks, L., 661,3477

Maksimov, S., 2366

Malamuth, C., 2283,2298,2301,
2304,2306,2478

Malaparte, C., 3478

Male, D.J., 1083

Malenkov, G.M., 3509,3679,
4124-25

Malevich, K.S., 2790

Malevsky-Malevich, P., 169-70

Malko, N., 2745

Malnick, B., 884

Malone, C.L., 313

Maloney, J.J., 596

Malsagoff, S.A., 1528

Maltzman, I., 4538

Mamatey, V.S., 3647

Manchouko, 3842

Manchuria, 3846

Mandel, W., 777,867,3812,4417

Mandelstam, N., 2372-73

Mandelstam, O.E., 2042,2367-73

Mandeville, J., 2345

Mannin, E., 490,4440

Manning, C.A., 3195,4221,4312-13

Manning, E., 2296,2439

Manton, S.M., 644

Mao Tse-Tung, 3852,3860,3873,

Marburg, E., 4035

Marchant, H.S., 491

Marchenko, A., 1529

Marcu, V., 4096

Marcus, J., 974

Marcuse, H., 1429

Marek, F., 4079

Marer, P., 200

Margolin, A.D., 4314

Margulies, S.R., 3648

Marie Fedorovna, Empress, 3242

Marienhof, A., 2374

Marion, G., 632

Markham, T., 610

Markov, A., 2145

Markov, P.A., 2693

Markov, S.V., 1959,2031,3240

Marks, S.J., 3649

Markstein, E., 1954

Marquess, H.E., 1511

Marr, N.J., 4568

Marshall, H., 2047,2169,2379,2384,2652,
2786,2834,2879

Martel, G., 588

Martin, K., 301

Martovych, O.R., 4315

Martynov, I., 2746

Marx-Engels - Lenin Institute, 4153

Marx, K., 1396,4557

Marx, M., 331

Marzani, C., 3765

Maslov, E.P., 1148

Maslov, S.S., 329

Masque, M.le, 2601,2606

Massachusetts Institute of Technology, 1865

Massie, S., 2032

Matejka, L., 2039

Matheson, H., 2149,2360-61,2619, 2628

Matich, O., 2277

Matossian, M.K., 4363

Matters, L., 2826,4467

Matthews, M., 918

Matthews, W.K., 4264

Matveyev, V., 2375-76

Mavor, J., 1149

Maximoff, G.P., 1530

Maxton, J., 4098

Maxwell, B.W., 1389

Maxwell, R., 171

May, A.N., 1658

Mayakovsky, V., 2377-87

Maybury, H., 466

Mayer, A.G., 3972

Mayer, A.J., 3766

Mayer, P., 3877

Mayfair, 320

Maynard, C.C.M., 3196

Mazlach, S., 4316

Mazour, A.G., 1150,4555-56

Mead, M., 1039

Meck, D.L., 981

Meck, G.von, 3241

Medlin, W.K., 41,4441-42

Medvedev, R.A., 1059,3289

Medvedev, Z.A., 1059,2590,4491,4515

Mehnert, K., 755,982,3878,4557

Mehring, W., 4171

Meiburger, A., 3767

Meierling, G., 738

Meijer, J.M., 4177

Meiksins, G., 4222

Meisel, J.H., 1390

Meissner, B., 919,1463

Meissner, H.O., 1656

Meister, J., 1736

Melgounov, S.P., 1532,3048

Melik-Shakhnazarov, A.S., 159

Melinskaya, S.I., 4516

Mellor, R.E.H., 268,1272

Melnyk, Z.L., 1111,1209

Melville, C.F., 3979

Mendelson, M., 1960

Mennonite Central Committee,
3142

Menon, K.P.S., 756,767,848,
3905

Meretskov, K.A., 1737

Merkulov, A., 2010

Merril, J., 2020

Merwin, W.S., 2369

Metaxas, A., 689,3879

Metlova, M., 694

Mexico, 366,4179

Meyendorff, A., 3049

Meyendorff, S.Z., 3108

Meyer, A.G., 1391,1430

Meyerhold, V.E., 2694,2705

Mezhakoff-Koriakin, I., 2059

Mickiewicz, E., 240,1531

Middle East, 96,463,1239,3687,
3816-35,4364-65

Mihajlov, M., 797,1961

Mikesell, R., 1273

Mikhailov, N.N., 269,277-80,
597,611,842,4205

Mikhelson, A.L., 3109

Mikolajczyk, S., 4025

Milenkovitch, M.M., 2791

Miles, F.J., 476

Miliukov, P., 1611,3145

Millar, J.R., 1084

Miller, A., 828

Miller, F., 975,3146

Miller, H., 1629

Miller, J., 668,827,849

Miller, M., 1196

Miller, M.O., 4558

Miller, M.S., 681

Miller, O.O., 3142

Miller, R.H., 3650

Miller, W.W., 740,798-99,843,2994

Milner-Gulland, R., 2033,2164,2166

Milson, J., 1738

Minz, I., 1739

Mirchuk, I., 4317

Mirov, N.T., 270

Mirsky, D.S., 4099

Mitchell, E.R., 4430

Mitchell, J., 561

Mitrov, Z., 2432

Moats, A.-L., 3479

Modell, D., 2595

Modelski, G., 1612

Moen, L., 866

Mogilevska, S., 2827

Mosley, N., 4178

Mostecky, V., 148

Mote, M.E., 1533

Moudry, V., 3942

Moussinac, L., 2728

Movsovic, M.I., 40

Mowat, F., 4469

Mstislavski, S., 2388

Muchnic, H.L., 1962

Mudie, D., 2284,4086

Muggeridge, M., 454

Muldavin, A., 398,4319

Munro, C., 1740

Muraka, D., 271

Muratoff, P., 3376-77

Murmansk, 3196,3386

Murphy, J.T., 1613,3656,4155

Murray, K.M., Duchess of Atholl
1007

Murray, N., 1659

Musatov, A., 2389

Mussolini, B., 4146

Myaskovsky, N.Y., 2742

Myles, N.W., 549


NKVD, 1641

Nabokoff, C., 4009

Nachsen, D., 2412

Nadejda, 3242

Nag, D.S., 1274

Nagel Publishers, 868

Nagibin, Y., 2390-92

Nagorski, Z., 1813

Nagy, F., 3935

Nahayewsky, I., 4320

Naik, J.A., 3906

Nalbandov, S., 2357,2359

Nansen, F., 1151,1741,4364

Narkiewicz, O.A., 1464

Narokov, N., 2393

Nasvytis, A.L., 732,3453

Nathan, P., 2043,2198

National Coal Board, 1211

National Peace Council, 3657

National Socialist Party, 2900,3358,
3364,3366,3923,3969,3981,3986,4256

National Union of Students, 631

Navrozov, L., 2323,2465,2499

Nazaroff, A.I., 256,550,726

Nazarov, P., 2394,4418

Neal, F.W., 3768

Nearing, S., 346,1152,1868,3658

Neelkant, K., 3907

Nehru, J., 3910

Neiswender, R., 3

Neizvestny, E., 2782

- 304 -

Nekrasov, V.P., 2395-98

Nekrich, A.M., 4561

Nelson, R.C., 1433,3002

Nelson, W., 2792

Nemec, F., 3942

Nemirovich-Danchenko, V., 2696

Nenarokov, A.P., 2996

Nenoff, S., 3769

Nerhood, H.W., 15

Nesterov, M.V., 2131

Nestyev, I.V., 2748-49

Netherlands, 4014

**Nettl**, J.P., 2997,3980

Neuberger, E., 1275

Neubert, K., 303

Neugebauer, K., 741

Neumann, W.L., 3659

Neuweld, M., 3495-96

'New York Herald', 3051

New York Public Library, 11

'New York Tribune', 3051

Newman, B., 504,711,811,1660-62,
3981,4223

Newman, E.M., 363

Newnham, R., 1999

Newsholme, A., 1098

Newth, J.A., 4419

Nichevo, 339

Nicholas, M., 2141

Nicholas, N., 2141

Nicholson, J., 593

Nicolaeiff, A., 2076,2643

Nicolaevsky, B., 1004,2998,3281

Niemeyer, G., 963

Nikiforoff, C.C., 272

Nikitin, M.N., 3359

Nikitin, P., 4321

Nikitina, A., 2768

Nikolayeva, G., 2399-2400

Nilin, P., 2401-02

Nilsen, V., 2729

Nimitz, A.E., 203,215-16,219,230,238,
1231-33,4492

Nixon, B., 2633

Nizhny, V.B., 2730

Nizovoi, P., 2403-04

Noah, H.J., 1869-70

Noble, J.H., 1023-24

Nodel, E., 4241

Nodel, W., 1276

Noe, A.C., 399

Noel-Baker, F., 1663

Nogee, J.L., 899,1575

Nolbandov, S., 2086

Nollau, G., 1614,3830

Norborg, C., 1465,3660

Nork, K., 3480

Normano, J.F., 1153

North Carolina, 706

North Pole, 2818,2820

North, R.C., 3807,3844

Norton, H., 742,4470

Norway, 4015-16

Novak, J., 727,900

Nove, A., 1154-57,1277,1317, 4419

Novikov-Priboi, A., 2405-07

Novomeysky, M.A., 4471

Novy Mir, 1949

Nowarra, H.J., 1742

Nurenberg, T., 426

Nutter, G.A., 1060

Nyarady, M., 4013


O'Ballance, E., 1743

Obolensky, S., 4294

Obraztov, S., 2697

Obruchev, V.A., 2408-10

Observer, 826

O'Connor, N., 4542-43

O'Conor, J.F., 3147

Octobriana, 1064

O'Dempsey, F., 2474

Odessa, 837,3347

Odom, W.E., 1040

Odoyevtzeva, I., 2411-12

Odulok, T., 2413

Ofer, G., 1212

O'Flaherty, L., 400

Ogareff, V., 120

Ogden, D., 2056

Oglander, D., 2329

Ogniov, N., 2414-15

Ognyev, V., 2034

Ogpu, 1477,1487,1508,1522-2

O'Hara, V., 338

Okudzhava, B., 2416

Olesha, Y., 2417-22

Olgin, V., 3873

Oliva, L.J., 3662

Olkhovsky, A.V., 2750

Omsk, 739

Onacewicz, W., 1698

Oras, A., 4224

Orga, M., 2000

Orgill, D., 1744,3417

Orloff, N., 2562

Orloff, V.G., 1534

Orlov, A., 3321,4156

Orme, A., 4026

Orrmont, A., 3160

Orvik, N., 4016

Osakwe, C., 1576

Osborn, R.J., 999

Oshmachka, T., 4322

O'Silver, J., 2365

Osipov, G.V., 952,1068

Osipov, K., 2423

Osipov, V., 2424

Ossetia, 4382

Ossorgin, M., 2425-26

Ostrovitjanov, K.V., 4529

Ostrovsky, N., 2427-30

Osusky, S., 901

Oswald, J.G., 3798-99

Othello, 2703

Oudendijk, W.J., 4014

Oulanoff, H., 1963

Outer Mongolia, 3846

Overseas Press Club of America, 598

Overstreet, B., 3661

Overstreet, H., 3661

Owen, L.O., 3079

Ozols, S.A., 100


P.T. 494

Paananen, L., 3951

Pabst, H., 3481

Pachmuss, T., 2275,2278

Pacific, 1254,4454

Padmore, G., 4206

Page, B., 1664

Page, M., 3510-11

Page, S., 3831

Page, S.W., 4101,4225

Pakistan, 3896

Palen, L.S., 3199-3200

Palencia, I. de, 4073

Palmer, G., 2898

Paloczi-Horvath, G., 3663,4068

Pamir, 2831

Paneth, P., 3418

Panfiorov, F., 2431-33

Pankhurst, S., 317

Pankratova, A.M., 2999

Panova, V., 2434-39

Papanin, I.D., 2828

Pares, B., 477,518,3664

Parijanine, M., 2829

Paris, 453,3285

Park, A.G., 4420

Parker, D., 2599

Parker, R., 612,2115,2559,2579

Parker, W.H., 857,3770

Parkhomov, M., 2440

Parkins, M.F., 1535

Parris, R.N., 2656

Parrish, M., 71

Parry, A., 1536,1745,2849,4518

Parson, H.L., 2912

Parsons, G., 2052

Parvilahti, U., 1026

Pasternak, B.L., 1950,1962,
2001,2441-63

Paterson, T.G., 3771

Pathet Lao, 3875

Patolichev, N., 1278

Patrick, G.Z., 2040

Patrick, M., 443

Paul, C., 2112,2126,2405,2407

Paul, E., 2112,2407

Paul, L.A., 1197

Paulus, F., 3401

Paustovsky, K., 2464-67

Pavlenko, P., 2468-71,3419

Pavlov, D.V., 3420

Pavlov, I., 4535,4539,4541

Pavlovsky, M.N., 3838

Payne, M.A., 3243

Payne, P.S.R., 2419,2460,4102
4157

Payne, T.R., 4544

Peach, L.du G., 2554

Pearce, B., 2310,2312

Pearlstein, E.W., 3051

Peck, I., 3052

Peking, 3186,3850

Pelenskyi, I.I., 104

Peltier, M., 669

Penkovsky, O.V., 1665,1684

Pennar, J., 902,1835,1871,3832

Pentony, D.E., 3665-66

Peppard, M., 2549

Percow, A., 1027

Pereira, M., 858

Perlo, V., 1158

Perrett, B., 1746

Perventzev, A., 2472-73

Peter the Great, 3662

Peterman, I.H., 4253

Peters, C.A., 1159

Peters, V., 4323

Pethybridge, A., 1537

Pethybridge, R., 3000,3053-54,3512,3936

Petrazhitsky, L.I., 1814

Petrograd, 3089-92,3102,3126

Petrosian, T., 1924

Petrov, E., 682

Petrov, V.M., 682,859,1028,1626,1628

Petrovich, G.V., 2850

Petrovich, M.B., 778

Petrunkevitch, A., 3055

Petsamo, 3956

Pettit, W.W., 3731

Phelps-Fetherston, I., 1615

Philby, E., 1666

Philby, K., 1634,1664,1666-67
1673,1677

Phillips, G.D.R., 4472

Piatakov, G.L., 3326

Piatigorsky, G., 2751

Pick, F.W., 4226

Pidhainy, O.S., 4324

Pidhainy, S.O., 1538,4325

Piehalkiewicz, J., 3929

Pietromarchi, L., 800

Pigido, F., 4326

Pikelner, S.B., 2851

Pilat, O.R., 1668

Pilnyak, B., 2474-78

Pim, A.W., 1008

Pinkevich, A., 1872-73

Piper, D.G.B., 2313

Pipes, R., 998,3056-57,3148

Pirogov, P., 621

Piroshnikoff, J.R., 1987

Pisar, S., 1279

Pismensky, A., 2479-80

Pistrak, L., 4069

Pitcher, H.J., 779,801

Pittman, J., 3667

Pittman, M., 3667

Pizer, D., 4206

Plamenatz, J.P., 1431

Plank, D.L., 2461

Platonov, A.P., 2481-82

Pliever, H., 743

Plivier, T., 3421

Ploss, S.I., 1234,1539

Podiachikh, P.G., 242

Poe, H., 829

Poggioli, R., 2041

Poignant, R., 1874

Pokrovsky, G.I., 1747

Pokrovsky, M., 2292

Pokshishevsky, V.V., 279,597

Poland, 1069,1207,1775,3372,4012,4017-30

Poland, Ministry of Foreign Affairs,
4027

Polevoi, B., 2483-88,3422

Poliakov, A., 3423

Polianovskaya, F., 2633

Politburo, 1461,1465,1473

Pollack, E., 3149

Pollack, J.C., 2913,3111-12

Polmar, N., 1748

Polovtsoff, P.A., 3201

Polunin, N., 401

Polyakov, A., 2489-91

Polyakova, L.V., 2752

Pomeroy, W.J., 903

Pomorska, K., 2001,2039

Ponafidine, E.C., 3112

Pondoev, G.S., 1099

Ponomarenko, P.K., 3424

Ponomarev, B.N., 1466,3322

Pontecorvo, B., 1658

Poole, E., 3080-81

Pope, A.V., 4122

Pope-Henessy, U.B., 505

Popescu, J., 758,853

Popoff, G., 1540,4258

Popov, G.A., 1100

Popov, I., 2492-93

Popov, N., 1467

Popov, V.M., 129

Poretsky, E.K., 1669

Porter, A., 347

Portisch, H., 4473

Portnoff, C., 2308

Portnoff, G., 2308

Pospielovsky, D., 953

Possony, S.T., 4103-04

Postgate, R.W., 1432

Potapov, L.P., 4465

Potichnyj, P.J., 954

Potsdam Conference, 3581,3712

Potter, G.E., 703

Powell, R.P., 211

Powell, R.T., 1210

Power, R., 3113,3244

Powers, F.G., 1670,1678

Prasad, B., 3908

'Pravda', 2791

Pravdin, M., 2494

Preobrazhensky, E., 1188

Price, E., 744

Price, G.M., 955

Price, H.T., 3245

Price, J.H., 2808

Price, M.P., 599,744,3114,4421

Price, R.A., 182

Price, R.F., 2535

Prilutskii, D.N., 66

Prishvin, M., 2495-2501

Pritt, D.N., 1541,1616,3668-69

'Problems of Communism', 3490

Proffer, C.R., 1965,2061,2117-18

Proffer, E., 2117-18

Prokofiev, M.A., 1875

1739,1743,1746,1752,1762-63,
2004,3263,3379,3390,3439,3949

Reddaway, P., 1058,1061,4105

Reddaway, W.B., 1302

Red Fleet, 3399,3408

Redl, H.B., 1876

Red Square, 736,813,833,1055,2791

'Red Star', 72

Reed, F., 2411

Reed, J., 3058

Rees, D., 3672

Reeve, F.D., 768,2003,2108

Refregier, A., 802

Reigart, H., 2366

Reilly, A.P., 1968

Reiners, W.O., 1046

Reiss, I., 1669

Reitlinger, G., 3361

Remhardt, G., 1671

Remington, R.A., 1749

Reshetar, J.S., 963,1395,1463,
1468,4327

Reshevsky, S., 1918

**Reswick, A. 3249**

Reve, K. van het, 1062

Reykjavik, 1901,1922

Riabchikov, E., 2852

Rich, V., 4287

Richards, D.J., 1919,2666

Richardson, J.H.C., 2281,2285

Richman, B.M., 930

Rickman, J., 962

Rieber, A.J., 1433,3002,3964

Ries, M.J., 1956

Rigby, T.H., 1496,3291,4159

Riha, T., 3003

Riis, S.M., 3115

Rimberg, J., 2711,2733

Robbins, J., 1997

Roberti, V., 830

Roberts, C.E.B., 319,3202

Roberts, C.M., 3773

Roberts, E.M., 4160

Roberts, H.L., 3774

Roberts, P.C., 1161

Roberts, S.E., 1969

Roberts, S.R., 2048

Robien, L.,Comte de, 3117

Robins, R., 3096,3767,3775

Robinson, J.M., 831

Robinson, T.W., 4530

Robinson, W.J., 428

Roche, C. de la, 2714

Rock, V.P., 3776

Roeder, B., 1030

'Rodina', 2825

Rodionoff, N.R., 17

Rodker, J., 2005

Rogers, F.B., 58

Rogers, T.F., 2023

Rokhlin, L., 1101

Rokitiansky, N., 41

Rokossovski, K.K., 3425

Rolland, R., 467

Romania, 1775

Romanov dynasty, 1263,3091,
3134,3260

Romanov, A.I., 1545

Romashkin, P.S., 1815

Romm, M., 2830

Ronbloom, H.K., 1672

Ronchey, A., 769,3514,3881

Rondiere, P., 807,4474

Ronimois, H.E., 1329

Ronin, S.L., 4216

Roosevelt, F.D., 3367,3582,
3659,3719,3730,3786

Root, E., 3777

Rosefielde, S., 1280

Rosen, S.M., 1877-78

Rosenbaum, K., 3982

Rosenberg, A., 1396

Rosenberg, J.N., 354,4328

Rosenberg, L.R., 77

Rosenberg, S., 2293,2466,2608

Rosenberg, W.G., 3203

Rosenfeld, B., 813

Rosenfeld, S., 813

Rositzke, H.A., 860

Roskin, A., 2249

Roslavleva, N., 2769-70

Rosmer, A., 3152

Rosovsky, H., 1213

Ross, E.A., 3116,3153

Rosser, R.F., 3673

Rossi, A., 3983

Rossif, F., 3060

Rostov, 3160

Rostow, W.W., 904

Rothberg, A., 1063,2592

Rothenberg, J., 2946

Rothschild, J., 3937

Rothschild, P., 814

Rothstein, A., 1330,1470,3004,3324,
3365,3674,4382

Roucek, J.S., 172

Rounault, J., 1031

Rounds, F., 645,654

Rowan-Hamilton, N., 382

Rowland, M.F., 2462

Rowland, P., 2462

Rowley, C.A., 445

Roy, M.N., 3059

Royster, V., 759

Rozanov, V.V., 1969

Rozanskas, E., 4273

Rozov, V., 2505

Rubakin, N., 161

Rubin, J.H., 455,3250

Rubin, R.I., 2947

Rubin, V., 455

Rubinstein, A.Z., 1577-78,3675

Rubinstein, S.L., 4544

Rubulis, A., 4234

Rudden, B., 1816

Ruge, G., 2463

Rudman, H.C., 1879

Ruggles, M.J., 148,157,1447

Ruhl, A., 4227

Rukeyser, W.A., 429

Ruksenas, K., 4273

Runes, D.D., 905

Rupen, R.A., 3882

Rupert, R., 1032

Rush, M., 1546,1720,3515,3520,
3676

Rusinek, A., 2948

Rusis, A., 4212

Russell, B., 1434

Russian Orthodox Church, 2891,2900-01,
2914,2918

Russian Soviet Federated Socialist
Republic, 184,1777,1782-83

Rybakov, A., 2506-08

Ryerson, E.L., 2797

Rykov, A.I., 3325

Ryss, Y., 2509

Rywkin, M., 4422


Sabaliunas, L., 4274

Sadecky, P., 1064

Sadleir-Jackson Brigade, 3205

St Antony's College, Oxford, 2927

St George, G., 992,2070,4475

Sakhalin, 4483

Sakharov, A.D., 1065

Salazar, L.A.S., 4179

Salisbury, H.E., 574,670,728,760,803,
3005,3016,3426,3451,3516-17,3883

Saltykov-Shchedrin State Public Library,
158

'Salyut', 2853

Samarin, V.D., 3363

Samarkand, 296,413,490,671,750-51,822,
4409,4413,4438,4440,4443-44

Samilov, M., 1989

Sammis, E.R., 3427

Samra, C.S.S., 3909

Samuel, C., 2755

- 314 -

Scott, W.E., 3965

Scott-Gatty, V., 2212

Scottish League for European
  Freedom, 4208

Seale, P., 1673

Seaton, A., 3430-31

Sedugin, P., 1818

Seduro, V., 4288

Seely, C.S., 3336

Segal, L., 542

Seibert, T., 430

Sejersted, F., 745,1880

Selznick, P., 1401

Semashko, N.A., 1102

Semenov, I.S., 2510

Semushkin, T., 4476

Senkevitch, A., 54

Senn, A.E., 4276-77

Serafimovich, A., 2511-12

Serapion Brothers, 1963

Serebrennikov, G.N., 993

Serge, V., 2513,3008,3061,
  3292-93,4127

Sergeant, P., 671

Sergeyev-Tzenski, S., 2514-15

Seroff, V.I., 2757

Servadio, G., 4477

Seth, R., 1674-75,3432-33

Sethi, S.S., 4161

Seton, M., 2735

Seton-Watson, H., 1617,3679-81

Settles, W.F., 832

Sevastopol, 3445

Sevruk, V., 3434

Seymour, J., 468

Shabad, T., 273,286

Shachtman, M., 1547

Shaffer, H.G., 1166,1402

Shafir, I.M., 4379

Shakespeare, W., 2454

Shakhnazarov, G.K., 1881

Shakhrai, V., 4316

Shamir, S., 3817

Shandruk, P., 4329

Shane, A.M., 2667

Shanghai, 1682

Shanin, T., 1086

Shapovalenko, S.G., 1882

Sharov, A., 2516

Sharpe, M.E., 1332

Sharpe, M.R., 2854

Shartse, O., 2079,2607

Shaw, G.B., 781

Shebunina, T., 1995,2150-51,2156,2566,
  2626,4581-82

Sheinin, L.R., 1819

Sheldon, C.S., 2855

Sheldon, R., 2519

Shelley, G., 340-41,2037,
  2147,2153,2345,2647

Shelton, W., 2856

Sheng Shih-Tsai, 3891

Sheng, Y., 3884

Sheridan, C.C., 320,3251,
  4330

Sherwood, D., 833

Shestov, L.I., 1969

Shih, Cheng-chich, 1883

Shimanskaya, E., 2611

Shimkin, D.B., 218,287

Shinkarev, L., 4478

Shipman,S.S., 1246

Shiryayev, P., 2517

Shishkov, V., 2518

Shklovsky, V., 2385,2519,
  3252

Shmelev, I., 2520-22

Shneerson, G., 2758

Shneerson, V., 2392,4346

Shneider, I.I., 2772

Shneidman, N.N., 1884

Sholokhov, M., 2024,2523-36

Shore, M.J., 1885

Shostakovitch, D., 2743,2746,
  2754,2757

Shotwell, J.T., 4028

Shryock, R.W., 3503

Shtemenko, S.M., 3435

Shteppa, K.F., 4563

Shternfield, A., 2857

Shub, A., 834,3528,3682,4106

Shukman, H., 2300,2986,3062,4107

Shulman, C., 850

Shulman, M.D., 3683

Shumilin, I.N., 1886

Shuster, G.N., 2880

Shvarts, E.L., 2537

Shvidkovsky, O.A., 2779

Siberia, 370,787,807,1036,1478,2819,
  2837,3157,3168,3176-77,3186,3191,
  3198,3211,3214-17,3229,3480,3486,
  4402,4405,4430,4447,4449-54,4456,
  4458-59,4464-66,4468-75,4477-78,
  4482,4484-85,4487

Sibley, R., 404

Sidorenko, A.A., 1761

Siere, M., 624

Sigerist, H.E., 1103

Silde, A., 1034,4229

Sillitoe, A., 782

Silver, B., 506,957

Silverlight, J., 3204

Silverman, S.N., 4108

Simirenko, A., 4531-32

Simmons, E.J., 174,1971-72,2024,4583

Simmons, J.S.G., 2,4,42

Simon, B., 1104-05,4546

- 317 -

Simon, E.D., 2805

Simon, G., 2915

Simon, J., 1105

Simonov, K., 2538-44

Simsova, S., 160-61

Simutis, A., 139,4278

Sinclair, L., 84

Sinclair, U., 2721

Singh, D., 4291

Singh, I., 633

Singleton-Gates, G.R., 3205

Sinha, S., 683

Sinkiang, 1253,3891

Sinor, D., 4424

Sinyavsky, A., 1056,2063,
2134,2545-50

Siomushkin, T., 2551-52

Sisson, E.G., 3119

Sizova, M.I., 2773

Skariatina, I., 456,3120

Skilling, H.G., 1548

Skoczylas, E., 2952

Skomorovsky, B., 3436

Skrebitzki, G., 2553

Skripnikova, A., 2906

Skrjabina, E., 3483

Skvirsky, D., 2388,2410,
2435,2507,4560

Slater, L.P., 2441,2444,2449

Slavutych, Y., 4348

Slesser, M., 2831

Sloan, P., 507,1403-04,3437

Slonim, M.L., 1967,1973

Slonimsky, J., 2774-75

Slusser, R.M., 1282,1557,1563,3580,3781

Smal-Stocki, R., 1618,4209-10

Smersh, 1674

Smirnov, I.I., 3009

Smirnov, I.N., 3327

Smirnov, N.A., 2927

Smirnov, V.G., 2554-55

Smirnova, N., 2556

Smith, A., 478,958

Smith, C.J., 3958

Smith, E.E., 4162

Smith, G.A., 1283

Smith, H., 784

Smith, I.H., 4180

Smith, J., 600,861,994

Smith, M.E., 457

Smith, S., 589

Smith, V.R., 1087

Smith, W.B., 622,3782

Smitham, F., 2091

Smits, R., 23

Smolansky, O.M., 3833

Smolar, B., 2953

Smolders, P.L., 2853

Smolensk, 1509,3383

Smolka, H.P., 2832,4479

Smulevich, B.I., 249

Smyslov, V.V., 1920

Snow, E., 558,1405,3438,3685

Snowden, E.A., 310

Sobel, R., 3783

Sobko, V., 2557

Sobol, A., 2558

Sobolev, L., 2559-63

Socialist Revolutionaries, 3082

Society for the Defence of
Freedom in Asia, 4211

Soderhjelm, H., 3959

Sokolnicki, A.J., 1618

Sokolnikov, G.Y., 1303,3326

Sokolnikova, G., 2564

Sokoloff, B., 1106

Sokolov, B., 2565,3253

Sokolov, N.A., 3147

Sokolovsky, V.D., 1751

Solasko, F., 2181,2296,2409

Solomon, M., 1549

Solomon, P.H., 39

Solonevich, I., 1550-51

Soloukhin, V., 808,854

Solovetsky, 1484

Soloveytchik, G., 575

Soloviev, M., 1752

Soloviov, L., 2566-68

Solovyev, O., 4564

Soltis, A., 1921

Solzhenitsyn, A.I., 1511,2001,2569-92

Somerville, J., 4584

Sonin, M.I., 247

Sontag, R.J., 3986

Sorenson, J.B., 959

Sorge, R., 1636

Sorlin, P., 906

Sorokin, P., 342,3063,3254,3784

Soutar, A., 3206

Southeast Asia, 3728,3811

Souvarine, B., 4163

Soviet Affairs Symposium, 3529-31

'Soviet News', 175

Spain, 4031-34

Spassky, B., 1901,1906,1912-13,1918,1921

Spector, I., 2930

Speier, H., 3987

Speirs, R., 4265

Spekke, A., 4259

Spielmann, K.F., 1708

Stewart, G., 3208

Stewart, J.M., 835

Stewart, P.D., 1553

Stipp, J.L., 3519

Stock, M., 4332

Stockwell, R.E., 1756

Stockwood, M., 672

Stoessinger, J.G., 1580,3787

Stoiko, M., 1757

Stokke, B.R., 1284

Stoklitsky, L., 2116,2307,2316

Stolt, R.G., 4533

Stolz, G., 30

Storry, G.R., 1636

Strakhovsky, L.I., 176,2042,
3209-10,3788

Stransky, J., 3943

Strauss, E., 907,931,1235

Street, L., 552,590

Strelsky, N., 2053

Strever, M., 2232

Strik-Strikfeldt, W., 3371

Strmecki, J., 4042

Strod, I., 3211

Strogov, S., 673

Strohm, L., 591

Strom, A., 479

Strong, A.L., 333,469,543,553,

1088,1475,3294,4443

Strong, J.W., 3532

Stroud, J., 2810

Strover, A.J., 2871,3799

Stroyen, W.B., 2918

Strube, W.P., 2919

Struk, D.S., 4349

Strumilin, S.G., 908

Struve, G., 1975

Struve, N., 2920

Stuart, R.C., 1089

Stucley, P., 492

Stukas, J.J., 4279

Stypulkowski, Z., 3484,4029

Sub-Carpathian Ruthenia, 3942

Sukhanov, N.N., 3123

Sullivants, R.S., 4333

Sulzberger, C.L., 684

Suny, R.G., 4369

Sun Yat-Sen University, 3884

Surguchiov, I., 2595-96

Suri, S.L., 3911

Sutton, A.C., 1170,3789

Suzdal, 822

Svanidze, B., 4125,4165

Svirski, A., 2597

Swan, E., 2309,2311

Trefousse, H.L., 3693

Treml, V.G., 31,196,1171–72,1336

Treniov, K., 2631

Tretyakov, S., 2632–33

Trevelyan, H., 4010

Trevor-Roper, H., 1677

Trifonov, Y., 2634

Trilling, L., 2083,2811

Triska, J.F., 1563,3694

Trivanovitch, V., 514

Troitse-Sergiyeva Monastery, 2867

Trotsky, L., 84,1183,1620,3065–66,
    3309,3847,4111–13,4166,4172–88,
    4380

Troubridge, U., 2350

Truman, H.S., 3727,3740

Trush, M., 3695

Tsamerian, I.P., 4216

Tschebotarioff, G.P., 785

Tseplyaev, V.P., 283

Tsiolkovsky, K., 2637

Tsvetayeva, M., 2635–36

Tsytovich, N., 2521

Tucker, R.C., 1437,3328,4167

Tucker, R.L., 695

Tuckerman, G., 447

Tukhachevsky, M.N., 3303

Tumulus, G., 4244

Turgeon, E.L., 224–26,228

Turin, S.P., 909

Turkestan, 385,4393,4406–07,4416,4420,
    4423,4430

Turkevich, J., 62,124

Turkey, 366,1253,1285,3235,3823,3830

Turner, C.B., 4534

Turner, J.E., 1387,2979

Turner, L., 2232

Turney, A.W., 3443

Tutaeff, D., 4359

Tuzmuhamedov, R., 4426

Tverskoi, K.N., 2812

Tweedie, Mrs. A., 370

Tweedie, O., 407

Tyazhelnikov, Y., 984

Tynyanov, Y., 2638–39

Tyrkova-Williams, A., 3067

Tyrmand, L., 845


Ueke, K., 3444

Ukraine, 104–06,129,185,213,924,1209,
    1327,2944,3155,3373,4060,4289–90,
    4292–96,4298–4302,4304–05,4307,4308–
    18,4320–22,4324–27,4331–35,4343,
    4347–48

Ukrainian Congress Committee of America,
    4334

Ukrainian Information Service, 4335

Ulam, A.B., 1438,3014,3521,3696,3791,
    4043,4168

Ulanova, G.S., 2763,2767,2773

Ullman, M.B., 243

Ullman, R.H., 4011

Umiastowski, R., 4012

Unbegaun, B.O., 42

Unger, H., 2759

U.S.S.R., Academy of Sciences, 37,
124-25,4488,4493,4523

U.S.S.R., Central Administration of
Economic and Social Statistics
of the State Planning Commission,
187-88

U.S.S.R., Central Statistical
Administration, 189-90,192-95
207

U.S.S.R., Council of Ministers,
2806,3367

U.S.S.R., Ministry of Foreign Trade,
201

U.S.S.R., Ministry of Higher
Education, 1890

U.S.S.R., State Planning Commission,
1349,1352,2806

U.S.S.R., Supreme Court, 3325-27

Unishevsky, V., 2838

United Arab Republic, 1285

United Nations, 1001,1570,1573,
1579-80,1645

United Nations, Economic and Social
Commission, 1576

U.S.A., 404,406,409,825,970,1095,
1158,1249,1285,1323,1486,1580,
1671,1686,1719,1773,1842,1874,
2707,2792,2814,2847,2855,3210,
3214,3224,3234,3367,3562,3712-
93,3975,4231,4314

U.S.A. Air Force Dept., 1761

U.S.A., Army Air Forces, 3416

U.S.A., Atomic Energy Commission, 63

U.S.A., Bureau of the Census, 244

U.S.A., Congress, House of Representatives, Foreign Affairs Committee, 3889

U.S.A., Congress, Joint Economic Committee, 1174

U.S.A., Dept. of the Army, 70,73,132,179

U.S.A., Dept. of Health, Education and
Welfare, 41,57,58,1889

U.S.A., Dept. of State, 16,32,82,89,118,
3792-93,3986,3989

U.S.A., Economic Research Service, 239

U.S.A., Geographic Names Board, 133

U.S.A., Library of Congress, 5,13,16,17,
23-27,46,56,64-68,99,130-31

U.S.A., Public Health Services, 59

U.S.A., Senate, Committee of Foreign Relations, 3725

U.S.A., Senate, Committee on the Judiciary, 36

Unterberger, B.M., 3214

Upits, A., 4266

Upton, A.F., 3961

Uralov, A., 3299

Urals, 526,530,975,1165,2096,3146,4398

Urban, G.R., 3874

Urch, R.O.G., 3256

Uspenskaya, Y., 2640

Uspenski, A.V., 2321

Uspenski, P., 2641

Ussuria, 2077

Utechin, S., 180,1439

Utley, F., 515,603

Uustalu, E., 4245,4248

Uzbekistan, 4402,4441


Vagin, P.I., 3359

Vakar, N.P., 103,910,4284

Vakhabov, A., 2931

Vakhtangov, E.B., 2685

Valentinov, A.A., 2883

Valentinov, N.V., 4117-18

Valeriy, I., 2642

Van der Post, L., 786,815

Vandervelde, E., 3068

Vandivert, R., 976

Van Doren, M., 2012,2235

Van Paassen, P., 674

Vanzler, U., 2146

Vardys, V.S., 4281

Varga, E., 1189

Varneck, E., 3215

Varney, J.C., 311

Vassiliev, M., 2860,4503

Vassiliev, V., 1286

Vatican, 2892

Veale, F.J.P., 4114

Verheul, K., 2064

Vernadsky, G., 4115

Vernon, F., 2321

Vernon, V., 2321

Vickery, W.N., 1957,1979,2398

Vicky, 304

Vidor, J., 371,1679

Vigdorova, F., 1891,2328,2644

Vigor, P.H., 14,1440

Viirsaule, E., 4246

Viktovich, V., 4433

Vining, L.E., 3257

Vinogradov, A., 2645-47

Vinogradov, N.A., 1107

Viollis, A., 372

Viriatino, 1072

Viroubova, A., 3258

Virski, F., 1762

Viser, F.J., 836

Vishwanathan, S., 3920

Vladimirov, L., 821,2861

Vlasov, A.A., 3370

Voaden, D.J., 1696

Vodarsky-Shiraeff, A., 128

Voegelein, L.B., 46

Vogel, L.E., 2109

Vogeler, R.A., 3485

Voinov, K., 1823

Volga, 758,809,2249,2689,
  3222,3478,4114,4365

Volga provinces, 319

Volgograd, 782

Volgyes, 2985

Volin, L., 1237

Voline, 3069,3155

Volochova, S., 2158

Volodin, A., 2643

Volsky, N.V., 4117-18

Volunteer Army, 3166,3190

Von Laue, T.H., 3015

Von Mohrenschildt, D.S., 3070

Von York, T., 3071

Vorkuta, 1033

Voronkova, L.F., 2648

Voronski, A., 2649

Voroshilov, K.E., 4189

Voss, A., 4261

Voyce, A., 2780

Voyetekhov, B., 3445

Voynow, Z., 2553

Voznesensky, A., 2650-53

Voznesensky, N.A., 1175-76,3374

Vronskaya, J., 2737

Vucinich, A., 921,4493

Vvedensky, A., 2320

Vyshinsky, A.Y., 1824


Wade, R.A., 3697

Wade, R.G., 1923-24

Wadekin, K.-E., 1238

Wagner, R., 3446

Wagner, W., 3925

Wainstein, E.S., 234

Walford, N., 2759

Walker, G.P.M., 150

Wallace, H.A., 4427

Walpole, H., 1025

Walsh, E.A., 1621,3072

Walsh, W.B., 181-82

Walter, E., 431,1350

Walter, J., 1687

Walter, K., 2364

Walton, G., 2497

Wandycz, P.S., 4030

Ward, E., 3962

Ward, H.F., 560,923,3339

Ward, J., 3216

Wardell, J.W., 4434

Warth, R.D., 3085,3698,4119,4169

Warp, H., 696

Washington, 1630

White, L., 4044

White, S., 55

White, W.C., 408

White, W.L., 233,563,613

Whiteside, T., 1681

Whiting, A.S., 3891

Whiting, C.M., 3849

Whiting, K.N., 183

Whitney, T.P., 731,762,1980,2574

Wicksteed, A., 460

Widstrand, C.G., 3608

Wiehe, J., 3830

Wiener, L., 2049

Wiesel, E., 2954

Wightman, O.S., 3124

Wigmans, J.H., 787,1036,3486

Wilber, C.K., 1177

Wilbur, C.M., 3850

Wilbur, W.H., 1412

Wilcox, E.H., 3125

Wilczynski, J., 1190-91

Wild, M., 3218

Wiles, P.J.D., 1178

Wilks, R., 2228

Williams, A., 2096

Williams, A.R., 355,495,545,
3126-27

Williams, E.W., 2814

Williams, F.E., 1108

Williamson, H.N.H., 3219

Willis, E.F., 3156

Willis, H.R., 1893

Willoughby, C.A., 1862

Wilson, H.C., 4430

Wilson, L.W., 1894

Wilson, W., 3766

Wilton, R., 3260,3128

Winks, R.W., 3702

Winn, R.B., 4548

Winner, T.G., 4435

Winter, E., 564,996

Winterton, P., 565,604,3301,3342

Wittlin, T., 1556,3487,4054

Wixley, A., 2078,2103

Wolfe, A., 2418

Wolfe, B.D., 1413,2251,3018,3047,3074,
3302,4047,4112

Wolfe, H.C., 3703

Wolfe, T.W., 1764-68

Wolin, S., 1557

Wolkonsky, Princess P., 3262

Wolkonsky, Prince S., 3261

Wollenberg, E., 1769

Wolycky, W., 4337

Wonlar-Larsky, N., 3264

Wood, S.H., 3019

Wood, W., 624

Woods, J.B., 4487

Woodward, D., 1770

Woodward, H., 3086

Woody, T., 1895

World Health Organization, 1576

Woronitzn, S., 28

Woronoff, O., 3265

Woroszylski, W., 2387

Wortis, J., 4549

Woytinsky, E., 3129

Woytinsky, W.S., 4381

Wraget, P., 874

Wrangel P.N., 3220

Wreden, N., 2165-66,2269

Wright, R., 432

Wu, A.K., 3851

Wukelic, G.E., 2862

Wurmbrand, R., 2923

Wurmbrand, S., 1037

Wykes, A., 3449

Wyndham, F., 4188

Wynne, G., 1684


X.Y., 4444


Yakhontoff, V.A., 3704

Yakir, P., 3331

Yakovlev, A., 2815

Yakutia, 4481

Yalta, 3554,3585,3653,3786,3812

Yan, V., 2654-55

Yanovsky, V.S., 2656

Yanowitch, M., 922,1192

Yanson, J.D., 1287

Yapp, Y., 2148

Yaresh, L.A., 1825

Yarkovsky, J.M., 3130

Yarmolinsky, A., 1981,2014,4217

Yaroslavsky, E., 4170

Yefimov, A., 1337

Yeghenian, A.Y., 4368

Yelyutin, V., 1896

Yenisei River, 2826,4467

Yershov, P., 2025,2708

Yezhov, A.I., 198

Yin, J., 3892

Yodfat, M., 3835

Yohel, N., 2555

Young, G., 3523

Yourievsky, _Princess_ C., 3266

Yuan, T'ung li, 93

Yudovich, M., 1916

Yugoff, A., 1179

Yugoslavia, 1191,1207,1259,
1775,1808,2535,4034-45

Yugov, A., 2657

Yugow, A., 1338

Yurasov, V., 2658

Yurlova, M., 3267

Yurovsky, L.N., 1305


Zablocki, C.J., 3893

Zabolotsky, N.A., 2659

Zacharoff, L., 3343,3450

Zaehringer, A.J., 2863

Zagorsk, 2867

Zagoria, D.S., 3894

Zagoria, J.D., 2998

Zagorsky, S., 1294

Zaitsev, B., 2660

Zakrevsky, M., 2199,2216

Zakrutkin, V., 2661

Zaleski, E., 1339-40,4521

Zalite, T., 4266

Zamyatin, E., 2662-67

Zander, W., 2955

Zarin, L., 2297

Zarine, L., 2649

Zatko, J.J., 2924

Zaubermann, A., 1341

Zavalani, T., 912

Zavalishin, V., 1982

Zawodny, T.K., 3375

Zebot, C.A., 1288

Zeitlin, I., 2503

Zelitch, J., 1826

Zeman, Z.A.B., 3992

Zenkovsky, S.A., 44,2932,4431

Zenzinov, V., 977

Zernov, N.M., 111,2925

Zetkin, C., 4120

Zhdanov, A.A., 1931

Zhelezhova, I., 2483

Zhigalova, O., 2668

Zhukov, G.K., 3451,4190-91

Ziedonis, A., 4233

Zieser, B., 3452,3488

Zilboorg, G., 2665

Zile, Z.L., 1771

Zimmerman, W., 1589

Zinoviev, G., 1476

Zinoviev, M.A., 1897,3327,3847

Zirkle, C., 4522

Zlatova, E., 4350

Zlotovski, K., 2669

Zoshchenko, M., 2670-74

Zoul, L., 1048

Zukhovitskaya, I., 2538
Zvorykin, A.A., 1932